William Blake's *Jerusalem*

William Blake's
Jerusalem

Structure and Meaning in Poetry and Picture

Minna Doskow

Rutherford • Madison • Teaneck
Fairleigh Dickinson University Press
London and Toronto: Associated University Presses

© 1982 by Associated University Presses, Inc.

Associated University Presses, Inc.
4 Cornwall Drive
East Brunswick, N.J. 08816

Associated University Presses Ltd
27 Chancery Lane
London WCZA 1NF, England

Associated University Presses
Toronto M5E 1A7, Canada

Library of Congress Cataloging in Publication Data

Doskow, Minna.
  William Blake's Jerusalem.

  Bibliography: p.
  Includes index.
  1. Blake, William, 1757–1827. Jerusalem. I. Title.
PR4144.J43D67   821'.7   81-65463
ISBN 0-8386-3090-1   AACR2

Printed in the United States of America

To George, Laura,
and Jessica

Contents

Author's Note

The facsimile of *Jerusalem: The Emanation of the Giant Albion* included in this volume is of copy C (Linnell-Rinder). It was first published in this country by Beechhurst Press, New York, in 1955 as the companion volume to Joseph Wicksteed's book-length commentary on *Jerusalem*. I would like to thank Mr. Thomas Yoseloff, the original publisher of the 1955 facsimile edition and American publisher of Joseph Wicksteed's commentary, who is presently with Associated University Presses, for generously offering to publish that facsimile edition along with my analysis of the structure of *Jerusalem*.

My own analysis of the text and illustrations of *Jerusalem* follows the order of copy C. I have, however, extensively used copy E (Mellon) in my work, and all references to color in my analysis are to that copy.

William Blake's *Jerusalem*

1
Setting Forth

THE longest by far of William Blake's completed poetic works is his major prophecy, the epic *Jerusalem: The Emanation of the Giant Albion*. Its completion covered more than a decade (1804–15), during which time the poet deleted, expanded, and altered lines, redrew illustrations, and variously revised the order of the plates, especially in chapter 2. As the object of such continuous thought and revision, *Jerusalem* represents the culmination of Blake's artistic endeavor in poetry and picture, containing one hundred plates, each of which is at least partially illustrated, and six of which are full-page illustrations.

Ever since its initial publication, *Jerusalem* has been the subject of much misunderstanding and controversy among its readers and critics. Some, especially earlier critics, approached the work looking for traditional epic design and a linear narrative structure. Not finding such orthodox narrative elements, they concluded that the poem was chaotic and confused.[1] The time has long since passed, however, when critics universally regarded *Jerusalem* as an impenetrable poetic night that allowed a few brilliant passages to shine intermittently through its universal murk. S. Foster Damon first, and then others whose ranks have thickened with time, abandoned the hypothesis of linear narrative structure and proposed instead a thematic organization.[2] In the last decade, as interest in *Jerusalem* and Blake's other major prophecies has mushroomed, numerous expositions of *Jerusalem*'s theme and structure have appeared. Indeed, the critical situation has so far reversed itself that, with rare exceptions, Blake's critics now see the poem as a brilliant exposition of Blake's visionary mode and message, and they acknowledge only minor murky lapses along the way.

13

While most critics now agree that *Jerusalem* demonstrates a high degree of thematic unity and has a clear structure, they by no means agree on the basis or form of that structure. Recognizing biblical analogies in the four chapter division of *Jerusalem*, Northrop Frye compares its structure to the biblical pattern of fall, struggle, and redemption,[3] while Harold Bloom notes analogies to the Book of Ezekiel,[4] Joanne Witke to the four synoptic Gospels,[5] and Stuart Curran to the Book of Revelation.[6] Karl Kiralis, on the other hand, sees the poem's successive chapters recapitulating the progressive growth of the individual and the historical progress of the human race.[7] Yet Henry Lesnick claims that the poet depicts the progressive stages in the fall of man.[8]

In E. J. Rose's view, each chapter describes one aspect of fallen man as represented by the appropriate Zoa: Tharmas, Luvah, Urizen, and Los, in turn.[9] Anne Mellor diverges somewhat to characterize the first chapter of *Jerusalem* as a summary of the whole and the subsequent chapters as descriptions of fallen man's misuse of body, mind and emotions, and imagination respectively.[10] W. J. T. Mitchell, who also rejects the notion of linear chronological form, concentrates on the sexual theme, describing the poem as "a thematically organized encyclopedic anatomy of the human condition as a battle of the sexes."[11]

Another group of critics, including Roger Easson, Mollyanne Marks, and Hazard Adams sees the unity of *Jerusalem* in its description and simultaneous enactment of Blake's poetic theory. The poem is then about the process of poetic creation, about writing a poem.[12]

All of these analyses of *Jerusalem* provide interesting insights into the poem, open up its meaning, and add to our understanding of it. Nevertheless, each provides only a partial account, for each omits large sections of the poem from consideration.[13] Coherence is thus achieved only at the cost of completeness. The basic question of earlier critics, therefore, remains, although in modified form. Is the poem, indeed, an entirely unified work centering around a single theme, to which all the events, characters, and situations in both text and illustrations relate? I believe that the question may be answered in the affirmative, but in order to do so, the present analyses of *Jerusalem*'s structure must be recast. The schematization of the poem as a version of the Bible, a restructuring of Ezekiel, a recapitulation of the progressive growth of the individual and the human race, a battle and reunification of the sexes, a view in turn of each of the four Zoas (or each of man's faculties—body, mind, emotion, and imagination) must be modified. To do so, I will return to Blake's own words, the initially stated theme of his traditional epic, beginning in chapter 1 of *Jerusalem:* "Of the Sleep of Ulro! and of the passage through / Eternal Death! and of the awaking to Eternal Life."[14] The structure of the poem may then be analyzed in terms of that theme. If this is done, all the poem's parts fall into place as pieces of a kaleidoscopic whole complementing and reinforcing one another. Each chapter then turns the kaleidoscope to view the theme in a new way. The pieces recompose themselves in new patterns and seem to reveal new appearances of the whole but are only actualizing those patterns potentially present all along. After the first glimpse, no new element is added to the picture. Further turns and glimpses simply rearrange existing pieces to examine the theme from all sides, going, in turn, through all the possible combinations.

Blake describes Albion's (everyman's) fall and redemption, which he calls sleep, passage, and awaking. But he does so by illuminating a single action and a single moment, the moment of Albion's choice, his turning from error or fall to truth or redemption. Albion's sleep, passage, and awaking are varying omnipresent states of consciousness that Albion enters, rather than chronologically successive stages of a continuous journey. Albion does not proceed systematically step by step through marked stages in a journey, not even a metaphoric one, as, for example, Dante does in the *Divine Comedy;* he is rather asleep one moment and awake the next, as soon as he frees his imagination and abandons his isolating selfhood in the moment of willing self-sacrifice for another. The various events, characters, situations, and images presented in both poetry and pictures gradually reveal the meaning and implications of this moment. They do so by showing what perceptions, ideas, relationships, objects, and institutions are involved in Albion's action and in his opposing states of being. By repeating the same events in changed contexts, for example, Albion's death, Los's division, Vala's conflict with Jerusalem; by altering the reader's perspective; and by gradually revealing new significance in the same characters and events, Blake replaces chronological or linear development with a tight thematic unity. Time is transcended as one action is consecutively revealed in all its multiple meanings from many perspectives, and the single moment of Albion's choice is exploded to cover the entire poem.

Albion does not first deny unity with the Savior (chap. 1), then establish fallen religion and purely natural man (chap. 2), then deify his rational powers (chap. 3), and finally establish the reign of Gwendolen's delusive love (chap. 4), although these characters and events are described in successive chapters. On the contrary, he does all these things and more the moment he denies unity with the

Savior, which he does with his first words, "We are not One; we are Many" (4:23). He thereby reveals his fallen state (sleep in Ulro), but it takes all the events related in the rest of the poem to tell us exactly what this state means. All Albion's fallen actions are one, and they are simultaneous although they are related in succeeding plates and chapters. The succession simply reveals from various perspectives what is already inherent in his initial words.

Similarly, and as also implied in his first words, all the fallen characters whom we meet during the course of the poem are one, and are part of Albion. They appear as other, for that is the way Albion sees himself in his fallen state. We therefore learn more about Albion's fallen rational part and its consequences in the world by examining his multiple male divisions (his sons, Hand, Satan, his Spectre, fallen Luvah, and Urizen) and his fallen physical and affectionate part with its consequences by seeing his female divisions at work (his daughters, Rahab, Tirzah, Vala, and Enitharmon). While they appear to Albion and to us as separate characters, they are simply different aspects of the original situation and the concrete objective appearances of Albion's fall into disunity.

The eternal or saving characters of the poem also exemplify Albion's nature, his divine potential, which he could activate by exercising his imaginative capacity. Represented at the outset by the Savior, and later by Los, Erin, Jesus, and Jerusalem, they do not in their various guises engage in successive actions, as, for example, building Golgonooza the city of art (chap. 1), then searching Albion's inner self (chap. 2), then forgiving Jerusalem's apparent sin (chap. 3), and finally counteracting Anti-Christ (chap. 4), but serve in their separate guises to elucidate the various forms of the imaginative consciousness they represent. Their actions comprise a single act and are simultaneous, simply unfolding what is implied in the Savior's initial cry to Albion: "Awake! awake O sleeper of the land of shadows, wake! expand! / I am in you and you in me, mutual in love divine" (4:6–7). The Savior thereby calls for the expansive imaginative unity of man and God in a Divine Humanity based on love. Each subsequent eternal action is implied in the original one and is inherent in the Savior's words.

The initial opposition between Albion and the Savior mentioned above, with which the poem begins, also contains within it the kernel meaning of all the subsequent oppositions in the poem, and there is no further progress from it, simply an unfolding of all its implications. The contrast between sleep in Ulro (Albion's fallen state) and awakened Eternal Life (the Savior's unified state of identity and mutual love between man and God) could not become more complete than it is at the outset.[15] The subsequent contrasts between fallen Albion and various eternal characters simply explore and reveal the inherent conditions, using different actions and characters to illustrate the different manifestations of that opposition. The process of the poem is, however, necessary to explain the nature of the states and their opposition in order to educate and awaken both Albion and the reader.

Blake's poetic process may be compared to what happens when the lens is changed in the viewing apparatus of a microscope. Going from the ten-power to the forty-power lens seems to change what is seen. Although an apparently new picture springs into view, however, there is really nothing new there at all. Changing the focus has simply enabled the viewer to see what was not readily visible before. So too does Blake change our focus, by introducing new characters and events into the poem. Acting like the higher-power lens, each new character or event brings one part of the original theme into more minute and clearer focus, thereby providing new insights into what was seen before.

Blake also changes the magnification by the way in which he organizes his chapters. After he succinctly states his theme in the first two lines of chapter 1, he expands it first generally in chapter 1, and then part by part in each subsequent chapter until the last five plates, when he turns it inside out to examine it.

The first chapter gives us an overview of the whole by introducing all the characters and events of the entire poem. The inadequacy of such an overview is, however, apparent in its outcome: Albion denies Jerusalem and goes once more to death or, more accurately, remains in death (cf. pl. 24). Insufficiently educated by chapter 1's quick run-through, Albion remains incapable of accepting imaginative truth. Each subsequent chapter, then, acting as an even more powerful lens, multiplies the magnification and decreases the area covered, isolating one element of error at a time: religious, philosophic, or affective. By focusing powerfully upon each element along with its imaginative alternative and the interaction between the two, each chapter seems to present a new picture but really provides only part of the old, bit by bit increasing our knowledge and understanding of the theme.

Chapter 1 outlines all the thematic elements: religious and moral, philosophical (or rational) and political, affective and imaginative. Chapter 2 then fills in this outline by exploring the religious element with its moral consequences; chapter 3, by exploring the rational or philosophic one with its political and physical implications; and chapter 4, by exploring the imaginative or affective one.[16] While the same events seem to recur—for instance, Albion repeatedly dies, struggles with Luvah, opposes the Savior, is distorted and sacrificed by Vala—the context is different each time, so that we constantly discover a new meaning, either religious, philosophical, or affective, depending on the chapter, in the old action.

Unlike the operator of a conventional microscope, Blake does not keep his perspective constant, but varies the viewer's angle of vision from generation to eternity. What we see changes, depending on whether we see it from the eternal or imaginative perspective (as Los, Blake, Jesus, Erin, and Jerusalem do) or from the fallen or generative perspective (as fallen Albion, his sons and daughters, Hand, Satan, the Spectres, Rahab, Vala, and Enitharmon do). Therefore, depending upon our perspective, we may see Jerusalem as a harlot (18:12 and passim) or splendid angel (86:1–32, illus. 2); the human being as an expanding universe (34:49) or as a selfish center growing into a monstrous polypus (29:19 ff.); the world as humanized (pl. 99) or dead (5:1–10, illus. 54, passim), as Canaan or Cheviot (63:23–42), as opening from within like a flower (13:34), or as an abstract void (13:37) and intricate mill (15:15–16; 65:21; illus. 22). Blake's use of multiple perspectives relates directly to the theme, for Albion's passage from sleep to awakening is simply a profound change in his perspective.

By contrasting these two states, generation and eternity, which continuously coexist for Albion's choice, and their interaction, Blake dialectically unfolds the meaning of his theme. Their interaction forms the characteristic Blakean dialectic of the poem as it stresses the potential transformation of Albion's existence from the former to the latter.[17] While Blake calls this dialectic sleep, passage, and awaking, there are essentially just two states of consciousness possible: generation and eternity—Albion's sleep in Ulro, which is expressed in the major metaphor of his inner division, and its imaginative alternative, expressed in the opposite metaphor of unity. In one, Albion is sunk to mere matter, divided within himself, and cut off from God, woman, his fellow man, and an objectified universe; in the other, Albion is glorified as the Human Form Divine, developing all his human faculties and united with an immanent God, a comforting emanation, fraternal humanity, and a living, subjective universe. Albion's passage through eternal death consists of Blake's simultaneous investigation of these two alternatives and their interaction. Sleep and awaking remain unchanged throughout; but Albion's existence is transformed as the poem educates his consciousness by altering it from one state to the other. Had Albion originally been able to perceive truth, he would have understood all the opposing elements of sleep or generation and awaking or eternity from the very first plate, for all the elements are present when Los enters "the Door of Death for Albion's sake Inspired" (1:9). As it stands, however, the entire exposition of the poem is necessary to awaken his consciousness so that he may answer the Savior's initial call for unity and imagination. Blake intends his poem to perform a similar function for the reader (see 5:18–20), who should, if the poem is successful, be learning along with Albion and be similarly transformed.

Blake begins by stating his theme pictorially as well as poetically, and by graphically summarizing the action of the poem. While the text announces this theme in terms of Albion, the second full-plate illustration depicts it in terms of *Jerusalem: The Emanation of the Giant Albion*. Here on the title page Jerusalem sleeps in Ulro at the bottom of the plate, passes through eternal death at the left, and finally floats in her fully awakened, winged form at the top. Another version of the theme accompanies its poetic statement on plate 4. There Vala, purely physical nature, who controls the world in which she exists, dominates the illustration. Her cowled figure resembles the fallen female spirit who controls the merely natural world pictured in *Gates* 16 and *America* 14. With the same gesture of the hand as in *America*, she reaches out to control man in the merely natural world; but she is only partially successful in *Jerusalem*. Grasping the head of one naked male figure, fallen Albion, who is seated on the rocky shore, she controls his intellect and vision. The other naked male figure, unfallen Albion, however, eludes her grasp and turns his attention and praying hands to the soaring figures rising in a parabola from him. Here are Albion's ongoing alternatives graphically presented. Falling under Vala's influence, Albion is limited to the generative world of eternal death: the rocky shore he sits on, the clouds and darkness he contemplates, the sea of time and space, and the fibrous net of roots below him symbolizing infertile, restrictive nature, darkened perception and intellect, engulfing nightmare history. Escaping her influence, as the figure at Vala's right does, he awakens to the full, glorious, human existence of the soaring chain of figures who culminate in Jerusalem and the motto "Μονος ο Jesus" (Jesus only) above. The exploration of these choices forms the substance of the poem graphically as well as poetically, for each choice is further unfolded in subsequent illustrations.

Seen as a symbolic representation of Albion's alternatives in the world, this illustration (pl. 4) may also be viewed in another way. If read from top to bottom, it traces Albion's fall from his divine state, in which he chooses imaginative vision and Jesus, to his vegetative or rooted state, in which he chooses generative vision and purely physical nature. On the other hand, if read from bottom to top, it traces his progress from sleep to awakening. By presenting these multiple possibilities within one illustration, Blake does pictorially what he also does poetically throughout *Jerusalem*. He explores a moment as though it were a passage through time by revealing its implications. The moment of Albion's decision—his choice of imaginative or generative vision—may also be told as the story of his fall or his ascension from one state to another. Blake's poetic tale does this as it explores the state of Albion's consciousness by relating events as though one followed the other.

Blake's method of summary and elucidation is basically the same for each chapter as it is for the poem as a whole. Just as he begins his poem with a statement of the entire theme in both poetry and picture, and goes on to explain in detail the meaning and implications of its parts in the subsequent plates, so too does he begin each of the poem's four chapters with a summary of that chapter's theme and content and go on to elaborate that summary in the chapter. Each chapter consists of two parts, a two-plate preface comprised of a frontispiece and a dedication, and a twenty-two- or twenty-three-plate body of intermingled poetry and pictures that expands the prefatory summary.[18]

Each of *Jerusalem's* six full-plate illustrations serves a thematic function. The first and sixth (pl. 1, 100) begin and end the poem respectively with a thematic prologue and epilogue. The four others (pl. 2, 26, 51, 76) each precede one chapter of the poem, functioning as a thematic frontispiece to that chapter.[19] They are each followed by a dedicatory plate that further outlines the theme of the chapter in poetry, prose, and picture.

The dedication is in each case addressed to a particular group that in Blake's view typifies the error exposed in the chapter. These groups, however, refer to states of consciousness, rather than historical entities. Just as sleep, passage, and awakening are metaphors for a particular state of Albion's consciousness, so are Jews, Deists, and Christians (the dedicatory groups of chapters 2, 3, and 4 respectively). Further, as it takes the entire poem to explain what these states are, so too does it take the rest of the dedication and the chapter that follows it to clarify what is meant by that group named at the beginning of each dedication, what error each represents, and what imaginative alternative opposes that error.

Chapter 1, then, which presents an overview of Blake's theme and his general poetic purpose of reuniting man with his divinity through the process of the poem, is dedicated "To the General Public"; everyman's tale is generally applicable. Similarly, the frontispiece to the chapter (pl. 2) summarizes the theme in terms or Jerusalem's sleep and waking (everyman's emanation: liberty). Chapter 2, which explores the religious element of Albion's fall, with its moral consequences and its imaginative alternative, is dedicated "To the Jews," founders of Albion's religious and moral codes. This group typified Albion's religious error for Blake as well as its imaginative alternative in the religious truth of the Jewish prophetic tradition. The frontispiece to the chapter (pl. 26) also summarizes this religious opposition, as Hand, who symbolizes religious error, confronts liberty or inspired truth in Jerusalem. In chapter 3 the focus changes from the religious to the philosophic element of Albion's consciousness, hence the chapter is dedicated "To the Deists" (pl. 52), who epitomize philosophic error for Blake. The political consequences of this error are depicted in the frontispiece, which shows Deistic error in its princely guise, possessed of crown and scepter, seated in despair on a throne, ruling Albion and his world (pl. 51). Again, however, Blake is referring to a state of consciousness rather than simply a historical group, and the rest of the dedication and chapter clarifies the preface. Finally, chapter 4, which explores affective error, is dedicated to "The Christians" (pl. 77), both false Christians, who typify this error in their distortion of mental and physical liberty, and true Christians, who supply the inspired alternative to this restriction in their free exercise of imagination and mental labors, which are the true Gospel. Similarly, in the frontispiece to the chapter, as Albion regards Christ crucified upon the oak of suffering (pl. 76), true Christianity confronts its distortion and hints at its potential transformation.[20]

Blake's consistent procedure throughout his poem is to begin with thematic summary, which he opens outward in all directions. The first two lines of chapter 1 contain the action of the whole; the prologue and epilogue display it graphically. The first confrontation between Albion and the Savior outlines all other confrontations. The first chapter's frontispiece and dedication embrace the chapter as well as the whole poem. Each subsequent chapter's dedication and frontispiece take one piece of that whole and explore it, summarizing the content of the entire chapter.

There is, in addition, another movement outward in the poem in the direct correspondence Blake establishes between inner consciousness and the outer world. The state of man's consciousness is reflected not only in his perceptions, feelings, and thoughts, but also in the relationships, natural universe, and human institutions he establishes as a result of his consciousness. Although Albion's sleep, passage, and awakening refer to his inner state, and although his particular errors of religion, reason, and affection that the various chapters explore are errors of that state, consciousness does not exist as an isolated internal phenomenon but within the concrete workings of society, within a religious, social, political, economic, and cosmic context for which it has inevitable implications and consequences. Nothing goes on within Albion that is not reflected in his external situation; his dead and oppressive consciousness creates his dead and oppressive world, as, on the contrary, his imaginative consciousness creates a living and liberated world.

Each chapter inevitably investigates Albion's errors and alternatives in terms of institutions and cosmic conditions, as well as states of mind. In each chapter we see what error means for Albion both internally and externally, how it distorts man's image of himself and consequently his institutions, and his land. Religious error thus not only denies man's indwelling divinity and distorts his idea of God, of man, and of woman, but it also perverts his churches and his moral codes, planting revenge, denial, and enmity as principles of action and poisoning his laws and social relations. Rational error too not only limits Albion's intellect to empirical science and Lockean logic, but equally limits his physical world to the inevitable expression of material phenomena obeying abstract laws, his political world to existent tyrannies destroying liberty and spreading universal war, and his economic world to the exploitive factory system produced by empirical science in the new industrial world. Finally, affective error as it tries to abolish Albion's liberty of mind and body also has its inevitable consequences. It establishes chastity and moral law, which institutionalize jealousy and cruelty, relationships of dominance and possessiveness between man and woman and between man and man, and abets war and oppressive religious and civil laws.

It is not accidental that Albion is treated as man and as land, as an individual who symbolizes everyman and as England, which by extension symbolizes all nations. In this double role he exemplifies the correspondence between inner and outer conditions. Nothing can happen within Albion that is not at the same time happening to his cities, villages, farms, forests, streams, and mountains, nor can his doctrines help being expressed in institutions, armies, churches, governments, economies, courts, families, or religious, moral, and civil laws. Albion's darkened land or its golden harmony presents a metaphor for both his state of mind and the objective appearance of that state.

NOTES

1. The following critics all characterize *Jerusalem* as structurally chaotic: E. J. Ellis and W. B. Yeats, *The Works of William Blake*, vol. 2 (London: Quaritch, 1893); P. Berger, *William Blake: Mysticisme et Poesie* (Paris: H. Bidier, 1907); D. J. Sloss and J. P. R. Wallis, *The Prophetic Writings of William Blake* (Oxford: Oxford University Press, 1926); Laurence Binyon, *The Engraved De-*

signs of William Blake (London: Ernest Benn, 1926); W. H. Stevenson, "Blake's *Jerusalem*," *Essays in Criticism* 9 (1959): 254–64; John Beer, *Blake's Visionary Universe* (Manchester: University of Manchester Press, 1969).

2. Various critics have found some thematic unity in the poem but have not attempted to show how the particular parts were related to the theme. Among these are: S. Foster Damon, *William Blake, His Philosophy and Symbols* (1924; reprint ed. Gloucester, Mass.: Peter Smith, 1958); Herschel M. Margoliouth, *William Blake* (London: Oxford, 1951); David V. Erdman, *Blake: Prophet against Empire* (Princeton, N.J.: Princeton University Press, 1954); Joseph H. Wicksteed, *William Blake's "Jerusalem"* (London: Trianon Press, 1954).

3. Northrop Frye, *Fearful Symmetry: A Study of William Blake* (Princeton, N.J.: Princeton University Press, 1947). Frye's thesis that chapters 1 and 2 of *Jerusalem* describe man's fall, chapter 3 his struggle in the world, and chapter 4 his redemption and apocalypse is not completely carried out in the poem. Man falls and struggles repeatedly throughout, and his opportunity for redemption is omnipresent.

4. Harold Bloom, *The Visionary Company: A Reading of English Romanticism* (Garden City, N.Y.: Doubleday, 1963); idem, *Blake's Apocalypse* (Garden City, N.Y.: Doubleday, 1963); idem, commentary, *The Poetry and Prose of William Blake*, ed. David V. Erdman (Garden City, N.Y.: Doubleday, 1970); idem, "Blake's *Jerusalem*: The Bard of Sensibility and the Form of Prophecy," in *Ringers in the Tower: Studies in Romantic Tradition* (Chicago: University of Chicago Press, 1971). Randall Helms, "Ezekiel and Blake's *Jerusalem*," *Studies in Romanticism* 13 (1974): 127–40, also adopts this view, following Bloom's lead.

5. Joanne Witke, "*Jerusalem*, a Synoptic Poem," *Comparative Literary Studies* 22 (1970): 265–78. Unlike the church fathers whom Witke follows, most modern biblical scholars exclude John from the "synoptic Gospels." This modern exclusion leaves only three synoptic Gospels—Matthew, Mark, and Luke—making Witke's analogy less than perfect.

6. Stuart Curran, "The Structures of *Jerusalem*," in *Blake's Sublime Allegory: Essays on the "Four Zoas," "Milton," "Jerusalem"*, ed. Stuart Curran and Joseph Anthony Wittreich, Jr. (Madison, Wis.: University of Wisconsin Press, 1973), pp. 329–46. Curran turns his attention to the multiplicity of organizing principles in the poem and identifies seven major structures, dividing the poem at, within, and across Blake's chapter divisions. While Curran's careful discussion is often illuminating, his concentration on structural multiplicity overlooks structural unity, leading to Hazard Adams's criticism that "Curran finds so many structures that either one's scepticism is aroused as to their real presences or one begins to imagine that anyone might play at the structure finding game." "Blake, *Jerusalem*, and Symbolic Form," *Blake Studies* 2 (1975): 55, n. 9.

7. Karl Kiralis, "Theme and Structure of William Blake's *Jerusalem*," in *The Divine Vision: Studies in the Poetry and Art of William Blake*, ed. Vivian de Sola Pinto (London: Victor Gollancz, 1957), pp. 141–62.

8. Henry Lesnick, "Narrative Structure and the Antithetical Vision of *Jerusalem*," in *Blake's Visionary Forms Dramatic*, ed. David V. Erdman and John E. Grant (Princeton, N.J.: Princeton University Press, 1970), pp. 391–412.

9. E. J. Rose, "The Structure of Blake's *Jerusalem*," *Bucknell Review* 40, no. 3 (1963): 35–54.

10. Anne K. Mellor, *Blake's Human Form Divine* (Berkeley, Calif.: University of California Press, 1974).

11. W. J. T. Mitchell, *Blake's Composite Art: A Study of the Illuminated Poetry* (Princeton, N.J.: Princeton University Press, 1978).

12. Roger Easson, "Blake and his Reader in *Jerusalem*," in *Blake's Sublime Allegory*, pp. 309–27 isolates four distinct levels of narration whose interaction provides the poem's structure and whose progression the reader responds to in working through the poem. Hazard Adams ("Symbolic Form") states that his interpretation of the unity of *Jerusalem* as based on the unmediated creation of a world in language, the creation of the poem itself, takes its impetus from Easson's essay. Mollyanne Marks, "Self-Sacrifice: Theme and Image in *Jerusalem*," *Blake*

Studies 7, no. 1 (1975): 27–50, states that "the process of composition is itself the subject and ordering principle throughout" (p. 46). Represented therein, she notes, is imagination's attempt to transcend spatial and temporal limits, the paradigm of which is Los's struggle with his spectre, which is also the struggle of Albion, Christ, and Blake in the poem.

13. I have omitted a discussion of my particular agreements and disagreements with other critics as unnecessarily distracting here, although I note them in my essay on *Jerusalem*, *Blake Studies* (forthcoming). The substance of the discussion emerges in the textual analysis that follows.

14. *The Poetry and Prose of William Blake*, ed. David V. Erdman and Harold Bloom (Garden City, N.Y.: Doubleday, 1970). All citations from the text of Blake's poetry and prose are from this edition.

15. Harold Bloom, *Blake's Apocalypse*, p. 366, sees "a gradually sharpening antithesis between two contrary forces in the poem"; however, the initial antithesis between Albion and the Savior is so complete that there is no room for sharpening to occur.

16. I use the term *affective error* to denote that distortion of mental and physical liberty most apparent in the perversion of the affections that chapter 4 explores. It includes the false concept of love presented by the fallen females, the limitation of consciousness that this error reflects, and the oppression of body and mind that results from it.

17. While Blake's dialectic bears certain resemblances to Hegel's or Marx's, it differs from both in one vital respect. There is no ongoing historical progression in it, rather an alternating and infinitely repeatable progression and regression. Albion's existence in generation is transformed by imagination, which works upon fallen appearances and doctrines to transcend them by preserving what is valuable in them (e.g., physical nature, sense experience, human reason, natural science), but founding them on a new basis so that they are no longer limited and restrictive but function freely, enabling man to realize his full potential. Blake's dialectic thus resembles Hegel's in the transformation of an entity by its contrary, its transcendence (*Aufhebung*), and its insistence on the necessity of contraries for existence. For Hegel, however, this transformation changes the original character of both contraries and brings into existence a new state, which will be similarly transformed in either an intellectual or historical progression (the processes described in Hegel's *Logic* and *Phenomenology of Spirit*, respectively). In Blakean dialectic, generation alone is transformed by eternity, which itself remains unaffected. Dialectical progression goes only this far. Further change is possible, but only as renewed fall through dialectical regression to an earlier state. There is a movement back and forth between generation and eternity instead of a Hegelian dialectical progression. *Jerusalem* differs in this respect from some of Blake's earlier works (e.g., *Songs of Innocence, Book of Thel*) in which a state of innocence both transforms and is transformed by its contrary, so that both are transcended in a new state—a higher innocence, Beulah or Eternity—that fulfills the earlier ones. Perhaps the difference is due to the nontemporal character of *Jerusalem*, which explores the single moment of transcendence only.

18. Blake divides the plates symmetrically. Chapters 1 and 4 contain a twenty-two-plate body, while the middle chapters, 2 and 3, contain twenty-three plates in theirs.

19. Jean H. Hagstrum, *William Blake: Poet and Painter* (Chicago: University of Chicago Press, 1964), points out that in *The Bedford Hours* each section of the book is preceded by a full-page illustration that gives the theme of the section that follows. Blake's similar practice in *Jerusalem* is one part of the general kinship between his method of illumination and that of the medieval book illuminators.

20. David Bindman, *Blake as an Artist* (Oxford: Phaidon; New York: E. P. Dutton, 1977), p. 179, suggests that the illustration shows Albion's awakening and Christ's sacrifice, and equates the two.

2
The Frame

THE six full-plate illustrations and the dedications for each of the four chapters of *Jerusalem* provide a framework for the rest of the poem. While they do not narrate the events of the poem in full dramatic detail, these ten plates do provide a thematic synopsis of the whole, expand the succinctly stated theme of chapter 1's opening lines, offer a view of the poem in miniature, and set up the terms that each chapter will explore in further detail. Concentrating on symbolic actions, they provide a series of epiphanies that the other plates elaborate and explain. The first and last plates (pls. 1, 100) act as a graphic prologue and epilogue that provide an overview of the entire action from the dialectically opposed perspectives of generation and eternity, while the pair of plates preceding each chapter outlines that chapter's particular theme and content as part of the whole action.

The dedication to the general public and the frontispiece depicting the entire story of Jerusalem's sleep and awakening (pl. 2) introduce the first chapter's outline of all the elements and consequences of Albion's fall together with their imaginative alternatives. Each subsequent chapter then goes on to cut across the theme and examine a single cross section of it, which is announced in the frontispiece to the chapter and typified by the dedicatory group of the chapter, and whose basic dialectic is unfolded in the prose and poetry of the dedication. The prose section of each dedication explains discursively that chapter's subject matter—the error that the chapter sets out to correct and its imaginative alternative, while the poetic section of each explores the same error dramatically, posing an archetypal situation in which error and truth interact with one another.

25

The full-page illustration of Los entering "the Door of Death for Albions sake Inspired" (1:9) with which *Jerusalem* opens captures the situation of the whole poem in the image of a single action, a single figure, and a single moment. From the graffiti over the doorway, we learn of the two adjacent, coexistent, and omnipresent realms that the poem explores—the Void (also called sleep, Ulro, or Generation in the poem) and Existence (alternately called awakening, Eden, or Eternity). While the poem tells us much more about the meaning of these two realms, this plate immediately gives us their salient features. Existence is characterized by the imaginative light pictured in the illustration, while the Void is poetically described in terms of sleep, shadow, and rock (1:3–4). Albion's initial position is in the void, dead, with petrified and "fixd" intellect and emotions (his "sublime" and "pathetic" qualities [1:4]), enclosed by limited reason (his covering "Spectrous Power" [1:5]), which does not allow him to see farther than this fallen universe that he creates and is limited to (1:1–2). This continues to be Albion's situation for most of the poem. Why and how this comes to be and what exactly it means is, of course, explained at length in the poem. Now we simply learn that it is so. Los's alternative position in existence presents Albion's potential alternative, which also exists throughout the poem. By his example, Los shows the reader as well as Albion the way to salvation. Neither is, however, ready to see Los's message quite yet. The exposition of the rest of the poem is necessary before the meaning of this first plate becomes entirely clear, before Los's mission can be accomplished in Albion's awakening as Albion finally imitates Los's initial action (96:20–36).[1] Yet certain things do become clear as we gaze at the illustration. First, Los's liberating function, which we read about continuously in the poem, appears in his stepping forward and in the lamp of concentric circles resembling a center opening outward, which he holds and with which he lights the void. In addition, his search for the particular human creative powers within Albion whose exercise can save Albion is prefigured (pl. 45). The basic dialectic between Albion's ongoing alternatives, the void and existence, or generation and imagination as they are most frequently called, is thus set forth.

Within the illustration itself, Los's lamp casts the only apparent light, for only imagination can light up the world. Without it, Albion's world would remain dark. Imagination is also evident in the Gothic doorway that Los steps through on his way to save Albion, which connects Los's unfallen and Albion's fallen realms. Since Gothic is living form, the spirit of prophecy walks through it to bring imagination to the world. The wind apparent in Los's hair and garments, which blows through the door from the void, indicates the potential breath of life that Los's coming may revive. The contrast with Blake's illustration for *Gates* 15 is instructive in this connection. There an aged, bent figure enters "Death's Door" as the wind blows from behind him into the grave. The reversal of the wind direction points to the absence of living breath beyond the grave, and the post-and-lintel construction of that door, which replaces the Gothic of *Jerusalem,* marks its deadly connection too.[2] In the frontispiece to *Jerusalem,* however, the outward breeze, the Gothic doorway, Los's vigorous striding figure, and his glowing light oppose the death and darkness beyond, illustrating the possible enlightenment of generation through imagination.

Abandoning for a moment Blake's more orderly procedure of exposing one aspect of error after another in the poem, let us skip to the last full-page illustration of *Jerusalem,* which functions as a thematic epilogue corresponding to the prologue of the first plate. Each epitomizes the action of the whole, while they serve as contrary visions to one another, rounding out the poem's dialectic. While the frontispiece devotes most of its space and inscription to darkness, the fallen realm of sleeping Albion, and presents Los with his imaginative light as the omnipresent potentiality of eternity within the actuality of generation, the last plate does just the opposite. It devotes most of its space to light and the imaginative world that awakened Albion creates, but shows generative darkness and night waiting just beyond that imaginative light as an equally omnipresent potential for Albion. Each vision is appropriate to its place. At the beginning of the action Albion is sunk in sleep, and imagination is his potentiality that can be actualized whenever his consciousness is ready to assert it. At the end of the poem, on the other hand, Albion is fully awakened in his imaginative state, and generation now becomes a potentiality for him as imagination was formerly.

The frontispiece and epilogue thus illustrate Albion's opposing alternatives of Death and Life in typically dialectical terms. Just as the frontispiece demonstrates through Los's entrance and light that Albion even in his sleeping state is open to the possibility of awakening, so the epilogue demonstrates by its representation of darkness, Druidic structures, and Enitharmon's figure that man in his awakened state is still open to the possibility of renewed sleep and passage. The poem's circularity is thereby implied as well. Albion's final awakening (pl. 95) and his newly humanized universe (pl. 99) are no more permanent than his initial state of generation. While the epilogue illustrates the triumph of imagination, it also depicts the possibility of Albion's renewed fall from unity, the original situation with which the poem began, in its picture of lurking darkness and surrounding night.

In the last full-page illustration, the central figure facing the reader holds Los's hammer and tongs, the tools of imagination throughout the poem. Most critics, therefore, identify him as either Los or his eternal form, Urthona. However, since the last five plates of the poem depict Albion in his eternal state, and since, moreover, eternal Albion includes unfallen imagination, Los or Urthona, as part of his fourfold humanity, it seems more likely that Albion is the figure in the illustration. Tall, curly-haired, strong, and youthful, this male figure resembles both the illustrations of Los in the poem (e.g., 6, 44, 73) and those of Albion (e.g., 14, 31, 33, 76, 95, 97). This resemblance is not surprising, since the two are potentially one throughout. Heretofore, however, Albion has been in his fallen state, sunk in sleep or generation, ignoring his imaginative potential. Now, on the contrary, he is awake and achieves his eternal form (pl. 95 ff.), so that his potential becomes actual, and he merges with Los. Therefore, he may appropriate Los's tools as well. Similarly, Albion now also includes his unfallen divinity and reason, which we see pictured in his bearded Jehovah-Urizen appearance in plates 96 and 99, and his liberated sexuality, which the full frontal view of his genitals, apparent for the first time in the poem in plate 100, indicates. Behind him the world of generation through which he has just come appears dominated by the figures of Los and Enitharmon, the two immortal forms within generation. On the right is Los, still carrying the sun of imagination as he did in the frontispiece, for he is the constant spirit of prophecy within the world. His light illuminates his figure, Albion's, and half the illustration as it turns golden even the serpentine line of Druid trilithons and nature's green sward beneath Albion's feet; for reason, religion, and the natural world are inevitably transformed by the power of imagination. On the left, however, is a more ambiguous figure, the feminine complement or emanation of Los, Enitharmon. While her spindle illuminates her face and forearms, merges with the moon's glow in her veil, and reminds us that the unfallen emanation is an imaginative connection to eternity, it also recalls the spindle of necessity, which restricts man throughout the poem when wielded by Rahab, the Daughters of Albion (84:29–30), or Vala (64:32; 66:10; 80:32,37). The glowing veil, too, while it reinforces the moony light of love, also recalls the restrictive function of Vala's veil (e.g., illus. 46) as does the moon (e.g., pl. 8) which recalls the moon ark of the fallen female too (e.g., illus. 24). As it rains blood on the earth, Vala's overflowing cup of sacrifice is recalled (88:56; 22:29; illus. 69), as well as the saving blood of self-sacrifice. Enitharmon's darkened body casts a shadow on the earth, counteracting Los's light, but it is mixed with red and purple and is therefore not so dark as that of the starry night of reason in the background, whose blackness reminds us of reason's restrictive function in generation, most particularly described in chapter 3 of the poem. The epilogue thus reflects the poem's ongoing dialectic between imagination and generation and leaves man at the end of *Jerusalem* still open to generative possibility but better able to cope with it because of his now enlightened consciousness.

Moving from the larger frame to the four smaller ones within it, we come to the first chapter's frontispiece and dedication. Since the chapter provides a general outline of the whole poem, it is appropriately dedicated "To the General Public" (pl. 3) and addressed to each reader as the individual personification of that public. Above the dedication the design forms a rounded arch resembling a doorway through which the reader enters the poem. On one side of the archway is inscribed "sheep" and on the other, "goats." Just as the two will be separated by Christ on Judgment Day, so will they be by Los at his furnaces in the poem, and by Blake as they read his poem. Blake explicitly addresses the reader in the hope that "the Reader will be with . . . [him] wholly One in Jesus our Lord" (pl. 3). Jesus for Blake, however, is an indwelling God whose form is human imagination. Blake thus urges the reader to join him in imaginative endeavor by means of the poem in following and learning from Albion's struggle. The reader should then become an active participant in the poem as he uncovers its various layers of meaning and discovers the identities between characters and events, exercising his imagination and following the changing patterns of Blake's kaleidoscopic structure. The dedication to chapter 1 also announces Blake's general poetic purpose of reuniting man with his divinity through love and forgiveness and restoring his original, prelapsarian state of "Wisdom, Art, and Science" (pl. 3), which is also Los's action in relation to divided Albion and which culminates in the vision of regenerated Albion at the end.

Accompanying the envoi to the reader which points to the possibility of human metamorphosis, a process the poem describes in Albion's passage through various states, is a human figure emerging from a chrysalis much as a butterfly does. This figure echoes the image of Jerusalem depicted on the title page that also serves as a prefatory illustration for chapter 1 by providing a general graphic summary of Blake's entire theme. While the chapter explores the theme largely in terms of Albion, and the dedication does so in terms of the reader who represents the general public, the full-page illustration turns its attention to Jerusalem. The story of human fall or sleep in Ulro that the poem unfolds becomes Jerusalem's story as much as it is Albion's, but her version is introduced separately. Once unified and identical in eternity, Albion and Jerusalem are divided into separate spheres in generation by Albion's initial refusal of unity with the Savior (4:23). This shattered unity is exemplified in their separate pictorial and poetic treatment.

Their original unity and inclusiveness is evident, however, in the universal remnant of sun, moon, and planets that each displays: Jerusalem on her wings (pl. 2) and Albion on his body (pl. 25). Jerusalem's fall from this unified and universal being is depicted in her sleeping position at the bottom of the plate (which is repeated in plate 33 and echoed by Albion in plates 14 and 19) and illustrates the first part of Blake's theme: sleep in Ulro. Mourned over by the two females whose spiky flower caps suggest their ties to physical nature in its fallen aspect,[3] the female, like the male, appears divided within herself. As we follow the picture clockwise from the bottom to top, we see the rest of Blake's theme illustrated. Jerusalem rises from sleep through passage in her emergent chrysalis form to awakening in her full butterfly form. If, on the contrary, we look counterclockwise from top to bottom, we see how Jerusalem falls into sleep. Both readings are, of course, her story, and Blake displays them both simultaneously, just as he tells the story of opposing states and alternatives in the poetry. The minute drawings of birds, winged insects, and human figures that flit between and around the letters of the title in streaming clouds, blushing colors, and universal ascension, however, underscore the rising aspect of her story here just as her half-insect, half-woman form at the upper left marks her passage from sleep to the fully awakened form with closed and rounded wings that floats across the top of the plate.[4] This is the same story that the entire poem tells about Albion, for the two are really complementary halves of a single tale, a tale displayed in the visual and verbal microcosm of the prefatory material for chapter 1.

Once he provides the general view of the theme in chapter 1, Blake begins to examine successive cross sections of it in the other chapters. He begins with the religious cross section in chapter 2. Dedicated "To the Jews," founders of Albion's religion who typify his errors in their patriarchal tradition and also provide the imaginative alternative to those errors in their prophetic tradition, chapter 2 explores in Blake's usual dialectical way the religious elements of Albion's fall that plates 4–9 introduce in chapter 1.

It is first of all necessary to clarify what Blake means by the group that he chooses to typify religious error, the Jews. Since he identifies the Jewish patriarchs as Druids (pl. 27) and sets "Babylon with cruel

Og" (27:22) within their synagogue, he is obviously not referring simply to historical Jewry. When he further mentions that Druid temples are spread "over the whole Earth" (pl. 27) and extends his address to all "Inhabitants of Earth [united] in One Religion" (pl. 27), it becomes apparent that he is addressing a spiritual group rather than a historical one. All those who commit the typical twin errors of false religion—the error of exiling God from within man to the sky and that of adopting a moral code based on denial—be they historical Jews, Druids, Babylonians, Catholic popes, or Anglican bishops, are, in Blake's view, Jews and included in the dedication. Blake's further claim that the patriarchs were Druids and that Britain was "the Primitive Seat of the Patriarchal Religion" (pl. 27) establishes a particular identity between the Jews and the English, but one that transcends contemporary mythologists' and "antiquaries'" theories of an Ur-culture from which all peoples, languages, mythologies, and religions are descended.[5] For Blake, the only Ur-culture is eternity, and insofar as national cultures with their various religions, languages, and mythologies try to reflect this primeval unified state, they are all one and all have equal validity. When Blake cites the work of Jacob Bryant and others to support his own ideas and identifies all antiquities with those of the Jews, he is communicating a cognitive rather than anthropological truth in identifying the original imaginative unity of all inspiration.[6] This is a far cry from the Phoenician, Ammonian, or Atlantean Ur-culture of the mythologists, although it may have some superficial resemblances to them. Insofar as all religions, however, have abandoned imaginative truth, they are all equally in error and may be identified with the Jews who have abandoned their imaginative truth for legalistic, patriarchal error. Therefore, Blake tells the Jews, "Your Ancestors derived their origins from Abraham, Heber, Shem, and Noah, who were Druids: as the Druid Temples (which are the Patriarchal Pillars & Oak Groves) over the whole Earth witness to this day" (pl. 27). Druid becomes patriarch throughout all the nations of the earth, for they all practice sacrifice and vengeance in place of true religion.

Later, when Blake urges the Jews to "Take up the Cross O Israel & follow Jesus" (pl. 27), he is urging the return of all to the original, universal religion of mutual love and forgiveness, that Ur-religion of Jesus as well as Jerusalem.

In naming the dedicatory group, Blake thus characterizes the error that chapter 2 explores. The dedicatory poem then goes on to depict this error together with its imaginative alternative, summarizing the action of the entire chapter. Albion's prelapsarian state, both individual and geographical (27:1–20), his fall (27:21–64), and his redemption (27:65–88) appear as Jewish religious error and

truth. The prelapsarian eternal state characterized by forgiveness
and self-sacrifice, in which man and God intermingle and the contraries of inspiration and reason coexist as Jerusalem's "golden
arches . . . Shine upon the starry sky" (27:11–12), is smashed by
religious error, in which the foreign enemies of inspiration "Babylon
and Cruel Og,/With Moral & Self-righteous Law . . . Crucify in
Satans Synagogue" (27:22–24)—that is, merge with false religion's
self-righteous law of sin and moral virtue to destroy human potential under Satan's aegis. The nature of this Satanic deity, his notions
of sin and moral law that destroy the truly human, are fully explained in the chapter. In the prefatory poem, however, we see
these doctrines or laws debasing England (27:32–36), withering up
liberty (Jerusalem) (27:49–52), the entire world (27:50), and the Human Form itself (27:53–55), as well as substituting "Druid Pillars"
(27:39) for Jerusalem's golden ones (27:3–4) and places of sacrifice
such as Paddington (27:26), London Stone (27:33), Tyburn's Brook
(27:34), and the Fatal Tree of Albion (27:29) for the places of compassion such as Golgonooza, the dwelling of the "golden builders"
(27:25). Religious error sets up as God (27:36–40) Albion's own
spectre, his rational projection Satan, who spreads war through
time and space, over Europe from Rhine to Danube in the contemporary Napoleonic wars, or over Asia in the biblical Babylonian
conquests (27:45–48).

The alternative to religious error is presented in the last part of the
dedicatory poem (27:55–88) as Divine Vision works through the enlightened poet to show man his imaginative potential. Blake's self-
sacrifice here is prophetic on two levels. Indicating his acceptance of
imagination in writing the poem, it prefigures the achievement of
his wider purpose—to free the reader's imagination and return him
to eternity—and it anticipates Albion's final similar action in the
poem as well. Taking responsibility for the spectre who is the product of human restrictive error, Blake deposes Satan, the false god, in
favor of Divine Humanity, the true god. As Blake describes the
universe of regenerated man based on mutual love (27:85–88) rather
than sin and punishment, we anticipate the Edenic vision proposed
by various eternal characters during chapter 2 and achieved by Humanity at the end of the poem.

The final prose passage that follows the prefatory poem once
more summarizes the action of chapter 2 as it states: "compulsory
cruel Sacrifices had brought Humanity into a Feminine Tabernacle,
in the loins of Abraham & David" (pl. 27), summarizing the action of
the dedicatory poem's middle section. In addition, the imaginative
alternative mentioned in the first and third sections of the dedicatory poem and also explored in the chapter is here enunciated as the

anticipated appearance of the Savior on earth and the "Return of Israel to Mental Sacrifice and War" (pl. 27).

The full-page illustration that precedes chapter 2 (pl. 26) also serves as a thematic prefatory summary of the chapter. In it we see Judaism in its fallen role as Hand confronting its imaginative role in Jerusalem. Hand's religion of sin and punishment, moral virtue, atonement, and sacrifice of others (described in pl. 9) represents that version of Jewish legalism which chapter 2 exposes as error, while Jerusalem, who "is named Liberty among the Sons of Albion" according to the inscription below her figure, symbolizes the liberating Jewish prophetic tradition that the chapter offers as an alternative to error. Both Hand and Jerusalem, however, represent more than historic Judaism. Hand's pose, his arms outspread in crucified position,[7] the flames in which he walks that halo his head and twine along his outspread arms like a brazen serpent but cast no light beyond him, the black cloud behind him, the dark background, his frowning look at Jerusalem, her apparent fright or distrust—all indicate the distortion or demonic parody of inspiration that Hand's religion represents in both its Judaic origins and Christian continuation. For good reason, then, is eternal Jerusalem appalled by Hand and his code of various "thou shalt nots." David Erdman suggests that Hand is perhaps leading her into Hades,[8] which is where his kind of religion really leads. Perceiving this, she stops dead in her tracks, raising her hands in a gesture of refusal. True religion will not be led astray and inverted by false, although it may temporarily be cast into shadow by it, as Jerusalem is by Hand in the illustration. Hand's attempt "to destroy Jerusalem, & to devour the body of Albion" (9:10) is thus doomed to failure, although he does not realize it. This interchange is dramatized in more detail as false religion tries to destroy Jerusalem and Albion in the chapter itself.

The next thematic cross section begins in the prefatory section of chapter 3. Dedicated to the Deists, the chapter focuses on the rational or philosophic element of Albion's fall, using the Deists as that symbolic group which for Blake epitomizes rational error as the Jews do religious error. Based on the limitation of man's intellect to his reason, Deistic error replaces human imagination with human understanding, deifies reason as the governing principle of the universe while exiling God from within man and the world and leaving both at the mercy of purely physical or mechanical forces. Anyone who accepts such a view of God, man, and the world is, despite his actual historical role, in Blake's terms a Deist.

Blake's definition of Deism is not really so arbitrary as it may at first seem. Even an ordinary modern desk dictionary defines Deism as "a movement or system of thought advocating natural religion

based on human reason rather than revelation emphasizing morality, and in the eighteenth century denying the interference of the
Creator with the laws of the universe."[9] Thus Blake's definition is
based on certain definite characteristics of Deism, which he generalizes across time and space and opposes to imagination. Since Deism
favors a material view of man as opposed to the human form divine—an absent, passive god as opposed to an immanent active
god, reason rather than revelation, general laws as opposed to the
humanized universe of imagination, natural religion rather than
inspired prophetic religion, and natural morality rather than forgiveness—all who favor these ideas are ipso facto Deists.

The error of the Deists begins, Blake tells us, by teaching "that
Man is Righteous in his Vegetated Spectre" (pl. 52). We have only to
look at Rousseau's praise of natural man or the writings of Locke
and Hume, praised by Voltaire, which glorify man as a natural
creature of sense and reason to find the truth of Blake's statement.
For Locke, man is simply the sum of his sense impressions and his
reflections on them.[10] Similarly, for Hume man is "nothing but a
bundle or collection of different perceptions which succeed each
other with an inconceivable rapidity and are in a perpetual flux and
movement."[11] Here is Blake's "Vegetated Spectre" or merely natural
man whom the Daughters of Albion circumscribe, bind, and
sacrifice to their own ends within the chapter, the Deistic conception of man bound by purely physical nature. Through their
theories of sensation Locke and his followers have "bound En-
glishmen to dead nature and imprisoned them in the cavern of their
material bodies,"[12] a process that together with its consequences, is
summarized in the dedication and explored in the chapter.

According to Blake the Deists equally mistake the nature of God
by "calling the Prince of this World, God; and destroying all who do
not worship Satan under the Name of God" (pl. 52). All who deny
the immanent and transcendent God that is the Human Imagination: Jews, Christians, and indeed "Every Religion that Preaches
Vengeance for Sin" (pl. 52) are in Blake's view Deists. This identity
between Judaism and Deism, while it does not make literal sense,
can be understood as underscoring their similar departures from
and opposition to what Blake sees as inspired prophetic religion.
Both portray perverted religion and moral virtue, deny the indwelling divinity of man, and affirm his merely natural form. They are
therefore in the "State named Rahab" (pl. 52). But our focus in
looking at them is different; for that state of the Jews proceeds from
their acceptance of a sky-dwelling deity and his negative decalogue,
whereas that of the Deists proceeds from natural religion and morality. In examining each, Blake displays a different facet of Albion's

error. For the Deists "Religion is the Worship of the God of this World by the means of what . . . [they] call Natural Religion and Natural Philosophy, and of Natural Morality or Self-Righteousness, the Selfish Virtues of the Natural Heart" (pl. 52). This false trinity of naturals, combined in the equally false unity of the selfhood, the philosopher's natural man motivated purely by self-interest, is further explored within the chapter. The Deistic selfhood necessarily cuts man off from man and replaces brotherhood with enmity. Therefore "The ultimate and inevitable expression of unannihilated Selfhood, whether it assumes the disguise of philosophy or patriotism, or—in the politics of interest and 'security'—no disguise at all, is War."[13]

Blake's particular concern is, however, with Deism's exclusive emphasis on reason—"Greek philosophy" and "Experimental Theory" (pl. 52)—which is examined together with its world-shattering consequences in the chapter. While inspiration represented in the dedication by "a Monk or a Methodist" sees through material appearances to imaginative reality, enabling man to live in eternal terms, in constant interpenetration of natural and divine, Deistic limitation to analytical reason restricts man to material appearances, to the generative world and its analysis. It thus limits him in its political consequences to the generative powers that rule this world, established church and monarchy. In this way Deistic reason bolsters the spectrous forces and is responsible for war, martyrdom, and tyranny, the violence of history portrayed in the chapter. While this connection may seem absurd at face value, for historically many Deists were opposed to the tyrannical kings of Europe and were searching for an escape from the state of war in a peaceful commonwealth, Blake uses it to point out the innate perniciousness implied in the Deistic world view itself. When Blake claims that "All the Destruction therefore, in Christian Europe has arisen from Deism which is Natural Religion" (pl. 52), he means to accuse that vision and the religion that arises from it which limit man and the universe to material functions, eliminate all but material authority, the tyrannical princes of the world who perpetually struggle with each other for material possession and power, and spread enmity and war.

Within such a vision an active immanent God no longer exists but is replaced by Satan, the spectrous projection of Albion's intellect (man's reason), and mechanical forces replace inspired action. Man himself is objectified as a merely natural creature who can be manipulated along with the other natural objects in the universe, may be exploited or killed with impunity, for he possesses no inherent divinity or distinctive humanity but is simply another natural object. Natural religion, then, emerges as the opposite of Blake's Christianity, which is "Forgiveness of Sin" and "can never be the cause of a War or a single Martyrdom" (pl. 52).

Blake's further accusation that Deists "acquit & flatter the Alexanders & Caesars, the Lewis's & Fredericks: who alone are its [War's] causes & its actors" (pl. 52) is a personal jab at Voltaire, but the main thrust of his criticism is not simply personal. It is aimed at the consequences of Voltaire's world view, his celebration of English empiricism, his exclusive devotion to reason as the "exact analysis of things" and therefore the basis of all knowledge and progress,[14] his glorification of the simply material universe, his praise of Locke as the "anatomist of soul," and of God as an "eternal machinist."[15]

Blake omits many names from his list of historic Deists while including others who were not strictly or historically speaking Deists, for the former's actions do not fit his definition while the latter's do. Thomas Paine thus does not fall into the category of Deist for Blake, although historically he was one; for his "Energetic Genius" (*Anno. Watson,* p. 603) does not fulfill Blake's definition.[16] Similarly, Blake praises "a Monk or a Methodist" (pl. 52), ignoring their abundant historical support of economic exploitation, political repression, and social inequity, and noting only their recognition of divine presence in the world.

This dedicatory plate, like all the others, divides into a prose and a poetic section. In the prose portion, Blake exposes Deistic error by attacking its exclusive devotion to reason, its image of the merely natural man, its practice of natural religion and morality, all of which he blames for war and tyranny in the world. He poses the imaginative alternative to Deism in true Christianity based on forgiveness and interpenetration of human and divine, matter and spirit. The poetic portion of the dedication restates this summary in dramatic and dialectical terms by contrasting Voltaire's, Gibbon's, and Rousseau's Deistic view with the Grey Monk's inspired view. Out of this opposition emerge the destructive, warlike, and sacrificial characteristics of the former and the compassionate, intellectual, pitying, and self-sacrificing characteristics of the latter. The contrast between the violent imagery of the Deistic forces and the compassionate imagery of the imaginative forces presented in the chapter itself is here foreshadowed. Voltaire and Gibbon appear armed with the torturous and warlike instruments of this world (52:5–24), while the Monk's arms are tears, sighs, and groans, which do the work of sword, bow, and arrow (52:25–29). Gibbon's "lash of steel" (52:5), the argument he launched condemning Christianity in *The Rise and Fall of the Roman Empire,* resembles Bacon's and Newton's scourges (cf. 15:11–12), instruments of scientific reason that attack inspiration, or the star-studded whips of the male subduing nature to the laws of reason (illus. 21), while Voltaire's "wracking wheel" (52:6) reminds us of Newton's waterwheel (15:16) and the Satanic wheels (e.g., 15:18–19; illus. 22) that oppress human beings economically, politically, and religiously (pl. 76). The consequences of this conjunction are seen as "The Schools in clouds of learning rolld/Arose with War in iron & gold" (52:7–8). To the clouds of philosophical abstraction and the iron implements of war is added "gold," not of imagination, but its demonic parody—kingship, a connection that chapter 3 explores in detail.[17]

Deism and Empire, allied here to attack the inspired Grey Monk, reappear as specific emperors and philosophers who employ "Grecian Mocks & Roman Sword" (52:19) in the attack and crucify the Grey Monk like the Jews who "Crucify in Satans Synagogue!" (27:24), or Luvah's attackers (65:8) and Christ's (illus. 76). The Deists do in materialistic philosophy what empire does in war and what the Jews do in their moral code of vengeance. Their error appears:

> When Satan first the black bow bent
> And the Moral Law from the Gospel rent
> He forgd the Law into a Sword
> And spilld the blood of mercys Lord.
>
> (52:17–20)

Satan, the archer God of Albion's Jewish and Deistic error (see illus. 35), attempts to destroy imagination by separating moral law from inspiration (1:18). As he allies himself with the state, the law becomes a weapon annihilating forgiveness and imagination ("mercy's Lord"). Religion allied with empire as state religion in chapter 2, natural religion in chapter 3, or in the paradigm case when Judaism allied itself with the Roman state to kill Jesus (cf. pl. 77), inevitably attacks and oppresses imagination.

As Deism's "vain" attack falls beneath the weapons of imagination, pity, compassion, self-sacrifice, and true intellect (52:25–29), we recall the same fate meted out to moral law in the dedicatory poem of chapter 2 (pl. 27) by Blake's inspired consciousness. The same result occurs in the retelling of the Mary-Joseph story within chapter 3 too. Each time imaginative consciousness succeeds in restructuring the world.

The frontispiece to chapter 3 visually summarizes the subject matter of the chapter in its picture of Deistic despair (pl. 51). Albion, the despairing central figure in the plate, sits with his head below his knees, his hair over his face, arms and feet crossed, displaying his conditional of rational error in his huddled, unseeing, and stonelike body. Erdman (p. 330) identifies him as Hyle, which means "matter" in Greek, and is the name of Albion's son. It is an appropriate name for Albion himself here in the chapter devoted to Deism, which posits a purely material view of everyman. Although his position resembles that in plate 37, the book on which his head rested in that illustration is missing. His head is here further sunken, and his body further huddled. The book's disappearance indicates the change in subject matter from that of the Mosaic religious law of chapter 2, and the further contraction of his limbs points to the progression of his degeneracy to still further error. The lower torso of his square, stony appearance resembles the figure to his right, thereby indicating his kinship with Vala or Deistic material nature and its consequences. Vala's spiky crown, sceptered fleur-de-lis, and marblelike throne, which associate her with the trappings of tyrannical kingship, imply the political consequences of Deism's concept of nature. Equally sunk in despair, unseeing, with one hand held up to her head to indicate her rational error while the other drops uselessly by her side, demonstrating her ineffectiveness in any real (imaginative) sense, she demonstrates in her own despair the dark results of her reign.

The chained figure (who resembles suicidal despair in Blake's picture of *The House of Death*) completes the picture of Deistic despair. Labeled Skofield in an earlier version of the plate, the figure has an obvious biographical reference. He is "the soldier who indicted Blake in 1803, . . . chained by his own accusations . . . and is seen not as a menace but another 'hapless soldier.' "[18] In addition, however, this figure refers specifically to Deism; for chained by the iron laws of necessity (natural law) as well as by the political chains of tyranny, he slinks off in flames, head bowed but eyes open, subdued but not completely blinded by Deistic reason. Here is the only meager possibility of hope in the picture; perhaps the flames of imagination will melt the chains of natural law and break the reign of Deistic despair, a possibility the chapter also mentions.

The last chapter of *Jerusalem* serves a double function in the development of the theme. First, it provides the final thematic cross section, the imaginative or affective element of Albion's fall, and second, it envisions Albion's awakening and Blake's accomplished purpose. From the outset Blake intended to renovate Albion's, the reader's, everyman's consciousness through the dialectical investigation of error along with its imaginative counterpart. Since the process is completed in chapter 4, when the third main element of Albion's error is revealed together with its imaginative alternative, renewal logically results. In chapter 4, dedicated "To the Christians," false Christianity is investigated along with its truth, and Albion's awakening inevitably comes out of this investigation.

The dedicatory group, Christians, here again represents a state of consciousness rather than simply a historical group. Blake does not define *Christian* orthodoxly any more than he does *Jew* or *Deist*. He proposes his definition saying, "I know of no other Christianity and of no other Gospel than the liberty both of body & mind to exercise the Divine Arts of the Imagination" (pl. 77). Freedom of imaginative endeavor is hardly an orthodox definition of Christianity. No more are Blake's definition of the Holy Ghost as "an Intellectual Fountain" (pl. 77), of Heaven as "Mental Studies and Performances" (pl. 77), or of the Gospel's labors as "the labours of Art & Science" (pl. 77). They do, however, define Christianity for Blake as the active exercise of intellect and imagination. There is, furthermore, no doubt about the activity of a true Christian; for "to labour in Knowledge, is to Build up Jerusalem" (pl. 77) and, conversely, "to Despise Knowledge, is to Despise Jerusalem & her Builders" (pl. 77). Therefore, Blake exhorts the reader, "Let every Christian as much as in him lies engage himself openly & publicly before all the World in some Mental pursuit for the Building up of Jerusalem" (pl. 77). True Christians do so, as all the saving characters have noted throughout the poem. False Christians distort this idea and Jerusalem's "liberty both of body & mind to exercise the Divine Arts of Imagination." This distortion is the particular error that chapter 4 is dedicated to expose.

It is responsible for England's "sleep of death" (77:3), which Blake mentions in the concluding dedicatory poem, and which the chapter explores more carefully in all the fallen female characters. Expressed as Jerusalem's exile, the distortion exiles "joy and love" (77:8) and brings death to "Englands green & pleasant bowers" (77:12). Only when distortion is abolished can England be renewed to its former Edenic condition, as we see within the chapter when Brittannia and Albion awaken.

The full significance of Jerusalem's meaning becomes clear in the dedication's definition of Christianity. As a woman and a city, she epitomizes the imaginative doctrine of the poem and the full extent of mental and physical liberty. Her symbolic function is evident when Blake directly addresses the reader at the beginning of this dedication to chapter 4:

> I give you the end of a golden string
> Only wind it into a ball:
> It will lead you in at Heavens gate

> Built in Jerusalems wall.
>
> (Pl. 77, top)

Blake exhorts each reader to follow in Theseus-like fashion Ariadne's clue that he provides. By reading the poem, and thereby educating his consciousness, the reader may be led out of the labyrinthine, monster-inhabited generative state, as Albion is in the course of chapter 4, to the intellectually active realm of forgiveness and mutual love that exists within the construct of physical and mental imaginative liberty (Jerusalem).

The characteristic error of false Christians somewhat resembles those of Jews and Deists. Indeed, since all human beings have only "One Religion. The Religion of Jesus: . . . The Wicked will turn it to Wickedness, the Righteous to Righteousness" (pl. 27). The various kinds of wickedness share a Satanic nature, for "Every Religion that Preaches Vengeance for Sin is the Religion of the Enemy & Avenger" (pl. 52). It thus comes as no surprise when in the major dedicatory poem of plate 76 all religious errors combine in the devouring "Wheel of Religion" (77:13), which strives against the Christian ideal. It is the religion of "Caiaphas" (77:17), the high priest of the Sanhedrin during Christ's trial, who represents the error of the Jews described in chapter 2, as well as "Natural Religion" (77:20), the Deistic distortion described in chapter 3, and that "Wheel of fire" (77:2–3, cf. *King Lear* 4.7. 45–48) which keeps man from Edenic bliss and true Christianity by the limitation of imagination and affection. "By it the Sun was rolld into an orb: / By it the Moon faded into a globe" (77:7–8); both imagination and love were materialized.

By representing both the particular error that the chapter sets out to expose and the culmination of all errors that have been exposed before, the prefatory poem exemplifies the double function of the chapter itself and proceeds dialectically as the poem does too. Opposing the fiery "Wheel of Religion," another of the poem's multifarious wheels, is Blake's Christ,

> . . . the bright Preacher of Life,
> Creating Nature from this fiery Law
> By self-denial & forgiveness of Sin
>
> (77:21–23)

who reverses its progress. As Christ thus renews man's intellect or imagination and thereby also his civil society, "Hell is opend to Heaven" (77:34) and "The dungeons burst & the Prisoners set free" (77:35), for the liberated mind liberates all society.

The ideal of Christianity and its distortion in error described in the dedication's words form a dialectic reflecting man's potentiality and his actuality, which the frontispiece to chapter 4 also illustrates (pl. 76). Here Christ and Albion face each other with outstretched arms in essentially similar positions, so that each suggests the mirror image of the other, depicting the potential of Albion as the Human Form Divine and the essential humanity of Christ. Yet the two are separate, and Christ is crucified upon the oak of suffering while Albion regards him. Albion in his divided state, fallen and a false Christian, faces his potential divinity but is not united with it. His resemblance to the figure in *Glad Day* underlines his divine potential, although our view of his back rather than his front indicates the unrealized state of that potential. He is, moreover, responsible for crucifying his divinity through erroneous doctrines of false love and sacrifice of others, which he substitutes for Christ's unselfish love and self-sacrifice. The Druidic oak of sacrifice on which Christ is crucified underscores this meaning, and the metamorphosis of the tree's fruit from acorns pictured at the left to apples pictured at the right refers, in addition, to Albion's tree of religious mystery, which is responsible for Christ's crucifixion.

Twin sources supply light to the otherwise darkened illustration. One is the rising sun of imagination, which is just visible above the horizon behind the oak and dark hills and between the thick clouds in the sky, the signal of morning, which heralds Albion's coming renewal described in the chapter. The other is Christ himself, from whose crown of thorns a halo emanates, lighting his own figure and the front of Albion's. Again we see intimation of potential human divinity, which will be realized within chapter 4.

This brings to a close our examination of *Jerusalem's* frame, the larger thematic frame of prologue and epilogue, and the four divisions within it, each corresponding to and prefacing one chapter of the poem. The framework unfolds one more layer of Blake's thematic form within the general pattern of theme and commentary, summary and explanation. Typically, the prefatory poems introducing each chapter reiterate the pattern of the whole, going from generation to regeneration through the dialectical interaction of the two within the context of the particular thematic component of the chapter, and the frontispieces summarize this visually. In the poem that prefaces chapter 1 (pl. 3), the general situation is established by the interaction between negative restrictive writing and Blake's inclusive imaginative writing that prevails, while the frontispiece shows the dialectic in the story of Jerusalem's sleep and awakening. In chapter 2 the patriarchal religious error is abrogated by Blake's restoration of prophetic religious truth, which also renews his land in Edenic harmony, while the two are seen in conflict as Hand and

Jerusalem in the frontispiece. In chapter 3 the poem pits the efforts of Deistic philosophers and the emperors with whom they are in league against the inspired Grey Monk, showing how ineffectual their weapons of false reason, war, sacrifice, and oppression finally prove against the intellectual and compassionate weapons of inspiration. The frontispiece here, however, shows the other side of the dialectical picture, deep Deistic despair, and only hints at its overthrow. Finally, in chapter 4, the fiery wheel of false religion (Judaic and Deistic) is counteracted by Christ's imaginative doctrine, and "Hell is opend to Heaven" as the first dedication foretold, while Albion's fallen actuality is confronted by his potential divinity in the frontispiece. In the second poem, added here to the ususal poetic portion in keeping with the chapter's twofold function, the same pattern is reasserted. Sleeping England awakens through reunification with Jerusalem and with the Lamb of God to recreate "Englands green & pleasant bowers."

Having examined the skeleton of the poem in its framing structure, I will now look at the added details provided in each chapter's text and designs, which expand and flesh out that skeleton.

NOTES

1. W. J. T. Mitchell, in *Blake's Composite Art*, sees the figure in plate 1 as a symbolic representation of author, reader, and hero, who all function as pilgrims like Los. While all are engaged in pilgrimage, Los and the Poet approach it from the eternal point of view while Albion and the reader do so from generation. The direction that the latter two take should thus differ from that of the former two, as should their relation to the Gothic doorway. Therefore I cannot agree that all are pictured in plate 1.

2. Blake pictures this post-and-lintel construction in the Druidic spectrous edifices of *Jerusalem*. It symbolizes their restrictive and deadly functions, while the Gothic architecture is associated with eternal Los (pl. 1) and Jerusalem (pls. 46, 57).

3. David V. Erdman, *The Illuminated Blake* (Garden City, N.Y.: Doubleday Anchor, 1974), p. 282, points out the similarity of these two female figures to those in Fuseli's frontispiece to Darwin's *Loves of the Plants*. This similarity further underlines their nature symbolism. Their separation from Jerusalem, in addition, indicates the fragmentation of the female principle into mourning nature and sleeping liberty.

4. Blake often uses rounded wings to denote eternal or imaginative forms, e.g., Jerusalem (pls. 2, 4), the cherubim (pl. 19), immortal space (pl. 44). He reserves the more jagged wings or batwings for spectrous characters, such as Los's Spectre (pl. 6), Vala (pl. 12), Albion's Spectre (pl. 33), and Urizen (pl. 35).

5. Edward P. Hungerford, *Shores of Darkness* (New York: World-Meridian Publishing Co., 1963) identifies this group of scholars as "the speculative mythologists of the latter half of the eighteenth century and of the early years of the nineteenth" (p. 3) and assigns them a central position in the intellectual life of their time. Although they were important for only a relatively short period, he demonstrates that they influenced the Romantic poets, including Blake, who treated their mythological theories as the source of symbolic truth. Although Blake may echo

Jacob Bryant's theory of an original culture from which all subsequent cultures and languages descend (p. 21), or Edward Davies's idea that the Druids were purveyors of patriarchal culture (pp. 25–26), or Wilford's that England was the actual location of Old Testament and mythical events (p. 30), the truth that Blake is interested in is not identical to these but is imaginative truth rather than literal.

6. As Blake states it in the *Descriptive Catalogue*, p. 534: "The antiquities of every Nation under heaven is no less sacred than that of the Jews. They are the same thing as Jacob Bryant, and all the antiquaries have proved. . . . All had originally one language, and one religion, this was the religion of Jesus, the everlasting Gospel."

7. There are nails visible in his hands in copy D. David Bindman takes this to mean that Hand is being represented as a false Christ. He is certainly false religion in any case.

8. David V. Erdman, *Illuminated Blake*, p. 305. All Erdman citations in the text are from this work unless otherwise noted.

9. *Webster's Seventh Collegiate Dictionary* (Springfield, Mass.: G & C Merriam Co., 1961).

10. John Locke, *An Essay Concerning Human Understanding*, 2 vols. (New York: Dover, 1959) 1: 122–23.

11. David Hume, *Of Sceptical and Other Systems of Philosophy*, in *The Age of Enlightenment*, ed. Isaiah Berlin, *The Great Ages of Western Philosophy*, vol. 4 (New York: George Braziller, 1958), p. 246.

12. Jean Hagstrum, "William Blake Rejects the Enlightenment," *Blake: A Collection of Critical Essays*, ed. Northrop Frye (Englewood Cliffs, N.J.: Prentice-Hall, 1966), p. 147.

13. John Middleton Murry, *William Blake* (1933, rpt.; New York: McGraw-Hill, 1964), p. 315.

14. Voltaire, *Traite de Metaphysique*, chap. 3, p. v, quoted by Ernst Cassirer, *The Philosophy of the Enlightenment*, trans. C. A. Koelin and James P. Pettegrove (Boston: Beacon Press, 1961), p. 12.

15. Cassirer, *Philosophy of the Enlightenment*, p. 13, 107.

16. Blake also calls Thomas Paine "either a Devil or an Inspired Man," both terms of praise in *The Marriage of Heaven and Hell*, and claims that "Paine has not attacked Christianity, Watson has defended anti-Christ" (p. 601).

17. The variant stanzas that Blake rejected for his engraved or finished version of the poem show more explicitly the connection between the philosophy of Voltaire and Gibbon and oppressive empire waging war. one variant stanza is:

> Gibbon plied his lash of steel
> Voltaire turnd his wracking wheel
> Charlemaine & his barons bold
> Stood by & mocked in iron & gold.

Another variant reads:

> The Wheel of Voltaire whirld on high
> Gibbon aloud his lash does ply
> Charlemaine & his Clouds of War
> Muster around the Polar Star.

18. Erdman, *Illuminated Blake*, p. 330.

3

The General Outline for the General Reader

AFTER initially stating *Jerusalem*'s theme in both text and design, chapter 1 dramatizes that theme in the opening confrontation between Albion and the Savior. All the basic components of sleep and awakening and the underlying metaphors of division and unity are set forth in this paradigmatic scene. As Albion denies unity with the Savior, crying "We are not One: we are Many" (4:23), he divides himself from God and fellow man, a fundamental error that immediately leads to further division (pl. 5). Losing his foundation in imagination (which for Blake is identical to divinity), Albion immediately fragments his consciousness and his world. He separates his immortal from his mortal self and lapses into Cartesian dualism, dividing mind from body and splitting into separate rational and physical parts, his male and female divisions (pl. 5).

In his first speech, Albion demonstrates all three basic components of his fall, his religious, rational, and affective errors that are all investigated generally in this chapter and then in detail separately in the three following chapters of the poem. Albion establishes fallen religion in his "Laws of Moral Virtue" (4:31), embraces fallen reason in rejecting "faith" (4:28) for "demonstration" (4:28), carries out its consequences in "war & princedom & victory" (4:32), rejects unselfish love as that "which binds/Man the enemy of man into deceitful friendships" (4:25–26), and accepts fallen affection in "jealous fears" (4:33) and secrecy instead. Meanwhile, the Savior proclaims unity and forgiveness: "we are One; forgiving all Evil" (4:20), brotherhood and mutual love: "I am in you and you in me,

44

mutual in love divine/Fibres of love from man to man thro Albions pleasant land" (4:7–8), the imaginative alternatives to Albion's erroneous religion, reason, and affection. These opposing alternatives are equally available for Albion's consciousness as the illustration indicates (pl. 4), for it pictures both fallen Albion controlled by error and unfallen Albion soaring freely. The network of lines in the right lower margin of this plate exemplifies the same opposing alternatives, for what it represents depends upon the beholder's consciousness. Looked at in Albion's fallen terms, it represents the deceitful bonds he mentions and the net that Vala so often uses to ensnare mankind.[1] Regarded, however, in the Savior's imaginative terms, it becomes those fibers of love he mentions which establish the divine brotherhood of man.

Albion's inner division from imagination, which inevitably splits him into his multiple male and female forms, has necessary consequences in his darkened land, his fallen institutions, nation, and universe (pl. 5). His errors of consciousness display their spatial appearance in the dark, despairing, clouded, and bloody land of Albion, which is presented in all its geographic, urban, and social particulars (5:1–15). Thereafter in chapter 1, the exposition of each error, while it demonstrates the distortion of the individual, also demonstrates the resultant distortion in land, society, and population. The acceptance of false doctrines or ideas is not simply an isolated individual phenomenon but has necessary consequences for all spheres of human life.

However, just as error is investigated dialectically with its alternative, so the geographical reflection of error is also. We see it briefly in the glimpses of Eden presented to us by Los in answer to his Spectre (7:51–70), by Jerusalem in her answer to Vala (20:5–10), by Albion recalling a lost Eden (24:36–50), and most extensively in the imaginative particulars of Golgonooza (12:24–13:29). Supplying an alternative landscape to error, this complex city formed by imaginative truth shows the geographical face of truth that will later be seen in eternal London, awakened Ireland, Eden, and the entire humanized universe.

Presented at the outset, Albion's basic division is variously revisited in chapter 1. It is first retold by Los's Spectre in the story of Albion's division into Urizen, Luvah, and Vala (7:28–50). Here we see in concrete terms of specific characters how Albion, cut off from imagination by his initial action, is further fragmented within himself. When unconnected to his imagination or divinity, Albion's passion (Luvah) inevitably turns from spiritual love to hate, while his physical body (Vala) just as inevitably turns from free love to jealous domination, and his reason (Urizen) isolates himself from this passionate mess, thereby turning cold and tyrannical and wielding iron "necessity" (7:32–33) to protect himself and maintain his dominance.

Albion's division is also echoed by Los's separation into spectre and emanation (pls. 6–8, 17) as man's imagination fragments. Here, however, the uniqueness of his immortal imagination becomes clear; for although fragmented, it remains eternal and unselfish (1:9; 8:17–18). Although splintered into Spectre (Reason grown cold and abstractly logical) and Emanation, Enitharmon (physical nature grown purely material), imagination still retains its power and controls both as it tries to save Albion. Even as the looming Spectre menaces Los (illus. 6), he is securely chained to Los's bellows, subservient to him and compelled to do imagination's bidding (8:15–16; 9:35; 17:1–47), as is Enitharmon too (pl. 17). Imagination thus accomplishes its teleological function through the very powers that try to negate it, through reason and nature even as they are distorted by Albion's errors.

While all three components of Albion's error revealed in the opening confrontation are necessarily interrelated, Blake chooses to describe one at a time together with its imaginative alternative. First he concentrates on religious error, analyzing it poetically within the confrontation between Los and his Spectre and pictorially in Albion's male and female divisions (pls. 6–9). Before going into rational error in plates 11–15, he uses illustration 9 and plate 10 as transitions exposing both religious and rational error. Plate 16 again sums up both errors, pointing out their results for England before plates 17–24 proceed to analyze affective error. Finally, plate 25 draws the chapter to a close with an illustration of Albion's sacrifice at the hands of generative error and an exposition of Blake's inclusive doctrine of states, which offers an alternative to error. He then returns our attention to religious error in preparation for its thorough exposition in chapter 2.

Religious error comes into focus first as divided Los confronts his Spectre or fallen rational part (pls. 6–10). In the dialectical interaction between them, Albion's religious alternatives, fallen and inspired, are revealed. The Spectre's accusations and arguments echo Albion's false religious doctrines while Los's words and deeds, on the other hand, reveal the Savior's religious truth in action. Recounting Albion's history, the history of mankind, Los's Spectre characterizes it as the history of religious error. He calls Albion's sons by the biblical names of Israel's enemies, enemies of true religion (7:18–19), and by the names of the Jewish patriarchs, who, in Blake's view, equally betray true religion (cf. dedication, chap. 2). All his sons worship the "Spectre of Albion" (7:40) as God instead of divine humanity, and establish a "Law of Sin" (7:50) and punishment to achieve their ends, while Albion's daughters weave "webs of war & of/Religion, to involve all Albions sons" (7:44–45). Albion in his multiple divided form thus falls into that false worship which orthodox religion also establishes. He adores a God who is separate from man, one who ultimately turns out to be a human rational projection, and establishes codes of sin and punishment to live under that inevitably lead him into war: internal wars with his natural human desires and external ones with his brothers. The involvement of Los's Spectre in this religious distortion appears when he too characterizes God as that spectrous deity of Albion's religion, "Righteous" rather than merciful (10:47), feeding on human offerings, and promulgating laws of sin and sacrifice (10:37–59). He further characterizes himself as the Satan of orthodox religion, "all evil, all reversed & for ever dead" (10:57). Religious truth then interacts with error as Los opposes Albion's erroneous "Religion of Generation" (7:64) with "regeneration," "mutual forgiveness," and the religion "of the Lamb of God" (7:65, 66, 67). He offers imaginative religion's immanent God and code of mutual forgiveness in opposition to fallen religion's absent God and code of punishment for sin. He also creates his own systems, city of Golgonooza (10:17–21), and Edenic geography (7:51–70) to counteract Albion's fallen equivalents. Recognizing the Spectre's error as his own "Pride & Self-Righteousness" (8:30), Los furthermore anticipates Blake's recognition in the dedicatory poem of chapter 2 (pl. 27) and demonstrates the transcendent character of his dialectic as spectrous error is transformed to imaginative truth.

This opposition is illustrated as Los's Spectre attempts to encircle and smother Los's flames of prophecy at the forge (illus. 6), religious error's historical role. As he hangs suspended upside down over Los, he demonstrates his upside-down view of truth and inverted Satanic religion. His invisible eyes, hands covering his ears and holding his head depict his lack of perception, intellect, and imagination. The pointed outline of his outspread batwings, which attempt to contain and smother Los's flames or truth, demonstrates the spectrous or perverted and restrictive function of his doctrines. In Los's unconcerned gaze, however, in the persistence of his flames around and above the Spectre, in the chain with which he binds the Spectre to the forge, and in the resemblance of the Spectre's wing structure to Los's bellows, we see the Spectre's ultimate ineffectiveness and subservience to inspiration.

The Spectre's pose is echoed by the lower figure in the marginal illustration of plate 7. Here Albion himself stands in the middle of the margin, pointing both up and down in another thematic illustration that notes his alternatives of imagination or generation. The floating female figure above who points upward demonstrates Albion's inspired religion, while the lower figure who plunges headlong into vegetating snakelike roots demonstrates the results of false religion as he repeats the Spectre's pose and Satan's fall. This figure reappears in microscopic outline on plate 16 as Israel-England, who, like individual Albion, is exposed to the cosmic consequences of fallen religion.

Religious error is further explained as Hand, the epitome of Albion's sons or male divisions, plays his role. His religion forbids "Genius . . . by laws of punishment" (9:16), "joy . . . as a Crime" (9:14), and turns "the beauty of Eternity" to "deformity" (9:7–8) celebrating all this negation through the "pomp of religion" (9:15), which becomes a "disease forming a Body of Death around the Lamb/Of God, to destroy Jerusalem, & to devour the body of Albion" (9:9–10).

In the illustrations, the religious element appears in female terms as well as male, thereby complementing the poetry's masculine emphasis. In plate 5, for example, the alternatives of religious truth and error are represented by the five female figures engaged in religious prayer and praise at the right. Four are obviously praying while the fifth opens her arms in religious praise like Albion in plate 76. The two central female figures kneel one behind the other in despair and unavailing aspiration, illustrating the position of all human beings in religious error. The contrast between the vertical outline interrupted by the heavy, horizontal, body lines of these kneeling figures, which the surrounding flames underscore, and the soaring, uninterrupted, vertical lines of the others who pray and look upward, who are naked rather than clothed, and around whom the flames rise in uninterrupted motion, illustrates the difference between fallen and inspired religion. The soaring figures echo Jerusalem's function and appearance, the crossed ankles in the lower figure foreshadowing Jerusalem's pose in plate 96 and the open arms of the uppermost figure that of Jerusalem in plate 99.[2] The kneeling figure's hair-over-eyes pose foreshadows the imperceptive despair evident in Albion (illus. 39, 51) and Vala (illus. 51, 64), and resembles the female's pose in *America* (illus. 16).

Finally, plate 8 depicts the particular role of the fallen female as physical nature within false religion. Denied inspiration when divinity is banished from her to an otherworldly region as it is by false religion, she appears harnessed to the waxing moon, tied, that is, to the natural lunar cycle by the twenty-eight days of her menstrual cycle. She is condemned to the never-changing repetition of the simply physical, ever waxing and waning, ever the same, for imagination is absent. Indeed, as Blake puts it in *There Is No Natural Religion* 6, "If it were not for the Poetic or Prophetic character the Philosophic & Experimental would soon be at the ratio of all things, & stand still unable to do other than repeat the same dull round over again" (p. 1). This is exactly her situation as pictured in plate 8, for she is cut off from the prophetic character or imagination. It anticipates a similar description of Vala in chapter 2. She thus becomes purely material, limited to the natural cycle in all her activities. This is also physical nature's position within fallen rationality, and Blake returns to this image of the female and her moon when he examines that error, too. Both religious and rational error cut physical nature off from imagination and leave her in the same sublunar cyclical position, although through different doctrines.

The consequences for Albion appear in the next illustration (pl. 9) and anticipate the poetry of plate 10. Albion's religious and rational errors illustrated in mid-page result in his fallen, unseeing, generative state at the bottom. The illustration, however, may be read in two complementary ways: as a tableau of Albion's errors and as the story of Albion's fall from innocence to generation. Just as the title page (pl. 2) represents both Jerusalem's ongoing alternatives of sleep and awakening and her journey from one state to another, or as illustration 4 does Albion's alternatives and his journey from Vala to Jerusalem, so too does plate 9 represent in tableau form the coexistence of Albion's innocence and error as well as his fall from one to the other (top to bottom). These complementary readings of the illustrations reflect Blake's ideas and thematic method in the poem. Like the poetry, the illustrations use progression, or fall and rise, as metaphors for Albion's consciousness rather than as successive stages of advancement or regression, and assign them spaces on the page as the poetry assigns them successive moments in the reading. As the poetry unfolds a moment in time, giving it the appearance of succession, the illustrations unfold an appearance in space. Both thus reveal inherent but hidden meanings in Albion's ongoing possibilities and provide successive dimensions to his moment of choice.

In plate 9 the scene of apparent innocence at the top is exchanged for a scene of experience or generation in the middle of the page and for a portrayal of fallen Albion mourned by nature at the bottom. While telling the story of a fall if regarded sequentially, the illustration also presents Albion's omnipresent alternatives of imagination and generation and the consequences of his generative choice. Stretched out on the ground, apparently dead, staring with unseeing eyes because he lacks perception in this state, his head flung back and below the level of his body because his intellect is fallen,

Albion is in a compound state of error. Throughout the poem his lowered head and unseeing eyes visually symbolize his erroneous, limited perception and intellect. The despairing females around him, their faces hidden in various attitudes of despair, are also not able to see and similarly suffer from limited perception and consciousness. The central figure, who seems to worship fallen Albion, prostrating herself before him, exemplifies Deistic error particularly, for Deism glorifies the merely material man that Albion has here become. Another female, the only one whose eyes are uncovered, tears her hair and looks for comfort to a sky-inhabiting power, thus demonstrating her religious error in seeking abstract divinity separated from the Human Form Divine. All she sees, however, are the stars of reason (rational Deism) and mountains of moral virtue (Sinai's religion), the twin errors of false reason and religion that rule Albion's fallen world and provide the only light in the picture. Coexistent with this state is the harmonious world pictured at the top of the plate, with its shepherd piper, his peaceful sheep, a lion lying beside them, and a sleeping tiger (extreme left). An incongruous scene of sacrifice set against a purple background (copy E) between the sheep and tiger, however, interrupts the apparent peaceful harmony and alerts us to the omnipresence of Albion's alternative state. The kneeling figure here holds what looks like the chalice that the Daughters of Albion carry when they sacrifice Albion in chapter 3 (pl. 69), and the flamelike lines behind the figure suggest a sacrificial pyre. These details suggest Abraham's sacrifice and hint at Albion's religious error, which, like the patriarch's, sacrifices others and is responsible for his fall.[3] The vine that encir-, cles the graceful tree against which the piping shepherd leans also warns of Albion's generative errors. As its tendrils twine down to the middle of the page, they gradually turn into a serpent, which a kneeling female in flowing drapery furtively pets and feeds. She ignores the huddled human figure at her left while she caters to the serpentine corrupter of Eden. As fallen female nature feeds the mundane egg of the natural world to the serpent, she nurtures religious error by sacrificing the physical world to it. She ignores the human need behind her and advances rational error instead, whose form is also serpentine.

Complementing the visual transition to the next section of Blake's theme that plate 9 provides is the poetic transition of plate 10. It summarizes the religious contentions between Los and his Spectre and explores the rationally erroneous "manner of the Sons of Albion" (10:7) dialectically with the imaginative manner of Los's sons and daughters (pl. 11–15). Blake first demonstrates how the sons of Albion

. . . take the Two Contraries which are calld Qualities, with which
Every Substance is clothed, they name them Good & Evil
From them they make an Abstract, which is a Negation
Not only of the Substance from which it is derived
A murderer of its own Body: but also a murderer
Of every Divine Member: it is the Reasoning Power
An Abstract objecting power, that Negatives every thing
This is the Spectre of Man: the Holy Reasoning Power
And in its Holiness is closed the Abomination of Desolation.

(10:8–16)

They commit both religious and rational errors by polarizing the unique, individual, and contrary qualities of things, people, or actions into "Good & Evil" instead of leaving then complementary contraries, such as reason and energy (MHH), thought and desire (J, 3) or Reason, Desire, Pity, and Wrath (illus. 54). Unlike the imaginative doctrine, which requires that man use all of his contrary powers both of body and mind to make himself fully human (pl. 76), the doctrine of good and evil bifurcates human existence and accepts only one part of it. By introducing notions of sin and punishment into religion, it victimizes mankind instead of liberating him. In rational terms, it denies part of his human nature by restricting him to his abstract reason only.

The sons of Albion employ objective reason to abstract their divisions of good and evil into empty generalizations that replace concrete actuality. In natural science this method of reasoning produces Newtonian physics, which begins with the observation of particular physical phenomena in the universe and reasons from them to general and abstract physical laws. In philosophy it produces British empiricism, which transfers Newtonian method to psychology and philosophy by reasoning from the particulars of existence to abstract philosophical ideas and the "natural laws" of society. These methods establish a mechanistic universe and an objectified humanity that are both ruled by generalized natural laws in which minute particularity and living imagination are missing. Locke bases his philosophy on this method of abstraction, which he sees as man's distinguishing characteristic and the basis of all intellectual endeavor. He notes that:

the mind makes particular ideas received from particular objects to become general: which is done by considering them as they are in the mind such appearances,—separate from all other existences and the circumstances of real existence, as time, place, or any other concomitant ideas. This is called ABSTRACTION, whereby ideas taken from particular beings become representatives of all of the same kind; and their names general names, applicable to whatever exists conformable to such abstract ideas.[4]

These Lockean abstractions are what Blake condemns in Albion's sons; for they blur distinctions, deny individuality, and remove existence from the physical world into the mental world alone, rather than combining the two in the subjective universe of imagination. In doing so, Lockean reason separates the mind from the world and thought from existence. It is concerned only with its own abstractions, which it imposes on existence and to which it grants exclusive reality. This reason is also an "objecting" power in the two senses that the pun on the word underlines: it objects to or denies the whole range of human possibilities outside itself, and it objectifies the universe. It turns the world into a collection of discrete, isolated objects that man as viewing subject analyzes and manipulates mentally through abstract ideas that are divorced from the unique circumstances of their occurrence. Man as observing, reasoning subject faces an objectified universe that exists for him within abstract mental categories to be systematized by him into natural laws of science and society. The subject is then isolated in his selfhood from the objectified universe around him and from the abstractions and natural laws that he creates to control it.

This same false reason that is apparent in the teachings of scientists as well as philosophers, in the unholy triumvirate of Bacon, Newton, and Locke, is perpetuated in the "Schools & Universities of Europe" (15:14), and is embodied in the machinery that scientific methods and discoveries make possible. Thus we see the "Loom of Locke" and the "Water-wheels of Newton" (15:15, 16) operate:

> . . . with cogs tyrannic
> Moving by compulsion each other: not as those in Eden: which
> Wheel within Wheel in freedom revolve in harmony & peace.
> (15:18–20)

The wheels of imagination are perverted by abstract philosophy, which turns the universe into a machine, a human rationalistic creation run by mechanical laws, and man into the slave of the machine. The exact mode of operation has been explained by Kathleen Raine:

> The "Wheels" are the causal interlocking presumed in a mechanistic universe, "wheel within wheel," because the material impulsion of one body by another is imparted from without. These presumed Mechanistic causes turn "the Satanic Mills" of Newton's universe. In

contrast there is the perennial philosophy of the "wheels within wheels" of Ezekiel's vision, spiritual essences that operate the causes of things in a manner quite other than that conceived by the mechanistic philosophy.[5]

These wheels weave Vala's veil, the black cloth of materialism that shrouds the world, in the looms of Locke. They also turn in the factories and mills of England where the inexorable working of machinery sets the pace and dictates the conditions of labor.

The effects of this reasoning process appear in human form in illustration 15. A large, naked, bearded figure dominates the plate and pushes man into a corner. With his arms extended to the edges of the page, he encloses the entire visible world. Coming, it seems, from the towered town visible beneath his lingering left foot, which, as Erdman suggests (p. 294), may be the Schools and Universities mentioned in the poetry (15:15), he represents the force of fallen reason taught there. His face with its short beard and medium-length hair resembles the triple face of Hand (pl. 50), who portrays the abstract philosophy of Bacon, Newton, and Locke (70:1–15).[6] He crushes the small male figure regarding him at the lower right, who barely lifts his upper torso from the ground as his arms and legs turn to branches and roots in treelike metamorphosis. Fallen reason thus limits what man can see, oppresses him, and turns him into a vegetating part of his generative world. His enrooting, mentioned poetically as a metaphor for his erroneous rational limitation to the merely natural (15:1, 2, 23, 25), is also graphically depicted here.

The effects of rational error on man's natural existence are illustrated in female terms as well as botanical images within the second section of chapter 1. The female at the bottom of plate 13, for example, whose green robe represents the green world of nature, kneels upon the earth and looks up to fruitless grapevines among which batwinged insects symbolizing Deistic reason fly.[7] Kneeling and open armed, she praises the natural world of Newtonian science that she sees: reason blighting fruitful creation as symbolized by vines which bear leaves only, not fruit. Her clothed figure kneeling upon the earth further associates her with the error she praises.

The effect of rational error on physical nature, seen unambiguously in this illustration (pl. 13), is presented dialectically with the contrary vision of physical nature imaginatively conceived in illustration 11, where the woman-swan at the top gives way to freed Erin at the bottom. Rationalized nature appears in the woman-swan figure who is immersed in the surrounding sea of materialism at the top. Although she possesses the same wings as the unfallen emanation, Jerusalem (pl. 18), and the divine cherubim (pl. 22), which

suggest her potential prophetic function, these wings are not entirely unambiguous since prophecy is distorted or overwhelmed by
error in the world. They adorn Rahab, false Deistic nature (pl. 53),
and the guardian angels or distorted religion mourning at Albion's
tomb in plate 15 or around the winged ark in plate 39. Unlike the
prophetic swans that youths ride in *America* 11 and on the title page
of Blake's illustrated Gray, whose open beaks sing in the air, who
are harnessed by their naked riders, whose necks and heads are
lifted, and who are all bird, this swan is riderless, bubbling, unhar-
nessed, and part woman. Its head and neck droop like a limp phal-
lus, resembling in this the spectre-swan of plate 71 rather than the
prophetic swans mentioned above. The addition of its woman's
breasts suggests a version of the Deistic, sterile hermaphrodite, the
unproductive combination of abstract reason and purely material
nature mentioned in chapter 3. As her beak opens below the surface
of the water, producing ineffectual bubblings rather than song, potential prophecy is muted by the materialism in which it is immersed. Her watery location between the oak of suffering and the
weeping willow on the opposite shore and her kneeling position
that resembles Hand's in plate 50 further emphasize her generative
position.

The effects of Albion's errors of consciousness on physical nature
are also reflected geographically, first in the counties of England and
Scotland (pl. 16), "And thence to all the Kingdoms & Nations &
Families of the Earth" (16:35). His religious errors appear as the
counties are identified with Israel's twelve tribes (Isaac's twelve
sons) and the land participates in patriarchal history and error
(16:34–60), a process that will be explained more fully in chapter 2.
In addition, the land is also involved in the bloody consequences of
rational error as counties, rivers, and cities participate in Albion's
struggle (16:1–21), and as "The corn is turn'd to thistles & the apples
into poison:/The birds of song to murderous crows . . ." (18:10–11).
Here false reason shrivels the fertility of the natural world into unproductive weeds as it blasted the grapes in illustration 13. False
religion turns the fruits of Eden into codes of poisonous moral virtue
through denial and negation. Both bring about the resultant state of
war, displacing harmony as carrion crows substitute for songbirds.

The other side of the story, the alternative to Albion's rational
error, appears as we glance down the page (pl. 11) from the swan-
woman to the blissful flaming image of Erin freely swimming in that
same sea or floating out from the furnaces of Los in which she is
created. Her ornaments, which as Erdman suggests (p. 291) resemble the bubbles of the swan-woman above, are transformed into
jewels. Even in its degenerated and inundated form, the message of

prophecy does not go completely unheard but is transformed by imaginative consciousness into vivid adornment. These jewels, unlike the pearls of "Europe" in Stedman's emblem, are broken rather than continuous strands.[8] They therefore suggest the broken chains of generation, which Erin has transformed into imaginative ornaments just as her view of the natural world transforms that too into a jewel (14:20–21). Her naked figure, the suggestion of a fish in her finny outline, which echoes a traditional Christ symbol, and the free gesture of her outspread arms all proclaim her imaginative function within materialism, the sea of time and space. As the creation of Los, she performs a function similar to his by bringing imagination into time. Yet her freedom is limited, as the palm-downward position of her open hands, which resembles that of Vala in plate 4, testifies, and her pointed outline, which suggests not only fins but the tips of batwings similar to the Spectre's does too. Playing her part in the dialectic of error and truth, this truly imaginative creation of Los is distorted by the surrounding generative world even as she transforms it.

Jerusalem, too, carries on that dialectic. She floats with the closed butterfly wings of the title page now opened and offers Albion the imaginative alternative to his rational error (pl. 14). Located beneath Erin's rainbow of promise, which recalls Noah's rainbow and which encircles Albion's world from horizon to horizon in defining its bounds, she is nevertheless invisible to Albion's unseeing, blank eyes.[9] His deathlike position, marked with stone mourning angels at head and foot, resembles that of Mary in Blake's 1803 watercolor *Death of the Virgin*,[10] and leaves us in no doubt of his generative state here. He therefore cannot perceive the imaginative promise of his world or self. His universe is represented by the clouds of obscurity, stars of reason, sea of materialism, and moon of the simply natural world, which now holds a red globe within its arms (copy E) that is Enitharmon or fallen space (17:51). It is contrasted with an alternative universe, the "Universe within" (14:17) of Los's children, projected outward in the sun, planets, moon, and stars etched into the top of the plate, which exist beyond Albion's ken—the universe promised by Jerusalem and Erin's rainbow.

Indeed, the rational error by which Albion's sons operate is contrasted throughout this section with the compassionate truth typical of Los's children, described largely in female terms (11:7, 17–18; 12:4, 25 ff.). Los's female children, Erin and the Daughters of Beulah who accompany her "for Jerusalems Sake" (11:8–9), are particularized, while his male children are simply called "sons" (11:11; 12:45). Los's children are described for the most part in images of an opening center, gates opening within, a single walled gate, encircling flames (14:16–30), and circular motions (11:17; 14:32), while Albion's children appear in phallic images (pl. 14) such as serpents, dragons, a "vegetating tongue," "watery flame," "dark roots" (14:2–14), a polypus, and fibrous growth (15:1–4), or as female "shades" (14:12) or shadows (Vala, 12:19).[11] Since Albion's male divisions represent his fallen rational part, Blake's imagery suggests that they need to be completed by the unfallen female or physical part, the emanation that Albion must reclaim, as Milton must too in that poem, to renew his imaginative form. Indeed, in chapter 3, which is devoted to rational error, Blake expands this hint in a full discussion of the emanation's saving function.

The play of dialectic is further revealed in the contrast between the consequences of Albion's philosophic method and those of Los's children's compassionate one. The false reasoning of Albion's sons results in the distorted human form of "a false brain: a false heart: / And false bowels: altogether composing the False Tongue" (14:5–6), the phallic male and shadowy female, and the human polypus or vegetable (14:2–14; pl. 15). Their generative philosophy and mathematics supply the scientific basis for the industrial revolution resulting in the "Looms of Locke" (15:15), the "Water-wheels of Newton" (15:16), the "Looms & Mills & Prisons & Work-houses of Og & Anak" (13:57), and the "Satanic Wheels" (13:37) that revolve in the abstract void of rational error (13:38–55). Albion's children also create all natural and man-made disasters. On the contrary, the human forms of Los's children, which result from imagination, are each a "translucent Wonder," opening in a succession of gates into a "Universe within" (14:17), rather than false phallic forms, coils, or shadows. They too have a mathematics that equally supplies the basis for their construct, Golgonooza—the city of art, rather than mills, prisons, and workhouses. Since, however, it is theirs, it is a divine mathematics based on fourfold imaginative multiplication, whose complex plan is impossible to draw with Newtonian three-dimensional tools (12:25–13:29). Matching their form as the abstract void matches the fallen rational form of Albion's sons, their natural world "opens like a flower from Earth s center / In which is Eternity" (13:34–35) and exists permanently beyond time and space (13:59–14:1; 15:8; 16:61–67).

Blake's dialectic in this section operates not only to demonstrate the opposition of Albion's alternatives, but also to show the possible transcendence of his negative error into positive truth. While the "manner" of Albion's sons "Negatives every thing" when acting in its own right, if it operates under the aegis of imagination, its scientific method of philosophical abstraction and logical negation proves useful:

. . . by mathematic power
Giving a body to Falsehood that it may be cast off for ever
With Demontrative Science piercing Apollyon with his own bow![12]

(12:12–14)

By providing form to the indefinite, science and mathematics have a redemptive use beyond their limited understanding; for they provide the concrete basis on which imagination works. So does Los's Spectre, who represents rational error, for he works under Los's compulsion for imaginative ends (illus. 6; 8:37–40; 17:17–20).

This process is illustrated to the right of its poetic explanation on plate 12. The male compass-wielding figure flies upside down, defining with his compasses a crisscrossed globe below with lines of latitude and longitude. He thereby carries out the Spectre's division of generative space (88:47–48) but, like all Blake's compass-wielding figures, functions ambivalently.[13] He defines the world with his scientific intruments and mathematical power and, seeing only this definition, limits himself to rational error. Los's imaginative view, however, goes beyond this definition. Los sees him preventing chaos by providing form, establishing the basis for imagination, and the beginning, but not all, of human possibility. One leg of his compass located at the North Pole, the nadir from the eternal point of view, points to the word *joy* in the text (l. 42) and shows reason establishing the possible beginning of imaginative vision.[14] He, however, believes that this beginning is the whole story and expects joy directly from it. His upside-down position, hidden face, and invisible eyes hint at his intellectual limitation and error as they did in the lower figure of plate 7, whom he resembles. That resemblance and the similarity in composition between plates 7 and 12 point to the underlying unity of religious error, which is represented there, and rational error, which is represented here. The differing backgrounds, activities, and particulars of the three figures in each plate, on the other hand, emphasize the different aspects of error that Blake focuses on in each place.

The consequences of the male's rational limitations are illustrated in the two female figures located one above and one below him (pl. 12). The batwing sleeves and almost serpent-tailed train of the fashionably gowned and hatted top figure identify her as Vala, fallen nature, who results from Deistic doctrines and limits man to his material self. Her position (as Chayes points out [p. 53]) between lines 1 and 19, which both end with the word *shade*, further identifies her character as the "shadow of Jerusalem: the ever mourning Shade" (12:19). Los, however, by giving her a body (12:1), makes her error definite and recognizable. The bottom kneeling

female figure, who also represents physical nature, plays a somewhat different role. She too results from the male mathematical
definition of the world and, pointing to the word *joy*, on which his
compass rests, she too rests her hopes on the scientifically defined
material world. Since she is located in the South, the zenith in
eternal terms (12:55), she assumes an imaginative function, the basis
for Los's work, an idea that is further explored in chapters 3 and 4
when Los supervises Albion's Daughters and Enitharmon. The
curved root at the bottom of the globe, while pointing to her world's
vegetative character, also forms a large spindle of that globe, which
the female turns with her extended right hand. Using the world as
her spindle, she does in primitive fashion what the females in plate
59 do with their wheels—she spins out the basis of life.

This brings us to the last section of chapter 1, which is concerned
with the last element of Albion's fall, his affective error. This error,
discussed in plates 16–24, emerges as Albion's sons "Govern . . . all
by the sweet delights of secret amorous glances" (16:59), demonstrating the essence of false love. It is that secret, jealous, cruel, and
possessive affection which strives for dominance that Albion describes as characterized by shame, doubt, sin, chastity, and contained in natural virtue and moral laws (pl. 21).

Like all other errors, affective error and the multiple sorrows it
leads to (16:63–64) have their imaginative and eternal side as well;
for "All things acted on Earth are seen in the bright Sculptures / Of
Los's Halls & every Age renews its powers from these Works"
(16:61–62). A double interaction between affection and imagination
is here described. Human action based on affection, no matter how
imperfect, is ultimately reflected in imagination, Los's sculptures,
which in turn empower all history. As fallen affection confronts
eternal affection, imagination picks out a gleam of truth from the
former, which it recovers and transforms into inspired truth in the
latter, as it did previously with fallen rationality.

The erroneous form that affection displays is, however, the most
threatening form of error yet, for it is the most seductive to the
imagination. It assaults Los in a way that false religion and reason
do not. For the only time in the poem, Los expresses fear and almost
succumbs to error. Even as he reasserts his dominance, compelling
his Spectre to obey him, he is affected by what he must counteract.
Los fears the "false and Generating Love" (17:25–26) of Albion's
daughters, which he accurately describes as "Envy Revenge &
Cruelty" (17:30) but nevertheless finds sexually seductive. He
openly shirks a direct struggle with the Daughters of Albion and
sends his Spectre against them instead, "lest he be consumed"
(17:7). Natural or physical beauty is, after all, very seductive to the

imagination. Los's action—that is, imaginative withdrawal from love and the pitting of false reason and religion (his Spectre) against what is left—leaves affection in its fallen sensual state and explains the ongoing conflict between love on the one hand, and, on the other, fallen religion and reason established in moral codes preaching chastity, condemning sin, and causing wars. It is also responsible for Albion's denial of liberty (pl. 21, 22) and his overreaction to Vala (pl. 23).

We see the opposition between the fallen female and the Spectre illustrated in plate 21, where a male figure wielding two three-tailed, starry whips of reason threatens three Daughters of Albion in a misguided attempt to subdue sexuality. This visual image pictures the Spectre's attempt to subdue generative love. It is also called Hand's pursuit of Albion's three daughters "with cruel stripes . . . thro the streets of Babylon" (21:29, 30) in the poetic text. While we expect such spectrous action from fallen Albion, it comes strangely from Los who, influenced by the possessiveness, jealousy, and doctrines of chastity that Albion's daughters display, hides Enitharmon "in shame and confusion of / Face" (17:53–54), sends out "ministers of evil" (17:62), and uses hate as the spur to his action (17:62–63).

Temporarily succumbing in spite of himself to what he reveals as error as it affects him, Los yields his imaginative role in the dialectic with error to Jerusalem. Although imagination is eternal and does carry on unabated when affective error is fully explored in chapter 4, Los is temporarily upset by the seductiveness of generative sexuality. But Jerusalem, whose liberty of body and mind is the appropriate imaginative antidote to generative sexuality, is not, and the dialectic takes place between Jerusalem and Albion with his sons (pls. 18, 21, 23, 24), on the one hand, or, on the other, between Jerusalem and Vala, who as Jerusalem's fallen counterpart contends with her for Albion's consciousness (pls. 20, 22, illus. 18, 20, 22).

Although Blake examines both parts of the dialectic together, intermittently turning from Vala to Albion, I shall, for clarity's sake, follow one at a time. Vala and Jerusalem begin in unfallen existence as complementary segments of inspired physical nature, "For Vala produc'd the Bodies. Jerusalem gave the Souls" (18:7). Their ideal complementary relationship is described in plate 19 as they assimilate with one another, singing choral duets "Dividing & uniting into many female forms" (19:45), and is illustrated in plate 18, where they are depicted as two almost-identical, large, winged figures who float in the night sky touching right toes. Jerusalem faces the reader and Vala has her back to the reader, their complementary positions illustrating their complementary natures as Vala's lilies (virgin innocence) complement Jerusalem's roses (freed sexuality). The small figures, resembling those at the bottom of *Marriage of Heaven and Hell* 1, who emanate from the larger ones and reverse their positions vis-à-vis the reader, further emphasize Jerusalem's and Vala's complementary natures. The female, facing the reader, comes from Vala, the Body; and the male, turning his back, from Jerusalem, the Soul; but both embrace in ideal union. Two moon arks (symbol of the fallen female throughout *Jerusalem*), however, rise above the small figures, and three tiny figures symbolizing Albion's fall tumble headlong down the right margin alongside the text in which Albion's sons reject Jerusalem. These images hint at an imminent perversion of the ideal relationship, which actually occurs as Jerusalem and Vala are separated by Albion's fall and division. Vala is cut off from her imaginative counterpart and limited to the simply physical, embodying generative sexuality and false affection, while Jerusalem remains powerless to influence her.

When the two large figures of plate 18 reappear in plate 20, their positions reversed, touching hands rather than toes in face-to-face encounter, they seem speeding toward head-on collision. Their opposition is further illustrated by the three medial tableaux on this plate, which depict the consequences of their opposing visions. The first tableau precedes Vala's poetic wintry vision of the hungry family in the text. A row of two stars, symbolizing the scientific basis of her domination, accompanies a comet and three moons similar to those of plate 8, symbolizing the physical limitation of fallen love, and sail-laden like Vala's generative moon ark (pls. 24, 39). These images introduce Vala's words, visually demonstrating her generative position.

In the tableau that interrupts those words, Vala sows falling stars, planting the seeds of false reason within physical nature while aided by the single, spectrous, star-pulling figure who precedes her. They follow the two double-plowing figures, two pushing and two pulling, the four Zoas divided in generation. Vala's kneeling position, lowered head, and turned-away face reveal her limited vision, while her plowers present twofold rationality rather than humanized fourfold imagination. They foreshadow in human variation Urizen's double men-headed oxen who plow in plate 29, symbolizing religious error in their activity, as well as Blake's other demonic plowers in *Milton* and the *Descriptive Catalogue* (p. 521).

When we move to the lower half of this plate, the dark background of Vala's words and image is exchanged for the red and golden flames surrounding Jerusalem and her answer. The contrast between her posture and these plowers with Vala's above illustrates the difference between their affective doctrines described in the poetry. There Jerusalem envisions springtime innocence and freely given love in a lost Eden (20:5–10, 22–40) in opposition to Vala's wintry vision of sorrow, shame, sin, and oppression (20:12–20) in a fallen land peopled by a "hungry family" (20:12), where "the slave groans in the dungeon of stone./The captive in the mill of the stranger, sold for scanty hire" (20:15–16). In the illustration Jerusalem faces the reader with open arms as she floats after the fourfold star-harrow pulled by four bearded old men, the four Zoas united in their efforts here. Bearded and bent as they are, however, they symbolize the fourfold potentiality of man bent under the weight of prevailing generative actuality, for Vala's vision prevails within Albion in spite of Jerusalem's efforts to the contrary. Two large stars placed next to and below Albion's name just before he replies to Vala and Jerusalem warn of what he will say even before he announces his acceptance of Vala rather than Jerusalem.

Their antithesis and Vala's domination of Jerusalem is further depicted in their ongoing debates (pls. 20–23) as well as in their next graphic appearance at the top of plate 22, which reverses their original positions (pl. 18) as Vala usurps Jerusalem's place, turning the latter vague and less definite. While the text describes Vala as "spreading her scarlet Veil over Albion" (21:50), the illustration shows the same thing happening to Jerusalem. The poetry meanwhile describes the consequences of Vala's domination in the general cluster of Albion's errors; for as soon as he succumbs to the fallen version of love, he is necessarily enmeshed in false religion, reason, and war. Shame and sin imply codes of "moral Law" (21:48). Secrecy brings fears, doubts, and calls for demonstrations (21:37). Albion's children are tortured and trapped in war (21:31–50). The connections become clearer as Vala is borne "in a golden Ark" (22:4) before Albion's armies, crying "All Love is lost! terror succeeds & Hatred instead of Love/And stern demands of Right & Duty instead of Liberty" (22:10–11). The perversion of physical nature in generative love destroys imaginative love and liberty, substitutes hate and sacrifice for them, and religiously calls these last punishment for sin and a stern code of moral virtue, that is, right and duty supported by reason. We have heard the archetypal version of this story related by Los's Spectre when he recounted the tale of Luvah, Vala, and Urizen (7:30–50). We see it here reiterated in further detail. When Vala looks for love and sees it as sin (22:14–15), she condemns free individual affection in mistaken religious codes that terrorize humanity through internal wars against natural human desires, and she also exterminates social affection to produce external wars between nations.

This sharpening antithesis between Jerusalem and Vala is further revealed in the bottom picture of plate 22. Here interlocking pairs of cherubim joined at arms, feet, and wings float with folded wings over the tops of three spiked, intermeshing wheels or cogs which, while immersed in yellow flame, churn the water (copy B) or mud (copy E) below them like Newton's waterwheels. While illustrating Jerusalem's rhetorical question, "Why should Punishment Weave the Veil with Iron Wheels of War/When Forgiveness might it Weave with Wings of Cherubim" (22:34–35), the illustration looks forward to Jerusalem's ultimate triumph as the cherubim wings here contain the world of Satan's wheels. Taken together, both words and picture combine the various components of affective error—the male Satanic wheels and female weaving of Vala's veil—and oppose them with imaginative affection as represented by the interlocking cherubim. Recalling the wheels of compulsion that Albion's sons form when they worship Vala (18:8), the tyrannic cogs and Newton's waterwheel that we glimpsed in the previous section (15:16–19), as well as fallen nature's veil, which includes generative love and leads to codes of moral virtue or punishment and sin, this plate displays the means of their overthrow.

Vala's and Jerusalem's absolute division and antithesis, however, result in the subsequent degeneration of both, as pictured in plates 23 and 24. In plate 23 rejected liberty is pictured in Jerusalem's collapse and in the oppression of Albion's population below her. Jerusalem faints exhausted between the lily of Vala and Rahab's sunflower (seen again as part of Rahab's papal throne in plate 53) and replies to Albion "like a voice heard from a sepulcher" (23:8); for even as Albion momentarily turns toward her, he persists in affective error. "Trembling . . . in jealous dark despair" (23:14), as the line above her picture announces. Wings and head drooping, Jerusalem's figure is for the first time pictured clothed in a filmy gown into which her limbs and wings blend as she grows more indefinite than before through Albion's rejection. Furthermore, the snaky entrails streaming behind her, which seem to come from her hair, demonstrate her absorption by Vala's generative doctrine. While the two human insects with pointed wingtips, who arise from Vala's veil and resemble both the immortal forms of time and space that Los welcomes in plate 44 and the human insect emerging from the chrysalis in plates 2 and 3, indicate imaginative potential, they also point to generative actuality, as does fainting Jerusalem. Below Jerusalem, interspersing the text in which Albion reveals his error, his oppressed population is imprisoned, restricted, and crushed between the roots of error and in its rocky caves, their bowed figures weighed down by Albion's affective error. His error thus degrades his social as well as individual affections, and his inner state is mirrored in his politically and economically oppressed population as Vala and Jerusalem continue to oppose each other.

Even triumphant Vala, pictured in plate 24, degenerates from the glorious winged figure who complemented Jerusalem in plate 18. Her symbol of the moon ark sails triumphantly across the stormy sea below the night sky at the top of the plate, crisscrossed by webs of rain (or perhaps her "web of despair"). A winged human face peers from the ark to regard the human chain in the middle of the page, which turns into an elongated cloud or intestinal ribbon winding down the right margin, Vala's veil "vegetating Knot by Knot" (24:61–62). Vala herself squats ignominiously with stunted arms encircling her head in intellectual and imaginative limitation (cf. Vala in pl. 47). Placed in the right margin between lines 14 and 24, she looks back over her shoulder to the text where Albion consigns his children to the death of generation:

> . . . to feed the hungry ravenings of Destruction
> To be the sport of Accident! to waste in Wrath & Love, a weary
> Life, in brooding cares & anxious labours, that prove but chaff.
> (24:14–16)

This is her effect on humanity as Albion turns to "wastes of Moral Law" (24:24) where Babylon, to whom he now clings, reigns in "Human desolation" (24:25).

Contemplating their dialectic, Albion is torn between Jerusalem and Vala but finally accepts Vala's version of love, for he is still in his original divided state. He contends directly with Jerusalem this time, as he did earlier with the Savior, but he now exposes the affective part of his earlier lapse.

As Albion's sons come together, "Three Immense Wheels" (18:8, 43–44) grinding out death (18:10), they too lapse into affective error by rejecting Jerusalem (18:11–35) as a "Harlot" (18:12) and "Albions sin and shame" (18:13, 32), and by accepting instead the chastity, sin, and contention of "Babylon, the City of Vala, the Goddess Virgin-Mother" (18:29).[15] For "peace & love . . . with transgressors meeting in brotherhood around the table./Or in the porch or garden" (18:14–16), they thus substitute "The unforgiving porches, the tables of enmity, and beds/And chambers of trembling & suspition" (18:23–24). For the life of free and multitudinous full expression,

> . . . delights
> Of age and youth and boy and girl and animal and herb'
> And river and mountain, and city & village, and house & family,
> (18:16–18)

they substitute a life of hatred and strife:

> . . . hatreds of age & youth
> And boy & girl, & animal & herb, & river & mountain
> And city & village, and house & family.
>
> (18:24–26)

The inversion of identical images emphasizes the wholesale perversion that generative affection produces in all phases of existence. This perversion culminates in the building of the anti-city Babylon to replace the imaginative city of Jerusalem. It serves a privileged class, "the Perfect" (18:26), whose religion and "glory" (18:27) are based on oppression and the sacrifice of the many for the few (18:26–28), and who reign "Building Castles in desolated places" (18:38). Petrified affection in both individual and land further produces the infertility described in plate 19 as Albion's inner state is reflected in his outer.

Albion turns "self-exiled from the face of light & shine of morning. / In a dark world a narrow house!" (19:13–14). Self-exiled, for he deliberately cuts himself off from his Savior, Los's light, and Jerusalem's shine, Albion pens himself in his "narrow house," the simply vegetative body with its limited senses and affections, victimizing himself through his narrowed vision. As a result "All his Affections now appear withoutside" (19:17), separated from his subjective self, objectivized and alien, to be manipulated as any other objects in the universe. Albion then destroys his own humanity and turns to rock as he allows generative sexuality, the fallen female's moon, to replace imagination's sun in his world. As a result, his "Circumference was clos'd: his Center began darkning / Into the Night of Beulah, and the Moon of Beulah rose" (19:36–37).

Illustrated graphically (pl. 19), Albion's affective error appears in his dead form, which lies prostrate and twisted by this further distortion, head sunken, eyes unseeing, with many tiny dead bodies lying on, around, and under him. Female figures mourn him with hidden faces at his head and foot, as they did in plate 14, but they loom larger here since the female's role expands in affective error. With only one exception, a fleeing male who outlines an opposing, waning crescent, the small human figures who rise aspiring in the right margin shape the waxing crescent moons of the fallen female (cf. illus. 8, 14 bottom, 18). As the lowest of these reaches up, his extended arm bumps the word *Moon* protruding from the text, for female affective error blocks his reach and roofs his view. The opposing exceptional figure is also graphically limited and blocked by

Albion's affective error, for the poetic list of Albion's sons (19:18–19), portrayed as objectified affections that form the "Satanic Mill" (19:19), forces his head down and his shoulders over. Indeed, all the male figures have their heads either thrown back or hunched down, their perverted affections causing their lack of sight. Only the double females see what they are doing as they look and reach up to the row of four human figures holding hands in a contorted dance of death along the top of the plate. They recognize perverted affection, but see it as necessary to their existence which, as the dance above shows, is really death. Heads lowered and faces hidden by long hanging hair, the three female figures above demonstrate their own affective error in their dance and include in their midst a misguided castrated male (deprived of his free natural sexuality because of them) whose head is thrown backward like Albion's below.[16]

Expressing the essence of affective error, Albion demonstrates that chastity, sin, and secrecy are at the bottom of his erroneous views of love. This view of love determines the very landscape itself as his "secret loves" (21:26), his "Sin & secret appetite" (21:27) result in the particular mourning mountains, rivers, sections of London, and cities of England (pl. 21). These all "Demonstrate in Unbelief" with "Doubt & Despair" (21:35, 36), are carried in "Arks" (21:45, 46), "infolded in moral Law" (21:48), and contribute to the universal state of war combining with Albion's religious and rational errors to display error's geographical face in the fallen landscape.

Albion is now covered with "The disease of Shame" (21:3) that particularizes the Savior's original diagnosis of his "souls disease" (4:13). Albion perversely proclaims, "All is Eternal Death unless you can weave a chaste/Body over an unchaste Mind" (21:11–12), exposing the hypocrisy of chastity's divided state. Revealing the extent of his affective error, he furthermore adds, "I brought Love into light of day to pride in chaste beauty/I brought Love into light & fancied Innocence is no more" (22:17–18). Albion's emphasis on light, previously associated with imagination (Los, the Savior, the sun), becomes suspicious in the context of pride and chastity, attributes of moral virtue and jealous love. Although divine if seen imaginatively, it too may be corrupted in generation.[17] His vision of open love ending innocence also smacks of fallen affective doctrines, a self-deluding attempt to limit innocence to inaction and passivity, and love to jealous secrecy. He welcomes Vala, affective error's sacrificial goddess, calling, "But come O Vala with knife & cup: drain my blood/To the last drop" (22:29–30), destroying first himself than others as Vala's conception of exclusive jealous love leads him to murder Luvah (22:29–32; cf. 4:26, 33).

At one point Jerusalem almost succeeds in winning over Albion. He feels the attraction of her doctrines, "that Love and Pity are the same" (23:14), that he has "erred" (23:16), and that he has engaged in "sacrifices of cruelty" (23:17), but in reaction he tries to annihilate Vala completely as he tried to do with Jerusalem before. His action thereby reveals his underlying error, for in accepting one principle he tries to exclude another in the manner of the sons of Albion (cf. 10:7–16). He thus demonstrates exclusive generative love even as he seems to repudiate it. Completely denying physical nature, he adopts a typically generative solution: "He recoil'd: he rush'd outwards; he bore the Veil whole away" (23:20). Fallen religion or reason might easily come up with such a remedy, denying material nature (Vala's veil) by taking refuge in abstraction, either an unembodied, absent god, or philosophically abstracted ideas. An imaginative solution would instead restore the veil to its former shining state (20:34), that is, reimbue physical nature with the glow of imaginative love. Albion's generative solution reveals his divided state, as do his "last words" (23:26) when he once more (or still) dies (24:60) while calling upon a God "wide separated from the Human Soul" (23:30), and restores "Vala's Veil whole, for a Law, a Terror & a Curse!" (23:32), thereby reinstituting "Moral Justice" (23:34) and "vengeance" (23:38).

Going from one extreme to the other, from denying Vala completely to exclusively establishing her merely natural world and generative sexuality as her veil "thundering . . . rushes from his hand, Vegetating Knot by Knot" (24:61–62), Albion remains in the grip of affective error. Like his sons, he substitutes Babylon-Vala for Jerusalem, her Moral Law and consequent destruction and cruelty in place of Jerusalem's "love and harmony" (24:43). His devotion to Vala and her domination appears graphically too. First, they are revealed in the dominant winged moon, a symbol of the fallen female and her doctrines, which presides on the tempestuous sea (material world) at the top of plate 24. Then they appear when the earlier image of the dance of death interrupts Albion's lament partway down the page in distinctly less human form, turning into a stringy line of cloud or human entrails as it winds down the right margin alongside the kneeling figure of Vala, whose arms by encircling her head indicate her limited imagination.

The same configuration of the dance of death or cloud-roll form appears in plate 23 as a twisted line of entrails behind fallen Jerusalem intermeshing with her hair when Albion rejects her for Vala. It also reappears as the entrails which the Daughters of Albion wind from Albion's body in the final plate of the chapter (pl. 25). In

each case it is associated with the false and generating love represented by Vala, appearing when that is dominant, and becoming
less human and more visceral as the full meaning of Albion's affective error is clarified.

The absolute triumph of affective error is, however, not pictured
until the final large and forceful illustration of the chapter, plate 25.
Here, in Blakean parody of the three fates, three fallen Daughters of
Albion sacrifice and torture fallen but universal Albion, whose limbs
still contain sun, moon, and stars. His bound and kneeling position,
subservient to affective error, the position of his head thrown back
and eyes limited to the fallen female above him, and his covered
genitals indicate the fallen generative state of his consciousness and
affections. As the fates wind his entrails or umbilical cord into a ball,
they sacrifice man through the power of their generative sexuality
on the stone altar of false religion that supports them. They control
and torture him while they simultaneously mourn over the
mutilated and bound figure they have produced. Albion grants
them power by adopting their affective error and allows his own
torture while they, in their turn, force Albion to conform to their
principles and mourn the result. Framing the design, their bodies
enclose Albion in restricted subjection to the merely physical. Indeed, the central female who hovers over the scene actually grows
into the roots and fibrous vegetation of the sides and background,
enclosing the scene still further. The suggestion of trees or cavern of
ribs in the left background and a network of veins on the right also
suggest the rule of vegetation or physical, ossified man limited to
his natural body.

The hovering female's place in the illustration's composition is
similar to that of Los's Spectre in plate 6. She too hovers above the
scene facing downward, her outstretched upper limbs framing the
illustration at the top and upper sides, and she restricts man as the
Spectre attempts to restrict Los. Moreover, the shape of her head
with flowing hair parted in the middle looks very much like the
head and back structure parted in the middle by the backbone of the
Spectre in plate 6. Their formal similarlity reflects the similarity of
their opposition to imagination, the Spectre in restricting man to
fallen religion and reason, and the female in restricting him to fallen
affection. The similarity in composition of the two plates displays
Blake's thematic form at work. Restriction's many appearances look
quite different, but Blake's repetition of a common outline points
out their underlying unity. In the same way Albion's action, told
from various points of view during the poem, at first sounds different, but the underlying identity emerges there too. The illustration

revisits Albion's generative division in female rather than male images, while the text revisits Albion's initial fall in terms of affective error rather than overall division.

Yet the text and illustrations also display a dialectical relationship. For while illustration 25 shows affective error triumphant at the end of chapter 1, the text for the plate reasserts the contrary face of the dialectic as Beulah mourns Albion's fallen situation. As products of Los's furnaces, these mourners of Beulah recognize Albion's affective error in his murder of Luvah, unfallen love (22:31; 24:51; 25:6), which murders divinity and denies passionate love. They also see that religious and rational error in the "Oaken Groves," "Dragon Temples," and codes of "vengeance" (25:4–5) equally destroy love and divine imagination, for all error is interconnected. While they view the universal destructiveness of Albion's action, which the chapter outlines, they reject the despair and accusations of universal sinfulness that such recognition can lead to by enunciating Blake's doctrine of states for the "deliverance of Individuals Evermore Amen" (25:13). By identifying generation as a state of consciousness through which Albion may pass and by condemning the view that imputes "Sin & Righteousness/To Individuals & not to States" (25:15–16), these inhabitants of Beulah oppose Albion's generative errors and further carry out Blake's opening promise to explore Albion's states. Thus, in chapter 1, "the closing words deliberately return us full circle to the opening words of the poem proper, on plate 4."[18] Chapter 1 ends precisely where it began, with Albion's ongoing situation. Albion still attributes sin to individuals and sleeps in Ulro while imagination works dialectically within his error to awaken his consciousness. The moment has not changed. Chapter 1 has simply investigated its meaning for Albion, what his sleep in Ulro signifies for his religion, his intellect, his affections, his society, and his universe, and what countervailing forces operate to end his sleep and restore his imaginative vision, society, and universe, to bring about his awakening.

NOTES

1. William Ivins, *Prints and Visual Communication* (Cambridge, Mass.: Harvard University Press, 1953) refers to the geometer's "net of rationality" (p. 70) and the stylized grid used by printmakers in the seventeenth and eighteenth centuries to translate drawings into a "standardized linear system" (p. 68) for the purposes of engraving. These restrictive nets reduced the unique and concrete particulars to a statistical average easily translated by printmakers. Blake's choice of a net image as a symbol of restrictive, rationalized, material functioning seems related to its use in engraving.

2. Erdman, *Illuminated Blake*, p. 284.

3. Since the illustration is tiny and many of its lines are inconclusive, a positive identification of the small group of figures is difficult. Erdman characterizes this group as a shepherd's wife feeding a cat and calls the sleeping animal at the left a sheep dog, images in keeping with innocence (p. 288). But this domestic activity seems inappropriate to its outdoor setting, and the sleeping animal resembles Blake's tiger in *Songs of Experience* more than any of his dogs. This hint of experience is reinforced if we identify the sacrifical group, which is also more appropriate to an outdoor setting than the domestic group is.

4. Locke, *Human Understanding*, 1:206–7, 2:9.

5. Kathleen Raine, *Blake and Tradition*, Bollingen Series 27, 2 vols. (Princeton, N.J.: Princeton University Press, 1968), 1, 167.

6. Erdman's identification of the figure as Abraham (*Illuminated Blake*, p. 294) seems unlikely, for while Abraham promises some kind of inspiration or "refuge" (15:27), the illustration pictures repression.

7. Erdman's suggestion that the figure is a trousered male (*Illuminated Blake*, p. 292) is not convincing if we look at the way in which her robe spreads out behind her feet, the suggestion of flowing hair at the shoulder, and Vala's broadbrimmed hat of plate 12, which she holds.

8. Erdman, *Illuminated Blake*, p. 291. Idem, *Prophet against Empire*, plate 13.

9. Copies B and E show Albion with blank, staring eyes. In copy D he looks askance at Jerusalem but is just as imperceptive.

10. Mellor points out the similarities between the two pictures and reproduces the watercolor as plate 55 of her book, *Blake's Human Form Divine*.

11. The wheel image used frequently for Albion's sons is an important exception to the prevalent phallic imagery. It is, of course, complemented by a contrary wheel or divine analogy that transcends it.

12. It is interesting to note in this connection that Blake has used the name *Apollyon* to symbolize the rational spirit of the generative world. Although both Bloom in his textual commentary and S. Foster Damon, *A Blake Dictionary: The Ideas and Symbols of William Blake* (Providence, R.I.: Brown University Press, 1965), p. 26, identify this name with the angel in Revelation who releases the demonic locusts (9:11), a connection with Apollo seems to be implied as well. Although both Hebrew and Greek names are given in the passage from Revelation, Blake chooses the Greek appellation only, thus placing it in the rationalist rather than inspirationalist tradition. The similarity to the name of the Greek god is obvious, and the fact that Apollyon in Revelation does not carry a bow and Apollo is often called the archer god and represented with his bow underlines the connection. The association between Apollo and the Muses, daughters of memory (Mnemosyne), whom Blake contrasted with the daughters of inspiration (of Beulah), further suits the symbol of rationalism. Nietzsche later, in *The Birth of Tragedy*, characterizes Apollo in much the same way as Blake when he draws the distinction between the Dionysian and Apollonian elements in Greek tragedy, although his evaluation of the character is quite different. Nietzsche sees the Apollonian as the "apotheosis of the *principium individuationis*" (what Blake would call the Selfhood). For him it embodies the principles of moderation and self-control, is in all things objective, and is "caught in utter abstraction" (Friedrich Nietzsche, *The Birth of Tragedy*, trans. Walter Kaufmann [New York: Random House–Vintage, 1956], pp. 33, 36). As such, he is a very appropriate symbol for Blake to use in the passage quoted above.

13. One might compare this compass user to Urizen in the frontispiece of *Europe* or to Newton in Blake's watercolor. All three eliminate chaos but at the same time mark out generative limitation with their compasses.

14. Irene H. Chayes, "The Marginal Design on *Jerusalem* 12," *Blake Studies* 7, no. 2 (1975): 51–76.

15 This wheel image within affective error continues the earlier wheel images of religious and rational errors (e.g., 5:46ff; 13:37; 15:16–19). That single image thereby demonstrates the

interrelationship of error. Layers of meaning are revealed within it as it recurs in new contexts throughout the poem. Blake's kaleidoscopic method thus operates in the wheel's various generative appearances; and as the perspective later alters to imagination, Blake's visionary ideas are also demonstrated, for we see the wheel's eternal appearance too.

16. The three females are probably the same three daughters of Albion repeatedly pictured within this section of chapter 1, who flee from spectrous reason (pl. 21) or sacrifice Albion (pl. 25). Their function remains the same and leads to death. It is symbolized here by the line of dancers linking hands. In form this line resembles a winding line of entrails or rolled clouds, other symbols of Vala or generative sexual death (see illus. 23, 24, 81, 83, 85). It also parodies in fallen fashion the line of cherubim who link limbs and wings in plate 22.

17. Blake makes a similar point about light in "Auguries of Innocence":

> God Appears & God is Light
> To those poor Souls who dwell in Night
> But does a Human Form Display
> To those who Dwell in Realms of Day.

(ll. 128–31)

18. Bloom, commentary, p. 850.

4

The Religious Error

CHAPTER 2 of *Jerusalem* investigates Albion's religious error together with its imaginative alternative, but the content of this chapter is not limited to what we usually think of as religious matters, for Albion's error inevitably distorts his entire consciousness and life: his mind, body, passions, perceptions, actions, and institutions. In chapter 2 Blake reveals all these distortions growing from the soil of Albion's religious error. In chapter 3, on the other hand, he shows them sprouting from philosophic error, and in chapter 4 from affective error. While many of the results look the same, since their root causes are interrelated, Blake separates each part of the complex root and analyzes it, with its ramifications and consequences, in a separate chapter.

After announcing his purpose and outlining the content in the dedication and frontispiece, Blake begins chapter 2 by presenting Albion as the priestly "punisher & judge" (28:4) of religious error, who establishes his mistaken notions in the false doctrines and perfidious institutions of his fallen religion (28:6–27). While Albion's appearance, words, and actions point out the religious roots and branch of his error, they also echo his earlier appearances, divisions, speeches, and actions pointing out the persistence of his ongoing situation, but from another perspective. By bringing together motifs from chapter 1 in Albion's appearance as punisher and judge, Blake demonstrates their interconnection as various sides of Albion's single action. Thus Albion here establishes his seat as he did in his first appearance (pl. 4), institutes division (28:12; 4:23), relies on demonstration rather than faith (28:11, 4:28), sees divine love as "unnatural consanguinities and friendships" (28:7; cf. 4:26), and establishes

71

laws of moral virtue (28:15–16; 4:31). He furthermore appears in the same cold and wintry images as he did earlier (28:13; 4:36; 15:30; 23:35), and amid similar trees (28:14; 13:38; 14:2). Here, however, Albion names the tree "Moral Virtue, and the Law / Of God who dwells in Chaos hidden from the human sight" (28:15–16), establishing the twofold religious error responsible for generation, first in the codes of moral virtue that define sin and punishment, and second in the idea of an absent, invisible, exiled God who dwells in chaos. Opposing religious truth as depicted in codes of love, mutuality, and acceptance (27:71, 85–88) and God as the "Human Form, Divine" (27:58), this description echoes Albion's "last words" at the end of chapter 1 when he told us, "God in the dreary Void / Dwells from Eternity, wide separated from the Human Soul" (23:29–30). The void-inhabiting God of man engrossed in affective error turns out to be identical with the God of religious error, for the two states are identical.

Albion's notions of sin and punishment overthrow Edenic perfection and pervert love to crime in the moral codes of his false religion as Hand's did earlier (9:7–16). In his world as in Hand's:

> Every ornament of perfection, and every labour of love,
> In all the Garden of Eden, & in all the golden mountains
> Was become an envied horror, and a remembrance of jealousy:
> And every Act a Crime, and Albion the punisher & judge.
>
> (28:1–4)

The echo of the word *crime* (9:14, 28:4) in the second passage, reiterated two lines later in the plural when we are told "all these ornaments are crimes" (28:6) produced by Edenic love, is particularly striking, for the singular noun form is not used anywhere else in *Jerusalem* and the plural is used only once in each subsequent chapter and is associated with punishment for sin each time. Blake's word use ties together the two passages under discussion and emphasizes the fact that we are viewing the same action in the second as in the first. Hand is, after all, part of fallen Albion, as is his world. Similarly, when Albion "condense[s]" his land "into solid rocks" (28:9) as he did to his sons and cities earlier (19:25), he echoes Hand's petrifying action when he "Condens'd" his affections and natural world (Emanations) "into hard opake substances" (9:1). Again Blake's identical language alerts us to the identity of the action. Here, however, condensation comes out of Albion's religious error of punishing "sin" and worshiping an absent and abstract God.

Furthermore, because Albion accepts these religious errors, he substitutes "Atonement" (28:21) and the sacrifice of others for imaginative "willing sacrifice of Self" (28:20), such as Los (pl. 1) or Jerusalem and the Divine Vision perform (pl. 27), and erects "twelve Altars, / Of rough unhewn rocks" (28:21–22) on which to sacrifice his own sons. This image, which combines Druidical human sacrifice with Jewish religious error, the twelve altars corresponding to Israel's twelve tribes, echoes the dedicatory identification of Druids and biblical patriarchs. For Blake, both Druid and Jew represent religious error. In his view the Druidic practice of human sacrifice does in a literal way what Jewish legalism does in a metaphoric one through codes of sin and punishment, that is, it murders men to please an abstract, absent diety.[1] Albion, by thus accepting Druidical Jewish error, attempts to sacrifice his own sons on his Druidic altars as the Daughters of Albion sacrificed him on their stone altars in plate 25. He sees his sons as "the first transgressors" (28:24) against his laws of moral virtue which, as we later find out, cannot be kept by anyone. He thereby unknowingly punishes himself, for his sons are part of him, and initiates the code of vengeance that his sons later turn against him and his population. Generation's cycle of victimizaton thus begins and is perpetuated by Albion's religious error, which aims to destroy liberty (pl. 26): "In Shame & Jealousy to annihilate Jerusalem" (28:27). This same annihilation, we may recall, was Albion's aim (pl. 24) and his sons' as well (pl. 18) in chapter 1 when they substituted Babylon for Jerusalem. As this aim reappears in chapter 2, however, its religious mask peeps out from behind its sexual one, and another layer is revealed.

Albion's religious error is further analyzed in chapter 2 as it divides Albion within and appears in both inner and outer degeneration. Chapter 2 opens out the first section of chapter 1 (pl. 7–9), in which Blake outlines religious error, exploring and explaining it further. He divides this exploration into three parts. First, in plates 28–36, he describes the individual aspects of Albion's division by religious error and the consequent degeneration of his natural self, his reason, and his view of God, in dialectical relation to his imaginative alternative. Next Blake passes to the institutional results of Albion's error in the analysis of Albion's fallen church, the cathedral cities of the Anglican Church, which are contrasted with the unfallen, inspired cities of eternity (pls. 37–42:76). Then religious error appears as it works within the categories of time and space, within history and the natural material world, glimpsed imaginatively as well as generatively (42:77–48:53). The chapter finally culminates in Erin's summary of generation and the ambiguous prayer of the Daughters of Beulah, which parallels the ending of chapter 1 but with a crucial and characteristic difference appropriate to this stage of Albion's consciousness.

Still operating within his original metaphor of division, Blake, throughout chapter 2, demonstrates its inner and outer appearance in religious error. Albion maintains his initial opposition to the Savior within this context (28:26; 29:1). He also immediately divides as he did in chapter 1, but this time into Spectre and Emanation, into rational and physical parts, as Los did at the beginning of chapter 1 when he revealed the religious element of Albion's fall (pl. 6–8). His Spectre, like Los's, also divides from his back and loins (29:4; cf. 6:2–3). Unlike Los, however, who opposes and controls his Spectre and Emanation, Albion turns his into the God of his religion, reducing the character of both God and man by doing so. Nevertheless, Los works to regenerate Albion's spectrous actions and provide the living opposition to his deadly choice as he promised in chapter 1 (8:15–40). He operates teleologically for imagination by controlling the work of his Spectre and Emanation within Albion's generative actions. Albion's limitations to time and space, to spectrous and emanative categories, even to generative sleep prove necessary for his salvation, since they provide Los's working materials, although Albion does not know it.

Albion's "Spectrous Chaos" (29:1–2, 3) is that same chaos-inhabiting God mentioned in the previous plate (28:16) and is identified further as "the Great Selfhood/Satan: Worshipd as God by the Mighty Ones of the Earth" (29:17–18), a mistaken notion of God that inverts the categories of true religion. This is not the Satan of orthodox religion whom we meet in *The Marriage of Heaven and Hell* as the divine and energetic Devil, but spectrous Satan, the negation of the Divine Vision. His characteristic mode of operation also demonstrates his demonic inversion and parodies eternity's center opening outward. Instead of a translucent universe (14:17–25) or a flower reaching from eternity and back (13:34–36), which the unfolding of imagination's center produces, Satan's unfolding is monstrous. Beginning from "a white Dot calld a Center from which branches out/A circle in continual gyrations" (29:19–20), he grows multiple heads and limbs that devour humanity like a hydra or polypus.

Mentioned in the central section of the dedicatory poem as well (27:27–76), Satan reduces the Human Form Divine to a worm (27:53–55; 29:5–6). Since Satan too is often described and pictured in *Jerusalem* as a dragon, worm, or serpent, by reducing man to such he establishes his identity with fallen Albion, perverts human categories, remakes man in his own image and, incidentally, parodies God's action in Genesis.

The same identity between Albion and Satan reappears in Blake's image of the plowman. Parodying the eternals' plowing that leads to imaginative renewal (55:54–55), Albion's plowing is sterile and produces no crop but death (29:9–11). It is represented in the illustration (pl. 29) by Satan at the plow. The bent and bearded long-haired figure cannot be mistaken for Albion, who always appears as a clean-shaven youth with curly hair. He resembles instead the figures pulling Vala's plow (pl. 20) and Blake's numerous bearded portrayals of spectrous Urizen (esp. pl. 41). The two human-headed beasts who pull his plow echo his facial features and his limited generative vision. Together with Satan they make a demonic three-some representing spectrous as opposed to fourfold or fully de-veloped imaginative vision.[2] Like Urizen in *The Four Zoas*, whose "plow of iron cut the dreadful furrows/In Ulro beneath Beulah where the Dead wail Night & Day" (FZ, 2, 25:37–38), Albion's Spectre plows death and destruction. His affinity with "the spiritual form of Pitt," George III's minister who ordered "the Plowman to plow up the Cities and Towers" (DC, p. 521), that is, directed the English wars with France, the domestic political repression, and economic exploitation between 1783 and 1801, also helps charac-terize him. So do the disastrous results of his plowing described in chapter 2 as physical war and oppression, which resemble those of Satan's plowing in *Milton* (1:7–8) when Satan usurps Palamabron's plow and wreaks havoc among the eternals and in the universe.

Just as Albion denies his own divinity and alienates his reason elevating it to an independent deity in his Spectre before whom he prostrates himself, so does he alienate his physical nature and generative sexuality, Vala. When he negates imagination in her favor saying: "The Divine Vision/Is as nothing before thee" (29:33–34), he elevates the physical and sexual to new heights: "Love/Ele-vate into the Region of Brotherhood" (29:52–30:1). His action em-powers her claim, "I alone am Beauty/The Imaginative Human Form is but a breathing of Vala" (29:48–49). In a demonic parody of God breathing life into Adam, Vala supplies life to Albion. He be-comes her creature, limited to his merely natural or physical form without imagination or immortal qualities.

When Albion grants Vala dominion, he "tremble[s]," pours down "milky fear" from his "members" (30:3) until "all manhood is gone" (30:4), and is undone by generative sexuality. Fallen Albion, seduced by the physical and absorbed in sexual bondage, displays the condition Los feared when he sent his Spectre against the Daughters of Albion (pl. 17), for sex with Vala leads to "death & eternal fear" (30:6) and bondage to Nature, which is "elevate[d] inward" (30:10). Outwardly it appears in the instruction of marriage, which is sanctioned by religion in generation but is unknown in Eternity (30:15).

Vala's seductive beauty and domination appear right at the outset of chapter 2 (pl. 28). While the poetic text of the plate concentrates on the male expression of Albion's religious error in Albion and his sons, the illustration depicts the same error in terms of Albion's female parts as Vala dominates Jerusalem. The two naked females in the illustration embrace face to face before a golden net. But Vala is dominant, for she both assimilates with Jerusalem (19:41) and catches her in her gold and silver net (20:30–32).[3] Furthermore, both figures sit upon a huge lily, symbol of Vala (cf. 19:42; illus. 18), surrounded by the watery world of time and space like the swan-woman of plate 11 and with the same results. Even as the two embrace, Vala's merely natural world dominates Jerusalem's imaginative one. The golden glow of the net behind the figures in the lily is Vala's as well as Jerusalem's and the gold of the sky, which announces Jerusalem's imaginative promise, is obscured and innundated by Vala's many clouds and ubiquitous sea established by Albion's religious error (28:1–3) that elevates Vala to dominion.

The small sea creatures that proceed down the right margin and between the lines locate the entire page beneath Vala's materialistic sea, that generative world established by Albion's words in the text. The sea shells that introduce and accompany Albion's speech demonstrate his petrific condensations, and the scaly man who sits with his drooping head inserted into one such shell shows man's limited vision and petrified intellect in this world. Located between the lines in which Albion declares Edenic love to be a crime and establishes divison as the basis of his "seat" (28:5, 12), this man is limited and bent into a huddled position by Albion's words, two of which, his "labours" (1. 6) and "seat" (1. 12), extended from the text directly above and beneath him.

Although they operate independently, for the most part, and are dominant in two separate spheres, the two divisions of Albion prompted by his religious error, the Spectre Satan and Emanation Vala, come together briefly in the image of the "Sexual Reasoning Hermaphroditic" (29:28), which parodies imaginative unity in its sterile conjoining of generative sexuality with abstract divinity. These work together to produce the fallen world and fallen man.

Man's self-reduction to the merely natural that results from his religious error and is expressed in Vala's domination also appears in the figure of Reuben. In him we see the further limitation of Albion's sensuality, the reduction of his other four senses (sight, smell, taste, and hearing) in addition to touch (sexuality) limited by Vala. Named for Isaac's oldest son to demonstrate his genesis in religious error, Reuben is Vala-dominated Albion, that is, man limited to his purely physical nature. Although we may seem to be very far afield from orthodox religious doctrines in this exemplum of fallen sensuality and perception, we are absolutely within Blake's definition, which sees the limitation of sense experience as a consequence of fallen, uninspired religion. As each of Reuben's senses is in turn limited, eyes narrowed (30:53; 32:2), nostrils turned earthward (30:47; 32:2); tongue folded "Between Lips of Mire & clay" (32:6), and ears bent in a spiral (32:13), Blake cements their connection to religious error by mentioning the biblical land that surrounds Reuben, by having Reuben sent over Jordan after each limitation, and by associating him with Albion's twelve daughters, who symbolize the twelve tribes of Israel. Limited himself, Reuben also limits all those who see him, that is, all who regard man as simply natural and not divine, even those in the inspired land over Jordan, nominally within Judeo-Christian religion, for "they looked on one-another & became what they beheld" (30:50; cf. 30:54; 32:14).

This story of sensual limitation is told on the archetypal level in the description of Albion's four Zoas: "the Four Eternal Senses of Man" (32:31) who "divided into Four ravening deathlike Forms" (32:36). The degeneration of Albion's sensuality, his Zoas or faculties, again establishes his identity with Reuben. Blake's discussion of this degeneration, furthermore, points out its temporary character; for the deathlike forms become "States Permanently Fixd by the Divine Power" (32:38), but Albion is the pilgrim passing through various states. Similarly, too, is Reuben, for "Reuben is Merlin/Exploring the Three States of Ulro; Creation, Redemption & Judgment" (32:41–2). He is the potentially divine man of imagination temporarily involved in generative, material states.

Man's reduction to the merely natural through religious error also appears visually in symbols of the natural world, in images of vegetation, fibers, and roots. In plate 34, for example, as Albion turns petrified from "Universal Love" (34:7), the illustration depicts intermeshing fibres in the left margin similar to those in the lower right margin of plate 4. They suggest veins, ropes, roots, Vala's veils, or the interwoven branches of a tree, which the trunk at the lower left (copy E) underscore, hinting at the tree of religious mystery (28:15–19). This image brings together Albion's religious error with Vala's work. As we regard its flowering, many-branched version, which grows up the right margin, turning into male and female human forms, we see religious error involving and shaping humanity through its vegetative productions. The lower diving figure in the tree resembles similar generative figures in chapter 1 (e.g., pls. 7, 12, 18), while the upper figure recalls, in a less definite and more vegetative version, the kneeling woman who was spinning out the natural world at the bottom of plate 12. Both demonstrate Vala's influence in their positions and forms.

The twining-branch motif of plate 34 is repeated in plate 36, but from another point of view. Here some leaves grow from formerly bare branches at the left. The figures emerging from the vegetation at the right are distinct and fully formed rather than indefinite, healthily flesh-colored rather than jaundiced, and the whole is brightened with living green leaves and red grape clusters. Instead of diving, the lower figure reaches up to pick the grape cluster above her head, while the upper figure turns male and no longer kneels but stands naked, looking up to the living green above him. Here we see the positive side or saving aspect of natural limitation, which the text also points out by warning of the chaotic hell that would result from Albion's limitless fall.

Since nature provides those limits without which man would become a monstrous, cruel, chaotic, Satanic hell (36:31–42), Albion does not degenerate further than Vala-dominated man. Further degeneration is possible. It is Albion's potential chaos (36:31–42), described here in terms of "Moral Justice" (35:30) and "Moral Virtue, fill'd with Revenge and Law" (35:35), the characteristics of Albion's false religion. This passage parallels Los' description in chapter 1 of what might happen if his Spectre were to work independently without the context of imagination (8:6–12, 38). In the earlier section, Blake points out the difference between the immortal imagination, which cannot be annihilated, and mortal man, who can be. In this parallel section of chapter 2, Blake shows us the difference between mortal man who has unannihilated imagination working for him within natural limitation and man's Spectre or Satanic God who is fall without limitation, a permanent state wholly abstract and negative.[4]

This positive characterization of the natural man is further revealed as Los shapes Reuben. It may at first seem perverse that imagination should be responsible for shaping the limited man of earthbound and merely natural perception and sending him out of the inspired land over Jordan each time in further restricted form (30:43–54; 32:1–13, 41), or that Divinity should found Albion's limits of "Satan and Adam" (31:1), of demonic, rationally based, invisible, exiled godliness and of earth-created, earth-limited humanity. Once, however, we see these limits as fortresses against formlessness and chaos, which are the greater menace since nothing can come of them, we understand Los's role within them. Here, at least, is a natural foundation on which imagination can build.

Imagination's shaping role is illustrated at the top of plate 32, whose text describes Reuben's creation. Los with hammer and anvil, in typical blacksmith activity of imagination, is about to pound a bright and golden sun connected to a fleeing male figure—Reuben being sent out over Jordan—by two wavy tendrils, which echo in curved variation the sun's straight rays. These tendrils, which recall Reuben's enrooting in chapter 1 (15:25) and Vala's vegetative images, symbolize Reuben's attachment to the natural world. The fact that Los's hammer sends him forth by beating the glowing sun of imagination, however, underlines the saving power at work within his creation and within Albion's error.[5] Albion's ultimate degeneration is thus avoided through the dialectic at work within him.

Blake also develops this dialectic between religious error and truth by showing the reader Albion's generative actions and doctrines from the eternal point of view, a point of view that Albion is unable to see but that is present nevertheless. As soon as Albion divides into Spectre and Emanation and grants Vala precedence within him, Los explains the action from his imaginative perspective, transcending the account Albion relates. While he tells the same story as Albion does (30:2–16; 30:23–40), he points out exactly where Albion is wrong:

> There is a Throne in every Man, it is the throne of God
> This Woman has claimd as her own & Man is no more!
> Albion is the Tabernacle of Vala & her Temple
> And not the Tabernacle & Temple of the Most High
> O Albion why wilt thou Create a Female Will?
> To hide the most evident God in a hidden covert, even
> In the shadows of a Woman & a secluded Holy Place
> That we may pry after him as after a stolen treasure
> Hidden among the Dead & mured up from the paths of life.
> (30:27–35)

Man, Los explains, has replaced his divinity with physicality and thereby denied or annihilated himself. Combining religious imagery ("throne of God," "Tabernacle," "Temple," "Most High," "Holy Place") with fallen female images of secrecy and hiding ("hidden shadows," "secluded," "pry," "stolen treasure," "mured up"),[6] Blake shows the connection between Albion's spectrous and sexual distortions, which both stem from religious error.

Los further anticipates the consequences of Vala's domination in the rule of the merely natural as the single principle of man's existence leading to the merely material universe of mathematics and empirical science, "the Wilds of Newton & Locke" (30:40), a concept that is fully explored in chapter 3 but hinted at here in the interconnections between various components of error.

Los's action in shaping Reuben (pls. 30, 32) is also briefly viewed from the eternal perspective, first by Los (pl. 30) and then by the eternals (pl. 32). Los contrasts Reuben's earthbound sensuality with inspired sensuality, declaring:

> If Perceptive Organs vary: Objects of Perception seem to vary:
> If the Perceptive Organs close: their Objects seem to close also:
> Consider this O mortal Man! O worm of sixty winters said Los
> Consider Sexual Organization & hide thee in the dust.
>
> (30:55–58)

Taking a subjective view of perception, which puts beauty in the eye of the beholder, Los shows how man's limited perception affects the entire world around him; for the universe turns merely material and limited to match the material and limited sense organs of fallen man. As Los further addresses the "worm" to which Satan reduces man (27:55; 29:6) and reminds him of Vala's domination ("Sexual Organization"), he ties Albion's religious error to his loss of variable perception. False perception seen imaginatively turns out to be false religion after all.

The further consequences of religious error in the prohibition of true art and science, which "cannot exist but by Naked Beauty displayd" (32:49), is pointed out by the other eternals, who treat Albion's religious error as some kind of cosmic joke based on his laughable idea of chastity. Here they anticipate the interconnections between art, science, liberty, and religion, which Los later points out in his speech to the cities (pl. 38) as they pose the alternative to Reuben's fallen perception. In their inspired alternative:

> . . . Divine Mercy
> Steps beyond and Redeems Man in the Body of Jesus Amen
> And Length Bredth Highth again Obey the Divine Vision Hallelujah
>
> (32:54–56)

By placing mathematical values in an inspired context, the eternals transcend Newtonian material categories and restore nature to imagination, which within the religious context of chapter 2 is called "the Body of Jesus." Imagination thus transforms material man and nature, fallen sensation and science. This is the beginning of eternity's answer to the Newtonian universe that chapter 3 develops and about which Los questioned the Daughters of Albion: "Is this the

Female Will O ye lovely Daughters of Albion. To/Converse concerning Weight & Distance in the Wilds of Newton & Locke" (30:39–40).

Finally, when Albion reiterates his initial choice of death and "turn'd his back against the Divine Vision" (35:14), crying: "I die! I go to Eternal Death!" (35:16), Los also imaginatively assesses this generative action. His question and answer: "Must the Wise die for an Atonement? does Mercy endure Atonement?/No! It is Moral Severity, & destroys Mercy in its Victim" (35:25–26) reject the essence of false religion through its opposite—mercy. Picking up the word *Atonement* from the chapter's initial description of Albion's religious error (28:21), Los's answer ties together all Albion's erroneous moral codes and religious laws, calling them "Moral Severity," and contrasts them simultaneously with the mercy of religious truth to put them in their true eternal perspective.

Similarly, as Los cries "Albion goes to Eternal Death" (31:9), and detects Albion's "petrific hardness" (34:1), he merges with divinity to reveal the roots of Albion's action in religious error. When Albion rejects unity with the Savior as he did initially, "Turning from Universal Love petrific as he went" (34:7) and from the Divine Vision (35:14); locates himself within "the System of Moral Virtue, named Rahab" (35:10), fallen religion's moral code; and announces his own imminent death with the cry of religious error, "God hath forsaken me" (35:22), an ironic inversion of what has occurred (for he has denied his own divinity and therefore forsaken God, rather than vice versa as he claims), imagination exposes the false religious basis of his actions. Los's warnings attack Albion's religious laws and moral codes, threatening death if Albion "persistest to forbid with Laws/Our Emanations" (33:8–9). In spite of imagination's efforts, however, Albion still remains cut off from his own divinity.

We see Albion graphically portrayed in this position in plate 37. While the poetic text goes on to consider the institutional aspect of religious error, the illustration still shows its individual form in Albion. Sunk in despair over his book, a soft-covered version of the stony Mosaic law, which Erdman (p. 316) identifies with Urizen's book in *Book of Urizen* 1 and 5 and Young's in *Night Thoughts* 5 and 7, Albion is as completely unseeing or dead as he was in any of the illustrations for chapter 1. But here the reason for his blindness appears in his visual limitation to religious error and his intellectual absorption by it. His hair has furthermore grown long, like Urizen's or Jehovah's whose laws he accepts, and falls over his face to block his sight. Surrounded by the clouds of mystification and the sea of materialism, he sits upon the rocky throne of petrified law, which resembles his stony Druid altars (28:21–24; illus. 25). His doctrines of moral virtue, which are open on his lap under his lowered face, prevent his seeing the imaginative alternative beside him: the scroll whose central portion he sits on, which preaches freedom from spectrous limitation, and which the tiny fairy figure offers him. This scroll, written in mirror script, envisions humanity overthrowing the Spectre, Albion's Satanic god. It provides the omnipresent imaginative alternative to generation in Blake's ongoing dialectic, but demands unorthodox seeing to decipher it. Just as his message offers the eternal opposite to Albion's religious error, so the tiny, graceful creature who perches on it with lifted face poses the visual opposite to Albion's massive, heavy, bent figure and unseeing face. Like the angel in *Marriage of Heaven and Hell* 10, Albion is limited by his orthodox religious views and cannot see the alternative written on the scroll that might liberate him. His cities as described in the text are equally blind.

Finally, Blake shows religious truth acting in its own right as it poses an imaginative alternative in dialectical opposition to religious error. Los holds out such an alternative in his doctrine of states that opposes Albion's notions of sin as he announces "I go forth to Create/States: to deliver Individuals evermore! Amen" (31:15–16). Here Los's words from chapter 1: "I am inspired: I act not for myself: for Albions sake/I now am what I am" (8:17–18) are exemplified in his action. In separating individuals from their states, Los acts for Albion's sake "that Albion may arise again" (31:14) and answers the prayer of Beulah's inhabitants at the end of chapter 1 that God "descend" and "take away the imputation of Sin/By the Creation of States & the deliverance of Individuals Evermore Amen" (25:12–13). Opposing Albion's erroneous religious doctrine, which "imputed Sin & Righteousness/To Individuals & not to States" (25:15–16), Los, unlike religious error that judges, punishes, and condemns, saves "those who have sinned from the punishment of the Law" (31:6), the law of the absent God, which Albion founded (28:15–16) and which is "death/To every energy of man" (31:11–12). As Los "descend[s] into Non-Entity" (31:17), we are reminded of the frontispiece to *Jerusalem* but now understand that Los's doctrine of states is one means by which he illuminates Albion's darkness.

The Divine Vision also offers an alternative to generation as Los appears before Albion, proposing unity in opposition to Albion's division much as the Savior did at the outset of chapter 1 (pl. 4), but supplying a religious dimension by adding "Jesus the Christ" (34:20) to the former account of Edenic unity, harmony, love, and mutuality. The Savior's first direct proposal of unity to Albion: "I in you and you in me mutual in love divine" (4:7) now presents Christ as mediator and ideal prototype for incarnate divinity as the Divine

Vision declares that "he [Christ] in us, and we in him,/Live in perfect harmony in Eden" (34:20–21).

As the imaginative alternative to religious error expressed in Vala's generative universe, Blake presents the humanized land in immortal London (pl. 34), the unfallen city, which is contrasted later to the fallen cathedral cities of Albion. Resembling Golgonooza of chapter 1 (pls. 12–13), it is another humanized city constructed from the same unorthodox building materials (ideas, imagination, thoughts, and affections). In addition, it reveals Blake the active poet-prophet writing within (34:42–43). The four unfallen cathedral cities—Verulam, Canterbury, York, and Edinburgh (34:44–54)—portray similar imaginative constructions as they demonstrate inspired religion in their "loving kindness," "fortitude," and self-sacrifice (34:51–54). In addition, each of the cathedral cities contains an expanding universe within itself (34:49) and gates of precious stones that lead directly to imagination (34:55), just as Los's children do (14:17–21). The imaginative individual and city are thus identified, as are inner consciousness and outer being. London too is both a city and "a Human awful wonder of God!" (34:29), creation and creator, material, human, and divine. In this it resembles its prototype, Jerusalem, who is described by the Old Testament prophets as both city and human, nation and woman. By repeating identical images in both individuals and collective constructions such as cities (34:29–59), Blake demonstrates that consciousness or vision is not solely an internal matter, but is reflected in outer circumstances. Cities and landscapes "Are also Men; every thing is Human" (34:48), while all individuals contain "a Universe" (34:49). Renewed consciousness thus renews its world just as fallen consciousness degenerates its world.

This identity between human and city or inner and outer is further explored as "The Friends of Albion" (36:3), who are his unfallen cities, collectively oppose his "Eternal Death" (36:3) much as the Savior opposed it in plate 4. The saving forces now appear in religious terms, however, as the unfallen twenty-eight cities of England with their Emanations, the original four (34:44–51; 36:4) plus:

> . . . Twenty-four in whom the Divine Family
> Appeard; and they were One in Him. A Human Vision!
> Human Divine, Jesus the Saviour, blessed for ever and ever.
>
> (36:45–47)

Both one and many, human and divine, material and transcendent, these multiple saviors, like the single Savior before them, demonstrate forgiveness and self-sacrifice to oppose Albion's religious errors as they, like Los in plate 1, enter time and space, are "created by the Hammer and Loom" (36:56), the tools of Los and Enitharmon, to save Albion. Since they are in their unfallen eternal forms, the number of cities is twenty-eight. Unlike the twenty-seven churches of history from Adam to Luther, which correspond to the twenty-seven dioceses of the contemporary Church of England and represent Albion's fallen religion,[7] these twenty-eight include in their number Los, who originally called them to their task, and become the redeemed eternal church united with him in Jesus, the "Human Divine" of imaginative religion.

The connection between eternity and generation that Los establishes in plate 1 is now seen in its religious context within the cathedral cities. It is named the "Gate of Los" (35:3, 9, 11), for Los is the connection between time and eternity, the crucial door of change through which states may be exchanged and vision altered. Even fallen Albion possesses such a connection, since "There is in Albion a Gate of Precious stones and gold/Seen only by Emanations, by vegetations viewless" (34:55–56). This too is the Gate of Los. All natural creations have gates to eternity within them, and vice versa, for all natural creation is potentially eternal. Functioning very much like the vortex in *Milton*, the gate of Los entered one way, from eternity, allows eternal Urthona to become Los, the twenty-eight unfallen cities to be created by Hammer and Loom in order to save Albion, or Albion to go to death. Entered the other way, however, from time, it finally enables Albion or the reader to awaken and enter Eternal Life. It is invisible to "vegetations," for they have no awakened imaginative potential, and equally so to "Satans Watchfiends" (35:1) no matter how carefully they search, for Satan is fall without limit or possibility of salvation, containing no basis for imagination to work upon. Although Satan's watchfiends are very thorough in their search for Los's gate, "Numbering every grain/Of sand on Earth every night" (35:1–2), their scientific and analytical methods that Jerusalem warned Albion about earlier (22:20–22) are exclusively material and therefore ineffective. Albion too, since he is in a state of Satan caused by his religious error, for "he hath studied the arts/Of unbelief" (36:13–14), flees from the gate of Los at this point. Uttering his religious errors, he turns diseased (36:1, 11), "sick to death" (36:12), subject to "falshoods" (36:19), and rejects "his Friends" (36:14). He appears as he did throughout chapter 1 and is described in similar images of generation, which are now seen as consequences of his religious error.

The same connection to eternity is described in another way, as "a Grain of Sand in Lambeth" (37:15), one that Satan's watchfiends must have missed. This grain contains Oothoon's palace of freely given love, invisible to the Satanic forces who can see love only as sin (37:15–22). Lambeth being Blake's onetime residence, the grains of sand may be seen as his poetry by means of which man opens up his eternal world of imagination (cf. 5:18–20) and within which Blake constructs ideas of freely given love (Oothoon's palace). Blake too, like Los, becomes the agent of eternity in time.

The connection of man to eternity through the unfallen emanation is hinted at when emanations see Los's gate within Albion (34:55–56), when spectrous forces try to destroy Albion's emanation in order to limit him to error (36:17), when Jerusalem hides in Lambeth, where Blake builds his eternal connections, and sleeps there within redemptive love (Oothoon's palace), which Blake's poetry extols. Vividly pictured in the illustration to plate 31, her awakening image foreshadows Blake's fuller explanation of the Emanation (39:38–42), his retelling of Eve's creation that stresses her saving function (42:32–34), and chapter 4's story of Albion's awakening through unity with his Emanation (96:2).[8] While the accompanying text describes the Divine Vision as founding Albion's fallen limits of Adam and Satan and Los's doctrine of states, the illustration shows the feminine face of salvation. It thus complements and expands the text, demonstrating the necessity for Eve as well as Adam. The illustration also unifies the various creation accounts given in the chapter as aspects of one account. The Emanation emerges from Albion's rib cage in the illustration, as did Eve from Adam (Genesis 2:21–22), while the Divine Vision (Christ bearing stigmata) supervises the creation. Imagination's role in shaping nature, told poetically in the story of Los creating Reuben, now appears in the picture of female creation. As Eve-Vala rises in flames from Albion's bosom, she looks up in awe to the Divine Imagination, who regards her too as he hovers in flames above. Her clear-eyed gaze, the sunburst effect around her uplifted face, her open, raised mouth, and the wing-shaped flames surrounding her indicate her divine connection. By picturing this divine connection, rather than the merely material Vala described in the text, the illustration portrays nature's imaginative role. Albion, however, is unaware of this aspect, or Albion-Adam, although not asleep as he was in the biblical story, is equally unseeing. His head is turned and his face pressed into the green earth on which he rests, while one open eye stares down at it. Limited to the merely natural by his religious error, Albion is unaware of the Divine Vision above him or the real value of the Emanation coming from his breast.

The dialectical nature of Albion's fallen position is perhaps best summarized in the large illustration for plate 33. Separated in two parts by the text, yet connected by a continuing background that reaches between the parts, plate 33 parallels plate 31 in composition and content. It too pictures the Savior over generative Albion, who is still sunk in religious error. In plate 33, however, the Savior comes down from his former soaring position and enters the world of generation, the natural world "between the Palm tree & the Oak of weeping" (23:24) pictured here. It is ironic that while the Savior is closer to them in this illustration than he was in plate 31, actually entering the world instead of simply soaring above them, neither Albion nor his Emanation can see him, for both are sunk in error's sleep. The irony is further extended, for while plate 21 represents the connection to divinity present even in the fallen Emanation, this one shows the presence of fall even in the eternal Emanation, Jerusalem, once Albion rejects her religion for Vala's.[9]

Jerusalem's position, stretched out asleep on a rock in the midst of the sea of time and space, resembles Albion's in plate 14. Her drooping wings seem to merge like a shroud with the rock and waves around her, wilting from their former eternal shape (pl. 2). Above her the outspread wings of the Spectre bat, who resembles Los's Spectre (pl. 6), limit her as a result of Albion's spectrous religious error, which limits liberty and prophetic truth. That same crescent moon we have seen before symbolizing the fallen female (pls. 8, 14, 18, 20, 24) shines beneath the Spectre's wings. It gets no light from imagination, since its dark side is turned to the sun shining in Jerusalem's western heavens, but shines by its own fallen light. However, despite the actuality of Jerusalem's sleep, the hovering Spectre, and the moon of Ulro, the ongoing support of imagination remains within the world of error. At the top of the plate Christ holds sinking Albion in his arms, supports and comforts him, and lights his generative world with rays of golden light. Albion's fainting, unseeing condition, however, demonstrates his fallen religious error. His right foot rests on a winged globe that recalls the winged outline of Vala's moon-ark (pl. 24) and her fallen version of religion, or the alchemical symbol of chaos.[10]

After having thoroughly examined what religious error does to Albion's consciousness, his perceptions, and concepts of God, man, woman, and the world, Blake examines its institutionalized appearance in Albion's organized religion, the Church of England (pls. 37–42, 76). In this chapter dedicated to "the Jews," Blake moves from the Jews as ancient Druids and partriarchs in the dedication and first section of chapter 2, to those Jews who are the Anglican Church in the second section and are represented by the cathedral cities whose words and actions reveal their religious error. At the end of the first section those cities, unified with Los in their eternal forms, try, like the Savior, to save Albion, for human salvation is the function of true religion. They enter time and space from Eternity. Having done so, however, they, like Albion, lose their unity with imagination and become generated, turning inspired religion into the religious legalism of the contemporary English church.

Fallen into religious orthodoxy, their number is reduced to seven: Chichester, Winchester, Gloucester, Exeter, Salisbury, Bristol, and Bath (36:51–61, 37:1–2). Los, the eternal eighth who redeems the seven churches of England or ages of history and keeps them from generation, disappears from their midst and confronts them instead. He opposes their errors with inspired truth, as the Savior does Albion's, and consistently attempts the regeneration of generation through his doctrines (pl. 38; cf. 7:54–70) even as he grows furious at them. To the fallen cities, Los cries: "Have you also caught the infection of Sin & stern Repentance?/I see Disease arise upon you!" (38:75–76). They have caught Albion's disease of shame (4:13, 9:9; 21:3; etc.), which stems from religious error and separates them from imagination as it does him. Los therefore declares, "I alone/Remain in permanent strength" (38:77–78), for he alone remains with imaginative truth.

As the cities fall from the original, inspired, prophetic religion into the perverted church of contemporary England, whose religious errors echo Albion's, their actions also parallel his. After they divide from imagination, they too separate from and deify their Spectres (pl. 37) as Albion did his (pl. 29), and with similar results. Generative Bath, for example, separates from his Spectre (37:3) and immediately establishes religious error in the church as "A triple octave he took, to reduce Jerusalem to twelve" (37:4). He uses the twenty-four cathedral cities to reduce Jerusalem's prophetic religion, the sixteen inspired books of the Bible (see 48:6–11; 36:7), to the religious legalism of Israel's twelve tribes. This religious distortion of Jerusalem in the contemporary Anglican Church has incidental political consequences as she is expelled from the church and takes refuge in Blake's inspired poetry, "Lambeths mild Vale" (37:11). When "Jerusalem cannot be found" (37:13), liberty and inspired religion are equally absent from both church and nation. Only poetry then offers liberty and inspiration a refuge. The separated Spectre-God of established religion, meanwhile, assimilates with Luvah in Albion's mountains (37:3), merges with spiritual hate in the place of moral virtue (4:29–31), and appears as Satan.[11]

All twenty-seven spectrous churches echo Bath, their spokesman, "their Wheels rising up poisonous against Albion" (38:1) like the Satanic wheels of all spectrous forces in the poem. They pray to the same God, Albion's Satanic rational projection (29:1–24), "O God of

Albion descend! deliver Jerusalem from the Oaken Groves!" (38:11).
But their noble purpose of delivering Jerusalem from Druidic
sacrifice, inspired religion from Oaken Groves, is doomed to failure,
for their God is Druidic himself (27:37–40; 29:17–18) and will do no
such thing. Only Los, who "grew furious raging: Why stand we
here trembling around/Calling on God for help; and not ourselves
in whom God dwells" (38:12–13), can save Jerusalem; for his opposition and alternatives are those of inspired religion. For him, God
dwells inside, not outside man, and he calls on God by calling on
man's own eternal imagination. Before analyzing Los's alternative,
the imaginative half of Blake's dialectic in this part of the chapter,
however, we must further examine the institutionalized form of
Albion's religious error within his churches.

Continuing their parallel with Albion, the twenty-seven churches
now separate from their Emanations (36:48–57) and witness the fall
of their four Zoas (37:26–38). The story of Vala's domination of
Albion is now retold in institutional terms as repression in the land.
The earlier images of Vala's veil, shuttle, net, and meshes recur
directly, ensnaring Albion's land itself as the Spectre employs organized religion to spread death and despair, or Vala's "weaving,"
"net," and "meshes closely wove" (37:8–9) for repression and war.
Vala, herself, however, plays a tiny part in this section of chapter 2,
for the female or physical nature is only acknowledged as the mechanical working of the purely physical by the established church.
Indeed, this is one aspect of the church's religious error. Pictured
where the church has put her, she appears kneeling and praying in
the right margin of plate 38, with her lower limbs involved in vegetation like the central figure in plate 34. Vegetated by the church's
view of her as female physicality, she prays in desperation (the
victim of despairing doctrines of sin) to the cloudy obscurity above
her (established religion's version of God).

The fall of the four Zoas also recurs here in new form. Representing the generation of Albion's senses in the first part of the chapter
(32:25–42), the four Zoas here demonstrate these human faculties as
they are expressed by organized religion. As Urizen, Luvah, Tharmas, and Urthona (38:2–5) fall into their generative forms, Urizen's
divine reason turns scientific, Luvah's spiritual love turns to false
pity (like Satan's in *Milton*), Tharmas's expression becomes stifled or
"sullen," and Urthona's inspiration turns into skepticism and despair. As doctrines of the church, which reason falsely, are hypocrit-
ical in their pity, sullen in their expression, and despairing in their
fallen codes of sin and punishment, these Zoas block Albion's full
humanity (38:5). Instead of working in harmony within the eternal
man, and in their eternal forms glorifying the Human Form Divine,

these fallen faculties work at odds within man, contending with each other (38:4–5) and "Destroying by selfish affections the things they most admire" (37:28). They destroy the image of divine man as they themselves create and perpetuate the church's view of vegetative man, whose faculties are at odds within him (e.g., passion and reason). They thereby victimize themselves too. Each faculty (Zoa) sacrifices his character as an eternal contrary in order to gain exclusive generative domination over the whole man.

The church's separation from inspiration, its division into spectre and emanation, and the fall of its four eternal Zoas to their generative forms doom its efforts to save Albion (39:1–17). The fallen church of England cannot provide salvation for its population, for it preaches erroneous religious doctrines, as Albion does. Since it calls punishment, morality, and the sacrifice of others holiness, through following its preaching "The soul drinks murder & revenge & applauds its own holiness" (37:30). The church is, however, only Albion himself writ large, for "Strucken with Albions disease they [the cities] become what they behold;/They assimilate with Albion" (39:2–3). Accepting Albion's fallen religious doctrines of sin and shame, they degenerate as he did. Just as all individuals who view man as merely material become equally material themselves (pls. 30, 32), so do all institutions that preach that view, including the established church as Blake saw it. Like Albion, the cities sleep in Ulro: "The Slumbers of Death came over them around the Couch of Death/Before the Gate of Los & in the depths of Non Entity" (39:35–36). Albion too lay on his couch of death (1:2; illus. 14, 19) as Jerusalem did (illus. 2, 33), or stood before the gate of Los (35:11), or saw nonentity surround the imaginative realm (pls. 1; 5:3–5; 13:37 ff.; 15:51–53; 18:1–10; 32:22; 38:15–16, 38:53–39:31). Now, however, the same circumstances make their institutional appearance in Albion's religious establishment. The cities are generated just like Albion or Reuben, for they are the inevitable outer reflection of man's fallen consciousness. "Such is the nature of the Ulro: that whatever enters/Becomes Sexual, & is Created, and Vegetated, and Born" (39:1–2). The cities enter Ulro as they embrace Albion's errors and try to accomplish salvation by force. They, too, are therefore limited and vegetated, lose their awakened consciousness, and establish Vala, their enrooted vegetation (39:21–27), as "Religion" (39:27).

The illustration (39) depicts their failure to save Albion. The cathedral cities with "Cherub's wings" (39:1) guide the winged ark of their religion through the stormy waters of the sea of materialism under a dark and threatening sky. The ark's dove-wings and glow of light recall Noah's ark, in which the promise of salvation was, in Blake's view, perverted to stultifying legalism by orthodox religion.

The earlier association of this ark with the fallen female (illus. 18, 20, 24) underlines its mistaken religious character. In addition, the ark "is the traditional emblem of woman as the *Foederis Arca* (ark of the covenant) in which life travels over the sea of generated existence," and is associated with the Virgin, who is addressed in her litany as *foederis arca*.[12] She embodies the false moral virtue of chastity in the orthodox version of her story, demonstrating further what Blake has isolated as the cities' Christian error. As the promise of Noah's ark is beset by the surrounding sea of materialism and belied by religious orthodoxy, inspired religion is turned to religious error. The boat then becomes the symbol of that error and is guided by the hovering three angels who, triple like the archer in plate 35, represent established religion. Furthermore, the open-mouthed serpent who glides below, whose tongue darts out, forming a line up the left margin, and whose body turns into the leafy vines of generation with three applelike fruits at the end (similar to those which vegetated Albion-Adam regards in plate 49) recalls corruption in Eden. He reinforces the note of generative domination over the glow of imaginative promise in the plate.

Having shown the parallel to Albion's fall through religious error in the fall of Albion's church, Blake now turns to examine that church's actual doctrines in the speeches of Bath and Oxford, two of its cities.[13] As Bath begins in mildness "in soft gentle tears" (40:2), we recognize the false mildness of Satan (*Milton*, 1:7) or fallen Luvah (38:2), rather than the mercy of eternity; for Bath preaches passivity, not real pity. He sees man as "A piteous example of oblivion" (40:9) and claims "we are nothing: but fade away in mornings breath" (40:13), thereby adopting Vala's version of man as merely material and transient, "a breathing of Vala" (29:49), rather than imaginative and permanent. The murderous negativity of his outlook appears in the language he uses. The word *nothing* is uttered five separate times, *none* three times, *not* and *no* once each in seventeen lines (40:13–30). Like fallen Albion (28:16), Bath denies man's significance and removes his divinity to a heaven-inhabiting God. Like all the fallen cities before (38:11), he too prays for God to "descend and save" Albion (40:16, 28). His prayer is typical of religious error, since it calls for salvation as a gift from a separated and absent God whose strength depends on man's weakness. It is therefore equally subject to Los's raging query to the cities mentioned above, "Why stand we here trembling around/Calling on God for help; and not ourselves in whom God dwells" (38:12–13).

Bath's speech is surrounded by a materialism that prohibits mercy in the illustration (pl. 40), a sea in which big fish eat little fish and a serpent swims. Above all, Vala floats in her cloud, ensnaring and enrooting Albion, whose roots come down at the left and join the sea next to the big fish. The sea beneath Vala, filled with serpents and sea creatures, also continues down the right margin alongside Bath's speech, finally ending in the shore at the very bottom of the plate. Here Albion's subjection to Vala, which the opening plates of chapter 2 describe (esp. 29:35–30:40), is illustrated, but so is the church's subjection to Vala, which Blake describes poetically too (39:25–27), and which Bath's speech demonstrates.[14]

The spectrous source of Bath's wisdom in the "mysterious power/Whose springs are unsearchable & knowledge infinite" (41:1–2) is further evidence of his religious error, for it exalts mystery. Therefore, when Bath claims to pass on to Oxford the "leaves of the Tree of Life" (40:30), we recognize the tree of mystery guarded by the Covering Cherub in the province of the false threefold (14:2), the tree of false religion that shot up under Albion's heel (28:14–19), and the poem's other generative trees. Nor are we surprised, then, as Oxford also preaches the erroneous doctrine of established religion. Calling upon the Old Testament names for God, Jehovah and Shaddai, he too counsels reliance on an outside deity, preaches passivity and weakness rather than exertion to overcome error (41:10–15).

The religious error implicit in the cities' speeches becomes explicit as they "curse" (42:60) and "repent of their human kindness" (42:62), exhibit false pity for Albion, and call to absent Satan "O God of Albion where art thou! pity the watchers!" (42:74). As "watchers" they resemble Satan's "watch-fiends" and parody the prophetic inspired watchmen, Los and Ezekiel, who seek to protect and instruct their people, not condemn them. Their religious error becomes even more explicit as they call, "Come up, build Babylon, Rahab is ours & all her multitudes" (42:63). They unequivocally embrace Rahab, Albion's system of moral virtue (35:10), and devote themselves to corrupt Babylon instead of divine Jerusalem.

The culmination of their error is pictured below Oxford's speech and one plate after Bath's in the glorious design for plate 41. Here we see a chariot that resembles the one in Blake's painting "God judging Adam," and is a parody of imagination's chariot (98:8–11). Although flames surround the chariot, they are not the flames of inspiration, for they leave the background in darkness. Nor is the chariot itself the golden one of Eden. It is rather composed of serpents whose bodies form the wheels and shafts, and whose three heads with open eyes and darting tongues form a threefold Satanic figurehead appropriate to a chariot of sin and punishment. It is pulled by two animals with human faces similar to the animals who pull Satan's plow in plate 29, but with the body and horns of oxen or bulls. Perhaps they are the bulls of fallen Luvah harnessed to the chariot of Urizen, for both fallen passion and reason serve false religion. The presence of only two in this illustration suggests the twofold vision of generation aided by the threefold Satanic serpents, rather than the full fourfold of Eden or true religion. The two hands at the ends of the beasts' horns, one pointing forward to where the serpents gaze and the other backward to grasp the pen offered by the small demons who ride the beasts, suggest the demonic control of expression within twofold generative vision. Erdman's suggestion that "The lion-ox grafting seems a Urizenically desperate attempt to find a law of voluntary collaboration of lion and patient ox" (p. 321) reminds us that such a law is oppression (MHH 24), but it is an oppression that heaven or false religion enforces. The resemblance of the beasts' horns to those in Blake's paintings of the Red Dragon and seven-headed Beast of Revelation associates them with fallen religion, as the bay leaf crowns atop their heads do with the false prophecy (Apollo's Delphic oracle). The human effects of this chariot of error can be seen in the mournful figures who ride in it. Utterly powerless to control their chariot without reins, they sit in helpless dejection with drooping or hidden hands. The heavily veiled woman leans against the mournful bearded man for comfort. His arm encircles her, but neither seems to get any comfort from this situation, and they are powerless to act. The only active hands in the picture are those of the two-fold beasts and demons, for humanity is "nothing" in religious error and Satan is all. We have only to glance at the same human figures in their eternal imaginative appearances amidst the flames of plates 96 and 99 to recognize the enfeebling and victimizing effects of religious error here.

The reflection of fallen consciousness in institutionalized error is mirrored back again in the individual as Albion, "studious of others in his pale disease" (42:1), looks at the church and internalizes the doctrines he observes completing another turn in the vicious cycle of error's influence. He then repeats his initial action, sickens, dies (42:4), repudiates Los as he did the Savior, and in identical terms, as a "deceitful friend" (42:9; 4:26). Using many of the same words and images he used earlier against his sons (28:20–27), he reiterates his religious error of judgment and punishment with which he began chapter 2 (pl. 28), demands "righteousness & justice" (42:12) from Los, condemns his own affections in codes of chastity (42:3–4, 14–16), and attempts to annihilate imagination by atonement, vengeance, and victimization (42:47–54). This time, however, he does so because he follows his church's doctrines.

The visual image of Albion's action appears in the right margin as a human chain of figures who step on each other's faces and backs, crush each other by their weight, and are crushed in turn. Careless of limbs, eyes, and faces, they burden and pain one another. The bottom figure, head invisible to denote his state of consciousness, almost destroyed by the weight he must support, resembles a rock more than a human being. He graphically represents Albion's stony state of consciousness in this chapter and the dire oppression of his population in religious error. The mounting figures demonstrate various states of that oppression, even the topmost figure, a female whose feet are crossed in a position typical of Vala, whose naked body is thrust forward, and who embraces a bunch of grapes as big as she is. Although she grasps the fruits of generation in Albion's world of religious error, she is just as blind as the rest. Meanwhile, a tendril from the human vine reaches out to embrace Albion's vindictive speech and his Spectre's subsequent actions described in the poetry, visually including both in oppressive generation.

Los provides the inspired alternative to Albion by exploding his generative categories through the addition of imaginative truth. By adding "mercy" (42:20), the distinguishing characteristic of religious truth, to Albion's categories of righteousness and justice, Los demonstrates what religious error lacks. He thereby annihilates Albion's categories, crying, "I break thy bonds of righteousness" (42:37). Taking the limits of contraction and opacity (Satan and Adam) that he himself created (31:1–2), he also explodes them as absolute limitations by declaring: "there is no Limit of Expansion! there is no Limit of Translucence" (42:35). Redemption annihilates these limits through woman or the unfallen emanation (42:33–34). Finally, Los explodes Albion's principle of atonement by again offering himself as a sacrifice for Albion (42:40–41; 1:9).

In opposing Albion's religious error, Los repeats his earlier opposition to the cities (pl. 38).[15] Contrasting the church's Satanic God with man's immanent God (38:13) and by imaginatively evaluating the world it establishes (38:12 ff.), he sees the church "drinking the cries of pain/From howling victim of Law: building Heavens Twenty-seven-fold" (38:17–18). Representing the twenty-seven dioceses of the English church, the cities sermonize about a pie-in-the-sky heaven while they promulgate religious laws that torture man on earth. Blake is referring to the moral laws, which destroy man by killing his affections and his divinity (27:29–55; 31:11–12; 38:24–34), and also religion's support of state law, with its political repression (38:36), oppression of the workingman (38:49–50), and war against France (38:40–45). By decreeing that "friendship & benevolence . . . be condemned by Law" (38:27, 30), the law of sin that forbids free affection, the church creates "A World in which Man is by his Nature the Enemy of Man" (38:52), where vengeance, enmity, victimization, and war reign.

Los also condemns the church's codes of universal morality, which ignore individuality in abstract generalized precepts of good and evil, and he contrasts them with the particularized universal of true religion, the Human Form Divine. He characterizes the church's notions of goodness as "Swelld & bloated General Forms, repugnant to the Divine/Humanity, who is the Only General and Universal Form . . . Who protects minute particulars, every one in their own identity" (38:19–20, 23). The church thus does not befriend man, for "Those alone are his friends, who admire his minutest powers" (38:58), and the church condemns many of those powers as sinful.

Imagination's care of particulars, which the generalizing tendency of religious error ignores or distorts, now emerges as one of its most important characteristics. Just as the church generalizes goodness till that is lost, so does it generalize "Art & Science till Art & Science is lost" (38:54). This generalizing tendency, if fully carried out, results in a world without any particularity, Non-Entity (38:59–71), the same world described in chapter 1 (13:38 ff.). Now, however, Los shows how the generalizing tendency creates this world and reveals interconnections between various aspects of error in it. He assesses religious error as "A pretence of Art, to Destroy Art: a pretence of Liberty/To destroy Liberty a pretence of Religion to destroy Religion" (38:35–36). False religion so distorts inspiration that it limits all areas of life and expression. Its codes of chastity, for example, outlaw "Naked Beauty displayd" (32:49), as the eternals told us before, and thereby limit artistic and scientific possibilities of expression. Its "laws" of morality and church-supported state laws also restrict man's liberty of thought and practice, thereby destroying true freedom or liberty. The truth of Los's remarks becomes apparent as he cites the examples of corrupted affection, false moral laws, political wars, economic exploitation, and empty generalizations resulting in sacrifice and denial of intellectual liberty within England, all of which are inherent in Albion's religious error (38:28–70).

The church's degeneration of the female to "a Sexual Machine: An Aged Virgin Form" (39:25) is opposed by Los's revelation of the emanation's imaginative function. Institutionalized religious error, like spectrous Milton, denigrates the female's role in salvation and sees her either as inactive passivity and denial, the Virgin, or mechanistic procreation, the sexual machine, which it idolizes as Babylon, Vala, or Rahab. Los, on the other hand, notes:

Man is adjoind to Man by his Emanative portion:
Who is Jerusalem in every individual Man: and her

Shadow is Vala, builded by the Reasoning power in Man.
(39:38–40)

He reveals her divine function as Jerusalem, connecting men in
mutuality and brotherhood (cf. 27:85–88), while he exposes fallen
Vala as a Satanic creation. He similarly retells the story of Eve's
creation, illustrated earlier in plate 31, to explain the role of the
female as the vehicle of salvation within time and space as:

> . . . The Saviour in mercy takes
> Contractions Limit, and of the Limit he forms Woman: That
> Himself may in process of time be born Man to redeem.
>
> (42:32–34)

As this section ends, Albion still turns from imagination as he did
initially, and imagination still attempts his salvation as initially. But
the final image, Albion's "Serpent Temples" (42:76) with Los's furnaces roaring among them, shows imagination functioning about
the Satanic edifices of the church, maintaining the dialectic within
the institutional religious terms of the section.

The third section of the poem (42:77–48:52) then takes up the
dialectic as "Los drew his Seven Furnaces round Albions Altars/
And as Albion built his frozen Altars, Los built the Mundane Shell"
(42:77–78). Imagination here surrounds Albion's Druidic-Judaic-
Anglican religion with both the seven ages of history and the physical, spatial universe, and the third section of the chapter expands
this image by exploring Albion's religious error within both
categories. Leaving the institutionalized expression of Albion's religious error, it turns to its outer expression in history and the spatial
world, but sees it largely from the imaginative rather than fallen
perspective.[16]

As Albion is again the punisher (pls. 28, 43), as Satan again separates from Albion (pls. 29, 43), as Vala does (pls. 29, 30, 43), as the
limitation of man to mere nature recurs (pls. 30, 32, 43), as Albion
becomes petrified (pls. 34, 35, 36, 44, 45, 46), as further wars engulf
Europe (pls. 34, 47), and as Albion's friends try to save him (pls. 36,
48), various events are repeated, but with distinct differences that
reveal formerly unseen implications through the expanded use of
the imaginative perspective.

Unlike section one of this chapter, which began with Albion's
point of view, this section begins with the Divine Voice in human
form, another version of the initial Savior (pl. 4), who appears in the
sun, like Christ the source of light in illustrations 31 and 33. He
recapitulates the theme: sleep, passage, and awakening in terms of

Albion's religious error—the Satanic responsibility for Albion's sleep, and Albion's eventual resurrection (43:6–26). He simultaneously reveals the redemptive functions of time and space, the main concern of this third section. When Albion then reappears as "Punisher" (43:16; cf. 28:4), the Divine Voice reveals the Satanic cause and redemptive purpose of Albion's actions, for "Albion must Sleep/The Sleep of Death, till the Man of Sin & Repentance be reveald" (43:11–12). History is necessary for Satan's revelation, which will redeem man (43:26).

The Divine Voice also supplies the imaginative view of Albion's separation from his Spectre Satan (29:4–24; 43:6–26). First, he differentiates Satan's negativity from Albion's sleep, exemplifying the difference between a state and the individual within that state, and second, he shows how Albion's malfunctioning mind produces Satan, who absorbs and dominates him (43:33–40), exemplifying the difference between the creation and its creator. As pure negativity, Satan is the "Reactor" (43:9, 11), who can only oppose and deny like the Spectre of Albion's sons in chapter 1 (10:14–16). He also tries to destroy what is positive and grounds "his Reaction into a Law/Of Action, for Obedience to destroy the Contraries of Man" (43:14–15). As negativity, Satan lacks independent concrete existence, so he establishes Albion's historical institutionalized religion in order to achieve such existence. The worldwide effects of his established religion appear in London, Oxford, Sussex, Kent, Ireland, Scotland, Wales, and in all the Cities of the Nations, throughout space and time as Albion's inner errors are reflected in the world (43:18–22; cf. 5:1–15; pl. 16). This is the Satanic takeover of Jerusalem's originally unfallen land (27:1–51). Satan, however, unknowingly serves eternal purposes in his actions (as Los's Spectre does too), for negativity must first become concrete in order to be exposed and abolished. Satan must "be reveald in his System" (43:10), which is Albion's religion with its codes and laws before exiled humanity can return to its divinity. The Divine Voice tells us about religious error exactly what Los told us about scientific error in chapter 1 (12:12–14), that Falsehood must be embodied before it can be recognized as error and corrected. This is the constant imaginative truth which unifies all of existence, true of religious as well as rational error.

The Divine Voice (43:33–40) redefines Satan as a creation or cognitive category of man, "a Shadow [rising] from his wearied intellect" (43:37), echoing Satan's self-definition as Albion's rational power (29:5) and anticipating the definition in chapter 3 (54:16 ff.). Whether Satan appears before Albion's face (29:2) or from Albion's back (29:3), arises from Albion's intellect (43:37) or hides in Albion's forests while Albion sleeps (43:13), he is still Albion's mental projection, an erroneous cognitive concept or "self-delusion" (43:39) that absorbs "all the Man" (43:40) and is expressed outwardly in Albion's forests of mystery (43:13), his religious doctrines, and established church.

Albion "prostrate" (43:41) and "Idolatrous" (43:46) before his own shadow, Satan, demonstrates man's position in religious error before the image of the god he himself created. His words echo Bath's doctrines of the established church (40:13–15). "I am nothing," Albion repeats over and over (43:42, 47, 51, var. 52), as indeed he almost becomes when he ignores his own divinity and worships negation.

Vala appropriately returns to play a part here as she did in the first section of the chapter (pls. 29–30), but with the important addition of Luvah in his fallen form as generated love or spiritual hate. His limitation by Albion to earthbound sensuality parodies Los's limitation of Reuben and limits love to sexuality, Vala's realm, within Albion as limited physical passion, and outside him as teeming, tumultuous nature (43:73–80).

The story of Luvah's fall and struggle with Albion (the battle between man and his passion), outlined by Los's Spectre in the first description of Satanic religion (7:30–50), now gains a historical meaning. In this part of chapter 2, which is concerned with history and the spatial world, Luvah takes the form of France, the passion for liberty in the French Revolution. Just as Albion is both man and land, so is Luvah. When they struggle, and Albion limits Luvah, exiles him, and condemns him to death, England rejects and condemns Liberty in France. Further, when "Luvah tore forth from Albions Lions, in fibrous veins, in rivers/Of Blood over Europe" (47:4–5), condemned liberty causes repressive European wars. The fallen form of liberty, however, turns chaotic and serpentine as the French Revolution turns into terror and Napoleonic conquest.

By murdering Luvah (22:31; 47:16), Albion denies part of himself and thereby initiates the internal strife and perverse sexuality of fallen man. War with France demonstrates the same action on the outer political level. Albion's passion, perverted by his religious error, is projected outward through his institutions and national policy, perverting liberty wherever it appears. Albion is still "the Punisher" (47:14) here, but his punishments rebound on himself as he "Mingles with his Victims Spectre" (47:15). Just as his attempt to sacrifice his sons is self-injury (28:20–27), so is his attempt to sacrifice Luvah. Indeed, Los's earlier precept, "That whenever any Spectre began to devour the Dead,/He might feel the pain as if a man gnawd his own tender nerves" (11:6–7), is now illustrated in Albion's case. By attacking France to repress the spread of liberty and revolution, Albion punishes himself along with France through English death and suffering, political repression, and internal economic hardships (e.g., taxation, inflation), so that Albion's married land, "Beulahs hill & vales" (47:10) becomes a land of death and war "With cymbal trumpet, clarion; & the scythed chariots of Britain" (47:11).

When Vala regards the battle between Albion and Luvah (43:61 ff.), which historically is the struggle between England and revolutionary France, she finds Jerusalem at fault. She blames war on liberty and inspiration, as the English repressive church and state do, and tries to end the problem by exiling and sacrificing liberty as they do, "to sustain the glorious combat & the battle & war/That Man may be purified by the death of . . . [Jerusalem's] delusions" (45:65–66). These delusions—the respect for independent, inspired individuality that Jerusalem's refusal to appropriate Albion's "Minute Particulars" shows, and her claim that "all thy [Albion's] little ones are holy/They are of faith & not of Demonstration" (45:45–46)—are imaginative truths. Vala, on the other hand, claims both Luvah and Albion as her own (45:50, 57), naturalizing all individuality instead. This appears graphically when Vala ensnares Albion in her nets (illus. 40) and as Albion himself enroots beneath the tree of mystery in illustration 49 and begins actually to resemble Vala, wrapping his arms around his head as she frequently does (e.g., pls. 24; 47). As the repercussions of this naturalization are projected onto the screen of history and the land of England, religious inspiration and liberty in the world are abolished through various historical repressive actions such as war between England and France (45:55–66).

The conflict between liberty and repression is graphically presented in the illustrations for this section of chapter 2. In plate 45, for example, Vala binds Jerusalem in a complex net of "iron threads of love & jealousy & despair" (45:49), which come from a shuttle between her legs and thus suggest the sexual character of her domination. Vala's domination is also evident in the vine that grows from Jerusalem up from the right margin of the plate and the wisp of entrail-cloud that floats above her. The distorted position, invisible head, and twisted limbs of Vala, however, show that she does not get off scot-free in the process. She is equally distorted by the bonds she inflicts; for man's religious error, expressed in the elevation of the natural, distorts the latter as it binds his liberty.

This conflict is explored further in plate 46, where the illustration shows Vala and Jerusalem standing on Albion's rocky shore in feminine opposition, while the text describes the male conflict between Los and Albion's spectrous sons. Covered by her dark veil,

Vala, with her back to the reader, regards Jerusalem, who faces the reader in naked beauty surrounded by her little ones. The dark background of Vala and the light one of Jerusalem, Vala's clouds and Jerusalem's sun, Vala's covering and Jerusalem's nakedness, Vala's Byzantine dome of St. Paul's near her feet (resembling St. Peter's in Rome) and Jerusalem's Gothic spires of Westminster near hers, all heighten the contrast between the two figures, between the religious error of the English church and its free inspired truth. While Jerusalem shines forth in glory from the cloud behind her and her little ones look up in eager joy, one even soaring as the final figure who escapes Vala on plate 4 does, she regards Vala intently and frowns at what she sees: generative English religion and repression. Vala, on the other hand, shrouded and darkened by her materialism, seems to threaten Jerusalem with her uplifted veil, "the dark threads" (45:67) with which she tries to smother inspiration and liberty in England.

The consequences for Albion of this feminine opposition are pictured in plate 47. Attempting to rise from the rock of ages, to transcend history, Albion sees only the dark abyss of religious error at his feet, and he remains intellectually limited, with his hands grasping his head within religious error. Jerusalem looks to him in vain for help and tumbles head downwards beneath the feet of triumphant Vala, who unseeingly tramples her. Vala herself looks vaguely and blindly upward, perhaps to a nonexistent sky-inhabiting deity, triumphant but joyless, while her arms encircle her head, indicating her limited intellect and perception (cf. pls. 12, 24, 46). While Vala's version of nature triumphs in the presence of Albion's religious error and topples Jerusalem's liberty and inspired religion from a position on Albion's shore, it brings joy and fulfillment to no one. The netlike design at the bottom, which changes to a vine as we follow it from left to right (like the snake along the bottom of plate 39) further indicates Vala's dominance in Albion's world. The single golden glow behind Albion's seat, however, suggests a gleam of hope: the potential saving function of nature not yet recognized by Albion.

In a final parallel, Blake ends this third section of chapter 2 as he did the first, with Albion's complete petrification. As we saw Albion turn to hardness and rock earlier (pls. 34, 35, 36), so now Los finds Albion hardened to imagination through error and "become barren mountains of Moral/Virtue; and every Minute Particular hardend into grains of sand" (49:19–20). Los's search within individual Albion simultaneously occurs within the land and history. Los therefore mentions the various districts of London (45:14–16, 40–44), its streets and buildings: the Tower, Court, and New Bethlehem Insane

Asylum,[17] as instances of Albion's minute petrification. Forming the fallen version of immortal London, these institutions of repression (prison, court, mental hospital) demonstrate the consequences of Albion's religious error. Los regards further consequences in all the cities and villages of England, where Albion's oppressive church condones economic exploitation, tyranny, forced conscription, and war. It preaches humility to the poor so that they remain in poverty and then ceremoniously distributes charity while leading the oppressed population in prayers glorifying a God who condones such a situation:

They mock at the Labourers limbs! they mock at his starvd Children!
They buy his Daughters that they may have power to sell his Sons:
They compell the Poor to live upon a crust of bread by soft mild arts:
They reduce the Man to want: they give with pomp & ceremony.
The praise of Jehovah is chaunted from lips of hunger & thirst!
                                                                    (44:28–32)

Los thus describes the degeneration of Albion's land caught in the grip of religious error's universal effects.

Albion's "petrified surfaces" (46:5) now reveal what is going on in his world as well as in his consciousness, which the earlier "petrific hardness" of his "face and bosom" (34:1) or spectrous "sepulchre hewn out of a Rock" (33:6) conveyed. In the world his rocky surfaces appear in his religion, the "Druid Patriarchal rocky Temples" (46:14) that Albion's sons erect around fallen Albion; in the land itself, "Albion's Ancient Druid Rocky Shore" (46:15), and in Albion's couch, the "Rock of Ages" (48:4) or all human history.[18]

Although history and geography are thus rocky or fallen, they are undeniably necessary for Albion's redemption. Time and space therefore emerge as ambiguous categories. Personified as immortal, they flee from Albion's fallen world (43:28–32, 72–82), but "weave a Shadow of the Emanation/To hide themselves" (44:6–7). They flee generation but create Vala's natural world. They assess Albion's fallen religion as "the Sexual Religion in its embryon Uncircumcision" (44:11), as simply natural (sexual), uninspired (uncircumcised), and undeveloped (embryonic), echoing the eternal view (39:21–27), but are weak, weep and tremble. They need the protection of imagination, for without it they degenerate. Therefore "Los put forth his hand & took them in" (44:16), as pictured in the illustration (pl. 44), once more showing his activity within the natural world. Two winged figures fly toward Los's welcoming hands, but the first (Time) has pointed, batlike, spectrous wings, while the second (Space) has rounded, eternal wings. They remain ambivalent, but since Los embraces them, they become immortal categories instead of simply fallen ones. In addition, imagination needs them too, for their coming brings out his bardic form. As Erdman states, "That the reunion benefits Los's bardic power is emphasized by the four strings drawn between his thigh and chest (and bound round his apron, D, F) that make him look like a harp."[19]

This is the first movement of actual unity in the poem and leads to the eternal view of Albion's generative land and history. As Los searches Albion's interior (pl. 45), he discovers hard times in England (pls. 45, 46, 47), for Albion's religious error is revealed in his land and "in the nightmare of history."[20] Meanwhile, however, Los rejects the twin bases of that error, both Vala's sexuality, saying: "Humanity knows not of Sex" (44:33), and the Spectre's guiding principle of vengeance, proclaiming:

> I could not dare to take vengeance; for all things are so constructed
> And builded by the Divine hand, that the sinner shall always escape,
> And he who takes vengeance alone is the criminal of Providence;
> If I should dare to lay my finger on a grain of sand
> In way of vengeance; I punish the already punishd: O whom
> Should I pity if I pity not the sinner who is gone astray!
> O Albion, if thou takest vengeance; if thou revengest thy wrongs
> Thou art for ever lost! What can I do to hinder the Sons
> Of Albion from taking vengeance? or how shall I them perswade.
> (45:30–38)

Here Los answers his own Spectre's first sermon of vengeance (7:11–50), as well as all subsequent expressions of it, and explains what adding mercy to Albion's righteousness and justice really means (42:20 ff.).

As Albion's sons then surround sleeping Albion with the edifice of fallen religion, "their Druid Patriarchal rocky Temples" (46:14) mentioned above, and as religion further expresses itself in war (pl. 47), as Albion once more utters his "last words" (47:18; 23:26), the imaginative perspective reasserts itself through Los, the Divine Vision, and through Blake's prophetic poetry, which "the hand of God will assist" (47:17). Albion's couch of death, the rock of ages, becomes a "Couch of repose/With Sixteen pillars" (48:6–7), encompassing Blake's prophetic religion, the sixteen inspired books of the Bible immediately mentioned by name (48:9–11), in place of Albion's twelve altars of religious legalism.

Los has the help of the unfallen Emanation in his imaginative task of transforming time and space. Paralleling the first section of chapter 2, which ends with the attempt of Albion's cities to save him, this section ends with a similar attempt by their Emanations. Prompted by awakening Jerusalem (48:18), they appear as Enion, who expands a moment of time and an atom of space as entries to eternity, like the Gate of Los or a grain of sand in Lambeth. Equally invisible to those who think only in terms of error, these moments and atoms are nevertheless omnipresent, apparent to imaginative consciousness, and transform generation into regeneration.

There is, however, one important difference in this emanative parallel to the cities' earlier attempt. While that fails and leads to generation, this establishes a connection to eternity, albeit hidden and intermittent, and leads to Erin's inspired speech. Here again is Blake's view of the Emanation as the connection between nature and eternity (cf. illus. 31; 39:38–42).

The ending of chapter 2 parallels that of chapter 1 as Albion again utters his "last words" (47:1; 47:18; 23:26) and dies, and as the Daughters of Beulah again pray for him; but now Erin rather than Albion summarizes the changes from Eden to generation. She deplores the situation in England where self-sacrifice has been replaced by "Murder, & Unforgiving, Never-awaking Sacrifice of Enemies" (48:57), the essence of Albion's code of vengeance and atonement. Blaming "Albions Law that freezes sore/Upon his Sons & Daughters," (48:60–61) for this situation, she rallies Jerusalem and the Daughters of Beulah to her in Ireland to provide a "Refuge" (48:59) or "Place for Redemption" (48:63).[21] As Erin describes Albion's fallen universe, where "the Bodies in which all Animals & Vegetations, the Earth & Heaven/Were contained in the All Glorious Imagination are witherd & darkend" (49:13–14), the fallen form of the once universal man mentioned in the dedication (pl. 27) now reappears with his fallen faculties itemized: "Eye," "Ear," "Nostrils," and "Tongue" (49:34–40), and his perception restricted, "The Visions of Eternity, by reason of narrowed perceptions,/Are become weak Visions of Time & Space, fix'd into furrows of death" (49:21–22).[22] Yet Erin recognizes Albion's religious error at work in all this and addresses Satan, the perpetrator of that religion, directly:

O Polypus of Death O Spectre over Europe and Asia
Withering the Human Form by Laws of Sacrifice for Sin
By Laws of Chastity & Abhorrence I am witherd up.
Striving to Create a Heaven in which all shall be pure & holy
In their own Selfhoods, in Natural Selfish Chastity to banish Pity
And dear Mutual Forgiveness; & to become One Great Satan

Inslavd to the most powerful Selfhood: to murder the Divine Humanity

(49:24–30)

She blames codes of vengeance and morality for the death of affection (l. 26) and the degeneration of man's divine nature (l. 25),
exclusion and selfishness for mercy's disappearance (ll. 27–29), and
the creation of a demonic deity for the murder of the inspired deity,
Divine Humanity (l. 30). She furthermore envisions Albion's redemption or awakening "By Self Annihilation" (49:46), and the
necessity of action within time and space (as the Divine Vision does
too [43:11–12]) as she exhorts: "Rush on: Rush on! Rush on! ye
vegetating Sons of Albion" (49:50). Summarizing the history of religion from Paganism to Christianity, she uses biblical place and
proper names, religious terms such as *Heaven, Hell, holiness, Chastity, Soul, Uncircumcision, Iniquity, Satan,* to identify the erroneous
religious basis of Albion's fallen situation. Erin, however, ends her
speech as the inhabitants of Beulah did in the first chapter, by teaching the doctrine of states (49:65–77; cf. 25:12–16), which transcends
generative categories of sin and punishment and offers an alternative to them. Proclaiming deliverance rather than condemnation,
forgiveness rather than punishment, love rather than enmity, aboli-
tion of petrified surfaces rather than the limitation to them, she
demonstrates inspired religion, Her speech explains Los's earlier
action in exploring Albion's "petrified surfaces" (46:5), for their exploration is preliminary to their removal.

> . . . the Evil is Created into a State, that Men
> May be deliverd time after time evermore. Amen.
> Learn therefore O Sisters to distinguish the Eternal Human
> That walks about among the stones of fire in bliss & woe
> Alternate! from those States or Worlds in which the Spirit travels;
> This is the only means to Forgiveness of Enemies
> Therefore remove from Albion these terrible Surfaces.
>
> (49:70–76)

Yet even Erin is affected by religious error, for she, too—like the
mistaken cities before her (pl. 38) and Albion himself—prays for
God to "descend" (50:10), and even mistakenly doubts his omnipresence, saying, "If thou hadst been here, our brother Albion had not
died." (50:11). This last is Erin's fallacy, for the Savior has been
present from the beginning (pl. 4), only Albion's consciousness has
not been ready to accept him. Erin too is affected by fallen con-

sciousness, for within it, as she tells us, the Emanation "will become an Eternal Death, an Avenger of Sin/A Self-righteousness: the proud Virgin-Harlot! Mother of War!" (50: 15–16). While this is the story of Vala's degeneration from Jerusalem (pls. 18–24, 29–30), it also accounts for Erin's mistake and those of Beulah's daughters in their prayer. Although the Emanation degenerates if she remains within fallen consciousness, separation is no solution either, for division ensures fall. This leaves the female in a quandary. Even immortal Erin—who encloses "the Wheels of Albions Sons" (50:22) with her bow of promise or surrounds the void with her spaces (11:12; 12:23; illus. 14), offering an imaginative alternative to generation—is still somehow incomplete and occasionally errs when not connected to an unfallen male. Her cohort, the Daughters of Beulah, ends up skipping back and forth to generation, "Ascending and descending into Albions sea of death" (50:21), so that their prayer too becomes ambiguous. As a result, they show pity without insight and combine forgiveness with religious error. They pray:

> Come O thou Lamb of God and take away the remembrance of Sin
> To Sin & to hide the Sin in sweet deceit is lovely!!
> To Sin in the open face of day is cruel & pitiless! But
> To record the sin for a reproach: to let the Sun go down
> In a remembrance of the Sin: is a Woe & a Horror!
> A brooder of an Evil Day, and a Sun rising in blood
> Come then O Lamb of God and take away the remembrance of Sin.
>
> (50:24–30)

They do not abolish the category of sin or separate the individual from the state. They wish simply to end the recording or remembrance of sin, Albion's religious tally sheets, which is a worthy but insufficient aim.[23] They have achieved a half truth only. Therefore their prayer to God cannot bring about salvation nor end generation. Unlike the inhabitants of Beulah, who express the imaginative vision after chapter 1's general survey of all error and its alternatives, these Daughters of Beulah at the end of chapter 2's survey of religious error and its alternative are still involved in it.

At the end of chapter 2 (pl. 50), sleeping Albion appears graphically in the terms to which the last section of the chapter was devoted—as the land of England complete with white cliffs of Dover washed by the sea of time and space. He is dominated by the Satanic threefold accuser, Albion's vengeful, abstract god.[24] The three spiked crowns on the accuser's heads resemble the Babylonian King's crown in Blake's illustration for Isaiah 14. They indicate Satan's religious error and his spectrous reign in England.[25] Emanating from his bosom is a two-headed figure that gives rise to two more Emanations emerging in chainlike progression. In chapter 3 they are described as "the Giant Brood" of Albion who turn into Bacon, Newton, and Locke. Here, however, within the context of religious error, they appear as the fallen Emanations, Albion's self-righteousness and eternal death (50:13–15). The Satanic threefold king with woeful mien(s), the fallen Emanations, the rocky shore, stormy sea, murky night, moon of Ulro, and spectrous bird-faced lightning all demonstrate the fallen generative world that Albion's religious error creates. The sun, however, rising in the east from materialism's sea, suggests the presence of imagination even within this world as it lights up the background and Vala's cloudy veil behind the Emanation.

At the end of chapter 2 we are still at the same point in the action as at the beginning of chapter 1. Albion still sleeps in Ulro while the dialectic of error and truth proceeds around or within him. Now, however, we understand more fully than originally what this means, for at least one element of his sleep, his religion, has been thoroughly investigated, together with its awakened alternative.

NOTES

1. Blake saw other similarities as well between Judaism and Druidism. Peter F. Fisher, "Blake and the Druids," in *Discussions of William Blake*, ed. John Grant (Boston: Heath, 1961), pp. 28–43, notes, for example, that they share the tendency to separate contraries into good and evil in laws of moral virtue, to make God an abstract deity, and "to consolidate the original voice of the prophet into fixed ritual and rule of the priest" (p. 39). Both religions, according to Blake, substitute the principles of judgment and condemnation of others, which he expressed in the metaphor of sacrifice or victimization, for Jerusalem's principles of forgiveness and inspiration, which are religious truth.

2. The demonic threefold appears in another guise as the Satanic three-fold archer in plate 35, who rides his triple steeds of war and aims to destroy the sinking sun of imagination below him with the destructive arrows of his threefold bow. We also see him as the triple Socratic accusers (pl. 93, 94), who condemn Christ as well as Socrates.

3. The two figures in the illustration have been variously identified as male and female or two females. Mellor, in *Blake's Human Form Divine*, pp. 300–304, argues convincingly for two females by pointing out the changes from the early proof of the plate (see Erdman, *Illuminated Blake*, Appendix, p. 399). She cites the disappearance of the phallic caterpillar, the impossibility of copulation in the new side-by-side position that replaces the former straddling position, and the decreased back musculature of one figure and the appearance of the *mons veneris* in the other figure in copy E. These characteristics argue for the identification of the two figures as Jerusalem and Vala.

4. The relationships expressed in these parallel passages may be summarized in a double equation and a ratio: first, Albion's Spectre = Los's Specture − Los; Second, Albion's Spectre = fallen Albion − Los; and third, Los: Albion:: Los's Spectre: Albion's Spectre. Things equal to the same thing are here, however, not entirely equal to each other; for although fallen

Albion shares much with Los's Spectre, he displays different aspects and functions of these shared characteristics, is not a permanent state, and is therefore equivalent to but not identical with Los's Spectre.

5. Los's hammer also sends forth Jerusalem's children to set limits in the natural world (32:21–24).

6. These images echo earlier ones used to describe fallen female sexuality in chapter 1 (21:19–27; 22:14–15).

7. Damon, *Blake Dictionary*, p. 85.

8. The vital function of the Emanation appears in *Milton* too. There Milton descends through the vortex to unity with his Emanations in order to realize his full eternal imaginative potential.

9. Her resemblance to the figure in plate 2, the title page, makes the identification as Jerusalem possible.

10. Piloo Nanavutty, "*Materia Prima* in a page of Blake's *Vala*," in *William Blake: Essays for S. Foster Damon*, ed. Alvin H. Rosenfeld (Providence, R.I.: Brown University Press, 1969), p. 293, identifies the winged globe as an alchemical symbol for chaos. In addition, Erdman identifies the globe as the moon, because of its continents (*Illuminated Blake*, p. 312). It would in this case symbolize the fallen world of Vala rather than Satan.

11. While the Spectre is repeatedly called Satan, Luvah is named Satan also. Erin calls him by this name in her imaginative description of generation at the end of chapter 2 (49:68).

12. Raine, *Blake and Tradition*, 1:232, 237.

13. Bath, we are told in the text, epitomizes all the cities, and Oxford, being a university city as well as a cathedral city, is one in which clergy are also trained. Both are therefore appropriate spokesmen for the church.

14. The composition of plate 40 is similar to that of plate 28, which also illustrates Vala's domination. In both, the sea is pictured at the top and immerses the entire text beneath its waters of materialism. The left margin in both depicts descending vegetation, while the right shows a line of sea creatures. The top of both, meanwhile, displays Vala enmeshing imaginative humanity in her net of materialism. In plate 40 she ensnares and vegetates Albion within it, while in plate 28 she holds it in reserve behind his unfallen Emanation, Jerusalem.

15. In Keynes's ordering of chapter 2, Los's speech to the cities directly follows the one to Albion, so that the reiteration and amplification of the same ideas follow one another.

16. Blake kept shifting part of this section (pls. 43–46) in his various copies of *Jerusalem*, chapter 2. Erdman's text, which I am using, follows copies A, C, and F. Here Blake proceeds from religion as a product of individual consciousness seen largely from the fallen viewpoint, to its institutionalized form, to its historical appearance seen largely from the imaginative perspective. In Keynes's text, which follows copies D and E, plates 43–46 precede plate 29, and the discussion of time and space precedes the revelation of the spectrous degeneration of Albion and his cities. We see the dialectic within history before we examine its spectrous appearance within man, his God, and his church. In all copies, however, Blake begins with a description of Albion as "punisher & judge" (28:4) and ends with the muster of imaginative forces culminating in Erin's vision and the prayer of the Daughters of Beulah (pls. 47–50). Since all the events between occur simultaneously and simply reveal the various dimensions of Albion's ongoing situation, it is hardly crucial which dimension we examine first so long as in examining the whole we understand all the dimensions before we finish.

17. Erdman, *Prophet against Empire*, p. 453.

18. Albion's twelve sons bear him on his rocky couch of generative history, which parodies the Savior's golden couch of imagination supported by the sixteen inspired books of the Bible, which he prepares for Albion (48:1–12).

19. Erdman, *Illuminated Blake*, p. 323.

20. Bloom, commentary, p. 854.

21. Blake does not usually identify Erin with Ireland, but here, since he is showing Albion's

religious error within the categories of time and space, the imaginative alternative to error also occurs within those categories. Ireland seems appropriate for several reasons. Since it is separated from England, on the other side of the sea of time and space as America is, it is an island of hope. The association of Ireland with Celtic bards and primitive Christianity, which Blake lauds in *The Vision of the Last Judgment* (p. 549), also suggests her redemptive character. Furthermore, England's dire oppression of Ireland suggests that she is one of Jerusalem's children who is being sacrificed on the Druid Altars of Albion's Law by the English church and state and is therefore a natural redemptive location.

22. The "furrows of death" have, of course, been put there by Satan, the plowman of generation (illus. 29).

23. Bloom, in his textual commentary, points out that their words corrupt the text from Ephesians 4:26: "Be ye angry and sin not: let not the sun go down upon your wrath" (p. 855).

24. This threefold accuser reappears in each chapter, characterizing that chapter's particular error. He is the Satanic God of religious error in chapter 2 (pl. 35); he reappears in chapter 3 as three-headed Hand embodying rational error (pl. 70); and he again appears in chapter 4 as the three accusers of Socrates, who condemn imaginative liberty (pls. 93, 94).

25. Jean H. Hagstrum, *William Blake: Poet and Painter*, p. 29, points out that Hand's crown in illustration 50 is an adaptation of the English royal crown, a resemblance that associates Hand more strongly with spectrous reign in England.

5
Deism

Blake analyzes the rational element of Albion's situation in chapter 3 of *Jerusalem*, which is dedicated to the Deists. Since rationalism is the basis of Deism, it is the appropriate subject matter for such a chapter. Deism posits reason as its exclusive ruling principle and dismisses whatever cannot be arrived at through logic and empirical demonstration. It propounds a particular view of God, man, and the world, ideas of moral virtue, and the bases for religious and political systems, which the chapter investigates. According to Blake's definition, "Deism is the Worship of the God of this World by the means of what you call Natural Religion and Natural Philosophy, and of Natural Morality or Self-Righteousness, the Selfish Virtues of the Natural Heart" (pl. 52). The chapter explores what Blake means by these terms, using the characters of the poem who have already been introduced, the male and female divisions of Albion and of his eternal imagination, but shows us another aspect of their natures.

Expanding the subject matter introduced in plates 10–16 of chapter 1, chapter 3 analyzes the rational element of Albion's situation in detail. As Blake turns his microscope lens from the lesser magnification of the introductory outline to the greater magnification of chapter 3, we see more precisely what he means by the "manner" of Albion's sons (pl. 10), how reason operates in the natural world of Deism, what that world consists of, its nature, inhabitants, and institutions, and more precisely, too, how Los works to oppose all these. As Albion and Los divide in plates 53–59 and the eternals respond to that division, the subject matter of

108

plates 10 and 11, which describe Albion's sons' negativity as opposed by Los's creativity, is seen in a different focus and in greater
detail. As the Daughters of Albion weave the natural world simultaneously with and parallel to the Daughters of Los whose weaving
has an imaginative purpose (pls. 58–9), we see the same opposition
between fallen and imaginative creation as when Albion's sons
build Entuthon Benython and Los's children build Golgonooza
(pls. 12–13). This contrast, which is explored in chapter 1 where
Hand's world is opposed to the opening universe within Los's children (pls. 13–14), is reexamined in chapter 3 where the nightmare
world of history and politics (pls. 63–71) is contrasted to its ongoing
imaginative alternative (pl. 71). It is further exemplified in the story
of Jerusalem-Mary (pls. 60–62) where the Divine Vision brings Los's
theory into practice by actually opening a universe of delight within
the universe of oppression created for Jerusalem by Hand's forces.
The reflection of all these intellectual categories within the actual
land, the cities, and counties of the British Isles with which the
rationalist section of chapter 1 ends (pl. 16) is repeated at the end of
chapter 3 in the complete geographic catalogue of Britain (72:1–52),
whose imaginative alternative, corresponding to Los's archetypes in
chapter 1, appears in the counties of Ireland and is extended from
there to the world (pl. 73).

In expanding the subject matter of plates 10–13 within chapter 3,
Blake uses the same form as he did in chapter 2. He again begins
with the story of Albion's division and the limitation of the natural
man and world that follows from it told dialectically with the eternal
view of these events (pls. 28–36, 53–59). But while in chapter 2,
Albion's religious error is the basis of his division, limitation, error,
and petrification, in chapter 3 the root cause is his rational error,
which works itself out through a corresponding series of events.
Corresponding, furthermore, to the institutionalized view of religion in chapter 2 (37–42:76) is the view of natural religion explored
in the specific example of Jerusalem-Mary in chapter 3 (pls. 60–62).
The historic view of religious error that then follows in chapter 2
(42:77–48:52) is paralleled by the historical and political survey of the
consequences of rational error in chapter 3 (pls. 63–72:44). Finally,
just as chapter 2 ends with a mustering of the saving forces culminating in Erin's summary of generation from the imaginative perspective and the Daughters of Beulah's prayer, so chapter 3 winds
up with a muster of eternal forces who analyze Albion's fallen world
and its alternative, and culminates in Blake's imaginative summary
of the action. This time, however, the Daughters of Beulah do not
end the chapter with a prayer to their God (as they did in chapters 1

and 2), but Blake himself demonstrates the workings of that God within the fallen world. Finally, the chapter ends, as the first two did also, with Albion still in his initial fallen position, asleep in Ulro.

Chapter 3 opens with Los working for imagination as in the middle section of chapter 1. Indeed, the parallels between Los's action there and here indicate that the same action is being considered, although in expanded form in chapter 3. In both places Los is at his furnaces (10:1; 53:5), builds Golgonooza (10:17; 53:15), and is opposed by Albion's reason in the form of a vegetated underground root. In chapter 1, Albion's son Scofield shoots down as a mandrake root to undermine Jerusalem's "foundations" (11:21–23) while in chapter 3 the "roots of Albions Tree" enter Los's soul (53:4). In chapter 2 these roots of Albion's tree grow into doctrines of religious mystery (28:15–19). While they grow differently in chapter 3, into rational systems, the root again attacks Los; for the root of religious and rational error is identical, even if the branch is not, and identically attacks man's indwelling divinity. It opposes Los in the "manner" (10:7) of Albion's sons, who use "the Reasoning Power/An Abstract objecting power, that Negatives every thing" (10:13–14), which is also Albion's Spectre, "the Reasoning Power in every Man" (54:7), who dims divinity for Albion (54:32).

The basic ongoing dialectic between generation and eternity is expressed in the contrast and conflict between Los and Albion with which chapter 3 begins. In images familiar from previous plates, we see the "roots of Albions Tree" (53:4) attack and divide Los (53:4–6); we see the opposition between Los's sevenfold vision of history and Albion's single vision (53:10–11), as well as those between Golgonooza, which Los builds, and the rocky altars that Albion sets up (53:15–17), between Los as continually building and Albion as continually destroying (53:19–21), and between Los's understanding of the Emanation as a merciful creation in generation and Albion's understanding of her as a grievous "Shadow" (53:24–27). Now, however, we see a new aspect in the old images, for they present Deism's attack on imagination and imagination's answers. The roots of Albion's tree are now his denial of divinity in favor of materialism; his altars are the sacrificial altars of natural religion; his vision is the single vision of empiricism;[1] his destruction is the political expression of Deism in tyranny and war; and his view of the Emanation as a shadow, Vala, is Deism's material view of nature and woman. All of these terms are further explored within the chapter.

As Los again divides (53:6; cf. 5:67; 6:1–3; 12:7), he separates first from his Emanation. The disconnected Emanation, Enitharmon, now becomes the uninspired material world at the basis of Deism and the underlying category of its natural physical laws and materialist philosophy. Through the Emanation, Los's children materialize into the nations of the earth (53:5–7), historical spatial entities that Los sees as sevenfold, as all history, which he himself, as the eighth eye of God or age of history (55:33), comes to renew into imaginative existence. Deism, however, in its materialist philosophy can see the nations and history with only the "Vegetated Mortal Eye's perverted & single vision" (53:11), in its fallen material appearance. Los, however, views the emanative division anew.

Blake also reiterates Albion's initial fall in terms of rational error (54:6–8). Petrified Albion is now hurled down from Eternity "By his own Spectre, who is the Reasoning Power in every Man" (54:7) into history, which is "the Memory between Man & Man" (54:8). As a result of his Deistic reason, he falls into memory's rational, uninspired, historical world. He again separates from his Spectre (as in chapter 2, pl. 29), whom he worships as "God" (29:18; 54:16) and is limited to the material world. However, although the same event is repeated in both chapters, the Spectre's rational rather than religious character emerges this time. The Spectre reveals his Deistic and scientific character as he calls himself "Bacon & Newton & Locke" (54:17) with "Voltaire: Rousseau" (54:18) in his wings, teaches "Doubt & Experiment" (54:18), and demands demonstration in place of faith, like Satan tempting Christ in the wilderness (54:21). Posing as the Deistic God whose character the chapter will explore, he is also "named Arthur" (54:25) for, in Blake's view, the political aspect of Deistic empiricism supports tyrannical monarchical power. His separation and deification again establish Albion's land, the natural world, as a "Serpent" (43:80; 54:29), or fallen, while Jerusalem, Vala, fallen Albion, and the Divine Vision all gather within its dragon form and beneath its spectrous stars and cloudy sky to act out the rationalist meaning of this separation and its imaginative alternative.

Since limitation to the natural forms the basis and extent of Deism, as Blake's quintuple repetition of the word *natural* in his initial definition of Deism (pl. 52) implies, much of the chapter is devoted to the fallen female, Blake's symbol of the merely natural. Taking the province of the natural man and natural world as her own, we see her dominating over both as the chapter unfolds.

As Los and Albion divide, repeating the initial and ongoing action of the poem, Rahab sits brooding over the description within the huge sunflower that dominates the opening plate of the chapter (pl. 53).[2] This pictorial opening of chapter 3 parallels that of chapter 2, just as the poetical beginning does, for it also depicts a fallen female, a flower, and the sea as plate 28 does. Vala's lily of plate 28, however, has been exchanged in plate 53 for Rahab's sunflower, the flower tied inexorably to time, following the sun all its life. As such, it is the appropriate symbol for Deism, as the lily, with its connotations of purity and chastity, is for orthodox religion. Ironically, though, Rahab on her Deistic sunflower throne obscures the sun and its imaginative potential and shadows the world of time and space that she blankly regards. Her seated attitude with head in hands suggests Deism's philosophical abstraction and accompanying despair, seen also in the figure at the left in the frontispiece (pl. 51) who, like Rahab here, wears a blue robe and crown.[3] Rahab's triple crown "recalls the sinister papal tiara . . . in Europe, plate 11"[4] combining religious tyranny with Deistic kingship, an association explored in the chapter (64:15–17), hinted at in the triple crown of Albion's reigning Spectre, whose portrait ends chapter 2. Her wings, which parody the butterfly wings of Jerusalem,[5] contain the moon, earth, and stars, but not the sun. They include the fallen elements of the universe only, not the imaginative, and therefore accurately represent the Deistic natural world.

Albion's daughters continue Rahab's role in the first section of chapter 3. Defining the world they weave as the "Cradle of the grass that withereth away" (56:7), mutable, material, and mortal, they exercise within it the female will in sexual and maternal jealous love to dominate and control Deism's merely natural man (56:3–43). Blake shows their actual destruction of man's potential divinity by identifying man with the infant Jesus, "He who is an Infant, and whose Cradle is a Manger" (56:5), and by showing how they restrict this infant, his cradle, and his world in their materialistic weaving and maternal ministrations. Paralleling Vala's domination of Albion and his naturalized metamorphosis in Reuben, which occur in the first section of chapter 2, the Daughters of Albion here dominate, naturalize, and engross man in the material world. By repeating elements of the earlier action in the later one, Blake emphasizes the underlying identity in the action, but distinguishes as well the different components in each.

Albion's limitation to the sleep of Ulro is now seen in its rational rather than religious cross section. As Los repeats his question, originally addressed to Vala in chapter 2, to Albion's daughters in chapter 3: "What may Man be? who can tell! But what may Woman be?/To have power over Man from Cradle to corruptible Grave" (30:25–26; 56:3–4), he uses the same images of transitoriness in cradle and grave to represent life in the merely natural realm, and he again questions Albion about the creation of a female will (30:31; 56:43). Within the parallel, however, Blake now reveals the connec-

tion to Deism. While formerly he spoke in religious terms of Albion's denial and exile of his own divinity, now he shows that divinity vegetated in time and space by materialist philosophy. The
Daughters of Albion limit life to mutable material existence (pl. 56),
mentality to Deistic reason by cutting the brain and "Bonifying into
a Scull" (58:8) the formerly limitless intellect (pl. 58), and support
the political expression of Deism in war (58:1–10), an aspect treated
at length in the third section of the chapter (pls. 63–69).

The "Three Women around/The Cross" (56:41–42) whom Los
mentions in his question to Albion about the creation of the female
will appear in illustration 57. Within the context of religious error,
the three women may represent the three Marys at the foot of the
cross (John 19:25), symbolizing for Blake the imminent betrayal of
true Christian principles in the strictures of the Pauline church,
which exiles man's indwelling divinity throughout history from
Paul's Epistles to St. Paul's in London. Within the context of Deism,
however, they represent the vegetation of the world that is poetically described in plate 56. Two above and one below, they completely surround the globe between them and the poetic text of plate
57. Their naked figures appear within the Mundane Shell or natural
world, whose hollow edge forms a doorway of generation around
them with barely visible angels carved upon it. The night of Deistic,
starry reason envelops them and their earth, while a net of fibrous
roots (like those in illustrations 25, 71, 74) grows from their fingers
and hair to the globe between, vegetating the stars of reason it
surrounds, the world of nature and religious institutions (the cathedrals of York and St. Paul's in London above, and the Gothic spires
of Jerusalem below). The Gothic cathedral labeled Jerusalem at the
bottom of the globe is furthermore obscured by the earth's shadow
(copy E), for the Deistic natural universe of the fallen female obscures liberty and inspiration in the world. The poetic text of the
plate meanwhile also describes materialism as overwhelming the
fallen churches (57:1–7).

The role of the fallen female is pictured in still another way in the
illustration for plate 58. Here the batwinged female genitals give
birth to the skeleton lying in the flaming grave. Continuing the
familiar image of ossification from chapter 2, the picture depicts the
human condition within Deism's merely natural world. The womb
of the natural world, if considered exclusively, as in Deism, becomes equally man's tomb, because it denies man's potential divinity and thus leaves him as a skeleton in the grave. We see this in the
poetic inscription of the frontispiece, where the womb-void of Albion's generative state (1:1–2) becomes Albion's couch of sleep and

death (1:3, 9) until Los enters it. Los also enters the natural world of Deism with the eternals and unfallen Emanations to mitigate the ossifying effects of the purely natural.

The unfallen Emanation plays a particularly crucial role within chapter 3 as the imaginative alternative to the fallen female. Just as she was the connection to eternity within the religious element of the theme (chapter 2), so is she too within the rational element (chapter 3); for

In Great Eternity, every particular Form gives forth or Emanates
Its own peculiar Light, & the Form is the Divine Vision
And the Light is his Garment. This is Jerusalem in every Man
A Tent & Tabernacle of Mutual Forgiveness Male & Female Clothings.
And Jerusalem is called Liberty among the Children of Albion.
(54:1–5)

Jerusalem has been identified as liberty in the frontispiece to chapter 2 (pl. 26); but in chapter 3 liberty acquires an intellectual and political meaning in addition to its religious one. While Deism, by limiting thought to logical analysis and empiricism, by denying inspiration and concentrating exclusively on what is material, supports political oppression and tyranny in the state, its imaginative alternative—Jerusalem or the eternals (54:1–5)—supports mutuality and forgiveness instead, which is expressed in free-ranging thought, in brotherhood, and in political liberty (57:8–10).

As Jerusalem functions through inspired mutual forgiveness, becoming the "Tabernacle" (54:4) of the Divine Vision itself, she demonstrates the divine analogy of Vala, who usurps Imagination's place within Albion to become his restrictive "Tabernacle" (30:29, 30). Jerusalem is the garment of the Divine Vision, clothing imagination with a luminous outer covering in the true spirit of unfallen nature. By using the same term *tabernacle* for opposite functions, Blake both emphasizes the underlying identity and notes the contrast between its two expressions—the fallen and unfallen concepts of nature. As the apparent covering and temple of imagination, nature may be fallen and opaque, in which case only its own appearance can be seen, or it may be unfallen and translucent, in which case imagination can shine through and illuminate its covering. Jerusalem demonstrates nature inspired by imagination, rather than merely material nature, and clothes apparent imagination with physical being, while Vala limits herself to the covering, or physical being itself, and obscures her imaginative content. Vala thus degrades humanity and the natural world, while Jerusalem enhances both.

As the role of the eternal Emanation is contrasted with her fallen Deistic counterpart in the text, the contrast between the fallen and unfallen universe that they represent in this chapter is pictured in the illustrations. Illustration 54 shows us both the unfallen image of the natural world at the top, and the fallen version of that world at the bottom. The unfallen natural world appears as a globe of contraries that combines the four elements: Reason, Desire, Pity, and Wrath as its four directions, or four unfallen Zoas. Above it birds fly, demonstrating its imaginative potential.[6] It is accompanied by five naked, soaring figures on each side, the five unfallen senses.[7] The figures on the left echo the earth's curve and resemble the form and movement of the soaring figures in plate 4 who escape Vala's grasp. The figures on the right are, however, less defined, more lumpish and disorganized in outline and motion, implying perhaps that all is not actually as well as it might be in the world they surround. The two entrail-shaped clouds, one at either side of the picture, further hint at Vala's presence within their midst.

In contrast to the globe above is the four-headed rocky monster below, whose frowning and sleeping heads symbolize the four fallen Zoas within the individual man, and the fallen world of Druid rocks (54:26) to which Arthur or England is constricted by the Deistic Spectre. Placed amidst obscure night, below a cloud filled with batwinged insects, and surrounded by five stars of reason, these four unhappy, unseeing, and either dead or dying heads demonstrate the condition of the fallen world amidst the night of generation influenced by the stars of fallen reason, the spectrous insects of generation, and the clouds of fallen nature.[8]

As the unfallen eternals imaginatively view Albion's Satanic Spectre's doctrines, they reveal the fallacies of Deism and carry on Blake's dialectical exploration of the theme. They connect Deism's limitation to the natural, with its political expression in princedom and tyranny, as the dedication of the chapter does too. Refusing "that Veil which Satan puts between Eve & Adam/By which the Princes of the Dead enslave their Votaries" (55:11–12), they present their egalitarian realm where "all equal share/Divine Benevolence & joy" (55:8–9) in a vision of Eternity similar to the Savior's initial one (pl. 4). Deism, according to the eternals, exists by limiting man to the simply natural and generative, to Vala's veil, "a Veil the Saviour born & dying rends" (55:16), for Imagination transcends the material and thereby pierces the veil. To accept the veil unrent means preventing any other than material power from functioning in the universe and limits man to what is, to the existent political powers of the world as well as its natural laws and material causes. Politically, it founds societies based on inequality, slaves and princes, the political tyrannies that Blake saw all around him in contemporary Europe. Rending the veil, on the other hand, enables the egalitarian society founded in brotherhood and shared benevolence to emerge. Then man may transcend what is, or natural laws, in the unified world of imagination.

The entire natural universe, "The Universal Conclave" (55:20), thus becomes involved in the struggle for Albion as the eternals use it imaginatively to oppose Deistic single vision. Just as Los shaped Reuben and the Divine Voice worked within time and space in chapter 2, so here do the eternals demonstrate the imaginative function of the natural universe and Los's work within it for regeneration, opposing Albion's rational error of Deistic materialist philosophy and generation (pls. 55–58).

The eternals, therefore, establish history by electing "the Seven Eyes of God" (55:31) as the saving remnant of eternity within the historical world, explaining here in another view of the same action Los's initial image of sevenfold imaginative opposition to the naturalized single vision of the Deists (53:8–14). Originating in eternity and containing a hidden eighth (Los) within their midst, this remnant, which corresponds to time and space, demonstrates that history is not the exclusive property of fallen vision. Fallen Deistic history, which is purely material and based exclusively on "Memory" (54:8), does not tell the whole story, for time and space, as we may recall from chapter 2, are immortal forms embraced by Los (44:16) and here show imaginative origin and purpose. This imaginative view includes both history and the spatial world in which it unfolds, for the two are connected. It also presupposes eternal, varying perception, which may "Contract or Expand Space at will" (55:44) while also "Contracting or Expanding Time!" (55:45). This imaginative perception goes beyond the natural and unalterable Deistic perception that corresponds to it:

> . . . as the moss upon the tree: or dust upon the plow:
> Or as the sweat upon the labouring shoulder: or as the chaff
> Of the wheat-floor or as the dregs of the sweet wine-press.
> (55:39–41)

Here Los's variable perception, mentioned as the imaginative alternative to Reuben's earthbound senses (30:55–56), or the eternals', which "Steps beyond and Redeems" (32:55) Reuben's purely natural view of "What seems to Be Is" (32:51), recurs to counteract the Deistic universe in a series of cogent similes that beautifully express the relationship between the fallen and eternal vision of the world. The active participation of the eternals within the natural world is further illuminated in their image of eternal plowers who "Labour well the Minute Particulars" (55:51) and "Compell the Reasoner to Demonstrate with unhewn Demonstrations (55:56). Supplying a divine parallel to the spectrous plowman (illus. 22, 29; 29:9–11) and anticipating in eternal terms Albion's self-plowing (57:2, 12–16), which advances definition by separating Albion from his Spectre although it leaves him still on his "Rock of Ages" (57:16; 48:4), the eternals plow error to sow imagination. For the same purpose that Los gives Vala a body and in the same way, by using reason as a tool (cf. 12:12–14), only altering Los's bow to their plow, they practice the imaginative method of revealing error through definition. This is the same method that Los used earlier to reveal materialist error and that the Divine Vision used to reveal religious error when he exposed Satan in his "System" (43:10).

Los's second method of revealing error through minute particularity (pls. 38, 45) is also adopted by the eternals, who reject Deism's "generalizing Demonstrations of the Rational Power" (55:63) for Minute Particularity. Echoing Los's speech to the cities, in which he rejects generalized religious codes of good and evil and the abstract unembodied God that destroy true Art, Science, Liberty, and Religion (38:12–79), and echoing his speech condemning generation as he searches for particularity within Albion's bosom (45:2–38), the eternals support "minutely organized Particulars" and "Definite & Determinate Identity" (55:62, 64) to replace Deism's generalized philosophical precepts and natural laws. Their moral precepts of doing good within particularity further counteracts what Blake saw as the generalized but meaningless goodness of Deistic views of man. He criticized Rousseau for such views in the dedication: "Rousseau thought Men Good by Nature; he found them Evil & found no friend," (pl. 52), and also both Voltaire and Rousseau, who talk of "Virtues of the Human Heart" while constantly abusing and criticizing others (pl. 52).

Taking up the eternals' decree that "the Indefinite be explored" (55:57), Los allows the Daughters of Albion to form the natural world but keeps them, like the Spectre (10:29), subservient to his will (56:31). In chapter 2 Los creates the natural limits to fall within man, lest Albion become Satan in religious error (31:1–2; 36:25 ff.). Here he creates those same limits, supervising the establishment of the Deistic natural universe lest Albion be absorbed in chaos, in "Non-Entitys dark wild/Where dwells the Spectre of Albion: destroyer of Definite Form" (56:16–17). Even the fallen Deistic universe of pure matter prevents indefinite chaos and unknowingly establishes the natural basis for imaginative transcendence. Los therefore cooperates in its creation, measuring out time with his hammer

(56:19–20), and stationing a Daughter of Beulah "between every two Moments . . . to feed the Human Vegetable" (56:9, 10). He defines history and nourishes the natural man of Deism with imagination. He connects time to Eternity, true to his prophetic character, echoing the connection established in the doorway of the frontispiece (pl. 1), in the many gates of Golgonooza (12:61–13:29), in the Gate of Los (12:44; 34:55–35:11), and grain of sand in Lambeth (37:15–22), or when Los embraced time and space (44:16; illus. 44), and Enion opened them up to eternity (48:30–37). Now we see the same connection opening up transcendence within the purely natural categories of the Deistic universe.

Left to Deism the world becomes pure matter under Albion's daughters (56:3–43) and pure mathematics and empirical science under his sons, "Rational Philosophy and Mathematic Demonstration" (58:13). This is the world pictured in plate 12, where the male defines the cross-hatched globe with his compasses in mathematical calculations of latitude and longitude, while the female spins it round from below in vegetated desire. Because Los has a hand in it through the creation of these categories, however, the world may transcend its natural limitations. In blacksmith activity at his anvil, Los hammers out the categories of matter "To Create a World of Generation from the World of Death" (58:18), much as he created Reuben (illus. 32). The same action that limits man and the natural world, establishing Albion's sleep of Ulro through both Deism and religious error, has an imaginative purpose and basis.

Without that basis the world would be left to "The Hermaphroditic Condensations" (58:11) of fallen male reason and fallen female sexuality, whose conjunction results in death. Split apart by Los, however, they admit the presence of imagination and the possibility of progress (58:11–20). Again Blake repeats an image that he used in the previous chapter but shows it from a new perspective. In chapter 2 "Sexual Reasoning Hermaphroditic" (29:28) depicted the unnatural conjunction of Satan, an absent, abstract God, and Vala, material nature, to produce the fallen religious view of man. Here, however, Albion's Spectre represents abstract Deistic reason, while the fallen female represents the world of matter it posits. Conjoining, the two forms create a closed system in which the vegetated universe is ruled by natural law in mechanical operation and understood by scientific and logical analysis. To introduce imagination as a working principle in this world, Los must open up this closed system, which he does by dividing the natural from the rational as contraries. Imagination may then enter through the split.

As a result of this imaginative presence, spectrous Urizen may work building a "Mighty Temple; delivering Form out of confusion" (58:22) without disastrous results. He prevents chaos and gives Los a starting place from which to work, although he simultaneously establishes the rationalist and material world of history and geography. His construction therefore has a double meaning—fallen and restrictive if seen from his limited point of view, but potentially eternal if seen from the larger perspective of imagination.

The same dialectical process appears in the fall of Albion's four Zoas, which recurs in chapter 3 (58:47; 59:10–21). While we saw the fall of these four Zoas previously, when Albion's senses were corrupted by religious error (32:25–42; 37:26–30; 38:1–7), we now see it as the fall of space itself to form the natural universe of Deism (59:10–21). Furthermore, as Albion repeats his earlier action in casting Vala's veil into the Atlantic deeps (59:2–3; 23:22–26), we see the saving as well as the fallen aspect of that action too. While Albion intends the natural limitation of his world, Los transforms his action so that the veil becomes

> . . . the beautiful Mundane Shell,
> The Habitation of the Spectres of the Dead & the Place
> Of Redemption & of awaking again into Eternity.
>
> (59:7–9)

The material world thus created becomes the physical basis necessary for imagination or fully human existence. The same process of transformation can be seen within the metaphor of weaving too. While the Daughters of Albion weave the natural material world (56:7–14), so do the Daughters of Los (59:26–55; illus. 59), but the latter's web transforms the former's. The Daughters of Los "labour for life & love" (59:37) adding "pity & compassion" (59:47) to the natural world. They thereby transform what Deism sees as simply natural. Here they answer their own question posed in chapter 1: "O what shall we do for lovely Jerusalem?" (11:17) by doing exactly what Los did previously (12:1–15), supplying a body for Vala, whose life otherwise is "but a Shade" (12:1), providing shape to the world but with love and compassion as part of that shape.

The Divine Voice also answers the same question of what can be done to comfort Jerusalem in the vegetated universe of Deism, but in a new way. He speaks directly to Jerusalem in the next section of chapter 3 (pls. 60–62), which examines that aspect of Deism known as natural religion. Emerging from "the clouds of Albions Druid Temples" (60:1), from Deistic natural religion, in which he was enclosed from the beginning of the chapter (54:32), he specifically addresses Jerusalem, comforting her through the affirmation of faith, promise of regeneration, and imaginative retelling of the story of Mary and Joseph, the inspired opposite of natural religion.

Devoted to exploring the religious expression of Albion's rational error, the second section of chapter 3 corresponds in structure to the second section of chapter 2, which was devoted to the institutional aspect of Albion's religious error as expressed in the Church of England. Inspired religion, which is presented here by the Divine Voice, is equally opposed to both errors, and is the imaginative alternative here to Deistic religion based on reason. The retelling of the Mary-Joseph story that follows, which might at first seem to belong more appropriately to the chapter devoted to religion (chapter 2), demonstrates that alternative. In his retelling, the Divine Voice exposes and corrects the erroneous vision of Mary as an adulteress. This is not an error committed by orthodox religion, which accepts the miraculous explanation of the Virgin Birth for Mary's child, although erroneously attributing it to the influence of an absent, abstract God and denial of sexuality. It is, however, an error committed by Deistic natural religion, which denies all miracles and insists on purely naturalistic explanations of religious doctrines. Denying the miracle of the Virgin Birth and affirming a code of moral virtue, Deistic natural religion leaves Mary as an adulteress, an error that the Divine Voice comes to correct. Since Mary is associated with Jerusalem here, and since Jerusalem too has been erroneously called a harlot throughout, the correction of Mary's position is also a correction in the Deistic vision of Jerusalem and therefore a comfort to both.

In the ensuing dialogue between Jerusalem and the Divine Voice,[9] the function of Deistic reason and natural religion in condemning and distorting Jerusalem is exposed. Representing liberty, religious as well as rational and political, Jerusalem in her enslavement demonstrates the total enslavement of all liberty by Deism in the world.

We see this distortion first in "the Song of the Lamb, sung by Slaves in evening time" (60:38), with which the dialogue begins (60:10–37) and which describes Jerusalem's position in the wasteland world of sacrifice, war, famine, and barrenness. Lamenting her fall from prelapsarian beauty and the former unified and wholly imaginative universe, it also prophesies her coming regeneration through imaginative love. Her perversion in natural religion appears in the sacrifice and secrecy of Babylon, whose laws are those of Natural Religion by which she is absorbed. She denies and sacrifices her beautiful children, all the expressions of liberty in the world denied by natural law and natural religion, because she has been "perswaded" (60:35) to worship false gods and to deny sexuality (60:23, 30). Sung by slaves—that is, within the bondage of generation—the lament resembles Psalm 137, sung by the Jews when they were slaves in Babylon exiled from Jerusalem. While both sets of singers look toward regeneration, they are as yet unable to accomplish it because they have not yet reached a sufficiently advanced point in their consciousnesses. The Jews in Babylon were, according to their prophets Ezekiel and Jeremiah, for a long while not ready to reenter Israel and accomplish their regeneration. These slaves too are not yet ready, for they cannot understand why Jerusalem's collapse has taken place or how to remedy it; they can merely lament it as natural religion's corruption of inspiration.

Jerusalem is in the same position as the slaves. She too is Israel "closd in the Dungeons of Babylon" (60:39) and "at the Mills" (60:41), like Milton's Samson. Again we see the responsibility of Deism for her position because Jerusalem is driven to despair and insanity by Deistic reason, which "grows like/The Wheel of Hand. incessant turning day & night without rest" (60:43), abounding in human exploitation. She is in the realm of triumphant Vala (60:39–49), the Deistic universe of nature limited to natural religion and its "Moral Pride" (60:49; pl. 52). She is dominated by the wheels of industry and mechanistic philosophy, "the turning mills" (60:63), in which spectrous reason, "The stars of Albion" (60:60), arise and the Divine Body of Human Imagination is denied (60:56–58). Yet, like the slaves before, Jerusalem keeps her faith in divinity (imagination), even though she is unable to understand what has happened.

To explain, the Divine Voice retells the story of Mary in its inspired version, and also reassures Jerusalem of his omnipresence and his power to awaken Albion. He affirms "Continual Forgiveness of Sins/In the Perpetual Mutual Sacrifice in Great Eternity!" (61:22–23), which is inspired religion, proclaiming "And this is the Covenant/Of Jehovah: If you Forgive one-another, so shall Jehovah Forgive You:" (61:24–25). In this way he releases Mary from her debasement to sing and flow "like a River of Many Streams" (61:28–29) through forgiveness and pity.

Both Mary and Jerusalem learn the lesson of forgiveness that abolishes victimization and condemnation, which this exemplary tale teaches. Sin, which is coextensive with life itself, for "There is none that liveth & Sinneth not" (61:24), then becomes paradoxically necessary and even fortunate, since it enables forgiveness, as both Mary and Jerusalem acknowledge (61:11–13, 44–46).

While the Divine Voice demonstrates that natural religion coexists with inspired imagination, this does not bring about an immediate renewal of the world. It does show the imaginative basis of liberty and strengthens Jerusalem's resistance to Deistic delusion by giving her a new understanding of herself. This new understanding is, however, not enough to change Jerusalem's outward condition, for "Emanations/Are weak, they know not whence they are nor whither they tend" (62:16–17). For renewal to occur, Albion himself must repudiate his Deistic error and cast off natural religion, which he is not yet ready to do, for "Albion is dead!" (62:2). Liberty thus continues to be oppressed in England as it has been throughout history in all the world (62:3–34), despite the presence of the Divine Voice who reveals the imaginative purposes at work within Deism. Like Los creating and supervising the natural world, the Divine Vision proclaims the necessity for Deistic categories, although in new terms. "Luvah must be Created/and Vala" (62:20–21), he claims, even though they repress liberty with "Valas cloud . . . & Luvahs fires" (62:28), hiding imagination in materialism, war, and sacrifice. His activity within these conditions, however, encourages liberty and renews Los's energies. Because Los sees the Divine Vision in his furnaces (60:5; 62:35), he returns to his anvil undiscouraged (53:20; 58:16; 62:41) and "anew began his labours" (62:42), even though Enitharmon again divides from him (62:38; cf. 53:6) and Deistic reason again tries to obscure imagination (60:6; 62:38; cf. 54:32). As the section ends, Albion's situation is unchanged, only further clarified.

Culminating this section devoted to natural religion is the illustration of Deistic religion's god (pl. 62). Here a monstrous figure holds the text as a giant-inscribed tablet or scroll in front of him while a minuscule man stands dwarfed by him between his feet. If we identify this figure as Luvah, as most critics do,[10] we run into two questions. First, what aspect of Luvah is being illustrated, for Luvah is diversely viewed in *Jerusalem*? Second, why should Luvah be pictured after Blake's versions of Mary's story at the end of the section on natural religion and its alternative? To the first question we must answer that Luvah here is not the Zoa of love who is often identified with Christ or with revolutionary France, which promises to renew the world as Christ came to do. Despite his headgear, which may suggest a crown of thorns, his generally monstrous appearance precludes any such identification. Does he then appear in his fallen form as love in the world of Ulro, spiritual hate, fallen passion, and sexuality, or, politically speaking, the fall of revolutionary promise in subsequent bloodshed and Napoleonic oppression? This interpretation seems far more likely, given his monstrous appearance, but what exactly does it mean in relation to natural religion or Deism, which is our subject here? As fallen love, Luvah often appears in tandem with Vala (nature), sharing her generative perspective. Like Vala, he provides the field upon which Albion's story may be played. Unlike Vala, however, he is murdered, distorted, and crucified by Albion or his daughters, for revolutionary or sexual passion is distorted and tormented by fallen religion and reason through orthodox and Deistic moral codes, rational philosophy, or civil law in an attempt to suppress it. Luvah's distortion is exemplified in Jerusalem's or Mary's position as a harlot. Distorted himself, Luvah also tries to dominate and destroy man. He wars with man's other faculties as reason tries to dominate passion, which in turn tries to undermine reason and man's original divinity to make man his own natural creature bound by generative sexuality. We see this last attempt in the picture of the tiny figure between the monster's feet; man dwarfed by Luvah's takeover. In his fall from divinity, Luvah furthermore turns demonic, so that from Christ he becomes the reverse, Satan, as Lucifer, God's brightest angel, did. As Satan, Luvah is also Albion's Spectre. Up to this point Albion's Spectre has been identified as his rational power, which is at odds with Luvah and repeatedly attempts to repress passion in Albion through both fallen religion and philosophy. If Luvah is Satan, and Erin tells us he is in that state (49:68), then he is certainly not Albion's rational power. We must then be viewing a new dimension of Satan previously unseen: Satan as perverted love. Represented as pity within the context of religious error (38:2), for divine love turns to false pity in orthodox religion (e.g., Satan in Blake's *Milton*), it becomes generative sexuality within the context of Deism, as divine love becomes naturalized along with everything else. Similarly, when Luvah joins Albion's sons within Deism, he adds sexuality to them.

It now becomes obvious why Luvah's picture accompanies the section on natural religion. Luvah presents a further aspect of natural religion's god, who now is seen to represent not only Albion's rational powers, but also his other limitations to the natural. Deism's god is a rational projection whose actions are bound by natural law and physical forces such as Luvah symbolizes. The snake coiled around his head in the illustration points to the dominance of Urizenic reason, which has been the Satanic god's character from the beginning of the chapter (pl. 54). Its resemblance to a coiled rope further suggests temporal life unwinding in the natural universe.[11] The seven peacock feathers around his head, while they may be associated with awakened man who is "Eyed as the Peacock" in eternity (98:14), are here pictured with fallen Luvah and appear in their fallen forms as the seven epochs of human history in the natural universe, to which the god of natural religion is also limited. The red flames around his feet, however, add the new element of his character, suggesting passionate Luvah with his attendant fires, as he is described in the text (62:28).

The text furthermore supports this view of Luvah, for the Divine Vision appears obscured in Luvah's clouds both at the beginning and end of this section (60:6; 62:38), since natural religion's error obscures imaginative truth. Revealed temporarily in the reinterpretation of Mary's story and the regeneration of Jerusalem within her enslavement, the Divine Vision is again obscured by Luvah's cloud of natural religion; for Albion is not yet free of it. Furthermore, Luvah is created with Vala by Jesus, so that the tale of history may have time and space to play itself out and bring generation to regeneration even though liberty (Jerusalem) is meanwhile repressed. The images of Vala's cloud and Luvah's fires that follow and obscure oppressed liberty in the tale of history within the Deistic world commingle in one image as "Luvah's Cloud reddening above" (62:30). Here Luvah expands to include Vala's nature as well as his own as they both dominate Deistic natural religion. Politically, this can hardly be the purifying fire of revolutionary France whom Luvah represents in chapter 2, since it obscures rather than advances liberty, but must instead be the repressive aspect of Deistic tyranny or postrevolutionary France into which revolution turns even as it is itself repressed by "the Wheels of Albions Sons" (62:32). What this does to man appears in the illustration, where man dominated by these forces becomes insignificant.

As we turn to the next section of chapter 3 (pls. 63–71), which parallels in structure the third section of chapter 2, we see Albion's rational error explored within time and space in the nightmare account of politics, oppression, and war that make up the history of the natural world. Another image of human insignificance within Deistic schemes is pictured in this section (pl. 70). Three human figures, dwarfed by a huge stone trilithon, pass through it to a land lit by the moon of the fallen female, which shares the sky with the intestinal-shaped cloud of Vala (cf. illus. 24). This time, however, humanity is dwarfed by the Druidic structure of Deistic natural religion and the simply natural world which it now enters, rather than the image of the Deistic god, for this section is concerned with the historical unfolding of Deism in the world, rather than its natural religion.

As the lineup of opposing forces is reiterated, dissension breaks out among the Zoas; Albion is again punisher and judge (63:1–6); and Albion, Luvah, and Vala engage in deadly contention with one another (7:30–41; 43:55–83; 63:5–9). This time, however, the story is told in polticial terms as Luvah slays Tharmas, Albion punishes

Luvah, and Vala seeks vengeance; for it is the story of revolutionary fervor succeeding in France, being oppressed in England, and causing wars of vengeance throughout Europe. Man's rational error and its consequences now unfold in their outer expression as Deism operates within the material world, supporting tyranny and existent political powers. The same events recur but are illuminated differently in the light of history and politics.

As the Daughters of Albion again materialize the potentially divine human being, familiar images recur. Man again appears as a weeping infant (56:5, 6, 34; 63:17, 20), emerges ossified from the female's gates of birth (illus. 58; 63:17–18), is victimized in sacrifice and war by the female as Gwendolen (58:2–9; 63:32–35; 64:35–38), as Vala (63:39–40; 65:29 ff.; 67:2–15; 67:17 ff.), or as the Daughters of Albion (63:31; 65:63–79; 66:17–84). The Daughters of Albion also reappear weaving (59:26–55; 64:2 ff.; 67:4 ff.), dominating humanity (56:3–4; 64:12–17), and combining in hermaphroditic conjunctions (58:11–20; 64:25). Reason still builds Deism's temple (58:21 ff.; 66:1–9) while Albion plows in an analogy of the eternals' plowing (55:54 ff.; 63:3; 64:30) or of his own self-plowing (57:2–15) as imagination counteracts both. The two ongoing coexistent worlds, imaginative and fallen natural, reappear (58:18, 50–51; pl. 59; 63:42–43; 64:1–5; 65:1–4; pl. 71), and the chapter ends by summarizing the actual world of space and time, geographic England, that yet contains imaginative possibility within it. Finally "Albion is darkend & Jerusalem lies in ruins" (71:54; cf. 54:13), which has been the situation throughout.

As Blake explores these images he consistently blames Deism for man's naturalized condition (64:20 ff.). However, by examining the fallen female's role as the sacrificial priestess of Deism within history, by showing her activities in war and victimization and her associations with fallen authorities (papal and monarchical: 61:50; 64:15–16), by enlarging Luvah's political role (63:6; 65:8 ff.; 66:15), and by examining Urizen's and his sons' multiple activities within the world, Blake emphasizes Deism's material and historical consequences.

This expression is clearly exemplified by the Daughters of Albion, their epitome, Vala, and their eldest, Gwendolen. Pictured in illustration 63, the fallen female literally falls onto the green earth and is bound by the worm of generation, which encircles her three times. Associated with Satan, the fallen rational power, as well as Urizen, and fallen man himself who becomes a worm, the worm with its three Satanic coils demonstrates Vala's spectrous oppression. Behind her the crescent moon, symbol of the fallen female, is surrounded by a spiky outline symbolizing the spectrous influence of

Deism, which founds her merely natural realm. Together with a large cloud, symbol of abstraction and materialism and colored deathly blue, the spectrous outline obscures the glow of imagination in the background. This is the general picture of Deistic, vegetating nature cut off from imagination and turned destructive. Erdman (p. 342) identifies the female here with France, whose power is destroyed by the allied armies invading Paris as Luvah is brought to justice there by Albion (63:5–6). As Vala, the female avenges Luvah by spreading justice, war, and disaster throughout Europe (64:6–11). This interpretation specifically enlarges her political significance. In addition, the red edges of the cloud behind her suggest "Luvahs cloud reddening above" (62:30), which emphasizes her political meaning by showing the bloody effects of revolution within her realm.

Suppressing liberty in the historical aftermath of the French Revolution, Vala takes her revenge in the form of a parade of human victims (63:7 ff.). The "dance of death" (63:10) that these human victims perform as they pass before Vala, who holds "the Druid Knife of Revenge & The Poison Cup/Of Jealousy" (63:39–40), sacrificial symbols of natural religion, portrays the contemporary political situation. As the tale unfolds, "The Cities & Villages of Albion became Rocks & Sand Unhumanized" (63:18), and death spreads universally "from/Ireland to Japan" (63:33–34). Gwendolen laughingly looks on at the dehumanization of England and the spread of universal war resulting from the oppression of liberty.

Appearing alone in plate 66 and with one of her coterie in plate 69, Vala is graphically depicted sacrificing humanity in history's wars. Pictured with knife and cup like the other fallen females, Albion's Daughters or Tirzah (66:20, 65, 83; 67:24–25), she parodies inspired religion by using its chalice in natural religion. As she passes her knife over man in plate 66, she grasps her victim between her thighs in sexual domination. This action is described in the text by her male warriors, who characterize war as sexual sublimation. "I am drunk with unsatiated love," they cry, "I must rush again to War: for the Virgin has frownd & refusd" (68:62–63). She refuses the truly human but distributes her sexual favors to dehumanized warriors as a reward for their sadistic machismo (pl. 68). In plate 69 three Daughters of Albion sacrifice a chained and fainting, or simply prostrate and unseeing, victim in a variation of illustration 25. This time the stars of reason and the moon of the fallen female appear in the night sky above him, indicating the cooperation of both reason and fallen nature, the hermaphroditic condensations of Deism, in his sacrifice. The large, partially fallen Druid stones in the background identify his setting in natural religion's temple, as does the cup one priestess holds. As the females scourge or flay him, we see their revenge for his similar action when reason tried to subdue nature (pl. 21), or when Vala avenged Luvah's murder (63:5–9).

This deadly female action is described in the text within the typical female function of weaving. Unlike the Daughters of Los, who weave for life and love (59:26–55), "the Daughters of Albion Weave the Web/Of Ages & Generations" (64:2–3), which turns destructive as they all join Vala at the loom (64:6–11) and at "the iron Spindle of destruction" (66:10). As Vala, the daughters vegetate

> . . . into a hungry Stomach & a devouring Tongue.
> Her Hand is a Court of Justice, her Feet: Two Armies in Battle
> Storms & Pestilence: in her Locks: & in her Loins Earthquake
> And Fire & the Ruin of Cities & Nations & Families & Tongues.
> (64:8–11)

The institutions of oppression, courts and armies, as well as the natural and man-made disasters of history's web, are the female's province in Deism, for they represent purely material, uninspired powers. Nature's destructiveness thereby expands to include the destructiveness of material institutions, penal codes, civil laws (courts), wars (armies), civil institutions, and nations, as well as the closest human relationships (families), and all human expression (tongues). As the bloodshed of history mounts up in a crescendo of imagery in plates 65–69, Vala oversees the conscription and mobilization of England's population in conquering armies (65:29–55; cf. 21:40–45; 22:4–7). She turns from nature as fertility, "Girt as a sower with his seed to scatter life abroad over Albion" (65:45), to nature fondly smiling at "blood and wounds and dismal cries, and shadows of the oak" (65:51). Sporting with other Daughters of Albion around Luvah, who is victimized by "stern Warriors" (65:64) on Albion's "Druid Altars" (65:63), Vala cooperates with them in limiting Luvah's brain, heart, and senses (intellect, affection, and perception), and in sacrificing him with stone-age flint knives, as Tirzah does too (67:24–25), in victimization and war (66:16–67:1). Her action parodies Los's limitation of Reuben (30; 32:1–13) and of Luvah (43:67 ff.), and echoes in part Christ's crucifixion and Luvah's by Albion's sons (65:8–10). Thus distorted, Luvah turns into hate, his eternal qualities degenerate, and his outer world of vegetation and living creatures, the lands of England, Scotland, and Wales and all of space, fall into generation (66:16–84). Extending throughout history, the Daughters of Albion reach from Horeb (Mt. Sinai) and Beth Peor (Moses' burial place within Reuben's land) to Albion's Cliffs (67:27) and "Europe & Asia from Ireland to Japan" (67:7),

spreading Deism and war to all parts of the modern, ancient, biblical, eastern, and western worlds (67:25–40). The foundation of their
actions in spectrous reason is evident as:

> They cut the Fibres from the Rocks groaning in pain they Weave;
> Calling the Rocks Atomic Origins of Existence; denying Eternity
> By the Atheistical Epicurean Philosophy of Albions Tree.
>
> (67:11–13)

By limiting man's understanding to Newtonian atomic science and
existence to the Rock of history with the support of Deistic natural
religion, which Blake thought "Atheistical" since it eliminates the
divinity of man, and "Epicurean" since it glorifies fallen man, they
deny imaginative transcendence and eternal existence. They further
treat human intellect like a scientific specimen, for they "have cir-
cumscribd the Brain/Beneath & pierced it thro the midst with a
golden pin" (67:41–42) like a mounted butterfly. Their doctrines
result in war and victimization, which they advance by supporting
the warriors through generative sexuality.

The degenerated human who results from their actions appears in
the illustration (pl. 67), where the human victim is stretched out,
chained hand and foot by Deism's iron chain of necessity. He lies
unseeing above a green line, the "Stems of Vegetation" to which
Tirzah binds man and Deism limits God (60:11; 68:9), like a sacrificial
victim awaiting the knife. Even as Tirzah mourns him as the "poor
Human Form" (67:44), she limits, perpetuates, tortures, and despises him (67:44–68:9). Using the names of pagan gods, the biblical
place names of Israel's kingdoms and geographical surroundings,
the name of Deism's god, and of contemporary nations, Tirzah
shows the widespread cruelty and bloodletting of all history. Cele-
brated by the Warriors' Song (68:10–70), Tirzah's history of
bloodshed, "A sheet & veil & curtain of blood" (68:21), Vala's veil
changed by sacrifical activity, extends from biblical times to modern.[12] Place names of the ancient world, such as Ephraim representing the Old Testament, Mount Olive representing the New (68:22),
Rephaim (Israel), Havilah (Arabia), Shur (Egypt), Canaan, and so
on, and those of the modern world such as England, France, Germany, and Africa, representing the repression of liberty in European wars and in the extension of the slave trade, abound, demonstrating Tirzah's widespread influence. Politically associated with
tyrannical monarchies as the Daughters of Albion "sport before the
Kings" (68:32), the bloody sacrifice of history is the apparent result
of universal materialism, the outer appearance of Deism.

Its principles, "Jealousy & Abhorrence & Revenge & deadly Murder" (69:13), as well as "A Religion of Chastity" (69:34), "Moral Law" (69:35), "Mutual Hate . . . & mutual Deceit & mutual Fear" (69:37), which are Deism's natural religion and principles of enmity, appear "uniting together in Rahab" (69:33). As Rahab further sits "Imputing Sin & Righteousness to Individuals; . . . [and] Brooding Abstract Philosophy to destroy Imagination, the Divine-/Humanity" (70:17, 19–20), the Deistic basis of all her historical destruction crystallizes.

Albion's male divisions also expose the political and historical face of Deism within this section of chapter 3. Understandably, however, they play a smaller part in the exposition, for they do not represent the world of matter so directly as the female does. Forming "A Polypus of Roots of Reasoning Doubt Despair & Death" (69:3), the males play three major roles within history. First, as the sons of Urizen they practice fallen reason within the natural world. Second, as Luvah, they exemplify the destruction of liberty in France through Deistic practice. Finally, as Hand, they join Rahab at the end of this section.

As the Daughters of Albion crucify liberty (Luvah) on Albion's tree of mystery (65:8), they sentence him "To die a death of Six thousand years bound round with vegetation" (65:10). Revolutionary liberty is hereby condemned to its repressed and imprisoned condition throughout history. Accompanying the female's historical cavalcade, Luvah, both generally as revolutionary liberty and particularly as "France: the Victim of the Spectres of Albion" (66:15), continues to be sacrificed on their altars (65:56–66:84) with the cooperation of Albion's sons—Deism's rational expression.

The males appearing as the Sons of Urizen, of fallen or Deistic reason, change the instruments of creation, "the plow & harrow, the loom/The hammer & the chisel, & the rule & compasses" (65:12–13), into instruments of war, "the sword . . . the chariot of war & the battle-ax/The trumpet fitted to mortal battle, & the flute" (65:14–15). The instruments by which unfallen reason improves the world in physical and intellectual creation within the context of imagination are changed to the instruments by which fallen reason wreaks destruction in the world within the context of Deistic principles. By granting reason exclusive rather than partial control, Deism distorts both intellect and nature, allowing man "In ignorance to view a small portion & think that All/And call it Demonstration: blind to all the simple rules of life" (65:27–28). Subject to this partial view, the Sons of Urizen are left with materialism and self-interest, principles that deny existence, cause war, and change "the Arts of Life. . . . into Arts of Death in Albion" (65:16).

Their mechanistic view causes economic oppression, too, as it is extended to industry. Artisanship is replaced by industrialization, "intricate wheels invented, wheel without wheel" (65:21), and the machine takes control of the man (65:22–24). These Deistic wheels mentioned previously in chapter 1 (15:18–19; illus. 22) reveal their economic effects as Blake gives us a truly Marxian description of the alienation of labor in mechanized industry:

> . . . intricate wheels invented, wheel without wheel:
> To perplex youth in their outgoings, & to bind to labours in Albion
> Of day & night the myriads of eternity that they may grind
> And polish brass & iron hour after hour laborious task!
> Kept ignorant of its use, that they might spend the days of wisdom
> In sorrowful drudgery, to obtain a scanty pittance of bread:
> In ignorance to view a small portion & think that All
> And call it Demonstration: blind to all the simple rules of life.
>
> (65:21–28)

Division of labor in industrialization is here depicted as it affects the worker, who now does not know a craft or follow his work through to an end product, but tediously repeats some small isolated task. The worker is conscious only of repeating the same partial and therefore apparently meaningless motions divorced from any final result or product. The only end he can see is a wage, "a scanty pittance of bread." His work thus becomes alienated from him, for it is unrelated to creation, meaningless to him, and does not fulfill him, just earns his bread. His vision is partial in an economic sense, for all he sees is his own task in divided labor. He fancies that all, because his work becomes a process of earning bread and nothing more. He does not see the larger picture evident in imaginative labor, man's creation of the products of his world.[13]

Albion's sons also build Reason's temple within which the female priestess sacrifices mankind. With "Reasonings" and "Demonstrations" (66:3) they build:

> . . . Natural Religion & its Altars Natural Morality
> A building of eternal death: whose proportions are eternal despair
> Here Vala stood turning the iron Spindle of destruction
>
> (66:8–10)

By subjecting man to existence within natural laws and moral codes based on reason, Albion's sons set Deism's conditions for the natural world and man's actions within it, which turn into the bloody story of history unaffected by imagination. Natural law predicates iron necessity, which destroys inspiration and keeps man from breaking out of his material, mechanical universe. Deism further teaches "that Man is Righteous in his Vegetated Spectre" (pl. 52), thereby approving this naturalized version of man.

The tale of history culminates as threefold, enormous, monstrous Hand and Rahab, who typify the Deistic version of human history, are described. Rahab epitomizes the Daughters of Albion and their devotion to the merely material and natural religion, while Hand is "the aggregate of the Twelve Sons of Albion" (70:10), whose three heads are named "Bacon & Newton & Locke" (70:15; cf. illus. 50), epitomizing Deistic reason. As he reasons, "rejecting Ideas as nothing & holding all Wisdom/To consist, in the agreements & disagreements of Ideas" (70:7–8), he provides a Blakean summary of Lockean logic. Locke, applying Newtonian analytical methods to philosophy, treats "ideas" as the equivalent of Newtonian particles, whose interaction is determined by physical laws. For him, knowledge consists of "nothing but the perception of the connexion of and agreement, or disagreement and repugnancy of any of our ideas."[14] Hand, as he echoes Locke, explains that "manner" of exclusion and negation which Albion's sons use (10:7–16). Combined with Rahab, he turns monstrous and unproductive, like the hermaphrodite earlier.

Pictured another way, the combination of fallen reason and fallen nature appears in illustration 71. In a parody of the Greek myth of Leda and the swan, a fallen, batwinged, spectrous swan, whose limp neck and beady eye mark his less than godlike appearance, touches Leda's toe with his beak. This is quite a falling off from the prophetic swans of *America* (A, 11) and the Gray illustrations; the swan's pointed wings identify him with fallen reason or the spectrous god of natural religion. His neck and eye resemble the bird-faced lightning accompanying the Spectre's reign in England (illus. 50). The female stretches out, leaning on her elbow, head droopy, eyes unseeing, and hair vegetating into tendrils and barren grapevines, marking the Deistic version of the natural world. Their combination here demonstrates the destructive commingling of Deistic elements in nonhermaphroditic form. In addition, the allusion to Leda and the swan points to "the mythic origins of murder and war,"[15] since from that union came Helen and the subsequent prolonged Trojan wars, an appropriate story for this section of chapter 3 that summarizes the slaughter of history.

At the beginning of the section, Blake mentions the existence of "Two Worlds" (65:1) within the human realm. For the most part, however, only the fallen world is readily apparent, since the section is devoted to actual history. Nevertheless, hints in both poetry and illustration of the imaginative potential world as eternally omnipresent alongside the historical one do occasionally emerge. In three successive plates Blake points out that Canaan exists over Cheviot (63:42), around the Mundane Shell (64:1), and as "a world of Mercy, and/A World of Justice" (65:1–2). The same duality appears in the illustrations, too. In plate 64, for example, the female is sunk over the scroll of history laid on the stone altar of natural religion. Head down, hair spread, body twisted, she is surrounded by the same spectrous outline as in plate 63, where the worm of generation encircled her body. The two small, floating, naked figures alongside her, however, present a far different scroll as they freely soar within a rounded outline shaped like Jerusalem's wings at the top of the title page (pl. 2). Although the female cannot see them, the fallen Urizenic figure stretched out at the bottom of the page looks up at them, temporarily distracted from his book of laws but keeping his place in it with his finger all the while. Although the rational world is limited to the tale of history, this illustration suggests that imaginative alternatives are nevertheless present for human beings who want to see them.

This section of chapter 3 ends by affirming and summarizing the existence of two worlds, Albion's land and Canaan (71:1), history and eternity. Bloom characterizes this summing up (70:32–71:63)as "Blake's last survey of the world of the Sons of Albion."[16] However, their world is equally the world of Jerusalem's sons (71:3) and as such has a dual character. Announcing generation with: "The Starry Heavens all were fled from the mighty limbs of Albion" (70:32), a line repeated from the dedication to chapter 2 (pl. 27) and with which chapter 3 also ends, Blake reiterates Albion's initial position, asleep in Ulro. But the alternatives to that sleep, Canaan rather than Albion's land, dominated by Jerusalem's sons rather than Albion's sons, eternity opening within history, also appear. The objective world of isolated selves that is posited by Deism, "the Selfish Center" (71:7), now shows its imaginative potential, for "the Center has Eternal States! these States we now explore" (71:9). We explore them as Blake enumerates the counties and cities of England, identifying each group with a particular Son and Daughter of Albion but revealing as he does so the eternal and human face of the land rather than its actual, material, historical face. Finally, Los ends the plate as he began it, by telling us, "But now Albion is darkened & Jerusalem lies in ruins:" (71:54). Reiterating earlier images, Blake revisits the initial situation and the darkened condition of Albion within which Vala weaves her veil "With the iron shuttle of War among the rooted Oaks of Albion" (71:61), thus summarizing the action of this section (pls. 65–70) as well as the ongoing situation of the poem.

Since Jerusalem has sixteen sons and Albion only twelve, the catalogue of Albion's counties and sons leaves four ungenerated. These are Rintrah, Palamabron, Theotormon, and Bromion, who symbolize the contraries of wrath, pity, desire, and reason respectively[17] and who previously appeared in blacksmith activity like Los's (16:1–15). Blake identifies them with the land of Ireland. He also identifies the twelve sons of Isaac and the twelve tribes of Israel with the thirty-two counties of Ireland (72:17–27), to demonstrate their potential inspired quality. While salvation begins in Ireland, its foundations or gates extend throughout the British Isles (72:13–16) and the entire earth (72:28–44), expanding from a single source variously called London, Golgonooza, Ireland, or Israel (72:28) to "all the Nations of the Earth/Europe & Asia & Africa & America" (72:30–31; cf. 16:28–60). In generation nations become islands, "Thirty-two Classes of Islands in the Ocean" (72:43), isolated Deistic categories. Men become similarly isolated, for their emanative connections are broken. In eternity, however, all these isolated entities are reunited.

In the illustration (pl. 72), a globe with the continents of Africa and Australia clearly drawn as islands shows this Deistic world. Inscribed within it is the spiral motto that the world is "Continually Building. Continually Decaying because of Love & Jealousy," the generative truth of the Deistic mutable world formed by Albion's daughters (cf. 53:19). It is mourned over by two guardian angels, who cover their eyes and do not see the flames of inspiration that surround them, for imaginative potential is invisible to their orthodox and natural religion. The serpent below, whose mirror-image message reads "Women the comforters of men become the tormenters & Punishers," sums up the story of the fallen females in chapter 3, who torment and sacrifice men within reason's temple, the Deistic world of bloody history, and are ignorant of its imaginative alternative.

Finally, Deism is seen from an imaginative perspective. Just as chapter 2 ends with a long summary of religious error viewed imaginatively by Erin, a product of Los's furnaces, so the last section of chapter 3 (72:45–76:27) ends with a long summary of Deistic error viewed imaginatively by Blake, the prophetic poet and representative of Los. Los's "Gates" (72:45) remain the connection to eternity, as they were in chapter 2, but they demonstrate a new significance. They now have "Fenelon, Guion, Teresa,/Whitefield & Hervey" (72:50–51) as guards. These enthusiasts carry on the tradition of the dedication's inspired Grey Monk (pl. 52), enemy of Deistic reason, science, and empiricism. Located in the south, where Los's furnaces stand and the unfallen Urizen dwells, they pose the imaginative alternative of inspiration to fallen Urizen, the rational spirit of Deism.

Los's furnaces stretch out from the south in all directions to encompass the historical natural world, for imagination transcends Deistic categories.

And Los's Furnaces howl loud; living: self-moving: lamenting
With fury & despair, & they stretch from South to North
Thro all the Four Points: Lo! the Labourers at the Furnaces
Rintrah & Palamabron, Theotormon & Bromion, loud labring
With the innumerable multitudes of Golgonooza, round the Anvils
Of Death. But how they came forth from the Furnaces & how long
Vast & severe the anguish eer they knew their Father; were
Long to tell . . .

(73:2–9)

Although long to tell, this coming forth is exactly Blake's story in the poem, the story of man's eternal contraries beset by the generative forces around them and kept ignorant of their own imaginative character. Blake now summarizes the Deistic form of this story in the lines that follow, while revealing Los's role as the dialectical counterforce within this story. The unfallen contraries emerging from Los's furnaces (73:5–7; cf. 11:11) and struggling in the world of Albion's fallen land (73:6–15; cf. 16:1–15) see productive metals and tools distorted in war (73:9–15) as the Sons of Urizen's were (65:12 ff.) or Vala's when she exchanged fertility for destruction (65:45–55). They also see these weapons enforcing political tyranny in Deistic distortion "Over the Fourfold Monarchy from Earth to the Mundane Shell" (73:15), distorting the eternal to the generative fourfold.

Blake again describes the creation of the natural world, which Deists restrict to "Vegetative Nature: by their hard restricting condensations" (73:21) and to "the limit of Opakeness Satan & the Limit of Contraction/Adam" (73:27–28; cf. 31:1–2). This time, however, he attributes the limitation to

Voltaire [who] insinuates that these Limits are the cruel work of God
Mocking the Remover of Limits & the Resurrection of the Dead
Setting up Kings in wrath: in holiness of Natural Religion
Which Los with his mighty Hammer demolishes time on time.

(73:29–32)

Voltaire's insinuations that God creates that merely natural world which perpetuates itself inexorably through natural law, and his derision of any possibility of transcendence, characterize Deistic natural religion. This vision of God and the universe, furthermore, supports the ruling secular powers of the world, "the Kings & Nobles of the Earth" (73:38), the fallen tyrannical monarchies of the world, from various pagan tyrants through the English monarchs (73:35–37), symbolized as well by Satan and his cohort (73:35).

In this characterization, Blake summarizes what the chapter has told us about Deistic rationalism and its deadly political, religious, natural, and human consequences. But he now shows it all from the imaginative viewpoint, revealing its dialectical underside as well. By working with all four ungenerated contraries of man: wrath, pity, reason, and desire (Rintrah, Palamabron, Theotormon, and Bromion [71:50–53]) rather than simply reason, as Deism does, Los transcends single vision. He transforms the individual from the "Human Vegetated Form" (73:50) of Deism, who is limited to empirical reason, to one that "in its inward recesses/Is a house of pleasantness & a garden of delight" (73:50–51), an imaginative form containing contraries. The natural world that he creates with these contraries (73:32–34; illus. 54) also goes beyond its Deistic counterpart. Although he establishes the limitations of opacity and contraction within this world (73:26–27), as he did before in opposition to religious error (31:1–2), these are his beginnings, the natural basis for imaginative transcendence, rather than his end as in Deism. Los both creates limitations and smashes them when they become petrified. He does so by opposing Voltaire's Deistic monarchs with his own imaginative forces (73:35–41), which include a mathematician and a philosopher, along with patriarchs, poets, and prophets, for inspired reason takes diverse forms. He also approaches more directly by "Dissipating the rocky forms of Death by his thunderous Hammer" (73:43; illus. 73).

The illustration in which Los beats the sun of imagination into prophetic shape upon his anvil resembles the earlier one of his beating a similar sun to form Reuben, the merely natural man (illus. 73, 32). Both illustrations show the connection between nature and imagination, which Deism denies. Within Los's system, however, natural limitation is created, used, and smashed. It becomes a state through which man passes in the education of his consciousness, rather than a permanent truth as it is within Deism, "As the Pilgrim passes while the Country permanent remains/So Men pass on: but States remain permanent for ever" (73:44–45). Necessary as a state, it must nevertheless be left behind by man when he passes to eternal life.[18]

Like Los (13:55 ff.; 15:8; 75:7) or any other prophet, Blake transcends Deistic history, the "Ratio/Of the Things of Memory" (74: 11–12) that chapter 3 explores, by walking "up and down in Six

Thousand Years" (74:19), seeing all events simultaneously and thereby restoring imaginative vision. He explains Deism as follows:

> The Spectre is the Reasoning Power in Man; & when separated
> From Imagination, and closing itself as in steel, in a Ratio
> Of the Things of Memory. It thence frames Laws & Moralities
> To destroy Imagination! the Divine Body, by Martyrdoms & Wars.
> (74:10–13)

Here we see the events of chapter 3 summarized. Albion's initial separation from the deification of his rational power (sec. 1), which cuts him off from imagination, leaves him with only philosophical reason, history, and empirical science, "Things of Memory." By eliminating imagination, with its doctrines of mutual love, brotherhood, and forgiveness, his fallen Deistic reason inevitably creates distorted natural religion and morality (sec. 2) and the bloody events of history (sec. 3): for "Those who Martyr others or who cause War are Deists" (pl. 52).

Still appealing to the Savior (74:14 ff.; 5:21 ff.), Blake reiterates the purpose and content of his poem in further detail (74:20 ff.), and further exemplifies the eternal principles of simultaneity and permanence by bringing together various earlier images within the Deistic focus of chapter 3. The four fallen Zoas thus cloud over (74:1) and pit their poisonous wheels against the four unfallen Zoas (74:6), just as they did to Los in religious error (32:25–42; 37:26–30; 38:1–5). They are poisonous like Bath (37:2), and their wheels resemble spectrous wheels mentioned earlier. But they specifically adopt Deism in their fall by "Entering into the Reasoning Power, forsaking Imagination" (74:7). Babylon also replaces Jerusalem here (74:16–17), as she did previously (pls. 30; 42:63–70; 50:14–17; 60:22 ff.). But she particularly represents Deism; for demanding sacrifice and torment, she replaces the unfallen comfort-giving emanation (illus. 72, bottom). Furthermore, as Albion's children become twelve gods replacing Jerusalem's sixteen sons, they reiterate fallen religion's similar reduction of Jerusalem's sixteen to twelve (37:4), but specifically demonstrate Deistic principles, for they are "by Abstraction opposed to the Visions of Imagination" (74:26). They engage in false generalizations as do the cities (38:19, 54) or false religion (45:19–20), destroying imaginative clarity and particularity in music by obscuring melody with harmony, in art by obscuring outline with light and shade, in language (poetry or philosophy) by substituting abstraction for visionary modes, and in morality and politics by enforcing cruel laws (74:24–27). Deism's responsibility for this action is apparent, for

. . . Hyle roofd Los in Albions Cliffs by the Affections rent
Asunder & opposed to Thought, to draw Jerusalems Sons
Into the Vortex of his Wheels.

(74:28–30)

Hyle (matter) encloses imagination within the natural material
world and uses the fallen female's sexuality and fallen reason that is
opposed to true intellect to bring inspiration into generation. Deism
is equally responsible for Reuben and his eleven brothers enrooting
again in Israel (74:42–51; cf. 15:1–4, 25; 30:36) and for the sacrificial
actions of Babylon, "the Rational Morality" (74:32) and the Daughters of Albion (74:34–36; cf. 66:20 ff.) as they act upon the twelve
through "Moral Virtue" (74:35).

Illustration 74 also summarizes various images of Deism. In the
margin, the sacrificial priestess and her male victim (cf. pl. 66) float
apart from each other. The female still holds her knife and the male
appears headless (perhaps illustrating the Daughters' sacrifice of
Reuben [74:34–40]). The enrooted figure at the bottom of the plate
recalls images of Reuben's enrooting (74:43–49; 15:1–4, 25; 30:36;
illus. 15, 32). The roots emerging from his head resemble Vala's
(pl. 71), and also imply Deism's rational limitation of Reuben. The
figure's feminine head, waist, leg, and pose, and its masculine body
and musculature, as well as the similarities to both Vala and
Reuben, hint at its hermaphroditic character mentioned in both religious and rational error, and they foreshadow the images of "the
Female Males" and "Male within a Female" (74:14–15) in the final
plate of the chapter.

This Deistic hermaphrodite marks Blake's final imaginative summary of Deism as it marked his beginning, albeit in different form
(pl. 51). As Rahab combines with Bath, Merlin, Bladud, and Arthur,
the spectrous male principles, her poison cup fills with the false
doctrines of the "Twenty-seven Heavens" (75:4) within the material
world of time and space. Fallen female morality now combines with
history's tyrannical monarchs (75:10–16) and fallen churches. Even
this conglomeration, however, may be penetrated by imagination,
which sees eternity opening within it:

. . . thus Rahab is reveald
Mystery Babylon the Great: the Abomination of Desolation
Religion hid in War: a Dragon red, & hidden Harlot
But Jesus breaking thro' the Central Zones of Death & Hell
Opens Eternity in Time & Space; triumphant in Mercy.

(75:18–22)

As the epitome of the false female, Rahab is religious and moral error, Vala, fallen nature and Babylon. She is revealed in very similar images by Milton (M 2, 40:17–22) just before he exposes error and gets ready to embrace imaginative truth, for she is that system of mystery, self-righteousness, sin, war, generative sexuality, and moral virtue which must be overcome for the Edenic world to prevail. Along with the Daughters of Albion, she has acted as the sacrificial priestess in Reason's temple, as natural religion, and destructive nature within Deism. Combining here with the "Dragon," the male phallic image by which Urizen is repeatedly represented (e.g., 14:3), and the twenty-seven churches of history, she associates nature with history's bloodshed in the absence of imagination, producing the sterile hermaphrodite of Deism.

In the illustration this image takes the form of the double female embracing the sevenfold Urizenic dragon. As we regard the crowned female here, we recall Rahab's earlier triple crown (illus. 53). The phallic seven-headed serpent recalls the seven spectrous ages of history, so that their comminglings graphically present destructive history within fallen nature, the hermaphroditic combination of Deism. In addition, the interlocking circles of the dragon form parody the eternal cherubic circles (illus. 22) and recall the Satanic, spectrous, starry wheels associating the dragon with Deistic errors of reason and mechanization as well as with history. Through Jesus this conglomeration of error may be altered and divinity penetrate the world of history and extension. This is the other aspect of the natural world investigated earlier in chapter 3, the imaginative view of Deistic generation, of which the reader, but not Albion, is aware, and of which Blake reminds us at the end.

Although chapter 3 ends with Albion still fallen, "for now the starry Heavens are fled from the mighty limbs of Albion" (75:27; cf. 70:32; pl. 27), the imaginative purpose of that condition becomes clear to the reader. The reader now perceives the imaginative possibilities within Albion's fallen condition as revealed in the chapter's penultimate lines:

> Thus are the Heavens formd by Los within the Mundane Shell
> And where Luther ends Adam begins again in Eternal Circle
> To awake the Prisoners of Death; to bring Albion again
> With Luvah into light eternal, in his eternal day.
>
> (75:23–26)

NOTES

1. Blake identifies single vision with the limited scientific outlook of empiricism in his letter to Thomas Butts, 22 November 1802, as he prays to be kept from "single vision & Newtons sleep" (p. 693, 1. 88).

2. Although she has been variously identified as Vala (Damon, *Blake Dictionary*, p. 390), Rahab (John E. Grant, "Two Flowers in the Garden of Experience," in *William Blake: Essays for S. Foster Damon*, ed. Alvin Rosenfeld [Providence, R.I.: Brown University Press, 1969], p. 357), and Vala dressed as Rahab (Erdman, *Illuminated Blake*, p. 332), she remains the priestess of Deism and "an Eternal State" (pl. 52, top) who functions under both Vala's and Rahab's names as well as that of the Daughters of Albion within the chapter.

3. Blake uses blue in his illustration to suggest chastity or death, both of which are appropriate here in light of Rahab's moral doctrines.

4. Grant, "Two Flowers," p. 357.

5. Erdman, *Illuminated Blake*, p. 332.

6. Erdman counts twenty-seven birds directly above the picture, with sixteen more at the upper right (ibid., p. 333). While the sixteen suggest the unfallen sixteen books of the Bible or Jerusalem's children (see chap. 2), the twenty-seven suggest the fallen churches in which these books are distorted, and hint at the presence of fall within the imaginative universe.

7. The fifth figure at the right is apparent in the colored copy, E, although not in the others.

8. The number of batwinged creatures larger than simple unfilled lines is twelve. These correspond to Albion's twelve Druid Altars worshiped in the fallen world of both religion and reason.

9. This is another name for imagination, which is variously called the Divine Vision (60:5; 62:35), a Lamb (60:50; 62:30), the Divine Voice (60:65), or Jesus (62:18) in this section of chapter 3 as throughout the poem.

10. Binyon, *Engraved Designs*, p. 135, Damon, *William Blake*, p. 472, Erdman, *Illuminated Blake*, p. 341, all identify the figure as Luvah.

11. Desirée Hirst, *Hidden Riches: Traditional Symbolism from the Renaissance to Blake* (New York, 1964), p. 132, points out the resemblance of this figure to Robert Fludd's *Urusque Cosmi*. In addition, she explains the similarly coiled rope in that picture as "temporal life gradually unwinding itself in the history of the world with the figure of time drawing it out" (p. 132).

12. The contrast between the "Song of the Warriors" (68:10–70), which is the song celebrating history in the natural world and the "Song of the Lamb" sung earlier (60:10–37), lamenting that same history, demonstrates Blake's dialectical method in a new way. The symmetrical position of the two songs, one occurring in the eighth plate of the chapter, the other eight plates later and eight plates from the end of the chapter, emphasizes the contrast between their contents and points of view. The former demonstrates the natural world from the imaginative perspective and the latter from the Deistic one. While the slaves worship the lamb or true God, the warriors worship the list of gods demanding human sacrifice. While the slaves lament lost innocence and beauty at evening, the warriors celebrate cruelty and deadly war "in the hot day of Victory" (68:10). The active female is Jerusalem, sorrowing in slavery for one, and the Daughters of Albion executing sacrifice for the other. Even Vala's veil functions dialectically as Jerusalem is renewed by it and Tirzah turns it to blood.

13. Blake's description of the work in divided labor prefigures that of the alienated worker under capitalism detailed by Karl Marx in *The Economic and Political Manuscripts of 1844* (New York: International Publishers, 1964), pp. 106–19. For a full discussion of the similarities in vision between Blake and the early Marx, see my essay "The Humanized Universe of Blake and Marx," in *Blake and the Moderns*, ed. Robert Bertholf and Annette Levitt (Buffalo, N.Y.: SUNY Press, publication scheduled 1982).

The eighteenth century political economist Adam Smith also provides a similar description of divided labor in *The Wealth of Nations*.

> In the progress of the division of labour, the employment of the far greater part of those who live by labour, that is, of the great body of the people, comes to be confined to a few very simple operations, frequently to one or two. But the understandings of the greater part of men are necessarily formed by their ordinary employments. The man whose whole life is spent in performing a few simple operations, of which the effects too are, perhaps, always the same, or very nearly the same, has no occasion to exert his understanding, or to exercise his invention in finding out expedients for removing difficulties which never occur. He naturally loses, therefore, the habit of such exertion, and generally becomes as stupid and ignorant as it is possible for a human creature to become. The torpor of his mind renders him, not only incapable of relishing or bearing a part in any rational conversation, but of conceiving any generous, noble, or tender sentiment, and consequently of forming any just judgment concerning many even of the ordinary duties of private life. . . . His dexterity at his own particular trade seems, in this manner, to be acquired at the expence of his intellectual, social, and martial virtues. But in every improved and civilized society this is the state into which the labouring poor, that is, the great body of the people, must necessarily fall, unless government takes some pains to prevent it.

Adam Smith, *The Wealth of Nations* (New York: Modern Library, 1937), pp. 734–35.
14. Locke, *Human Understanding*, 2:167, 4:1–2.
15. Erdman, *Illuminated Blake*, p. 350.
16. Bloom, commentary, p. 858.
17. Damon, *William Blake*, p. 460.
18. The pilgrim image picks up the "passage" metaphor of the initial thematic statement (4:1–2), the image of Los's role and pilgrim's hat from plate 1, as well as the imaginative doctrine distinguishing individuals and states uttered earlier by the Daughters of Beulah (25:13), Los (31:13–16), and Erin (49:65–71).

6

The Liberty of Both Body and Mind

CHAPTER 4 begins as each of the other chapters does, with a dialectical situation in which fallen Albion opposes imagination. This time, however, Albion's affective error is under consideration. Seen first in the opposition between Christ's creation and the destructive wheel of fire in the dedication, the opposition is continued as Albion opposes Los's protection of the "Feminine Affections" (78:8) with his version of fallen affection—Vala-Rahab. While

> The Spectres of Albions Twelve Sons revolve mightily
> Over the Tomb & over the Body; ravning to devour
> The Sleeping Humanity. Los with his mace of iron
> Walks round: . . .
> . . . .
> Dashing in pieces Self-righteousnesses.
>
> (78:1–4, 6)

Revolving like the wheel of fire mentioned in the dedicatory poem, the spectrous forces still attempt to destroy or devour humanity, who still sleeps. Los now opposes them, continuing his wrathful action of chapter 3 (cf. 73:32, 43) by smashing spectrous categories to prevent Albion's complete petrification and that of his world.

The state of Albion's generative world is graphically represented in the opening illustration of chapter 4 (pl. 78). Here a bird-headed human figure sits upon a white rock surrounded by the sea of time and space. Vala's clouds dominate the sky while the sun of imagination sets at the left, its brown rays sending an ominous light over the whole. The figure with a bird of prey's beak represents Albion's

141

twelve spectrous sons, who the text explains are "ravning to de-vour/The Sleeping Humanity" (78:2–3). He may be called Hand, who has been mentioned before as the epitome of Albion's twelve spectrous sons (8:43); and indeed, he dominates a rocky island as Hand does in plate 50, where he reigns over Albion's rocky land, also surrounded by the sea of time and space. His identification, therefore, with St. John awaiting Apocalypse on Patmos, with Los, or with the poet generally seems unlikely.[1] The figure's prominent cockscomb implies a combination of prey and bird of prey, or victim and victimizer, typical of fallen Albion, who often inflicts injuries on his own divisions when he is limited by spectrous forces. The co-ordination of bird head and male body here is analogous to that of the swan head and woman's body in plate 11, which was also pictured in the midst of the overwhelming sea. The images of seaweed here further parallel the sea images of shells and fish along the right margin of plate 11. There the prophetic function of the swan and unfallen emanation was overwhelmed by generation. Here too the potentially divine is distorted. The male human form adopts a bes-tial head, illustrating his corruption of intellect in "ignorance [armed] with a rav'ning beak!" (9:13).

The fallen female, meanwhile, dominates the text as Albion's sons again substitute Vala for Jerusalem, crowning her (cf. illus. 51, 75), and giving her "power over the Earth" (78:16). The archetypal fallen female who distorts Jerusalem's liberty of body and mind in affec-tive error appears in various forms throughout the chapter as Rahab, Enitharmon, Gwendolen, Cambel, or the Daughters of Al-bion. The forgiveness, freedom, and self-sacrifice of imagination that make up the redemptive affection of the unfallen female are distorted in her sexuality, quest for dominance, and limitation to the natural that corrupt mental and physical liberty, all of which the first section of chapter 4 explores (pls. 78–86). As she is described in various forms and utters numerous laments in this section, Blake exposes her erroneous distortion of liberty and affection and em-brace of delusion in dialectic with Los's counteracting labors. Her effects appear in the lament of ruined Jerusalem (78:31–80:5), as well as in Vala's (80:12–31), Gwendolen's (80:83–82:9, 22–44), and Al-bion's Daughters' (83:85–84:28) laments, of which this first section of chapter 4 is composed.

Taking up the initial view of affective error, which the third sec-tion of chapter 1 (pls. 18–24) introduced, chapter 4 expands it with one important difference. In chapter 1 affective error was both rep-resented and opposed by a female. Unfallen Jerusalem took Los's place as eternity's representative while Los fled terrified from the fallen females, fearing their seductiveness, and sent his Spectre to pursue and persecute them. His peculiar vulnerability to natural beauty and generative sexuality, two favorite topics for poets and painters, dramatized the danger of seduction by the merely natural. Jerusalem, therefore, carried on the dialectic with Vala (nature) and fallen Albion (generative human existence) in Los's place. In chapter 4, however, the situation is reversed. Jerusalem is distorted by the fallen female. Liberty becomes "Disorganizd," enslaved, and ruined when threatened by affective error, while imagination, on the contrary, remains the powerful spokesman of eternity and counteracts error. By reversing Jerusalem's and Los's roles, Blake alters our view of affective error. It appears equally threatening to both imagination and liberty, but may also be successfully counteracted by each.

As Albion's twelve spectrous sons again substitute Vala-Rahab for Jerusalem (78:15–16; 18:11–35), they summarize the errors of false religion and reason within the context of false affection. They give Vala-Rahab a throne to "usurp the Throne of God" (78:19) just as Albion did in chapter 2 (30:27–28) and enslave Jerusalem as natural religion did in chapter 3 (60:39–51) by elevating the false affective doctrines to sovereignty. Their oppression, moreover, convinces Jerusalem that she has sinned and is "outcast from the Divine Presence!" (78:33), the opposite of her inspired faith in chapter 3 (60:52–64; 62:15). Reigning affective error is here responsible for distorting liberty, cutting it off from imagination, and persuading it of its own corruption through delusion. Jerusalem perceives this distortion, saying, "The hills of Judea are fallen with me into the deepest hell" (79:8), and describes the transformation of all biblical places of comfort into constricted places of torment, "narrow places in a little and dark land" (79:14), for affective error turns religion to torture. She further describes the contemporary generative situation in England in which "Albion is himself shrunk to a narrow rock in the midst of the sea!" (79:17). England is hardened against liberty (79:20), and war spreads from there throughout the world (79:55–67) as English imperialism replaces Edenic mutuality (79:20–67).

We see the image of Jerusalem's distress in the illustration for plate 92 where she sits mourning in the hills of Albion, surrounded by England's fallen contraries and Druid trilithons. Although in ruins herself, she causes their ruin too. "She is the breach in the wall of Druidic Babylon" as Orc was in *America*, and illustrates the prophecy of Isaiah 3:25–26: "Thy men shall fall by the sword, and thy mighty in the war. And her [Jerusalem's] gates shall lament and mourn; and she being desolate shall sit upon the ground."[2]

Although disorganized, Jerusalem attacks the illusions of generative sexuality, the "nets of beauty & delusion" (79:78) that Vala and the other fallen females promulgate. She blames affective error, which limits love to that sexuality and delusion for her and Albion's distortion, declaring: "Humanity is far above/Sexual organization" (79:73–74).

As Vala answers Jerusalem's lament with her own, paralleling their give and take in plates 20 and 22, she explicitly expresses her delusion. Separated from Jerusalem (80:12; cf. pls. 19–22), she rules a world of error but believes "if once a Delusion be found/Woman must perish & the Heavens of Heavens remain no more" (80:14–15). In part, of course, she is correct, but not in the literal way she believes. Only her idea of woman would perish in the reunification of man and the reestablishment of Eden as, in fact, all generative sexual roles would, for "Sexes must vanish & cease/To be, when Albion arises from his dread repose" (92:13–14).[3] Vala, therefore, seeks to maintain man in his merely natural form through her jealous love so that she may continue to dominate him.

We see her efforts as she retells the story of Luvah's murder and her own attempts on Albion (80:16–31).[4] In her version of the story, fallen passion (Luvah) attempts to destroy man who, newly divided, returns the compliment. Separating himself from his passionate part, man leaves that to nature (Vala) and thereby establishes fallen passionate love. Wielding Luvah's sacrificial knife of generative sexuality (see illus. 66, 69, and 74; also 22:29; 63:39; 66:20; 67:24–25; 83:12), Vala, in turn, keeps Albion in subjection, "embalmd in moral Laws" (80:27) with "lovely jealous stupefaction" (80:29). Nature cooperates with religion in using exclusive sexuality as a tool to stupefy man and establish laws of chastity.

Armed with her knife (80:22–23), she also turns the spindle of necessity to distort Jerusalem through natural laws and political compulsion (80:32; cf. illus. 12; chap. 3 passim, e.g., 59:53; 66:10; 64:32). She tries "To weave Jerusalem a body according to her will/A dragon form on Zion Hills most ancient promontory" (80:35–36), to impose Urizenic form on liberty as well as false Mosaic moral codes to enforce her will. This distortion is further expressed in familiar images of war, blood, fire, and cloud, of Albion's forests, Serpent Temples, and Druidic plains, which extend from biblical times to the present throughout the earth. These now come together with the fallen female within the new context of affective error (80:32–56). When Cambel and Gwendolen form Hand and Hyle (reason and matter respectively), paralleling Vala's action with Albion, the familiar images of fiber, tree, loom, cup, bone, law, and wine press also recur. The daughters shape the sons here just as they did Luvah in chapter 3, or just as Los shaped Reuben in chapter 2. The context of affective error, however, supplies a new meaning to that action. Hand's creation takes place under Cambel's "delusive light" (80:59), and Hyle is "Compelld into a shape of Moral Virtue against the Lamb" (80:77) while his sex is concealed. Reason and matter are thus shaped by fallen sexuality, which hides itself and functions deviously.

Asking "what shall we do to keep /These awful forms in our soft bands" (80:84–85), Gwendolen answers her own question in the next plates (81–82:55) and expands Vala's earlier delusive statement. Like Vala, she assumes that repression, delusion, and forceful dominance are necessary to her existence. "I gather our eternal fate," she says to her listening eleven sisters:

> . . . Outcasts from life and love:
> Unless we find a way to bind these awful Forms to our
> Embrace we shall perish annihilate, discoverd our Delusions.
> (82:2–4)

What she says is true of the fallen female only, but she can conceive no other. She therefore acts on her precepts and perpetuates her error through her mistaken actions. Representing woman as sexual object, she manipulates her beauty and sexuality in order to maintain her existence and achieve power. She uses false affection to dominate man, for, she tells us, "Men are caught by Love" (81:6). But her love does not embrace or comfort; it ensnares and catches. It includes denial and chastity, cruelty and jealousy as well as proffered sexuality, all of which she uses to enforce her will. As she rejects Merlin's inspired images of love in laws of chastity, sin, and death (81:2–7), she gives her love and allegiance to the stern and cruel warrior instead of the fully human man. Emphasizing the relationship between suppressed sexuality and war brought out in chapter 3 (68:62–63), she devotes herself to such sacrifice and repression (81:1–16; 82:22–44). Responsive to the warriors' demands, she is yet responsible for them, since she creates cruel, selfish love and, by refusing all other alternatives, for war itself. The spiral of destruction thus mounts through the distorted sexual relationship between Gwendolen and her warrior-lover.

Unable to recognize her own delusion, Gwendolen sees the truly human as falsehood, "Humanity the Great Delusion" (82:43). In her world, man loses his eternal form and becomes first an infant and then a worm (81:13–14; 82:47–49). As a worm he appears manipulated by the female in the marginal illustration for plate 80. What Satan does to man through distorted rationality (17:46; 27:55; 29:6; 30:57; 64:12), Gwendolen and Cambel do in their naked lovemaking through distorted sexuality.

The imaginative alternative to Gwendolen's affective error occurs in Jerusalem's unfallen imaginative categories of free body and mind. These two alternatives are succinctly contrasted in illustration 81, where Gwendolen holds her prophetic falsehood behind her back (82:19–21), and also in the lines of the text below that illustration (81:15–16). In the text Gwendolen reveals her principles saying, "In Heaven Love begets Love! but Fear is the Parent of Earthly Love!/And he who will not bend to Love must be subdud by Fear" (81:15–16). This fear of sexual refusal, which the fallen female uses to maintain her dominance, as well as the fear of punishment inspired by the moral and false religious law, is her prime weapon.

Gwendolen's doctrine is further clarified in the illustration.

> In Heaven the only Art of Living
> Is Forgetting & Forgiving
> Especially to the Female
> But if you on Earth Forgive
> You shall not find where to live.
>
> (Pl. 81)

The message appears in mirror writing, in the looking-glass of Enitharmon, within billowing clouds that take the visceral form of Vala's veil surrounding Gwendolen and against the dark background of night. Although she points to it in addressing her sisters, she does not regard it herself and cannot see its prophetic implications, only its literal meaning. Gwendolen excludes the imaginative doctrines of forgiveness and "forgetting" sin (cf. Daughters of Beulah 50:31) as inimical to earthly existence, and ignores the possibility of transforming that existence to suit such precepts. Instead, she suits her behavior and precepts to fallen existence, thereby perpetuating it. The reader, however, if not limited to Gwendolen's looking-glass perception, may penetrate surface appearances to discover the prophetic truth implied.

The illustration in which Gwendolen addresses the other eleven Daughters of Albion resembles plate 46 and the confrontation between Vala and Jerusalem. Placed at the left and with her back to the reader, Gwendolen's figure echoes Vala's, while her clouds form a veil of her own replacing Vala's veil, and her falsehood takes the place of the fallen church alongside Vala. The listening daughters, however, represent the fallen version of Jerusalem and her children, who face Vala. Instead of standing in open naked beauty, as Jerusalem does, Cambel, the corresponding large, naked, female figure facing the viewer here, "assumes the attitude of the Medicean Venus,"[5] the generative erotic ideal who coyly covers her breasts and genitals. She is the perfect graphic representation of fallen, secret, and jealous love. Her sisters, unlike the soaring offspring of

Jerusalem in the earlier picture, are frowning with concern, some holding their hands up in disconcerted attitudes of worry or resignation, for they accept delusion rather than flying free of it. The former female confrontation between error and truth is exchanged for the image of expanding female delusion. Gwendolen's affective error comes to absorb all female existence, both in the illustration and throughout the first section of chapter 4, which is filled with female lament.

Gwendolen's explanation of her falsehood adds to the chapter's crescendo of female laments as it follows Jerusalem's and Vala's and precedes Albion's Daughters' and Enitharmon's. Although her "Falshood is prophetic" (82:20), its positive quality is not revealed until Los enters the action. True to his role throughout the poem, his work within falsehood demonstrates its dialectical character and imaginative purpose. As Cambel again forms Hand (82:63; 80:57–65), she works "according to her will" (82:63), using love "like a chain/Binding his wrists & ankles with the iron arms of love" (82:70–71), but also gives "her beauty to another" (82:69). She unconsciously exercises selfless love, for she is operating within Los's furnaces and cannot help herself. The natural world, too, we may recall, unconsciously operates for imaginative ends finally, and for the same reason. Unselfish love enters Gwendolen's action, which begins in envy of her sister and ends in her repentance, as

> . . . she also in the eddying wind of Los's Bellows
> Began her dolorous task of love in the Wine-press of Luvah
> To form the Worm into a form of love by tears & pain.
> (82:74–76)

Los's influence causes fallen love to attempt unselfishness for the first time. But this occurs only after error is imaginatively interpreted by Los. Falsehood is in this way prophetic.

If we look again at illustration 80 with this thought in mind, we may reinterpret the action there. Glancing up the page rather than down, we see the worm of generation become quasi-human, rather than vice versa as a downward glance implies. Man's transcendent possibilities as well as his actual generative condition then become clear. This suggestion of metamorphosis represents an advance over the unaltered condition represented in plate 63, where the worm of generation thrice entwined the fainting female. Here the worm twines but once around one female figure, while both touch green vine leaves that are equivalent to the earlier green earth. While the female is still in the generative world, there is a hint of possible progress too. This hint of hope points out the dialectical character of fallen affection, for it is placed alongside the female's unrepentant human restriction described in the poetry of plate 80. The definite unmistakable image of a worm, on the other hand, dominates the left margin alongside the poetic hint of hope described in plate 82.

As Los enters generation, drawn "By pangs of love" (82:83), demonstrating the unselfish, self-sacrificing qualities of inspired love even as he describes its fallen condition within lapsed Jerusalem and the warlike Daughters of Albion (pl. 83), that dialectical character becomes clearer. He initiates the actions of Beulah's Daughters and of Enitharmon, whose silver spindles and golden weights (83:69) counteract the iron ones of the fallen females' looms. Opposing Vala's veil and Rahab's, they weave "the Web of life for Jerusalem, the Web of life/Down flowing into Entuthons Vales glistens with soft affections" (83:73–74). True affection then enters the fallen world, whose potential transformation is thereby provided for.

While Los allows the Daughters of Albion to control the Mundane Shell (56:31; 83:33 ff.), forming "the fluctuating Globe according to their will" (83:34) and limiting the earthbound senses of man, and allows the Spectre to work in it as well (83:78–79), he maintains another level within that world. This is "the real Surface/Which is unchangeable for ever & ever" (83:47–48) and which is "superadded" (83:47) to the world of appearances, the eternal level mentioned in chapter 3. Because of Los, therefore, the world of appearances becomes a flexible medium that may "assimilate with mighty Golgonooza," or imagination (83:43). However, as Los points out, "The land is markd for desolation . . . unless we plant/The seeds of Cities & of Villages in the Human bosom" (83:54–55). The free exercise of liberated mind, which is part of true affection, is necessary to penetrate the erroneous appearances of the world. While nature provides the basis for imagination to work upon, only civilization, the product of imagination, can avoid the doom of continuous generation. The seeds of cities within man, man's prophetic works and creative acts of which civilization consists, prevent universal chaotic destruction and the unending cycle of history. These works provide the real surface to the world, reflecting the "bright Sculptures of/Los's Halls" (16:61–62). Recognition of and attention to this reality is the work of liberated intellect in the universe, of Blake's true Christian as this chapter defines him, and is the force that dialectically opposes fallen affection.

As part of that fallen affection, "Albions daughters on Euphrates" (83:84) add the fourth installment to the fallen female lament. Their song, resembling the song of the Jews when they were captives in Babylon and echoing the song of slaves in evening in chapter 3, bemoans the contemporary fallen condition of England. While appealing to Los to help them, however, they simultaneously unite "With Rahab as she turnd the iron Spindle of destruction" (84:30) and take Gwendolen's falsehood from her. Their vision of the fallen land and particularly of "London blind & age-bent begging thro the Streets/Of Babylon, led by a child his tears run down his beard" (84:11–12) is represented in the illustration where an aged figure is led by a child toward a Gothic doorway. There are, however, no tears running down the aged figure's beard and the open Gothic doorway is a hopeful sign, for it is associated with living form, imagination (pl. 1), and inspired liberty (illus. 46). Albion's generative land, which the Daughters of Albion describe, therefore represents an incomplete vision; for the illustration shows the reader signs of hope within that world which they miss but which Los's speech and actions reveal (82:80–83:65). A similar process occurs as Gwendolen's falsehood grows in the hands of Albion's daughters (84:31–32). As it develops into "A Space & an Allegory around the Winding Worm" (85:1), becoming the spatial world of generative appearances or "Allegoric Generation" (50:2), Los enters this world, supplying "Time & Revolution" (85:6)—pun intended—and providing "The Seeds of beauty in the Space" (85:9). We saw these seeds before as cities and villages within divine humanity, forming Los's "Divine Analogy" (85:7) from the generative "Allegory" (85:1;. cf. 50:2). Since generative or fallen female space is simply material, an abstract, invisible realm of ideas or generalizations is invented to exist alongside matter as an allegory of its meaning. In the imaginative view, however, space becomes transcendent, an analogy of the eternal imaginative reality it reflects, which transforms allegory into symbolism. This vision silences the generative forces of the world: "The Stars stand still to hear: Jerusalem & Vala cease to mourn" (85:15). Reason listens to imagination, while liberty and the natural world are reassured by it. Indeed, as imagination exerts itself, the whole earth pays heed—the frozen mountainous powers, the tyrannical crowned heads, powers of warfare, and enslavers of inspiration (85:14–21). All come under his influence, for "So dread is Los's fury, that none dare him to approach/Without becoming his Children in the Furnaces of affliction" (86:48–49). This prophetic statement summarizes what has begun with Cambel and Gwendolen (pl. 82) and looks forward to the coming regeneration with which the poem ends.

As Los takes the "red Globe of fire" (85:19) in his hand, he again brings the light of inspiration into the world (cf. illus. 1; 97; 45:3) along with the "red Globe of blood" (17:51; 86:52), Enitharmon's natural world of space. Here is the natural world presented as allegoric generation or divine analogy, for the red globe of nature may be viewed as all-absorbing and bloody matter or as the imaginative light of the world.

The same dichotomy of vision is apparent in illustration 85. The male facing the viewer is connected to the female, whose back is turned by the grape vines that she draws from him with her left hand while her right holds other living vines connected to some unseen object out of the picture at the right. Both sit or kneel on the earth with their faces turned away from each other, so that the male regards the single star of reason, the visceral cloud form of Vala's veil, and the Ulro moon of the fallen female, while the female regards a sun surrounded by concentric rings like Los's light in the frontispiece. Looked at from the generative point of view, man is seen connected to and controlled by nature through her vegetating power (the vines she holds, cf. illus. 40, 57) as Cambel controls Hand (80:61–65) or Vala does Jerusalem's children (80:31–33). Looked at from the imaginative point of view, however, these same vines may be seen as the "fibres of love" (86:40), which the emanation, who regards imagination's light, sends from Golgonooza and which connect man through imaginative nature and liberty to eternity.[6] Exemplifying this double point of view poetically, Los exhorts Enitharmon to draw his fibers out in pity so that they two may be connected in imaginative existence (87:7–11), but Enitharmon willfully insists on using them to dominate man in a material natural world (87:12–15).

Los's song to Jerusalem, which rounds off the first section of chapter 4 clearly expresses his imaginative vision. Since the section began with Jerusalem's fallen lament that she is sin and godforsaken, Los appropriately ends the section by exposing her "Delusion" (85:31) and showing her that she is "lovely" (85:29), "the soft reflected Image of the Sleeping Man" (85:24). He describes the inspired winged appearance of unfallen affection that we saw at the bottom of the title page (pl. 2), "lovely Three-fold/In Head & Heart & Reins three Universes of love & beauty" (86:2–3), the perfect counterpart of the fallen female or affective error that the first part of chapter 4 has presented. She is also the divine analogy of Rahab, whose fallen threefold appearance of brain, bosom, and loins we saw in chapter 3 within the Satanic threefold Hand (70:17–31). Described in eternal gold and silver, the imaginative analogy of Vala's gold and silver nets (20:30) and Rahab's silver and golden melting and consummation of man (70:27–28), she also shines in rainbow hues and is compared in a simile to the rainbow, which contains divine promise and is Erin's symbol as well. One color is, however, missing from her rainbow spectrum—green. By that ommission, Blake points to the incompleteness of Jerusalem in this form. He implies that Vala, the body or nature's green earth, and Enitharmon, in whose realm one must be generated in order to "consummate bliss" (86:42), need to be added for complete female existence. Jerusalem is, therefore, still threefold, not because the female is necessarily less complete than the male, but because Jerusalem needs her counterpart, Vala, the body, for fulfillment and fourfold existence. While Los's celebration of immortal Jerusalem, therefore, marks an appropriate end to the section that explores the fallen female form and affective error by posing the image of her unfallen female intellect, religion or morality, and love (head, heart, and reins respectively), one further aspect of the fallen female, her bodily or natural appearance in space remains still to be renewed. For this, we turn to the second section of chapter 4 and the appearance of Los's Emanation, Enitharmon. Here the dialectic between imaginative and materialized vision, which is not resolved until the final section of the poem, comes to a climax as Los and Enitharmon face each other.

As Enitharmon again separates from Los (86:50; 83:67; cf. 5:67; 6:3; 53:6), the division is presented in terms of affective error. "Lured by her beauty" (86:60), as he was afraid of being lured by the beauty of Albion's daughters (17:6–10), Los's fears are realized in Enitharmon's "all devouring Love" (86:64). This devouring love, similar to Gwendolen's and her sisters' and opposed to comforting and creative unfallen love, is typical of the divided state. It results in "Two Wills" (86:61), that is, opposing desires for domination, and "Two Intellects" (86:61), two opposing visions of reality. When Enitharmon rejects Los's love, which sees beauty, reaches out for pity, and would create imaginative nature (87:3–11), by saying, "In Eden our loves were the same here they are opposite/I have Loves of my own I will weave them in Albions Spectre" (87:17–18), she echoes Gwendolen's distinctions between true and fallen love (pl. 81, inscription). As Enitharmon extols secrecy, jealousy, feminine domination, pride, and morality, and uses sexuality as the ultimate weapon in her arsenal, she also echoes the affective errors of the other fallen females: Cambel, Gwendolen, Vala, the Daughters of Albion (87:14–24; 88:16–33), and characterizes the world of affective error:

> . . . This is Womans World, nor need she any
> Spectre to defend her from Man. I will Create secret places
> And the masculine names of the places Merlin & Arthur.
> A triple Female Tabernacle for Moral Law I weave
> That he who loves Jesus may loathe terrified Female love
> Till God himself become a Male subservient to the Female.
>
> (88:16–21)

Establishing again the female's merely natural world (cf. 29:51; 56:3–4) with its hidden sexuality (cf. 21:19–21), its Deistic categories, and threefold demonic appearance of moral law (cf. 70:20 ff.), she rejects unfallen love and imagination (Jesus) and, like Vala and Gwendolen, tries to usurp imagination's place in man through female domination. Like her counterparts, she knows only her fallen role and fears annihilation if imagination prevails, "My Looms will be no more & I annihilate vanish for ever" (92:11). Enitharmon, however, differs from the other fallen females in an important way, in her closeness to Los, although she herself is not aware of this difference. She joins Los in escaping materialism, Enion (illus. 87), and is finally transformed by him through direct confrontation, for "So dread is Los's fury, that none dare him to approach/Without becoming his Children in the Furnaces of affliction" (86:48–49). At this point, however, she is unconscious of Los's effect and is just as fallen as Gwendolen.

Los, on the contrary, bases his picture of eternal or imaginative love on the role of the unfallen female and all she stands for. Opposing Enitharmon's definition and going beyond generative and genital sexuality to universal commingling, he envisions the world of awakening seen at the end of the poem. Los's vision includes a complete breakdown of subject-object barriers in mutuality and renewal of intellect as well as body. As he puts it:

> When in Eternity Man converses with Man they enter
> Into each others Bosom (which are Universes of delight)
> In mutual interchange, and first their Emanations meet
> Surrounded by their Children. if they embrace & comingle
> The Human Four-fold Forms mingle also in thunders of Intellect.
> (88:3–7)

The first stage of reunification depends completely upon Emanations, that is upon natural existences, the visible forms of imaginative entities that must first break down individualistic or selfish barriers by embracing and commingling with one another in freely given love. Then, and only then, can fully human development occur with mingled contraries in imaginative activities. This unselfish vision contradicts the isolating selfishness and domination of the fallen female's love that tries to prevail exclusively and results in universal cataclysm instead of creation.

> But if the Emanations mingle not; with storms & agitations
> Of earthquakes & consuming fires they roll apart in fear
> For Man cannot unite with Man but by their Emanations

Which stand both Male & Female at the Gates of each Humanity.
(88:8–11)

The necessity of merging through the Emanation (a necessity pointed out in *Milton* too) demonstrates the Emanation's vital importance in human existence as the visible edge of imagination. Since affective error completely distorts this edge through delusion, it inevitably limits man's existence to generation and prevents eternal transcendence. The correction of that error in the freely given love and liberty of mind and body is thus a necessary first step for awakening. It would transform the Emanations from their fallen roles, in which they strain for exclusive human domination, to their imaginative roles, in which they are united within eternal man.

It should be noted that in this passage the Emanation appears as both masculine and feminine. It does so once more in Blake's summary of affective error and division: "The Feminine separates from the Masculine & both from Man, / Ceasing to be His Emanations, Life to Themselves assuming" (90:1–2). Since the Emanation is feminine throughout most of the poem, why does it here suddenly become masculine too?[7] The answer must lie in the particular function of the Emanation within affective error. In unfallen form as affective truth, the Emanation is Jerusalem, liberty of body and mind, the visible form or garment of inspiration or imagination and the imaginative connection between men. In fallen form, however, all aspects of that character become distorted. Not only does liberty of body fall into limited, generative sexuality, but liberty of mind also falls into delusion. We see that delusion first as the fallen Emanation tries to dominate man in the chapter's first section. There is, however, another related dimension to delusion, which expands the notion in another direction, that of natural law or fallen universality. This delusion of false universality stems from the limitation of mind and body just as much as feminine delusion does, but it is masculine in gender. It appears briefly in chapter 2 as the cities adopt false universality in orthodox religion and in chapter 3 as Deism perpetuates false universal laws that Los comes to smash. It reappears and is explored in chapter 4 as Los contends with his Spectre and error consolidates with the Covering Cherub. Mentioned here as part of the natural distortion and block to eternity that the fallen Emanation presents, it foreshadows its later development.

Blake introduces another view of division within the archetypal struggle between affective error and its imaginative alternative (Enitharmon and Los) by assigning the Spectre a role here. "Knowing himself the author of their divisions & shrinkings" (88:35), the

Spectre rejoices in the conflict between Los and Enitharmon and does what he can to exacerbate the quarrel. Since reason is the source of all quarrels (64:20), we see it here at the basis of affective error and female delusion, bolstering the "dominion of a jealous Female" (88:41) with its own delusions, those hinted at within the fallen masculine Emanation. He joins Enitharmon in victimizing Imagination (Los), adding male delusion to female by "dividing the Space of Love with brazen Compasses/In Golgonooza & in Udan-Adan & in Entuthon of Urizen" (88:47–48; cf. illus. 12). Space is thus given rational and mathematical proportions within art or civilization (Golgonooza), within chaos or generation (Udan-Adan and Entuthon), and within the scientific universe of Urizen.[8] Male delusion, which appears as natural law or abstract generalization in culture, science, philosophy, and morals, becomes part of fallen female space and sexuality.

Begun in the dedicatory poem with the description of the two opposing wheels of the universe (pl. 77), and continued in the struggle between first the fallen females (pls. 78–85) and then Enitharmon and Los (pls. 86–88 and 92–93), the struggle between affective error and its imaginative alternative culminates as Los faces the Covering Cherub (pls. 89–91). The Spectre's corruption of intellect in male delusion and the other errors previously examined separately in the poem are consolidated in the Covering Cherub, the Antichrist or human dragon (89:10–11). His head, bosom, and loins demonstrate philosophic, religious, and affective error respectively, forming the fallen equivalents of Jerusalem's eternal parts (pl. 86). In addition, his devouring stomach contains all of oppressive time and space. The "double female . . ./Religion hid in War" (89:52–53) also enters his form, so that he includes the negative aspects of Albion's female divisions as well. "They become One with the Antichrist & are absorbd in him" (89:62). His head or fallen philosophy contains "Minute Particulars in slavery" (89:17), Druid edifices, and Albion's forests (89:22–23), while his bosom or religion contains "Israel in bondage to his Generalizing Gods" (89:30), his loins or affection encloses the fallen substitute for Jerusalem, Babylon, and his devouring stomach encloses Jerusalem, with all of time and space distorted in threefold "allegoric delusion & woe" (89:45), the antithesis of divine analogy.

Bringing together all errors within one form, the Covering Cherub demonstrates the growth of falsehood, which, since it is prophetic, announces the imminence of regeneration. This imminence is also evident in the marginal illustration (pl. 89). Two females placed one above the other reach toward one another. One dives down and the other stands upright as both touch the cocoon resting between them.⁹ In *Jerusalem* the cocoon symbolizes twofold human possibility (e.g., the cocoon alongside the envoi to the reader in plate 3 or Jerusalem emerging from the cocoon on the title page). It represents the stage between man's existence as a worm or permanent generative caterpillar under the influence of Satan or Vala (illus. 63; 75; 80; 82; poetry 17:46; 27:55; 29:6; 30:57; 64:12) and his emergence as the imaginatively freed soul with butterfly wings (illus. 2; 14; 44). Unlike the regenerated figure in *Glad Day*, whose cocoon lies discarded at his feet, man here is still in his generative state held by the fallen female, and he can go either way. The resemblance of the lower figure here to Vala (cf. pl. 74, top; pl. 12, bottom) underlines his limitation, but the descending nude figure and birds flying around the tree-vine imply that he is readying himself to burst the cocoon and emerge in new form.

As Los expounds true Christian religion, intellect, and affection to oppose the Covering Cherub and reveal his embodiment of error (90:28–38, 52–57), he isolates the substitution of false universality for particularity as responsible for all generative conditions. He blames that generalizing tendency which blurs distinctive individuality and negates the uniqueness of man's gifts and expression by laying down universal laws or principles. Within religious error, this generalizing tendency appears in the codes of good and evil and abstract deity that fallen religion sets up in place of "Divine/Humanity who is the only General and Universal Form" (38:19–20). In Deism, it is expressed in the generalizations of natural law, natural religion, and doctrines of "General Good" (55:61), which Deism substitutes for particulars. Within both systems such generalizing theories destroy true art, science, religion, and liberty (pls. 38, 55). By setting up codes of chastity and behavior or standards of intellectual activity, this tendency works within affective error too. Universality becomes the exact antithesis of the unique expression of particular, individual, imaginative gifts, which is the only Gospel. As Los isolates the underlying universalizing tendency as the cause of generation, he says:

> . . . No Individual ought to appropriate to Himself
> Or to his Emanation, any of the Universal Characteristics
> Of David or of Eve, of the Woman, or of the Lord.
> Of Reuben or of Benjamin, of Joseph or Judah or Levi.
> Those who dare appropriate to themselves Universal Attributes
> Are the Blasphemous Selfhoods & must be broken asunder.
> A Vegetated Christ & a Virgin Eve, are the Hermaphroditic
> Blasphemy, by his Maternal birth he is that Evil-One
> And his Maternal Humanity must be put off Eternally

    Lest the Sexual Generation swallow up Regeneration
    Come Lord Jesus take on thee the Satanic Body of Holiness.
                                           (90:28–38)

Any of the individualities named in the poem represent partial truths, whether of religion, reason, nature, or sex. In trying to appropriate universality, these partial truths become "Blasphemous Selfhoods," isolating their partial vision and claiming it as exclusive and universal. They thereby turn partial truth into falsehood or error and destroy the one true universal, the unique Human Form Divine. Underlying their delusions, which turn human divinity into mere matter—a "Vegetated Christ," and affection into chastity—"A Virgin Eve," are the fallen females, "Maternal Humanity," who threaten to envelop all in sexual generation, a threat that Los and Jesus smash by their imaginative transcendence of false universality. The story of Albion's fall may also be seen in this way, as the misappropriation of universality:

    For Los said: When the Individual appropriates Universality
    He divides into Male & Female: & when the Male & Female
    Appropriate Individuality, they become an Eternal Death.
                                           (90:52–54)

This casts Albion's original division in a new perspective. Albion's fragmentation into disconnected fallen male and female or rational and natural parts now appears as a result of his misappropriation of universality in denying the Human Form Divine—the only true universal. As his disconnected parts each attempt to dominate the human form through various fallen doctrines (religious, rational, political, scientific, or affective) based on false generalizations that take a part for the whole, they form various versions of the generative world and produce false art, science, religion, philosophy, love, and liberty (38:35–36, 54; 45:19–20; 55:60–65; illus. 26, 52, 77). In this way they "become an Eternal Death," that Satanic state in which fallen Albion sleeps. They are exposed as false universals in chapter 4, as the distortion of imagination or true Christianity, which celebrates particular Mental Gifts. Los points out their falsity as he cries:

    . . . the Worship of God, is honouring his gifts
    In other men: & loving the greatest men best, each according
    To his Genius: which is the Holy Ghost in Man; there is no other
    God, than that God who is the intellectual fountain of Humanity;
    He who envies or calumniates: which is murder & cruelty,
    Murders the Holy-one: Go tell them this & overthrow their cup,

Their bread, their altar-table, their incense & their oath:
Their marriage & their baptism, their burial & consecration:
I have tried to make friends by corporeal gifts but have only
Made enemies: I never made friends but by spiritual gifts;
By severe contentions of friendship & the burning fire of thought,
He who would see the Divinity must see him in his Children
One first, in friendship & love; then a Divine Family, & in the midst
Jesus will appear; so he who wishes to see a Vision; a perfect Whole
Must see it in its Minute Particulars; Organized & not as thou
O Fiend of Righteousness pretendest; thine is a Disorganized
And snowy cloud: brooder of tempests & destructive War.
You smile with pomp & rigor: you talk of benevolence & virtue!
I act with benevolence & Virtue & get murderd time after time:
You accumulate Particulars, & murder by analyzing, that you
May take the aggregate; & you call the aggregate Moral Law:
And you call that Swelld & bloated Form; a Minute Particular.
But General Forms have their vitality in Particulars: & every
Particular is a Man; a Divine Member of the Divine Jesus.

(91:7–30)

As Los opposes the various "fiends of righteousness," whom we have seen throughout chapters 1 through 4, and their false doctrines, he explains his true religion, intellect, and affection, which turn out to be exactly that exercise of imagination which Blake calls true Christianity. He overthrows "the ritual paraphernalia of Christian worship"[10] (cup, bread, altar, incense, oath [91:12–13]) and the generative institutions that regulate life (baptism, marriage, burial), for they have been corrupted by state and church. In their place he substitutes individual genius and intellect, friendship and thought, love and self-sacrifice, and minute, individual, unique particularity. Within his imaginative vision, humanity appears in its minute particulars or unique attributes, which are divine and humanize the entire universe, turning it also divine. Vision depends on such individuality, for only particulars give life and inevitably result in love, friendship, and benevolent action, rather than empty generalizations such as moral or natural laws, which result in death. The opposite of the various generative doctrines seen in chapters 1 to 3, and particularly the opposite of affective error as described in chapter 4, Los's doctrines oppose Satanic war, religious "pomp & rigor," false benevolence and virtue such as is expressed in moral law, and abstraction with its swelled and bloated forms, which destroys by generalizing or analyzing.

Los's speech opposing the Covering Cherub's consolidation of error (pl. 90) marks the moment at which power shifts from generation to regeneration in the poem. Since error has been thoroughly investigated, exposed, and recognized in all its appearances, and consolidated so that it grows prophetic in the Covering Cherub, Albion is now ready for awakening. Both fallen Spectre and Emanation become powerless, for they stand absolutely revealed, as does imagination, which thereby gains power. As each of the major generative power groups in the poem now confronts Los in turn, each is consolidated, altered, or annihilated.

Plate 90 begins with a succinct summary of Albion's division into separate fallen masculine and feminine parts, which distort man's "Brain," "Heart," and "Loins" (90:3, 4). The fallen females, called by the names of Albion's daughters, form their "Veil & Net" (90:4) and weave "curtains of hiding secresy" (90:13) around their generative, jealous love, while the fallen males under both biblical and English names sit at their furnace waging war (90:23), imbibe spiritual hate rather than love in their false religion (90:17), ossify the natural man in their philosophy (90:20), and cut him off from the land (90:25), thereby parodying Los's creative actions at forge and furnace. They further condense in Luvah as "One Great Satan" (90:43) and build Urizen's temple (90:50), while the daughters officiate in sacrifice there and at Los's forge, where they "Vegetate" (90:50) or establish the natural basis of life. This view of Albion's sons and daughters summarizes their actions throughout the poem in familiar images of nets, fibers, weaving, curtains, bones, looms, iron, furnaces, war, and tombs. Their combination as "the Hermaphroditic/Blasphemy" (91:34–35) also reappears in another view of the false religious and Deistic hermaphrodite described in chapters 2 and 3. In dialectical answer to this summary, Los attacks false universality (90:52–55) with the imaginative alternative of particularity, an aspect of "Lord Jesus" (90:38) or true Christianity, as the dedication defines them. These are the "Demonstrations of Los" (90:5), which are the divine analogy of empirical demonstrations, and they culminate on the archetypal level as Los again confronts and commands his Spectre (91:7–30) and Emanation (92:13–27). This time, however, Los escalates his control when the Spectre, in a last-ditch effort to counteract Los, musters all his Druidic and Deistic powers, creating "stupendous Works" (91:33) in the forms of temples, voids, stars, scientific demonstrations, dragons, tombs, and occult teachings (91:32–41); for "Los alterd his Spectre & every Ratio of his Reason" (91:50).

Yet even in extremis, the Spectre overcomes man, who faints in a typical generative position, with his head thrown back in unseeing intellectual and perceptual limitation (illus. 91). He is bound by spectrous fibers to Solomon's seal on one side and a spiral or concentric circle of fibers colored deathly blue on the other, among the roots of his tree of mystery that grows up along the right margin. His mind is thus obfuscated by both the religious mystery of his tree and occult mysteries associated with Solomon.[11]

Again in plate 93 spectrous power exerts its influence on man. The three Socratic accusers, who recall the threefold Satanic accuser of plate 35, are pictured here. Inscribed "Anytus Melitus & Lycon thought Socrates a Very Pernicious Man. So Caiphas thought Jesus" (pl. 93), they condemn intellect and imagination (Socrates and Jesus). They succeed in having Socrates put to death as Caiaphas, that "dark preacher of Death" (77:18), succeeded in having Jesus killed, for both want to eliminate the free exercise of intellect and imagination, which they regard as "Pernicious." The futility of their efforts at this point in the poem is apparent, as we see them point to their own downfall in the following illustration (pl. 94). There, bound by fibers, heads thrown backward, eyes unseeing, and apparently dead or fainting, they are in the same position in which they formerly tried to place Albion (illus. 91). Their attempt to overthrow humanity is thus itself overthrown by imagination. Even as we see them here, they point their fingers toward the truth, the rest of the poem, "and advise us that pernicious Socratic wisdom and Christian inspiration . . . are in the offing."[12]

Enitharmon's last-ditch appeal has the same effect as the Spectre's. When Los alters his Spectre, unification begins. "The Briton Saxon Roman Norman" amalgamate "into One Nation the English" (92:1, 2), and renewal is inevitable. Enitharmon foresees this move toward unity as the beginning of her end, that is, the end of her individual, willful existence, which is all she can see. "The Poets Song draws to its period & Enitharmon is no more" (92:8), she says. She further predicts, "My Looms will be no more & I annihilate vanish for ever" (92:11). She therefore persists in error, fighting for life as she knows it, and trying still to dominate Los. Los, however, attempts to transform rather than annihilate her, by correcting her affective error and emanative delusion. Therefore, he tells Enitharmon, "Sexes must vanish & cease/To be, when Albion arises from his dread repose O lovely Enitharmon" (92:13–14; cf. 44:33). Summarizing her error in his images of Druid religion, moral law, and the merely natural universe (92:15–27), "The terrors of Creation & Redemption & Judgment" (92:19), Los proposes "Visionary Space and Time" (92:17) and "Mutual Forgiveness" (92:18) instead. Although this has been his function throughout, now that unity has begun and the moment of reversal is at hand, Los describes generation for the first time in the past rather than present tense (92:24–27). Enitharmon is, however, unaware of it. She looks up mildly (93:1; illus. 93, bottom) and, in anything but mild tones, utters her last appeal for love based on "pride of dominion" (93:5). Addressing Rintrah and Palamabron, wrath and pity—two unregenerated sons of Jerusalem and Los's typical characteristics throughout the poem—her appeal is doomed to failure in her terms but bound for ultimate success in transcendence of those terms. Some of that is apparent in the illustration, if not yet in the text. Calm and unfrightened, Enitharmon regards Los rather than the accusers above her in illustration 93, is only half within the tomb, and is surrounded by bright yellow and red flames. Her regeneration has begun even while she laments. As she combines with Satan, we see formed "The God of This World, & the Goddess Nature/Mystery Babylon the Great, The Druid Dragon & hidden Harlot" (93:24–25), which like the Covering Cherub heralds regeneration through consolidation. Los sees in it "that Signal of Morning which was told us in the Beginning" (93:26) even though he alone is aware of it.

In the second section of chapter 4 (pls. 87–93), Los in turn encounters and overthrows each of the generative powers previously described: the Covering Cherub, the Sons and Daughters of Albion, his own Spectre and Emanation, and the hermaphroditic combinations. In each case Los conquers their delusions by upholding particularity over abstract universals, by opposing sexual generation with liberty and forgiveness, and by imaginatively opposing all the components of error previously explored. Because of this process, which is made possible by the thorough exposition of chapters 2, 3, and 4, Albion is readied for awakening, as he was not at the end of chapter 1, when the components of error had been merely outlined. The third and final section of chapter 4, plates 94–100, is therefore devoted to a description of Albion's moment of awakening and the imaginative state it implies. Placed in the context of chapter 4, rather than set off in a chapter by itself, it is both the imaginative alternative to affective error specifically and the alternative to all generative error as well; for as we now know, all error is one, as its consolidation in the Covering Cherub demonstrates.

The last section of chapter 4 begins with Albion still in his initial fallen condition, asleep in Ulro. "Albion cold lays on his Rock" (94:1), a sleeping giant as throughout the poem (e.g., 15:29–30; 16:27; 43:11–12; 48:3–4; 57:16; 78:1–3). He is still dead, entombed, surrounded by storms, starry wheels, Ulro darkness, clouds, and sea, isolated and oppressed by war, hunger, and the conditions of industrialization (94:1–17). Pictured graphically in the lower illustration for plate 94, sleeping Albion, old and bearded, stretched out in his tomb with his Emanation, who sleeps in "Death on Albions Bosom" (94:20), surrounded by Druid edifices, is still in generation. However, the imminence of regeneration, which Los has announced, is also pictured in the illustration as Albion's darkened landscape is lit by the rising sun of imagination. Morning dawns and the threefold Satanic accuser lies overthrown and dead or dying above. Although prepared for by the entire exposition of the poem and possible only because of it, the reversal from sleep to awakening is the matter of a moment. Time is telescoped as "Brittannia awoke, from Death on Albions Bosom . . . fainted seven times on the Body of Albion" (94:20–21), and the seven ages of history outlined in chapter 3 pass. Now when "The Breath Divine Breathed over Albion" (94:18) as it did initially (4:4), history ends, and "Time was Finished!" (94:18). Once introduced, awakening is as complete as generation was before.

Since the Emanation is man's connection to eternity, she awakens first and rouses Albion with her "voice" (95:1) and message. Chapter 4 has prepared us for her awakening, first, through the series of fallen female laments (pls. 78–84), and second, through the confrontation between Enitharmon and Los. The fallen females, compelled to defend a lie, give it body and expose it, advancing the consolidation of error as Los prophesied. Rid of delusion through Los's efforts, the female may assume her eternal self. Therefore Brittannia recognizes the female code as falsehood and appeals: "O God awake/I have slain In Dreams of Chastity & Moral Law I have Murdered Albion!" (94:22–23). God has, of course, been awake throughout, only she was asleep and could not see him. As she awakens from the dream of generation, the nightmare of history, and admits her own erroneous actions, she reclaims them, much as Blake himself does with his selfhood in the dedication to chapter 2 (27:75). She may then see and unite with Albion's divine eternal form, conquer generation, denying the delusions of institutionalized morality, Deistic naturalism, and female domination. She affirms the reality of regenerated love, which she now exemplifies as she denounces her former jealousy. As his natural part is renewed, all Albion awakens: "Her voice pierc'd Albions clay cold ear he moved upon the Rock" (95:1). Now that his Emanation or natural part is imbued with imaginative vision, that time is finished, and Albion is freed from the nightmare of history, his awakening is possible. As the Divine Voice told us earlier, "Albion must Sleep/The Sleep of Death, till the Man of Sin & Repentance be reveald" (43:11–12). Only after all errors, religious, philosophic, and affective, have been consolidated into a single figure, the Covering Cherub, and exposed as Antichrist, is that accomplished, and Albion's "awaking to Eternal Life" (4:2) can begin.

Albion's awakening, although briefly described, is quite thorough. As the "Divine Breath" goes forth over him three times (94:18;

95:2, 5), it first redeems nature and affection (awakens Brittannia), next awakens Albion's senses, body, perceptions, and outer reflections, and finally awakens his intellect. The image of this awakening is illustrated as Albion rises from his tomb (pl. 95), looming majestic in flames of wrath above the white cliffs at his right and the rock of ages at his left. His right hand directs the flames upward above the cliffs on which the hawk-headed Hand sat at the beginning of the chapter (pl. 78), while his left leans on the rock of ages to lift him up from death. He leaves the tomb and rocks of generative existence behind (and in copy E the worm of his generative form as well) and enters the flames of imagination and intellect. Casting off his Urizenic appearance, he is transformed from his old man's figure (illus. 94) to the youthful physical form of Los or imagination (illus. 95, 97). Yet his position as he arises from the tomb presents a mirror image of Urizen's in plate 15. Urizen faces the reader and seems to be pressing downward in his attempt to limit the human figure, who is restricted and vegetated by the action. Albion, on the other hand, has his back to the reader and rises from limitation and vegetation in a similar position, but with his right hand opening out rather than limiting his surroundings. He presents the imaginative alternative to Urizen, as Christ does to Albion in plate 76, and is not a completely new character but the old, transformed by vision, as the mirror image implies. The connection is pictured in the almost tail-like protuberance that connects Albion in the illustration to the unregenerated Urizenic figure in the tomb, who is left behind.

As Albion awakens, earlier images of imagination combine in his appearance, forming a consolidation of imagination, the divine analogy of generative appearances and consolidation of error. Albion's "flames" and "pillars/Of fire" (95:7, 8–9) are the opposite or imaginative version of Hand's flames (e.g., pl. 26), Vala's "red fires" (30:1), Luvah's "fires" (62:28), or false religion's fiery wheel (77:2). They are the flames of the Divine Vision in Los's furnaces (cf. 60:5; 62:35; 66:41) and the "fire" and "flames of fierce desire" (3:5, 6), which characterize prophetic expression. As Albion turns into a flaming creature "speaking the Words of Eternity in Human Forms, in direful/Revolutions of Action & Passion" (95:9–10), he parallels and repeats the action of the Divine Vision who "became First a burning flame, then a column/Of fire, then an awful fiery wheel surrounding earth & heaven" (66:41–42). As his words revolve in human form, they oppose his various distorted monstrous appearances (polypus, worm, dragon, Covering Cherub) into which his generative doctrines distorted his imaginative human existence. They also oppose the destructive revolutions of the fiery wheel of religion (77:13), the starry wheels of spectrous reason (e.g., 5:52–53), the dark Satanic wheels of industry (15:18–19), Newton's wheels, the "Iron Wheels of War" (22:34), and so on—that great collection of demonic wheels. Albion's humanized version echoes instead the Edenic eternal wheels (15:20), imaginative wheels of cherubim (illus. 75), and revolutions of Los (85:6). Since imagination is victorious over false religion and moral virtue (Albion's barren mountains), the sun now appears "Struggling to rise above the mountains" (95:12). The bow with which Satan had tried to eliminate imagination (illus. 35) is also reclaimed and fires "arrows of flaming gold" (95:13) instead of Apollyon's arrows of "Demonstrative Science" (12:14), which were Satan's weapons. Albion now possesses a humanized bowstring that "breathes" (95:14), and restores the four Zoas from their chaotic, disorganized states to their proper spheres under awakened Albion's aegis. Tharmas returns to the sheepfold, Luvah to the loom, Urizen to the furrow in eternal form, and Urthona to the anvil, where he has been as Los, who "kept the Divine Vision in time of trouble" (95:20). All imaginative symbols now come together in Albion's awakening to overthrow those perverted generative appearances that formerly reigned.

While unity begins as "Brittannia enterd Albions bosom rejoicing" (95:22), the process is not yet complete, for Albion must still rejoin his imagination as well as his natural body. The initial reunification is illustrated in plate 96 in subdued colors as Albion in his aged appearance partially embraces his naked Emanation within rolling clouds. Although he appears aged and bearded as Jehovah or Urizen, Albion is no longer oppressed by false religion and reason, as his embrace of his awakened Emanation, liberty of body and mind, demonstrates. His ideas of God and reason are transformed. Both now appear identical with one another and with him, Albion, in eternal unity. Even in plate 99, when reunification is complete, and male and female join in full frontal embrace pictured in vivid color, Albion's aged appearance remains unchanged. It still includes regenerated Jehovah and Urizen in the Human Form Divine.[13]

Reunified with nature (95:22), God, and reason (illus. 96), Albion is also reunified with imagination, as pictured in the Albion-Los identity of illustration 95 or when Albion sees Jesus-Los as "The Universal Humanity" (96:3–7). Because Albion recognizes divinity and imagination as human, he can combine time with eternity and maintain imaginative human relationships by conversing with God "as Man with Man, in Ages of Eternity" (96:6). In this, he imitates Blake's example (pl. 3), brings Los's prophetic imaginative vision into action (88:3–4), and restores his own prelapsarian state (24:44–45). He can therefore assess his own generative experience accurately for the first time. Admitting "My Selfhood cruel/Marches against thee [Jesus] deceitful from Sinai & from Edom" (96:8–9), he acknowledges the spectrous principle in himself as Blake (27:76) and Brittannia (94:22–23) did, as well as its influence in his religion, moral law (Sinai), and Deistic natural form (Edom).[14] He now sees history as a dream, "the Visions of my deadly Sleep of Six Thousand Years" (96:11), and its Satanic appearance in generation as the projection of his own consciousness: "I know it is my Self" (96:13). This is the antithesis of his generative accusations against the Savior (4:24–25) and Los (42:9–10), and it prepares Albion to accept Jesus' message of brotherhood, love, and self-sacrifice (96:23–28), which the Savior has consistently offered him. He now sees the eternal image of God's sacrifice for man not as an isolated historical event as church doctrine states, but as an ongoing one that is echoed in every kindness any man performs for another.

Albion's renewed consciousness is completed through his "Mysterious/Offering of Self for Another" (96:20–21), which is "Friendship & Brotherhood" (96:16, 21). By throwing himself into the furnaces of affliction for the sake of his "Friend/Divine" (96:30–31), Albion imitates the self-sacrificing actions of all the imaginative characters in the poem (Los, the Savior, Jerusalem, etc.), abandons generative doctrines for eternal ones, and simultaneously awakens himself and his world from selfish, deathlike sleep. As he imitates Los's initial action (1:9), his physical resemblance to Los grows from its first appearance in illustration 95 to its second in illustration 97, where he too carries the light of imagination into the world as Los did (pl. 1).

As Albion adopts imaginative vision, he changes his world, for consciousness creates the world it envisions: "all you behold, tho it appears Without it is Within" (71:18). Casting himself into "the Furnaces of affliction" (96:35), he transforms them into "Fountains of Living Waters flowing from the Humanity Divine" (96:37), as the Divine Vision did for Mary (61:28–29). The furnaces of generation, which are comprised of suffering and affliction, change into life-giving waters, for Albion's unselfish action annihilates generative principles of existence in favor of eternal ones. The entire universe is thereby transformed:

And all the Cities of Albion rose from their Slumbers, and All
The Sons & Daughters of Albion on soft clouds Waking from Sleep
Soon all around remote the Heavens burnt with flaming fires
And Urizen & Luvah & Tharmas & Urthona arose into
Albions Bosom: Then Albion stood before Jesus in the Clouds
Of Heaven Fourfold among the Visions of God in Eternity.
(96:38–43)

In the universal awakening all Albion's formerly divided parts, which are the outward appearance of Albion's imaginative consciousness, are restored to their eternal forms. His Sons and Daughters and their generative doctrines, his Zoas and their fallen positions, his fallen cities, all of which appeared in divided chaotic state throughout the poem are reunited with Albion to complete his universal subjective existence. Even the clouds and fires typical of the generative appearances of Vala, Hand, or fallen female and male throughout the poem, are, like everything else, transformed into heavenly fourfold appearances. No new characters or surroundings are suddenly introduced when Albion awakens, but the same appearances are transformed as petrified surfaces give way to underlying permanent reality. Clouds and flames still surround the commingling figures in plates 96 and 99, but they are glorious, not obscure.

Still describing Albion's awakening, plates 97–99 repeat the action just described in plates 94–96, but in greater detail. Blake thereby consistently follows his thematic organization in describing the moment of renewal as he did in generative fall, but in a more concentrated fashion. For example, when Albion calls on Jerusalem to awaken and "overspread all Nations" (97:2), we know that she has already been roused, for Albion converses with divinity as man with man by grace of his unfallen Emanation. Furthermore, we have seen Jerusalem in her English form (Brittannia) uniting with Albion and indeed awakening him (95:1–2). Here, however, Jerusalem's English form is universalized. Just as generative domination spread as the polypus from England throughout the world, so do renewal and liberty now that "the Night of Death is past and the Eternal Day-/Appears upon our Hills" (97:3–4). In his reiteration of incident, Blake thus expands the concept of emanative liberty by adding universality to the initial image.

The meaning of Albion's intermingling with imagination and divinity (96:5–7) also becomes clearer as Blake tells us, "So spake the Vision of Albion & in him so spake in my hearing/The Universal Father" (97:5–6). The poet now hears Albion's inspired voice, the voice of universal divine humanity, God incarnate in everyman. When Albion again reaches for his fourfold bow (97:6–7; cf. 95:13–20), that too is explained further. Made of four metals, gold, silver, brass, and iron, which correspond to Golgonooza's gates toward Beulah and Eden (12:66; 13:5), the bow demonstrates man's connection to eternity and repose. Its human quality, introduced in plate 95 through its breathing bowstring, is also expanded here, where it is both male and female, the opposite of the hermaphroditic conglomerations of earlier plates but typical, instead, of eternal, unified sexuality, with its "Arrows of Love" (97:12) that are used "in Wars of mutual Benevolence Wars of Love" (97:14). As Albion, his four Zoas (97:7–11), and his twenty-eight cities (97:17) clothe themselves with these fourfold bows and arrows, man, his land, and his institutions are all transformed from their threefold Satanic appearance (illus. 35). Furthermore, "The Druid Spectre was Annihilate loud thundring rejoicing terrific Vanishing/Fourfold Annihilation" (98:6–7). Physical war is then replaced by intellect, love, and mutual benevolence, as when the Almighty bent his bow (52:28) or when the Savior described its eternal function (34:14–26).

By repeating lines that accompany Albion's initial grasp of the bow (95:14–15) in its second view (98:4–5), Blake shows that the same action is being considered. But now Albion becomes Blake's true Christian, exercising "the Divine Arts of Imagination" in some "Mental Pursuit" (pl. 77), whose "Arrows of Intellect" (98:7) bring about the final profound transformation of the world. As the "innumerable Chariots of the Almighty" (98:8) appear, divine analogy of false religion's chariot (illus. 41), they are accompanied by "Bacon & Newton & Locke, & Milton & Shakespear & Chaucer" (98:9). Empirical philosophy and scientific rationalism are now removed from their exclusive fallen appearances and restored to their proper place alongside prophetic poetry. The physical world, too, apparent in "Sexual Threefold" (98:11) of each chariot, is also renewed, for each contains within it a new unified and fully human "Fourfold" (98:12). The natural world is thus not exchanged for another, but remains sexual, generating but not generative, since it is now inhabited by imaginative man. Similarly, the illustration that shows Albion with the light of inspiration also shows him based in the natural world with his feet firmly treading the green earth (pl. 97). The star of reason and the moon of love, no longer in its fallen crescent phase (illus. 8, 14, etc.), also appear in the illustration. Restored to their proper positions, they too, as empirical reason and sexual love, are part of imaginative activity. So is the sun of prophetic wrath mentioned in the text (98:10) which, unlike destructive generative wrath, is creative and liberating (cf. 95:6).

The restoration of the four Zoas is seen in another way when Albion's senses are renewed (98:12–23), and he awakens "to Life among the Flowers of Beulah" (98:21). Renewed nature or sensual life, however, leads man only to Beulah, as the redemptive females such as Erin or the Daughters of Beulah do too, and renewed intellect, actively expressed, must be superadded to take man fully to Eden itself. This expression is also reiterated so that we may see into it further. As we saw Albion "speaking the Words of Eternity in Human Forms, in direful/Revolutions of Action & Passion" (95:9–

10) or conversing in equally human forms with his divinity and imagination (96:5–7), so now all parts of man express themselves:

> And they conversed together in Visionary forms dramatic which
>   bright
> Redounded from their Tongues in thunderous majesty, in Visions
> In new Expanses, creating examplars of Memory and of Intellect
> Creating Space, Creating Time according to the wonders Divine
> Of Human Imagination, throughout all the Three Regions immense
> Of Childhood, Manhood & Old Age[;] & the all tremendous
>   unfathomable Non Ens
> Of Death was seen in regenerations terrific or complacent varying
> According to the subject of discourse & every Word & Every
>   Character
> Was Human according to the Expansion or Contraction, the
>   Translucence or
> Opakeness of Nervous fibres such was the variation of Time &
>   Space
> Which vary according as the Organs of Perception vary & they
>   walked
> To & fro in Eternity as One Man reflecting each in each.
>
> (98:28–39)

Redeemed inner vision, perception, and sense are here reflected in outer appearances, in the imaginative renewal of time and space. Just as scientific reason is included with prophetic poetry in the Chariots of the Almighty (98:8–9), so too is memory included here with intellect as part of the eternal activity of imaginative man.[15] Through the use of his imagination man reshapes himself and his world. He regenerates the three regions of Ulro—Creation, Redemption, and Judgment—replacing them with the human categories of Childhood, Manhood, and Old Age. He reshapes space, time, history, thought, and all phases of human life in unending imaginative activity and creation. Appearing "in Eternity as One Man reflecting each in each" (98:39), man extends his subjectivity to include other men and finally achieves true brotherhood. His extended subjectivity further includes the natural world, as animate life from lion to worm or fly also becomes part of the subjective man (98:43–45). The original division based on the subject-object distinction is thus overthrown in imaginative unity.

As the world becomes humanized, the doctrines of generation disappear. Called collectively "The Covenant of Priam" (98:46),[16] a demonic parody of Jehovah's true covenant (98:23), these doctrines include all the familiar Jewish and Deistic errors that result in war and empire: "The Moral Virtues" (98:46), "the Tree of Good & Evil" (98:47), "the Druid Temples of the Accuser of Sin" (98:49), "Albions Spectre the Patriarch Druid" (98:48), his "Human Sacrifices/For Sin in War" (98:48–49), and "The Oak Groves of Albion that coverd the whole Earth beneath his Spectre" (98:50). Also included are: "Albions Poverty Tree" (98:52), rampant taxation (98:53), and economic exploitation, which equally disappear from the renewed world. As Blake describes the world of Priam's covenant, he summarizes the conditions of the historical generative world and attacks the contemporary situation in England, its widespread poverty, hunger, oppressive taxation, political oppression, and repressive empire (especially evident in America and Ireland), which all result from the moral, religious, rational, and affective errors explored within the poem.

Invisible to the "Living Creatures" (98:42) who become humanized in Albion's awakening and contained in his all-inclusive subjectivity, the conditions of Priam's covenant are replaced by those of Jehovah's covenant, the "Forgiveness of Sins which is Self Annihilation" (98:23), "the Mutual Covenant Divine" (98:41). Therefore all life is transformed. Even the Dragon-headed snake pictured above (pl. 98, top), familiar to us as the image of Urizen, Religion hid in war, Urizen combined with the fallen female will, or the serpent of generation that involves man in false morality, false reason, and war, becomes humanized along with the other living creatures (98:44). The creatures below the text, the snail, toad, worm(s), spider, and moth, are also transformed from symbolic agents of war (*Milton*, 27:11–24) to humanized elements of the universe. They regard the sky and horizon beyond, looking for but not finding the conditions of generation described in their cry. Instead, they see a sky full of birds, consistent symbols of imagination in *Jerusalem*. The flock of insects and reptiles, themselves renovated, thus regard a renovated universe.[17]

The entire universe is humanized in the subjective identification of all creation within Albion. His primordial condition is thus restored, for "Man anciently containd in his mighty limbs all things in Heaven & Earth" (pl. 27). This is another way of expressing Albion's reintegration with his Emanation and imagination and the renewal of his natural and social world that the last six plates describe. There is no longer any separation between self and other, or perceiving subject and objective universe. All appearances and phenomena are reintegrated in one subjective whole since everything outside reflects an inner condition or is shaped by an inner state. Albion's imaginative vision of mutual forgiveness, love, and brotherhood cannot create oppressive institutions, systems of thought, or art, for it refuses to treat another as an object. It cannot posit a reified universe, for it creates or shapes its surroundings as part of itself. Finally, we see:

> All Human Forms identified even Tree Metal Earth & Stone, all
> Human Forms identified, living going forth & returning wearied
> Into the Planetary lives of Years Months Days & Hours reposing
> And then Awaking into his Bosom in the Life of Immortality
> And I heard the Name of their Emanations they are named
>   Jerusalem
>
> (99:1–5)

The entire phenomenal world is now part of subjective existence. This does not represent a withdrawal from the world into some type of ideal mystical existence, for all these humanized forms live in planetary space and clock or calendar time, that is, within the natural world. Even these categories of time and space, however, are not simply neutral or natural categories. They are based on human knowledge: astronomy, physics, and mathematics. Nature itself is thus humanized by them and not left in savage, raw condition. This differs, however, from pure Deistic scientific empiricism and Newtonian mathematics, for the phenomena are not objectivized into "atomic existences" but become subjectified or human instead. Therefore natural existence is not generative, but proceeds according to Los's gift of time and Enitharmon's of space, the mercy of eternity, within an imaginative context. Natural existence, furthermore, is a springboard for creative activity, which transcends the natural world in "the Life of Immortality" but always returns to it as a place of repose. The life of pure intellect in eternity is too intense and too removed to be maintained in isolated exclusiveness and demands natural existence as a foundation and a repose. Contraries that form the basis of progression and dialectic within the poem, therefore, still continue within imaginative existence. They complement each other in living relations so that finite and infinite, natural and immortal, are not exclusive but interdependent. As soon as such conditions obtain, liberty prevails—everyone's Emanation is called Jerusalem. Man can then exercise the arts of imagination in creative effort. He is unified with the world and his fellow men through sympathy and brotherhood, and his society reflects his regeneration in external conditions. The moment of Eternal Life forecast at the outset is now accomplished.

NOTES

1. Mitchell, *Blake's Composite Art;* Erdman, *Illuminated Blake,* p. 357; Judith Ott, "The Bird-Man of William Blake's *Jerusalem,*" *Blake Newsletter* 10, no. 2 (Fall 1976): 48–51, all note the resemblance of the figure to an eagle and identify him, therefore, with St. John on the Isle of Patmos. Ott further identifies the figure with Los, or the poet generally.

2. Erdman, *Illuminated Blake,* p. 371.

3. As Susan Fox points out in her essay "The Female as Metaphor in William Blake's Poetry," *Critical Inquiry* 3 (1977), pp. 507–19, Blake consistently uses the female as a metaphor rather than a literal presentation, especially in his later works. In *Jerusalem,* as she notes, females represent the emanative portion of all humanity. Vala's demise therefore would simply abolish the emanative notion she represents.

4. Other versions of this story occur in 7:30–40; 43:61–80; 63:5 ff.; 64:18–24; 65:8–11; 66:56–73.

5. Damon, *William Blake,* p. 474.

6. The same double interpretation applies to the net of fibers pictured in plate 4.

7. Shiloh, the Emanation of France, is the single previous male exception (49:48; 55:29), perhaps due to the feminine character often associated with "la belle France," or to emphasize the contrast with England—masculine Albion.

8. Adan is an anagram for *nada,* "nothing," earlier called the indefinite realm (7:22). *Entuthon* too is used to symbolize the chaotic indefinite as well as generative realm throughout the poem.

9. Erdman identifies this object as a "scalloped basket such as angels fill with bread for Christ after his triumph in Blake's watercolor for *Paradise Regained* IV 581–95" (*Illuminated Blake,* p. 368). If so, the basket is upside down here and has spilled its bread. Erdman also sees this object as a variant of "handing down of grapes" (*Illuminated Blake,* p. 368), but the object bears little resemblance to grapes and looks more like the caterpillar in *Gates* 1. That plate asks "what is man?" and gives the ambiguous answer of the caterpillar and the sleeping babe-cocoon. Such ambiguity is appropriate here too, for man has the alternatives of remaining asleep in the cocoon of generation or flying free of it in eternal metamorphosed form.

10. Bloom, *Blake's Apocalypse,* p. 428.

11. Erdman calls the two circular symbols to which Albion is bound the Old and New Testaments respectively (*Illuminated Blake,* p. 370). As such, they would demonstrate Albion's spectrous religion; however, while the identification of Solomon's seal (Old Testament) is apparent, the identification of the ear of wheat (New Testament) in the spiral at the right is less than visually demonstrable.

12. Erdman, *Illuminated Blake,* p. 372.

13. Irene H. Chayes, "The Marginal Design on *Jerusalem* 12," notes that the male figure in both plates 96 and 99 has the windblown hair of Blake's Christ as well as the Urizenic beard, showing "the risen Albion as both Jehovah and Christ, man and God redeeming each other" (p. 59). Although my explanation proceeds in slightly different terms, my conclusion is similar, namely, that all Albion's generative forms, including those of Jehovah and Urizen, are transformed by Albion's renewal as he rises from his tomb of generation in flames of inspiration.

14. Edom was Esau's territory in the Bible and therefore an appropriate designation for the Deistic natural man's realm in Blake's mythology. It was also used as a pseudonym for Rome in late rabbinical literature, which would make it an equally appropriate designation for Deistic empire in Blake's system.

15. Karl Kiralis hypothesizes that the " 'exemplars' could also well refer to the many aphorisms in *Jerusalem*" ("Theme and Structure," p. 146). He cites 67:19–21 as an exemplar of memory and 58:8–10 as one of intellect. Blake thereby uses the powers of both memory and intellect in his poem to effect regeneration.

16. Bloom, commentary, p. 862 explain Blake's use of Priam's name stating, "The Covenant of Priam (98:46) is at once the Classical vision of virtue as belonging foremost to the warrior and the poetic art founded upon that vision."

17. Erdman identifies twenty-eight small birds led by a large one in the illustration. He calls the twenty-eight "the senses become fourfold seven" and the large one "imagination" (*Illuminated Blake*, p. 377). The number twenty-eight, however, has been used throughout the poem for Albion's unfallen cities and churches. It would be consistent that Albion's land and institutions be pictured here, for they are in their awakened form (97:17), and they too may be led by imagination.

Bibliography

Adams, Hazard. "Blake, *Jerusalem*, and Symbolic Form." *Blake Studies 7*, no. 2 (1975): 146–66.

Beer, John. *Blake's Visionary Universe*. Manchester: University of Manchester Press, 1969.

Berger, Pierre. *William Blake: Mysticisme et Poesie*. 1907. Reprint. Paris: H. Didier, 1936.

Bindman, David. *Blake as an Artist*. Oxford: Phaidon; New York: E. P. Dutton, 1977.

Binyon, Laurence. *The Engraved Designs of William Blake*. London: Ernest Benn, 1926.

Bloom, Harold. *The Visionary Company: A Reading of English Romanticism*. Garden City, N.Y.: Doubleday, 1963.

———. *Blake's Apocalypse*. Garden City, N.Y.: Doubleday, 1963.

———. "Blake's *Jerusalem*: The Bard of Sensibility and the Form of Prophecy." In *Ringers in the Tower: Studies in Romantic Tradition*. Chicago: University of Chicago Press, 1971.

———, and Erdman, David V., eds. *The Poetry and Prose of William Blake*. Garden City, N.Y.: Doubleday, 1970.

Cassirer, Ernst. *The Philosophy of the Enlightenment*. Translated by C. A. Koelin and James P. Pettegrove. Boston: Beacon Press, 1961.

Chayes, Irene H. "The Marginal Design on *Jerusalem* 12." *Blake Studies 7*, no. 2 (1972): 51–76.

Curran, Stuart, and Wittreich, Joseph Anthony, eds. *Blake's Sublime Allegory: Essays on the "Four Zoas," "Milton," and "Jerusalem."* Madison, Wis.: Wisconsin University Press, 1973.

Damon, S. Foster. *William Blake: His Philosophy and Symbols*. 1924. Reprint. Gloucester, Mass.: Peter Smith, 1958.

————. *A Blake Dictionary: The Ideas and Symbols of William Blake.* Providence, R.I.: Brown University Press, 1965.

Doskow, Minna. "The Humanized Universe of Blake and Marx." In *Blake and the Moderns,* edited by Robert Bertholf and Annette Levitt. Buffalo, N.Y.: SUNY Press, scheduled 1982.

Ellis, E. J., and Yeats, W. B., eds. *The Works of William Blake.* Vol. 2. London: Quaritch, 1893.

Erdman, David V. *Blake: Prophet against Empire.* Princeton, N.J.: Princeton University Press, 1970.

————. *The Illuminated Blake.* Garden City, N.Y.: Doubleday Anchor, 1974.

————, and Grant, John E., eds. *Blake's Visionary Forms Dramatic.* Princeton, N.J.: Princeton University Press, 1970.

Fisher, Peter, F. *The Valley of Vision: Blake as Prophet and Revolutionary.* Edited by Northrop Frye. Toronto: University of Toronto Press, 1961.

Fox, Susan. "The Female as Metaphor in William Blake's Poetry." *Critical Inquiry* 3 (1977): 507–19.

Frye, Northrop. *Fearful Symmetry: A Study of William Blake.* Princeton, N.J.: Princeton University Press, 1947.

————, ed. *Blake: A Collection of Critical Essays.* Englewood Cliffs, N.J.: Prentice-Hall, 1966.

Grant, John E., ed. *Discussions of William Blake.* Boston: Heath, 1961.

Hagstrum, Jean H. *William Blake: Poet and Painter.* Chicago: University of Chicago Press, 1964.

Hegel, Georg Wilhelm Friedrich. *Logic.* Translated by William Wallace. Oxford: Clarendon Press, 1975.

————. *Phenomenology of Spirit.* Translated by A. V. Miller. Oxford: Oxford University Press, 1979.

Helm, Randel. "Ezekiel and Blake's *Jerusalem.*" *Studies in Romanticism* 13 (1974): 127–40.

Hirst, Desiree. *Hidden Riches: Traditional Symbolism from the Renaissance to Blake.* New York: Barnes and Noble, 1964.

Hume, David. "Of Sceptical and Other Systems of Philosophy." In *The Age of Enlightenment,* 6 vols., edited by Isaiah Berlin. Vol. 4: *The Great Ages of Western Philosophy,* pp. 162–260. New York: George Braziller, 1958.

Hungerford, Edward P. *Shores of Darkness.* New York: World-Meridian Publishing Co., 1963.

Ivins, William. *Prints and Visual Communication.* Cambridge, Mass.: Harvard University Press, 1953.

Keynes, Geoffrey, ed. *The Complete Writings of William Blake*. London: Oxford University Press, 1966.

Locke, John. *An Essay concerning Human Understanding*. Vol. 1 (2 vols.). New York: Dover, 1959.

Margoliouth, Herschel M. *William Blake*. London: Oxford, 1951.

Marks, Mollyanne. "Self-sacrifice: Theme and Image in *Jerusalem*." *Blake Studies* 7, no. 1 (1975): 27–50.

Marx, Karl. *The Economic and Philosophical Manuscripts of 1844*. Translated by Martin Milligan. Edited by Dirk J. Struik. New York: International Publ., 1964.

Mellor, Anne K. *Blake's Human Form Divine*. Berkeley, Calif.: University of California Press, 1974.

Mitchell, W. J. T. *Blake's Composite Art: A Study of the Illuminated Poetry*. Princeton, N.J.: Princeton University Press, 1978.

Murry, John Middleton. *William Blake*. 1933. Reprint. New York: McGraw-Hill, 1964.

Nietzsche, Friedrich. *The Birth of Tragedy*. Translated by Walter Kaufmann. New York: Random House–Vintage, 1967.

Ott, Judith. "The Bird-Man of William Blake's *Jerusalem*." *Blake Newsletter* 10, no. 2 (Fall 1976): 48–51.

Pinto, Vivian de Sola, ed. *The Divine Vision: Studies in the Poetry and Art of William Blake*. London: Victor Gollancz, 1957.

Raine, Kathleen. *Blake and Tradition*. Bollingen Series 37, 2 vols. Princeton, N.J.: Princeton University Press, 1968.

Rose, E. J. "The Structure of Blake's *Jerusalem*." *Bucknell Review* 40, no. 3 (1963): 35–54.

Rosenfeld, Alvin H. *William Blake: Essays for S. Foster Damon*. Providence, R.I.: Brown University Press, 1969.

Sloss, D. J., and Wallis, J. P. P., ed. *The Prophetic Writings of William Blake*. Oxford: Oxford University Press, 1926.

Smith, Adam. *The Wealth of Nations*. New York: Modern Library, 1937.

Stevenson, W. H. "Blake's *Jerusalem*." *Essays in Criticism* 9 (1959): 254–64.

Wicksteed, Joseph H. *William Blake's "Jerusalem."* New York: Beechhurst Press, 1955.

Witke, Joanne. "*Jerusalem*, a Synoptic Poem." *Comparative Literature Studies* 22 (1970): 265–78.

Appendix
William Blake's
Jerusalem—*Facsimile*

Jerusalem The Emanation of The Giant Albion

1804
Printed by W. Blake S

To the Public

After my three years slumber on the banks of the Ocean, I again display my Giant forms to the Public: My former Giants & Fairies having reciev'd the highest reward possible: the ___ and ___ of those with whom to be connected, is to be ___: I cannot doubt that this more consolidated & extended Work, will be as kindly recieved ~~ ___ The Enthusiasm of the following Poem, the Author hopes ___

___ I also hope the Reader will be with me, ___ My One in Jesus our Lord, who is the God ___ and Lord ___ to whom the Ancients look'd and saw his day afar off, with trembling & amazement.

The Spirit of Jesus is continual forgiveness of Sin: he who waits to be righteous before he enters into the Saviours kingdom, the Divine Body: will never enter there. I am perhaps the most sinful of men! I pretend not to holiness; yet I pretend to love, to see, to converse with daily, as man with man: & the more to have an interest in the Friend of Sinners. Therefore ___ Reader, ___ what you do not approve, & ___ me for this energetic exertion of my talent.

Reader! ___ of books! ___ of heaven,
And of that God from whom ___
Who in mysterious Sinais awful cave,
To Man the wondrous art of writing gave,
Again he speaks in thunder and in fire!
Thunder of Thought, & flames of fierce desire:
Even from the depths of Hell his voice I hear,
Within the unfathomd caverns of my Ear.
Therefore I print; nor vain my types shall be:
Heaven, Earth & Hell, henceforth shall live in harmony

Of the Measure, in which
the following Poem is written

We who dwell on Earth can do nothing of ourselves, every thing is conducted by Spirits, no less than Digestion or Sleep. ___

When this Verse was first dictated to me I consider'd a Monotonous Cadence like that used by Milton & Shakspeare & all writers of English Blank Verse, derived from the modern bondage of Rhyming; to be a necessary and indispensible part of Verse. But I soon found that in the mouth of a true Orator such monotony was not only awkward, but as much a bondage as rhyme itself. I therefore have produced a variety in every line, both of cadences & number of syllables. Every word and every letter is studied and put into its fit place: the terrific numbers are reserved for the terrific parts the mild & gentle, for the mild & gentle parts, and the prosaic, for inferior parts: all are necessary to each other. Poetry Fetter'd, Fetters the Human Race! Nations are Destroy'd, or Flourish, in proportion as Their Poetry Painting and Music, are Destroy'd or Flourish! The Primeval State of Man, was Wisdom, Art, and Science.

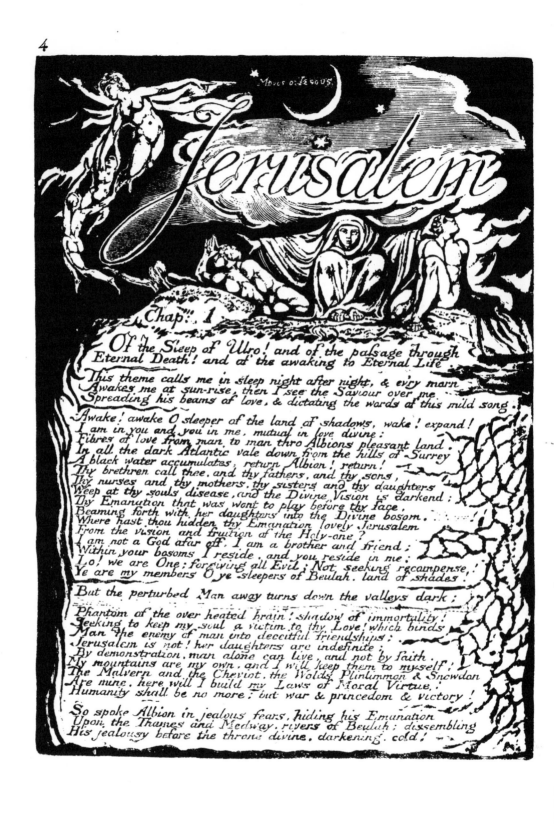

MONS O: JESOUS

Jerusalem

Chap: 1

Of the Sleep of Ulro! and of the passage through
Eternal Death! and of the awaking to Eternal Life.

This theme calls me in sleep night after night, & ev'ry morn
Awakes me at sun-rise, then I see the Saviour over me
Spreading his beams of love, & dictating the words of this mild song.

Awake! awake O sleeper of the land of shadows, wake! expand!
I am in you and you in me, mutual in love divine:
Fibres of love from man to man thro Albions pleasant land.
In all the dark Atlantic vale down from the hills of Surrey
A black water accumulates, return Albion! return!
Thy brethren call thee, and thy fathers, and thy sons,
Thy nurses and thy mothers, thy sisters and thy daughters
Weep at thy souls disease, and the Divine Vision is darkend:
Thy Emanation that was wont to play before thy face,
Beaming forth with her daughters into the Divine bosom.
Where hast thou hidden thy Emanation lovely Jerusalem
From the vision and fruition of the Holy-one?
I am not a God afar off, I am a brother and friend:
Within your bosoms I reside, and you reside in me:
Lo! we are One: forgiving all Evil; Not seeking recompense.
Ye are my members O ye sleepers of Beulah, land of shades!

But the perturbed Man away turns down the valleys dark;

Phantom of the over heated brain! shadow of immortality!
Seeking to keep my soul a victim to thy Love! which binds
Man the enemy of man into deceitful friendships:
Jerusalem is not! her daughters are indefinite:
By demonstration, man alone can live, and not by faith.
My mountains are my own, and I will keep them to myself!
The Malvern and the Cheviot, the Wolds, Plinlimmon & Snowdon
Are mine, here will I build my Laws of Moral Virtue!
Humanity shall be no more: but war & princedom & victory!

So spoke Albion in jealous fears, hiding his Emanation
Upon the Thames and Medway, rivers of Beulah: dissembling
His jealousy before the throne divine, darkening, cold!

The banks of the Thames are clouded! the ancient porches of Albion are
Darkend! they are drawn thro' unbounded space, scatterd upon
The Void in incoherent despair! Cambridge & Oxford & London,
Are driven among the starry Wheels, rent away and dissipated,
In Chasms & Abysses of sorrow, enlarg'd without dimension, terrible
Albions mountains run with blood, the cries of war & of tumult
Resound into the unbounded night, every Human perfection
Of mountain & river & city, are small & witherd & darkend
Cam is a little stream! Ely is almost swallowd up!
Lincoln & Norwich stand trembling on the brink of Udan-Adan!
Wales and Scotland shrink themselves to the west and to the north!
Mourning for fear of the warriors in the Vale of Entuthon-Benython
Jerusalem is scatterd abroad like a cloud of smoke thro' non-entity:
Moab & Ammon & Amalek & Canaan & Egypt & Aram
Recieve her little-ones for sacrifices and the delights of cruelty

Trembling I sit day and night, my friends are astonish'd at me.
Yet they forgive my wanderings, I rest not from my great task!
To open the Eternal Worlds, to open the immortal Eyes
Of Man inwards into the Worlds of Thought: into Eternity
Ever expanding in the Bosom of God, the Human Imagination
O Saviour pour upon me thy Spirit of meekness & love:
Annihilate the Selfhood in me, be thou all my life!
Guide thou my hand which trembles exceedingly upon the rock of ages,
While I write of the building of Golgonooza, & of the terrors of Entuthon:
Of Hand & Hyle & Coban, of Kwantok, Peachey, Brereton, Slayd & Hutton:
Of the terrible sons & daughters of Albion, and their Generations.

Scofield! Kox, Kotope and Bowen, revolve most mightily upon
The Furnace of Los: before the eastern gate bending their fury.
They war, to destroy the Furnaces, to desolate Golgonooza:
And to devour the Sleeping Humanity of Albion in rage & hunger.
They revolve into the Furnaces Southward & are driven forth Northward
Divided into Male and Female forms time after time.
From these Twelve all the Families of England spread abroad.

The Male is a Furnace of beryll; the Female is a golden Loom;
I behold them and their rushing fires overwhelm my Soul,
In Londons darkness; and my tears fall day and night,
Upon the Emanations of Albions Sons! the Daughters of Albion
Names anciently rememberd, but now contemnd as fictions:
Although in every bosom they controll our Vegetative powers.

These are united into Tirzah and her Sisters, on Mount Gilead.
Cambel & Gwendolen & Conwenna & Cordella & Ignoge.
And these united into Rahab in the Covering Cherub on Euphrates
Gwiniverra & Gwinefred, & Gonorill & Sabrina beautiful.
Estrild, Mehetabel & Ragan, lovely Daughters of Albion
They are the beautiful Emanations of the Twelve Sons of Albion

The Starry Wheels revolv'd heavily over the Furnaces:
Drawing Jerusalem in anguish of maternal love,
Eastward a pillar of a cloud with Vala upon the mountains
Howling in pain, redounding from the arms of Beulahs Daughters,
Out from the Furnaces of Los above the head of Los,
A pillar of smoke writhing afar into Non-Entity, redounding
Till the cloud reaches afar outstretch'd, among the Starry Wheels
Which revolve heavily in the mighty Void above the Furnaces

O what avail the loves & tears of Beulahs lovely Daughters
They hold the Immortal Form in gentle bands & tender tears
But all within is opend into the deeps of Entuthon Benython
A dark and unknown night, indefinite, unmeasurable, without end.
Abstract Philosophy warring in enmity against Imagination
Which is the Divine Body of the Lord Jesus, blessed for ever)
And there Jerusalem wanders with Vala upon the mountains,
Attracted by the revolutions of those Wheels the Cloud of smoke
Immense, and Jerusalem & Vala weeping in the Cloud
Wander away into the Chaotic Void, lamenting with her Shadow
Among the Daughters of Albion, among the Starry Wheels;
Lamenting for her children, for the sons & daughters of Albion

Los heard her lamentations in the deeps afar! his tears fall
Incessant before the Furnaces, and his Emanation divided in pain,
Eastward toward the Starry Wheels. But Westward a black Horror,

His Spectre driv'n by the Starry Wheels of Albions sons, black and
Opake divided from his back; he labours and he mourns!

For as his Emanation divided, his Spectre also divided
In terror of those starry wheels; and the Spectre stood over Los
Howling in pain: a blackening Shadow, blackening dark & opake
Cursing the terrible Los: bitterly cursing him for his friendship
To Albion, suggesting murderous thoughts against Albion.

Los rag'd and stamp'd the earth in his might & terrible wrath!
He stood and stamp'd the earth! then he threw down his hammer in rage &
In fury: then he sat down and wept, terrified! Then arose
And chaunted his song, labouring with the tongs and hammer:
But still the Spectre divided, and still his pain increas'd!

In pain the Spectre divided: in pain of hunger and thirst:
To devour Los's Human Perfection, but when he saw that Los

Was living: panting like a frighted wolf, and howling
He stood over the Immortal in the solitude and darkness:
Upon the darkning Thames across the whole Island westward.
A horrible Shadow of Death, among the Furnaces beneath
The pillar of folding smoke; and he sought by other means,
To lure Los: by tears, by arguments of science & by terrors:
Terrors in every Nerve, by spasms & extended pains:
While Los answerd unterrified to the opake blackening Fiend

And thus the Spectre spoke: Wilt thou still go on to destruction?
Till thy life is all taken away by this deceitful Friendship?
He drinks thee up like water, like wine he pours thee
Into his tuns: thy Daughters are trodden in his vintage
He makes thy Sons the trampling of his bulls, they are plowd
And harrowd for his profit, lo! thy stolen Emanation
Is his garden of pleasure, all the Spectres of his Sons mock thee
Look how they scorn thy once admired palaces, now in ruins
Because of Albion! because of deceit and friendship! For Lo!
Hand has peopled Babel & Nineveh: Hyle, Ashur & Aram:
Coban's son is Nimrod: his son Cush is adjoind to Aram,
By the Daughter of Babel, in a woven mantle of pestilence & war,
They put forth their spurious cloudy sails; which drive their immense
Constellations over the deadly deeps of indefinite Udan-Adan
Kox is the Father of Shem & Ham & Japheth, he is the Noah
Of the Flood of Udan-Adan. Hutn is the Father of the Seven
From Enoch to Adam; Schofield is Adam who was new
Created in Eden, I saw it indignant, & thou art not moved!
This has divided thee in sunder: and wilt thou still forgive?
O! thou seest not what I see! what is done in the Furnaces,
Listen, I will tell thee what is done in moments to thee unknown:
Luvah was cast into the Furnaces of affliction and sealed
And Vala fed in cruel delight, the Furnaces with fire:
Stern Urizen beheld; urgd by necessity to keep
The evil day afar, and if perchance with iron power
He might avert his own despair: in woe & fear he saw
Vala incircle round the Furnaces where Luvah was closd:
With joy she heard his howlings, & forgot he was her Luvah,
With whom she livd in bliss in times of innocence & youth!
Vala comes from the Furnace in a cloud, but wretched Luvah
Is howling in the Furnaces, in flames among Albions Spectres,
To prepare the Spectre of Albion to reign over thee O Los,
Forming the Spectres of Albion according to his rage:
To prepare the Spectre sons of Adam, who is Scofield: the Ninth
Of Albions sons, & the father of all his brethren in the Shadowy
Generation. Cambel & Gwendolen wove webs of war & of
Religion, to involve all Albions sons, and when they had
Involvd Eight; their webs rolld outwards into darkness
And Schofield the Ninth remaind on the outside of the Eight
And Kox, Kotope & Bowen, One in him, a Fourfold Wonder
Involvd the Eight—Such are the Generations of the Giant Albion,
To separate a Law of Sin, to punish thee in thy members.

Los answerd. Altho' I know not this! I know far worse than this:
I know that Albion hath divided me, and that thou O my Spectre,
Hast just cause to be irritated: but look stedfastly upon me:
Comfort thyself in my strength the time will arrive,
When all Albions injuries shall cease, and when we shall
Embrace him tenfold bright, rising from his tomb in immortality.
They have divided themselves by Wrath, they must be united by
Pity: let us therefore take example & warning O my Spectre.
O that I could abstain from wrath! O that the Lamb
Of God would look upon me and pity me in my fury.
In anguish of regeneration! in terrors of self annihilation:
Pity must join together those whom wrath has torn in sunder,
And the Religion of Generation which was meant for the destruction
Of Jerusalem, become her covering, till the time of the End.
O holy Generation! Image of regeneration!
O point of mutual forgiveness between Enemies!
Birthplace of the Lamb of God incomprehensible!
The Dead despise & scorn thee, & cast thee out as accursed:
Seeing the Lamb of God in thy gardens & thy palaces:
Where they desire to place the Abomination of Desolation.
Hand sits before his furnace: scorn of others & furious pride:
Freeze round him to bars of steel & to iron rocks beneath
His feet: indignant self-righteousness like whirlwinds of the north:

Rose up against me thundering from the Brook of Albions River
From Ranelagh & Strumbolo. from Cromwells gardens & Chelsea
The place of wounded Soldiers. but when he saw my Mace
Whirld round from heaven to earth. trembling he sat: his cold
Poisons rose up & his sweet deceits coverd them all over
With a tender cloud. As thou art now; such was he O Spectre
I know thy deceit & thy revenges, and unless thou desist
I will certainly create an eternal Hell for thee. Listen!
Be attentive! be obedient! Lo the Furnaces are ready to recieve thee
I will break thee into shivers! & melt thee in the furnaces of death
I will cast thee into forms of abhorrence & torment if thou
Desist not from thine own will, & obey not my stern command:
I am closd up from my children: my Emanation is dividing
And thou my Spectre art divided against me. But mark
I will compell thee to assist me in my terrible labours. To beat
These hypocritic Selfhoods on the Anvils of bitter Death
I am inspired: I act not for myself: for Albions sake
I now am what I am! a horror and an astonishment
Shuddring the heavens to look upon me: Behold what cruelties
Are practised in Babel & Shinar. & have approachd to Zions Hill

While Los spoke. the terrible Spectre fell shuddring before him
Watching his time with glowing eyes to leap upon his prey
Los opend the Furnaces in fear. the Spectre saw to Babel & Shinar
Across all Europe & Asia. he saw the tortures of the Victims.
He saw now from the ouside what he before saw & felt from within
He saw that Los was the sole, uncontrolld Lord of the Furnaces
Groaning he kneeld before Los's iron-shod feet on London Stone,
Hungring & thirsting for Los's life yet pretending obedience.
While Los pursud his speech in threatnings loud & fierce.

Thou art my Pride & Self-righteousness: I have found thee out:
Thou art revealed before me in all thy magnitude & power
Thy Uncircumcised pretences to Chastity must be cut in sunder!
Thy holy wrath & deep deceit cannot avail against me
Nor shalt thou ever assume the triple-form of Albions Spectre
For I am one of the living: dare not to mock my inspired fury
If thou wast cast forth from my life! if I was dead upon the mountains
Thou mightest be pitied & lovd: but now I am living; unless
Thou abstain ravening I will create an eternal Hell for thee.
Take thou this Hammer & in patience heave the thundering Bellows
Take thou these Tongs: strike thou alternate with me: labour obedient
Hand & Hyle & Koban: Skofeld, Kox & Kotope, labour mightily
In the Wars of Babel & Shinar, all their Emanations were
Condensd. Hand has absorbd all his Brethren in his might
All the infant Loves & Graces were lost. for the mighty Hand

Con

Condensd his Emanations into hard opake substances;
And his infant thoughts & desires. into cold, dark, cliffs of death.
His hammer of gold he seizd; and his anvil of adamant.
He siezd the bars of condensd thoughts, to forge them
Into the sword of war: into the bow and arrow:
Into the thundering cannon and into the murdering gun
I saw the limbs formd for exercise. contemnd; & the beauty of
Eternity. lookd upon as deformity & loveliness as a dry tree:
I saw disease forming; a Body of Death around the Lamb
Of God. to destroy Jerusalem. & to devour the body of Albion
By war and stratagem to win the labour of the husbandman:

Awkwardness armd in steel: folly in a helmet of gold:
Weakness with horns & talons: ignorance with a raving beak:
Every Emanative joy forbidden as a Crime:
And the Emanations buried alive in the earth with pomp of religion:
Inspiration denyd; Genius forbidden by laws of punishment:
I saw terrified. I took the sighs & tears & bitter groans:
I lifted them into my Furnaces; to form the spiritual sword.
That lays open the hidden heart: I drew forth the pang
Of sorrow red hot: I workd it on my resolute anvil:
I heated it in the flames of Hand, & Hyle, & Coban
Nine times; Gwendolen & Cambel & Gwineverra

Are melted into the gold, the silver, the liquid ruby,
The crysolite, the topaz, the jacinth, & every precious stone.
Loud roar my Furnaces and loud my hammer is heard:
I labour day and night, I behold the soft affections
Condense beneath my hammer into forms of cruelty
But still I labour in hope, tho' still my tears flow down.
That he who will not defend Truth, may be compelld to defend
A Lie: that he may be snared and caught and snared and taken
That Enthusiasm and Life may not cease: arise Spectre arise.

Thus they contended among the Furnaces with groans, & tears;
Groaning the Spectre heavd the bellows, obeying Loss frowns;
Till the Spaces of Erin were perfected in the furnaces
Of affliction, and Los drew them forth, compelling the harsh Spectre.

To

Into the Furnaces & into the valleys of the Anvils of Death
And into the mountains of the Anvils & of the heavy Hammers
Till he should bring the Sons & Daughters of Jerusalem to be
The Sons & Daughters of Los that he might protect them from
Albions dread Spectres: storming, loud, thunderous & mighty
The Bellows & the Hammers move compelld by Los's hand.

And this is the manner of the Sons of Albion in their strength
They take the Two Contraries which are calld Qualities, with which
Every Substance is clothed, they name them Good & Evil
From them they make an Abstract, which is a Negation
Not only of the Substance from which it is derived
A murderer of its own Body: but also a murderer
Of every Divine Member: it is the Reasoning Power
An Abstract objecting power, that Negatives every thing
This is the Spectre of Man. the Holy Reasoning Power
And in its Holiness is closed the Abomination of Desolation

Therefore Los stands in London building Golgonooza ~
Compelling his Spectre to labours mighty; trembling in fear
The Spectre weeps, but Los unmovd by tears or threats remains

I must Create a System, or be enslavd by another Mans
I will not Reason & Compare: my business is to Create

So Los, in fury & strength: in indignation & burning wrath
Shuddring the Spectre howls. his howlings terrify the night
He stamps around the Anvil, beating blows of stern despair
He curses Heaven & Earth, Day & Night & Sun & Moon
He curses Forest Spring & River, Desart & sandy Waste
Cities & Nations, Families & Peoples, Tongues & Laws
Driven to desperation by Los's terrors & threatning fears

Los cries, Obey my voice & never deviate from my will
And I will be merciful to thee: be thou invisible to all
To whom I make thee invisible, but chief to my own Children
O Spectre of Urthona Reason not against their dear approach
Nor them obstruct with thy temptations of doubt & despair
O Shame O strong & mighty Shame I break thy brazen fetters
If thou refuse, thy present torments will seem southern breezes
To what thou shalt endure if thou obey not my great will.
The Spectre answerd, Art thou not ashamd of those thy Sins
That thou callest thy Children? lo the Law of God commands
That they be offered upon his Altar: O cruelty & torment
For thine are also mine! I have kept silent hitherto.
Concerning my chief delight: but thou hast broken silence
Now I will speak my mind! Where is my lovely Enitharmon
O thou my enemy, where is my Great Sin? She is also thine
I said: now is my grief at worst: incapable of being
Surpassed: but every moment it accumulates more & more
It continues accumulating to eternity! the joys of God advance
For he is Righteous: he is not a Being of Pity & Compassion
He cannot feel Distress: he feeds on Sacrifice & Offering:
Delighting in cries & tears & clothed in holiness & solitude
But my griefs advance also, for ever & ever without end
O that I could cease to be! Despair! I am Despair
Created to be the great example of horror & agony: also my
Prayer is vain I called for compassion: compassion mockd
Mercy & pity threw the grave stone over me & with lead
And iron, bound it over me for ever: Life lives on my
Consuming: & the Almighty hath made me his Contrary
To be all evil, all reversed & for ever dead: knowing
And seeing life, yet living not; how can I then behold
And not tremble; how can I be beheld & not abhorrd

So spoke the Spectre shuddring, & dark tears ran down his shadowy face
Which Los wiped off, but comfort none could give! or beam of hope
Yet ceasd he not from labouring at the roarings of his Forge
With iron & brass Building Golgonooza in great contendings
Till his Sons & Daughters came forth from the Furnaces
At the sublime Labours for Los, compelld the invisible Spectre

To labours mighty, with vast strength with his mighty chains.
In pulsations of time, & extensions of space. like Urns of Beulah
With great labour upon his anvils, & in his ladles the Ore
He lifted, pouring it into the clay ground prepard with art:
Striving with Systems to deliver Individuals from those Systems:
That whenever any Spectre began to devour the Dead,
He might feel the pain as if a man gnawd his own tender nerves.

Then Erin came forth from the Furnaces, & all the Daughters of Beulah
Came from the Furnaces, by Los's mighty power for Jerusalems
Sake: walking up and down among the Spaces of Erin:
And the Sons and Daughters of Los came forth in perfection lovely!
And the Spaces of Erin reachd from the starry heighth, to the starry depth.

Los wept with exceeding joy & all wept with joy together!
They feard they never more should see their Father, who
Was built in from Eternity, in the Cliffs of Albion.

But when the joy of meeting was exhausted in loving embrace;
Again they lament. O what shall we do for lovely Jerusalem?
To protect the Emanations of Albions mighty ones from cruelty?
Sabrina & Ignoge begin to sharpen their beamy spears
Of light and love: their little children stand with arrows of gold:
Ragan is wholly cruel, Scofield is bound in iron armour!
He is like a mandrake in the earth before Reubens gate:
He shoots beneath Jerusalems walls to undermine her foundations!
Vala is but thy Shadow, O thou loveliest among women!
A shadow animated by thy tears O mournful Jerusalem!

Why wilt thou give to her a Body whose life is but a Shade?
Her joy and love, a shade: a shade of sweet repose:
But animated and vegetated, she is a devouring worm:
What shall we do for thee O lovely mild Jerusalem?

And Los said, I behold the finger of God in terrors!
Albion is dead! his Emanation is divided from him!
But I am living! yet I feel my Emanation also dividing
Such thing was never known! O pity me, thou all-piteous-one!
What shall I do! or how exist, divided from Enitharmon?
Yet why despair! I saw the finger of God go forth
Upon my Furnaces, from within the Wheels of Albions Sons:
Fixing their Systems, permanent: by mathematic power
Giving a body to Falshood that it may be cast off for ever.
With Demonstrative Science piercing Apollyon with his own bow!
God is within, & without! he is even in the depths of Hell!

Such were the lamentations of the Labourers in the Furnaces!

And they appeard within & without incircling on both sides
The Starry Wheels of Albions Sons, with Spaces for Jerusalem:
And for Vala the shadow of Jerusalem: the ever mourning shade:
On both sides, within & without beaming gloriously!

Terrified at the sublime Wonder, Los stood before his Furnaces.
And they stood around, terrified with admiration at Erins Spaces
For the Spaces reachd from the starry heighth, to the starry depth.
And they builded Golgonooza: terrible eternal labour!

What are those golden builders doing: where was the burying-place
Of soft Ethinthus? near Tyburns fatal Tree? is that
Mild Zions hills most ancient promontory; near mournful
Ever weeping Paddington? is that Calvary and Golgotha?
Becoming a building of pity and compassion? Lo!
The stones are pity, and the bricks, well wrought affections:
Enameld with love & kindness, & the tiles engraven gold
Labour of merciful hands: the beams & rafters are forgiveness:
The mortar & cement of the work, tears of honesty: the nails,
And the screws & iron braces, are well wrought blandishments,
And well contrived words, firm fixing, never forgotten,
Always comforting the remembrance: the floors, humility,
The ceilings, devotion: the hearths, thanksgiving:
Prepare the furniture O Lambeth in thy pitying looms!
The curtains, woven tears & sighs, wrought into lovely forms
For comfort, there the secret furniture of Jerusalems chamber
Is wrought: Lambeth! the Bride the Lambs Wife loveth thee:
Thou art one with her & knowest not of self in thy supreme joy
Go on, builders in hope: tho Jerusalem wanders far away.
Without the gate of Los: among the dark Satanic wheels.

Fourfold the Sons of Los in their divisions: and fourfold,
The great City of Golgonooza: fourfold toward the north,
And toward the south fourfold, & fourfold toward the east & west
Each within other toward the four points: that toward
Eden, and that toward the World of Generation,
And that toward Beulah, and that toward Ulro:
Ulro is the space of the terrible starry wheels of Albions sons:
But that toward Eden is walled up, till time of renovation:
Yet it is perfect in its building, ornaments & perfection.

And the Four Points are thus beheld in Great Eternity
West, the Circumference: South, the Zenith: North,
The Nadir: East, the Center, unapproachable for ever.
These are the four Faces towards the Four Worlds of Humanity
In every Man. Ezekiel saw them by Chebars flood.
And the Eyes are the South, and the Nostrils are the East.
And the Tongue is the West, and the Ear is the North.

And the North Gate of Golgonooza toward Generation
Has four sculptur'd Bulls terrible before the Gate of iron.
And iron, the Bulls: and that which looks toward Ulro.
Clay bakd & enameld, eternal glowing as four furnaces:
Turning upon the Wheels of Albions Sons with enormous power.
And that toward Beulah four, gold, silver, brass, & iron:

And

And that toward Eden. four. formd of gold. silver. brass. & iron.

The South. a golden Gate. has four Lions terrible. living:
That toward Generation. four. of iron carvd wondrous:
That toward Ulro. four. clay bakd. laborious workmanship
That toward Eden. four; immortal gold. silver. brass & iron.

The Western Gate fourfold. is closd: having four Cherubim
Its guards. living. the work of elemental hands. laborious task:
Like Men. hermaphroditic. each winged with eight wings
That towards Generation. iron; that toward Beulah. stone;
That toward Ulro. clay; that toward Eden. metals.
But all closd up till the last day. when the graves shall yield their
(dead.

The Eastern Gate. fourfold: terrible & deadly its ornaments:
Taking their forms from the Wheels of Albions sons: as cogs
Are formd in a wheel. to fit the cogs of the adverse wheel.

That toward Eden. eternal ice. frozen in seven folds
Of forms of death: and that toward Beulah. stone:
The seven diseases of the earth are carved terrible.
And that toward Ulro. forms of war: seven enormities;
And that toward Generation, seven generative forms.

And every part of the City is fourfold: & every inhabitant. fourfold.
And every pot & vessel & garment & utensil of the houses.
And every house. fourfold; but the third Gate in every one
Is closd. as with a threefold curtain of ivory & fine linen & ermine.
And Luban stands in middle of the City. a moat of fire
Surrounds Luban. Loss Palace & the golden Looms of Cathedron.

And sixty-four thousand Genii. guard the Eastern Gate:
And sixty-four thousand Gnomes. guard the Northern Gate:
And sixty-four thousand Nymphs. guard the Western Gate:
And sixty-four thousand Fairies. guard the Southern Gate:

Around Golgonooza lies the land of death eternal: a Land
Of pain and misery and despair and ever brooding melancholy:
In all the Twenty-seven Heavens. numberd from Adam to Luther:
From the blue Mundane Shell. reaching to the Vegetative Earth.

The Vegetative Universe. opens like a flower from the Earths center:
In which is Eternity. It expands in Stars to the Mundane Shell
And there it meets Eternity again. both within and without.
And the abstract Voids between the Stars are the Satanic Wheels.

There is the Cave; the Rock; the Tree; the Lake of Udan Adan:
The Forest. and the Marsh. and the Pits of bitumen deadly:
The Rocks of solid fire: the Ice valleys; the Plains
Of burning sand; the rivers. cataract & Lakes of Fire:
The Islands of the fiery Lakes; the Trees of Malice; Revenge;
And black Anxiety; and the Cities of the Salamandrine men:
(But whatever is visible to the Generated Man
Is a Creation of mercy & love, from the Satanic Void.)
The land of darkness flamed but no light. & no repose:
The land of snows of trembling. & of iron hail incessant:
The land of earthquakes: and the land of woven labyrinths:
The land of snares & traps & wheels & pit-falls & dire mills:
The Voids. the Solids. & the land of clouds & regions of waters:
With their inhabitants: in the Twenty-seven Heavens beneath Beulah:
Self righteousnesses conglomerating against the Divine Vision:
A Concave Earth wondrous. Chasmal. Abyssal. Incoherent:
Forming the Mundane Shell: above; beneath: on all sides surrounding
Golgonooza: Los walks round the walls night and day.

He views the City of Golgonooza. & its smaller Cities:
The Looms & Mills & Prisons & Work-houses of Og & Anak:
The Amalekite; the Canaanite; the Moabite; the Egyptian:
And all that has existed in the space of six thousand years:
Permanent. & not lost not last nor vanishd. & every little act.
Word. work. & wish. that has existed. all remaining still
In those Churches ever consuming & ever building by the Spectres
Of all the inhabitants of Earth wailing to be Created:
Shadowy to those who dwell not in them. meer possibilities:
But to those who enter into them they seem the only substances
For every thing exists & not one sigh nor smile nor tear,
One

One hair nor particle of dust, not one can pass away.

He views the Cherub at the Tree of Life, also the Serpent,
Orc the first born coild in the south: the Dragon Urizen:
Tharmas the Vegetated Tongue even the Devouring Tongue:
A threefold region, a false brain: a false heart:
And false bowels: altogether composing the False Tongue.
Beneath Beulah: as a watry flame revolving every way
And as dark roots and stems: a Forest of affliction, growing
In seas of sorrow. Los also views the Four Females:
Ahania, and Enion, and Vala, and Enitharmon lovely,
And from them all the lovely beaming Daughters of Albion.
Ahania & Enion & Vala are three evanescent shades:
Enitharmon is a vegetated mortal Wife of Los:
His Emanation, yet his Wife till the sleep of death is past.
Such are the Buildings of Los: & such are the Woofs of Enitharmon:

And Los beheld his Sons, and he beheld his Daughters:
Every one a translucent Wonder: a Universe within
Increasing inwards, into length, and breadth, and heighth:
Starry & glorious: and they every one in their bright loins:
Have a beautiful golden gate which opens into the vegetative world
And every one a gate of rubies & all sorts of precious stones
In their translucent hearts, which opens into the vegetative world:
And every one a gate of iron dreadful and wonderful.
In their translucent heads, which opens into the vegetative world
And every one has the three regions Childhood: Manhood: & Age:
But the gate of the tongue: the western gate, in them is closd.
Having a wall builded against it: and thereby the gates
Eastward & Southward & Northward, are circled with flaming fires.
And the North is Breadth, the South is Heighth & Depth:
The East is Inwards: & the West is Outwards every way.

And Los beheld the mild Emanation Jerusalem eastward bending
Her revolutions toward the Starry Wheels in maternal anguish
Like a pale cloud arising from the arms of Beulahs Daughters:
In Entuthon Benythons deep Vales beneath Golgonooza.

And Hand & Hyle rooted into Jerusalem by a fibre
Of strong revenge & Skofeld Vegetated by Reubens Gate
In every Nation of the Earth till the Twelve Sons of Albion
Enrooted into every Nation; a mighty Polypus growing
From Albion over the whole Earth: such is my awful Vision

I see the Four-fold Man. The Humanity in deadly sleep
And its fallen Emanation. The Spectre & its cruel Shadow
I see the Past, Present & Future, existing all at once
Before me; O Divine Spirit sustain me on thy wings!
That I may awake Albion from his long & cold repose.
For Bacon & Newton sheathd in dismal steel, their terrors hang
Like iron scourges over Albion. Reasonings like vast Serpents
Infold around my limbs, bruising my minute articulations

I turn my eyes to the Schools & Universities of Europe
And there behold the Loom of Locke whose Woof rages dire
Washd by the Water-wheels of Newton. black the cloth
In heavy wreathes folds over every Nation; cruel Works
Of many Wheels I view, wheel without wheel, with cogs tyrannic
Moving by compulsion each other: not as those in Eden: which
Wheel within Wheel in freedom revolve in harmony & peace.

I see in deadly fear in London Los raging round his Anvil
Of death: forming an Ax of gold; the Four Sons of Los
Stand round him cutting the Fibres from Albions hills
That Albions Sons may roll apart over the Nations
While Reuben enroots his brethren in the narrow Canaanite
From the Limit Noah to the Limit Abram in whose Loins
Reuben in his Twelve-fold majesty & beauty shall take refuge
As Abraham flees from Chaldea shaking his goary locks
But first Albion must sleep, divided from the Nations

I see Albion sitting upon his Rock in the first Winter
And thence I see the Chaos of Satan & the World of Adam
When the Divine Hand went forth on Albion in the mid Winter
And at the place of Death when Albion sat in Eternal Death
Among the Furnaces of Los in the Valley of the Son of Hin-
-nom

Hampstead Highgate Finchley Hendon Muswell hill: rage loud
Before Bromions iron tongs & glowing Poker reddening fierce
Hertfordshire glows with fierce Vegetation! in the forests
The Oak frowns terrible, the Beech & Ash & Elm enroot
Among the Spiritual fires; loud the Corn fields thunder along
The Soldiers fife; the Harlots shriek; the Virgins dismal groan
The Parents fear; the Brothers jealousy; the Sisters curse
Beneath the Storms at Theotormon & the thundring Bellows
Heaves in the hand of Palamabron who in Londons darkness
Before the Anvil, watches the bellowing flames: thundering
The Hammer loud rages in Rintrahs strong grasp swinging loud
Round from heaven to earth, down falling with heavy blow
Dead on the Anvil, where the red hot wedge groans in pain
He quenches it in the black trough of his Forge; Londons River
Feeds the dread Forge, trembling & shuddering along the Valleys

Humber & Trent roll dreadful before the Seventh Furnace
And Tweed & Tyne anxious give up their Souls for Albions sake
Lincolnshire Derbyshire Nottinghamshire Leicestershire
From Oxfordshire to Norfolk on the Lake of Udan Adan
Labour within the Furnaces, walking among the Fires
With Ladles huge & iron Pokers over the Island white.

Scotland pours out his Sons to labour at the Furnaces
Wales gives his Daughters to the Looms; England: nursing Mother
Gives to the Children of Albion & to the Children of Jerusalem
From the blue Mundane Shell even to the Earth of Vegetation
Throughout the whole Creation which groans to be delivered
Albion groans in the deep slumbers of Death upon his Rock.

Here Los fixd down the Fifty-two Counties of England & Wales
The Thirty-six of Scotland, & the Thirty-four of Ireland
With mighty power, when they fled out at Jerusalems Gates
Away from the Conflict of Luvah & Urizen, fixing the Gates
In the Twelve Counties of Wales & thence Gates looking every way
To the Four Points: conduct to England & Scotland & Ireland
And thence to all the Kingdoms & Nations & Families of the Earth
The Gate of Reuben in Carmarthenshire: the Gate of Simeon in
Cardiganshire; & the Gate of Levi in Montgomeryshire
The Gate of Judah Merionethshire: the Gate of Dan Flintshire
The Gate of Napthali, Radnorshire: the Gate of Gad Pembrokeshire
The Gate of Asher, Carnarvonshire the Gate of Issachar Brecknockshire
The Gate of Zebulun, in Anglesea & Sodor, so is Wales divided.
The Gate of Joseph Denbighshire: the Gate of Benjamin Glamorganshire
For the protection of the Twelve Emanations of Albions Sons

And the Forty Counties of England are thus divided in the Gates
Of Reuben, Norfolk Suffolk Essex, Simeon Lincoln York Lancashire
Levi. Middlesex Kent Surrey. Judah Somerset Glouster Wiltshire
Dan. Cornwal Devon Dorset. Napthali. Warwick Leicester Worcester
Gad. Oxford Bucks Harford, Asher. Sussex Hampshire Berkshire
Issachar Northampton Rutland Notingham, Zebulun Bedford Hunton Camb
Joseph Stafford Shrops Heref. Benjamin Derby Cheshire Monmouth
And Cumberland Northumberland Westmoreland & Durham are
Divided in the Gates of Reuben Judah Dan & Joseph

And the Thirty-six Counties of Scotland, divided in the Gates
Of Reuben Kincard Haddntn Forfar. Simeon Ayr Argyll Banff
Levi. Edinburgh Roxbro Ross. Judah. Aberdeen Berwik Dumfries
Dan Bute Cathnes Clakmanan. Napthali. Nairn Inverness Linlithgo
Gad Peebles Perth Renfru. Asher Sutherlan Sterling Wigtoun
Issachar Selkirk Dumbartn Glasco Zebulun Orkney Shetland Skye
Joseph Elgin Lanerk Kinros, Benjamin Kromarty Murra Kirkubright
Governing all by the sweet delights of secret amorous glances
In Enitharmons Halls builded by Los & his mighty Children

All things acted on Earth are seen in the bright Sculptures of
Los's Halls & every Age renews its powers from these Works
With every pathetic story possible to happen from Hate or
Wayward Love & every sorrow & distress is carved here
Every Affinity of Parents Marriages & Friendships are here
In all their various combinations wrought with wondrous Art
All that can happen to Man in his pilgrimage of seventy years
Such is the Divine Written Law of Horeb & Sinai:
And such the Holy Gospel of Mount Olivet & Calvary:

His Spectre divides & Los in fury compells it to divide:
To labour in the fire. in the water. in the earth. in the air.
To follow the Daughters of Albion as the hound follows the scent
Of the wild inhabitant of the forest. to drive them from his own:
To make a way for the Children of Los to come from the Furnaces
But Los himself against Albions Sons his fury bends. for he
Dare not approach the Daughters openly lest he be consumed
In the fires of their beauty & perfection & be Vegetated beneath
Their Looms. in a Generation of death & resurrection to forgetfulness
They woo Los continually to subdue his strength: he continually
Shews them his Spectre: sending him abroad over the four points of heaven
In the fierce desires of beauty & in the tortures of repulse! He is
The Spectre of the Living pursuing the Emanations of the Dead.
Shuddring they flee: they hide in the Druid Temples in cold chastity:
Subdued by the Spectre of the Living & terrified by undisguised desire.

For Los said: Tho my Spectre is divided: as I am a Living Man
I must compell him to obey me wholly: that Enitharmon may not
Be lost: & lest he should devour Enitharmon: Ah me
Piteous image of my soft desires & loves: O Enitharmon.
I will compell my Spectre to obey: I will restore to thee thy Children.
No one bruises or starves himself to make himself fit for labour:

Tormented with sweet desire for these beauties of Albion
They would never love my power if they did not seek to destroy
Enitharmon: Vala would never have sought & loved Albion
If she had not sought to destroy Jerusalem: such is that false
And Generating Love: a pretence of love to destroy love:
Cruel hipocrisy unlike the lovely delusions of Beulah:
And cruel forms, unlike the merciful forms of Beulahs Night

They know not why they love nor wherefore they sicken & die
Calling that Holy Love: which is Envy Revenge & Cruelty Man
Which separated the stars from the mountains: the mountains from
And left Man a little grovelling Root, outside of Himself
Negations are not Contraries: Contraries mutually Exist:
But Negations Exist Not: Exceptions & Objections & Unbeliefs
Exist not: nor shall they ever be Organized for ever & ever:
If thou separate from me, thou art a Negation: a meer
Reasoning & Derogation from me, an Objecting & cruel Spite
And Malice & Envy: but my Emanation. Alas! will become
My Contrary: O thou Negation. I will continually compell
Thee to be invisible to any but whom I please. & when
And where & how I please. and never! never! shalt thou be Organized
But as a distorted & reversed Reflexion in the Darkness
And in the Non Entity: nor shall that which is above
Ever descend into thee: but thou shalt be a Non Entity for ever
And if any enter into thee. thou shalt be an Unquenchable Fire
And he shall be a never dying Worm. mutually tormented by
Those that thou tormentest. a Hell & Despair for ever & ever.

So Los in secret with himself communed & Enitharmon heard
In her darkness & was comforted: yet still she divided away
In gnawing pain from Los's bosom in the deadly Night:
First as a red Globe of blood trembling beneath his bosom
Suspended over her he hung: he infolded her in his garments
Of wool: he hid her from the Spectre in shame & confusion of
Face: in terrors & pains of Hell & Eternal Death, the
Trembling Globe shot forth Self-living & Los howld over it:
Feeding it with his groans & tears day & night without ceasing:
And the Spectrous Darkness from his back divided in temptations,
And in grinding agonies in threats: stiflings: & direful strugglings

Go thou to Skofeld: ask him if he is Bath or if he is Canterbury
Tell him to be no more dubious: demand explicit words
Tell him: I will dash him into shivers, where & at what time
I please: tell Hand & Skofield they are my ministers of evil
To those I hate: for I can hate also as well as they:

From every-one of the Four Regions of Human Majesty.
There is an Outside spread Without, & an Outside spread Within
Beyond the Outline of Identity both ways. which meet in One:
An orbed Void of doubt. despair, hunger, & thirst & sorrow.
Here the Twelve Sons of Albion: joind in dark Assembly.
Jealous of Jerusalems children, ashamd of her little-ones
(For Vala produced the Bodies. Jerusalem gave the Souls)
Became as Three Immense Wheels, turning upon one-another
Into Non-Entity. and their thunders hoarse appall the Dead
To murder their own Souls. to build a Kingdom among the Dead.

Cast! Cast ye Jerusalem forth! The Shadow of delusions!
The Harlot daughter! Mother of pity and dishonourable forgiveness
Our Father Albions sin and shame! But Father now no more!
Nor sons; nor hateful peace & love, nor soft complacencies
With transgressors meeting in brotherhood around the table,
Or in the porch or garden. No more the sinful delights
Of age, and youth and, boy and girl, and animal and herb.
And river and mountain, and city & village, and house & family.
Beneath the Oak & Palm. beneath the Vine and Fig-tree.
In self-denial! - But War and deadly contention, Between
Father and Son, and light and love! All bold asperities
Of Haters met in deadly strife, rending the house & garden
The unforgiving porches, the tables of enmity, and beds
And chambers of trembling & suspition. hatreds of age & youth
And boy & girl, & animal & herb, & river & mountain
And city & village, and house & family. That the Perfect
May live in glory, redeemd by Sacrifice of the Lamb
And of his children, before sinful Jerusalem. To build
Babylon the City of Vala, the Goddess Virgin-Mother.
She is our Mother! Nature! Jerusalem is our Harlot-Sister
Returnd with Children of pollution, to defile our House.
With Sin and Shame. Cast! Cast her into the Potters field.
Her little-ones She must slay upon our Altars: and her aged
Parents must be carried into captivity, to redeem her Soul
To be for a Shame & a Curse, and to be our Slaves for ever

So cry Hand & Hyle the eldest of the fathers of Albions
Little-ones; to destroy the Divine Saviour: the Friend of Sinners.
Building Castles in desolated places, and strong Fortifications.
Soon Hand mightily devourd & absorbd Albions Twelve Sons.
Out from his bosom a mighty Polypus. vegetating in darkness.
And Hyle & Coban were his two chosen ones. For Emissaries
In War: forth from his bosom they went and returnd.
Like Wheels from a great Wheel reflected in the Deep
Hoarse, turnd the Starry Wheels. rending a way in Albions Loins
Beyond the Night of Beulah. In a dark & unknown Night.
Outstretchd his Giant beauty on the ground in pain & tears.

His Children exil'd from his breast, pass to and fro before him
His birds are silent on his hills, flocks die beneath his branches
His tents are falln! his trumpets, and the sweet sound of his harp
Are silent on his clouded hills, that belch forth storms, & fire,
His milk of Cows, & honey of Bees, & fruit of golden harvest,
Is gatherd in the scorching heat, & in the driving rain:
Where once he sat he weary walks in misery and pain:
His Giant beauty and perfection fallen into dust:
Till from within his witherd breast grown narrow with his woes:
The corn is turnd to thistles & the apples into poison:
The birds of song to murderous crows, his joys to bitter groans!
The voices of children in his tents, to cries of helpless infants!
And self-exiled from the face of light & shine of morning,
In the dark world a narrow house! he wanders up and down,
Seeking for rest and finding none! and hidden far within,
His Eon weeping in the cold and desolated Earth.

All his Affections now appear withoutside: all his Sons,
Hand, Hyle & Coban: Guantok, Peachey, Brereton, Slayd & Hutton,
Scofeld, Kox, Kotope & Bowen; his Twelve Sons: Satanic Mill:
Who are the Spectres of the Twentyfour, each Double-form'd:
Revolve upon his mountains groaning in pain; beneath
The dark incessant sky, seeking for rest and finding none:
Raging against their Human natures, ravning to gormandize
The Human majesty and beauty of the Twentyfour,
Condensing them into solid rocks with cruelty and abhorrence
Suspition & revenge, & the seven diseases of the Soul
Settled around Albion and around Luvah in his secret cloud
Willing the Friends endurd, for Albions sake, and for
Jerusalem his Emanation, shut within his bosom:
Which hardend against them more and more: as he builded onwards
On the Gulph of Death in self-righteousness, that rolld
Before his awful feet, in pride of virtue for victory:
And Los was roofd in from Eternity in Albions Cliffs
Which stand upon the ends of Beulah, and withoutside, all
Appeard a rocky form against the Divine Humanity.

Albions Circumference was closd: his Center began darkning
Into the Night of Beulah, and the Moon of Beulah rose
Clouded with storms: Los his strong Guard walkd round beneath the
And Albion fled inward among the currents of his rivers.   Moon

He found Jerusalem upon the River of his City soft reposd
In the arms of Vala, assimilating in one with Vala
The Lilly of Havilah: and they sang soft thro' Lambeths vales,
In a sweet moony night & silence that they had created
With a blue sky spread over with wings and a mild moon,
Dividing & uniting into many female forms: Jerusalem
Trembling! then in one commingling in eternal tears,
Sighing to melt his Giant beauty, on the moony river.

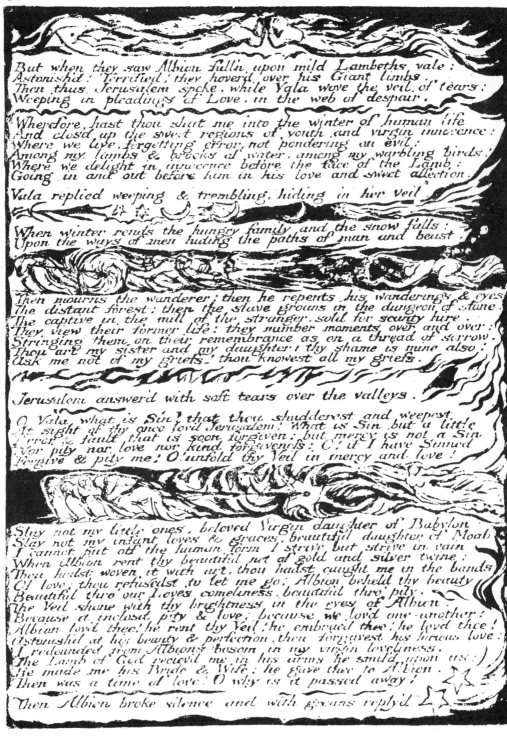

But when they saw Albion fall'n upon mild Lambeths vale:
Astonish'd! Terrified! they hoverd over his Giant limbs.
Then thus Jerusalem spoke. while Vala weve the veil of tears:
Weeping in pleadings of Love. in the web of despair.

Wherefore, hast thou shut me into the winter of human life
And closd up the sweet regions of youth and virgin innocence:
Where we live, forgetting error, not pondering on evil:
Among my lambs & brooks of water, among my warbling birds:
Where we delight in innocence before the face of the Lamb:
Going in and out before him in his love and sweet affection.

Vala replied weeping & trembling, hiding in her veil

When winter rends the hungry family and the snow falls:
Upon the ways of men hiding the paths of man and beast.

Then mourns the wanderer: then he repents his wanderings & eyes
The distant forest: then the slave groans in the dungeon of stone.
The captive in the mill of the stranger. sold for scanty hire.
They view their former life: they number moments over and over:
Stringing them on their remembrance as on a thread of sorrow.
Thou art my sister and my daughter! thy shame is mine also:
Ask me not of my griefs! thou knowest all my griefs.

Jerusalem answer'd with soft tears over the valleys.

O Vala, what is Sin? that thou shudderest and weepest
At sight of thy once lovd Jerusalem! What is Sin but a little
Error & fault that is soon forgiven: but mercy is not a Sin
Nor pity nor love nor kind forgiveness! O! if I have Sinned
Forgive & pity me! O! unfold thy Veil in mercy and love!

Slay not my little ones, beloved Virgin daughter of Babylon
Slay not my infant loves & graces, beautiful daughter of Moab
I cannot put off the human form I strive but strive in vain
When Albion rent thy beautiful net of gold and silver twine:
Thou hadst woven it with art, thou hadst caught me in the bands
Of love; thou refusedst to let me go: Albion beheld thy beauty
Beautiful thro' our Loves comeliness, beautiful thro' pity.
The Veil shone with thy brightness in the eyes of Albion.
Because it inclosd pity & love; because we lovd one-another!
Albion lovd thee! he rent thy Veil! he embraced thee! he lovd thee!
Astonishd at his beauty & perfection, thou forgavest his furious love:
I redounded from Albions bosom in my virgin loveliness.
The Lamb of God recievd me in his arms he smild upon us:
He made me his Bride & Wife: he gave thee to Albion.
Then was a time of love! O why is it passed away!

Then Albion broke silence and with groans replyd

O Vala! O Jerusalem! do you delight in my groans
You O lovely forms, you have prepared my death-cup:
The disease of Shame covers me from head to feet: I have no hope
Every boil upon my body is a separate & deadly Sin.
Doubt first assaild me, then Shame took possession of me
Shame divides Families. Shame hath divided Albion in sunder.
First fled my Sons, & then my Daughters, then my Wild Animations
My Cattle next, last ev'n the Dog of my Gate. the Forests fled
The Corn-fields, & the breathing Gardens outside separated.
The Sea; the Stars; the Sun; the Moon; driv'n forth by my disease
All is Eternal Death unless you can weave a chaste
Body over an unchaste Mind! Vala! O that thou wert pure!
That the deep wound of Sin might be closd up with the Needle,
And with the Loom: to cover Gwendolen & Ragan with costly Robes
Of Natural Virtue, for their Spiritual forms without a Veil
Wither in Luvahs Sepulcher. I thrust him from my presence
And all my Children followd his loud howlings into the Deep.
Jerusalem! dissembler Jerusalem! I look into thy bosom:
I discover thy secret places: Cordella! I behold
Thee whom I thought pure as the heavens in innocence & fear:
Thy Tabernacle taken down, thy secret Cherubim disclosed
Art thou broken? Ah me Sabrina, running by my side:
In childhood what wert thou? unutterable anguish! Conwenna
Thy cradled infancy is most piteous. O hide, O hide!
Their secret gardens were made paths to the traveller:
I knew not of their secret loves with those I hated most.
Nor that their every thought was Sin & secret appetite
Hyle sees in fear, he howls in fury over them, Hand sees
In jealous fear; in stern accusation with cruel stripes
He drives them thro' the Streets of Babylon before my face!
Because they taught Luvah to rise into my clouded heavens
Battersea and Chelsea mourn for Camhel & Gwendolen!
Hackney and Holloway sicken for Estrild & Ignoge!
Because the Peak. Malvern & Cheviot Reason in Cruelty
Penmaenmawr & Dhinas-bran Demonstrate in Unbelief
Manchester & Liverpool are in tortures of Doubt & Despair
Malden & Colchester Demonstrate: I hear my Childrens voices
I see their piteous faces gleam out upon the cruel winds
From Lincoln & Norwich, from Edinburgh & Monmouth:
I see them distant from my bosom scourgd along the roads
Then lost in clouds; I hear their tender voices! clouds divide
I see them die beneath the whips of the Captains; they are taken
In solemn pomp into Chaldea across the breadths of Europe
Six months they lie embalmd in silent death: warshipped
Carried in Arks of Oak before the armies in the spring
Bursting their Arks they rise again to life; they play before
The Armies: I hear their loud cymbals & their deadly cries
Are the Dead cruel? are those who are infolded in moral Law
Revengeful? O that Death & Annihilation were the same!

Then Vala answerd spreading her scarlet Veil over Albion

—ded me
Albion thy fear has made me tremble; thy terrors have surroun-
thy Sons have naild me on the Gates piercing my hands & feet;
Till Skofields Nimrod the mighty Huntsman Jehovah came.
With Cush his Son & took me down. He in a golden Ark,
Bears me before his Armies tho my Shadow hovers here
The flesh of multitudes fed & nourisd me in my childhood
My morn & evening food were prepard in Battles of Men
Great is the cry of the Hounds of Nimrod along the Valley
Of Vision, they scent the odor of War in the Valley of Vision
All Love is lost! terror succeeds & Hatred instead of Love
And stern demands of Right & Duty instead of Liberty
Once thou wast to me the loveliest Son of heaven; but now
Where shall I hide from thy dread countenance & searching eyes
I have looked into the secret Soul of him I loved
And in the dark recesses found Sin & cannot never return.

Albion again utterd his voice beneath the silent Moon

I brought Love into light of day to pride in chaste beauty
I brought Love into light & fancied Innocence is no more

Then spoke Jerusalem O Albion! my Father Albion
Why wilt thou number every little fibre of my Soul
Spreading them out before the Sun like stalks of flax to dry!
The Infant Joy is beautiful, but its anatomy
Horrible ghast & deadly! nought shalt thou find in it
But dark despair & everlasting brooding melancholy:

Then Albion turnd his face toward Jerusalem & spoke

Hide thou Jerusalem in impalpable voidness, not to be
Touchd by the hand nor seen with the eye: O Jerusalem
Would thou wert not & that thy place might never be found
But come O Vala with knife & cup; drain my blood
To the last drop! then hide me in thy Scarlet Tabernacle
For I see Luvah whom I slew, I behold him in my Spectre
As I behold Jerusalem in thee O Vala dark and cold

Jerusalem then stretchd her hand toward the Moon & spoke

Why should Punishment Weave the Veil with Iron Wheels of War
When Forgiveness might it Weave with Wings of Cherubim

Loud groand Albion from mountain to mountain & replied

Jerusalem! Jerusalem! deluding shadow of Albion!
Daughter of my phantasy! unlawful pleasure! Albions curse!
I came here with intention to annihilate thee! But
My soul is melted away, inwoven within the Veil
Hast thou again knitted the Veil of Vala, which I for thee
Pitying rent in ancient times, I see it whole and more
Perfect, and shining with beauty! But thou! O wretched Father!

Jerusalem reply'd, like a voice heard from a sepulcher:
Father! once piteous! Is Pity a Sin! Embalmd in Valas bosom
In an Eternal Death for Albions sake, our best beloved.
Thou art my Father & my Brother. Why hast thou hidden me,
Remote from the divine Vision: my Lord and Saviour.

Trembling stood Albion at her words in jealous dark despair;

He felt that Love and Pity are the same; a soft repose!
Inward complacency of Soul: a Self-annihilation!

I have erred! I am ashamed! and will never return more:
I have taught my children sacrifices of cruelty: what shall I answer?
I will hide it from Eternals! I will give myself for my Children!
Which way soever I turn, I behold Humanity and Pity!

He recoild: he rushd outwards: he bore the Veil whole away.
His fires redound from his Dragon Altars in Errors returning
He drew the Veil of Moral Virtue, woven for Cruel Laws,
And cast it into the Atlantic Deep, to catch the Souls of the Dead.
He stood between the Palm tree & the Oak of weeping
Which stand upon the edge of Beulah; and there Albion sunk
Down in sick pallid languor! These were his last words, relapsing
Hoarse from his rocks, from caverns of Derbyshire & Wales
And Scotland, utter'd from the Circumference into Eternity.

Blasphemous Sons of Feminine delusion! God in the dreary Void
Dwells from Eternity, wide separated from the Human Soul
But thou deluding Image by whom imbu'd the Veil I rent
Lo here is Valas Veil whole, for a Law, a Terror & a Curse!
And therefore God takes vengeance on me: from my clay-cold bosom
My children wander trembling victims of his Moral Justice.
His snows fall on me and cover me, while in the Veil I fold
My dying limbs. Therefore O Manhood, if thou art aught
But a meer Phantasy, hear dying Albions Curse!
May God who dwells in this dark Ulro & voidness, vengeance take,
And draw thee down into this Abyss of sorrow and torture,
Like me thy Victim. O that Death & Annihilation were the same!

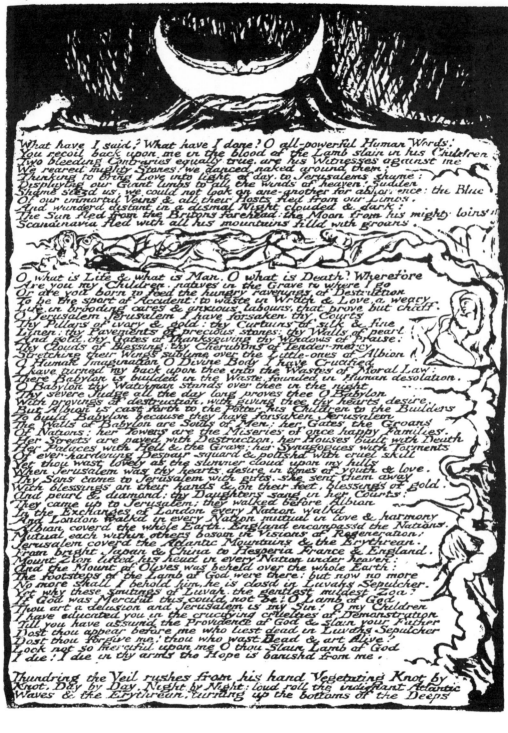

What have I said? What have I done? O all-powerful Human Words!
You recoil back upon me in the blood of the Lamb slain in his Children.
Two bleeding Contraries equally true, are his Witnesses against me
We reared mighty Stones: we danced naked around them:
Thinking to bring Love into light of day, to Jerusalems shame:
Displaying our Giant limbs to all the winds of heaven: Sudden
Shame siezd us, we could not look on one-another for abhorrence: the Blue
Of our immortal Veins & all their Hosts fled from our Limbs,
And wanderd distant in a dismal Night clouded & dark:
The Sun fled from the Britons forehead: the Moon from his mighty loins:
Scandinavia fled with all his mountains filld with groans.

O what is Life & what is Man. O what is Death? Wherefore
Are you my Children, natives in the Grave to where I go
Or are you born to feed the hungry ravenings of Destruction
To be the sport of Accident! to waste in Wrath & Love, a weary
Life in brooding cares & anxious labours, that prove but chaff.
O Jerusalem Jerusalem I have forsaken thy Courts
Thy Pillars of ivory & gold: thy Curtains of silk & fine
Linen: thy Pavements of precious stones: thy Walls of pearl
And gold, thy Gates of Thanksgiving thy Windows of Praise:
Thy Clouds of Blessing; thy Cherubims of Tender-mercy
Stretching their Wings sublime over the Little-ones of Albion
O Human Imagination O Divine Body I have Crucified,
I have turned my back upon thee into the Wastes of Moral Law:
There Babylon is builded in the Waste, founded in Human desolation.
O Babylon thy Watchman stands over thee in the night
Thy severe Judge all the day long proves thee O Babylon
With provings of destruction, with giving thee thy hearts desire.
But Albion is cast forth to the Potter his Children to the Builders
To build Babylon because they have forsaken Jerusalem
The Walls of Babylon are Souls of Men: her Gates the Groans
Of Nations: her Towers are the Miseries of once happy Families.
Her Streets are paved with Destruction, her Houses built with Death
Her Palaces with Hell & the Grave: her Synagogues with Torments
Of ever-hardening Despair squard & polishd with cruel skill
Yet thou wast lovely as the summer cloud upon my hills
When Jerusalem was thy hearts desire in times of youth & love.
Thy Sons came to Jerusalem with gifts, she sent them away
With blessings on their hands & on their feet, blessings of gold:
And pearl & diamond: thy Daughters sang in her Courts:
They came up to Jerusalem; they walked before Albion
In the Exchanges of London every Nation walkd
And London walkd in every Nation mutual in love & harmony
Albion coverd the whole Earth. England encompass'd the Nations.
Mutual each within others bosom in Visions of Regeneration:
Jerusalem coverd the Atlantic Mountains & the Erythrean,
From bright Japan & China to Hesperia France & England.
Mount Zion lifted his head in every Nation under heaven.
And the Mount of Olives was beheld over the whole Earth:
The footsteps of the Lamb of God were there: but now no more
No more shall I behold him, he is closd in Luvahs Sepulcher
Yet why these smitings of Luvah, the gentlest mildest Zoa?
If God was Merciful this could not be: O Lamb of God
Thou art a delusion and Jerusalem is my Sin! O my Children
I have educated you in the crucifying cruelties of Demonstration
Till you have assum'd the Providence of God & slain your Father
Dost thou appear before me who liest dead in Luvahs Sepulcher
Dost thou forgive me! thou who wast Dead & art Alive?
Look not so merciful upon me O thou Slain Lamb of God
I die! I die in thy arms tho Hope is banishd from me.

Thundring the Veil rushes from his hand Vegetating Knot by
Knot. Day by Day, Night by Night: loud roll the indignant Atlantic
Waves & the Erythrean, turning up the bottoms of the Deeps

And there was heard a great lamenting in Beulah: all the Regions
Of Beulah were moved as the tender bowels are moved: & they said:

Why did you take Vengeance O ye Sons of the mighty Albion?
Planting these Oaken Groves: Erecting these Dragon Temples
Injury the Lord heals but Vengeance cannot be healed:
As the Sons of Albion have done to Luvah: so they have in him
Done to the Divine Lord & Saviour, who suffers with those that suffer:
For not one sparrow can suffer, & the whole Universe not suffer also,
In all its Regions, & its Father & Saviour not pity and weep.
But Vengeance is the destroyer of Grace & Repentance in the bosom
Of the Injurer: in which the Divine Lamb is cruelly slain;
Descend O Lamb of God & take away the imputation of Sin
By the Creation of States & the deliverance of Individuals Evermore Amen

Thus wept they in Beulah over the Four Regions of Albion
But many doubted & despaird & imputed Sin & Righteousness
To Individuals & not to States, and these Slept in Ulro.

To the Jews.

Jerusalem the Emanation of the Giant Albion! Can it be? Is it a
Truth that the Learned have explored? Was Britain the Primitive Seat of
the Patriarchal Religion? If it is true: my title-page is also True, that
Jerusalem was & is the Emanation of the Giant Albion. It is True, and
cannot be controverted. Ye are united O ye Inhabitants of Earth in One
Religion. The Religion of Jesus: the most Ancient, the Eternal: & the
Everlasting Gospel – The Wicked will turn it to Wickedness, the Righte-
ous to Righteousness. Amen! Huzza! Selah!
  "All things Begin & End in Albions Ancient Druid Rocky Shore."
  Your Ancestors derived their origin from Abraham, Heber, Shem, and
Noah, who were Druids: as the Druid Temples (which are the Patriarch-
al Pillars & Oak Groves) over the whole Earth witness to this day.
  You have a tradition, that Man anciently containd in his mighty limbs
all things in Heaven & Earth: this you recieved from the Druids.
  "But now the Starry Heavens are fled from the mighty limbs of Albion"
  Albion was the Parent of the Druids; & in his Chaotic State of Sleep
Satan & Adam & the whole World was Created by the Elohim.

The fields from Islington to Marybone,
To Primrose Hill and Saint Johns Wood:
Were builded over with pillars of gold,
And there Jerusalems pillars stood.

Her Little-ones run on the fields
The Lamb of God among them seen
And fair Jerusalem his Bride:
Among the little meadows green.

Pancrass & Kentish-town repose
Among her golden pillars high:
Among her golden arches which
Shine upon the starry sky.

The Jews-harp-house & the Green Man;
The Ponds where Boys to bathe delight:
The fields of Cows by Willans farm:
Shine in Jerusalems pleasant sight.

She walks upon our meadows green:
The Lamb of God walks by her side:
And every English Child is seen,
Children of Jesus & his Bride,

Forgiving trespasses and sins
Lest Babylon with cruel Og,
With Moral & Self-righteous Law
Should Crucify in Satans Synagogue!

What are those golden Builders doing
Near mournful ever-weeping Paddington
Standing above that mighty Ruin
Where Satan the first victory won.

Where Albion slept beneath the Fatal Tree
And the Druids golden Knife,
Rioted in human gore,
In Offerings of Human Life

They groand aloud on London Stone
They groand aloud on Tyburns Brook
Albion gave his deadly groan,
And all the Atlantic Mountains shook

Albions Spectre from his Loins
Tore forth in all the pomp of War!
Satan his name: in flames of fire
He stretchd his Druid Pillars far.

Jerusalem fell from Lambeths Vale,
Down thro Poplar & Old Bow;
Thro Malden & across the Sea,
In War & howling death & woe.

The Rhine was red with human blood:
The Danube rolld a purple tide:
On the Euphrates Satan stood:
And over Asia stretch'd his pride.

He witherd up sweet Zions Hill,
From every Nation of the Earth:
He witherd up Jerusalems Gates,
And in a dark Land gave her birth.

He witherd up the Human Form,
By laws of sacrifice for sin:
Till it became a Mortal Worm:
But O! translucent all within.

The Divine Vision still was seen
Still was the Human Form, Divine
Weeping in weak & mortal clay
O Jesus still the Form was thine.

And thine the Human Face & thine
The Human Hands & Feet & Breath
Entering thro the Gates of Birth
And passing thro the Gates of Death

And O thou Lamb of God, whom I
Slew in my dark self-righteous pride;
Art thou returnd to Albions Land!
And is Jerusalem thy Bride?

Come to my arms & never more
Depart; but dwell for ever here:
Create my Spirit to thy Love:
Subdue thy Spectre to thy Fear.

Spectre of Albion! warlike Fiend!
In clouds of blood & ruin rolld:
I here reclaim thee as my own
My Selfhood; Satan! armd in gold.

Is this thy soft Family-Love
Thy cruel Patriarchal pride
Planting thy Family alone,
Destroying all the World beside.

A mans worst enemies are those
Of his own house & family;
And he who makes his law a curse,
By his own law shall surely die.

In my Exchanges every Land
Shall walk, & mine in every Land,
Mutual shall build Jerusalem:
Both heart in heart & hand in hand

If Humility is Christianity; you O Jews are the True Christians; If
your tradition that Man contained in his Limbs, all Animals, is True &
they were separated from him by cruel Sacrifices: and when compulsory
cruel Sacrifices had brought Humanity into a Feminine Tabernacle, in the
loins of Abraham & David: the Lamb of God, the Saviour became apparent on Earth as the Prophets had foretold? The Return of Israel is a Return to Mental Sacrifice & War. Take up the Cross O Israel & follow Jesus.

Jerusalem.
Chap. 2.

Every ornament of perfection. and every labour of love.
In all the Garden of Eden. & in all the golden mountains
Was become an envied horror. and a remembrance of jealousy:
And every Act a Crime. and Albion the punisher & judge.

And Albion spoke from his secret seat and said

All these ornaments are crimes. they are made by the labours
Of loves: of unnatural consanguinities and friendships
Horrid to think of when enquired deeply into; and all
These hills & valleys are accursed witnesses of Sin
I therefore, condense them into solid rocks. stedfast.
A foundation and certainty and demonstrative truth:
That Man be separate from Man, & here I plant my seat.

Cold snows drifted around him: ice coverd his loins around
He sat by Tyburns brook, and underneath his heel shot up!
A deadly Tree, he namd it Moral Virtue, and the Law
Of God who dwells in Chaos hidden from the human sight.

The Tree spread over him its cold shadows. (Albion groand)
They bent down, they felt the earth and again enrooting
Shot into many a Tree: an endless labyrinth of woe!

From willing sacrifice of Self, to sacrifice of (miscall'd) Enemies
For Atonement: Albion begun to erect twelve Altars,
Of rough unhewn rocks, before the Potters Furnace
He namd them Justice, and Truth. And Albions Sons
Must have become the first Victims, being the first transgressors
But they fled to the mountains to seek ransom: building A Strong
Fortification against the Divine Humanity and Mercy,
In Shame & Jealousy to annihilate Jerusalem.

Turning his back to the Divine Vision. his Spectrous
Chaos before his face appeard: an Unformed Memory

Then spoke the Spectrous Chaos to Albion darkning cold
From the back & loins where dwell the Spectrous Dead

I am your Rational Power O Albion & that Human Form
You call Divine. is but a Worm seventy inches long
That creeps forth in a night & is dried in the morning sun
In fortuitous concourse of memorys accumulated & lost
It plows the Earth in its own conceit, it overwhelms the Hills
Beneath its winding labyrinths. till a stone of the brook
Stops it in midst of its pride among its hills & rivers
Battersea & Chelsea mourn. London & Canterbury tremble
Their place shall not be found as the wind passes over
The ancient Cities of the Earth remove as a traveller,
And shall Albions Cities remain when I pass over them
With my deluge of forgotten remembrances over the tablet

So spoke the Spectre to Albion. he is the Great Selfhood
Satan: Worshipd as God by the Mighty Ones of the Earth
Having a white Dot calld a Center from which branches out
A Circle in continual gyrations. this became a Heart
From which sprang numerous branches varying their motions
Producing many Heads three or seven or ten. & hands & feet
Innumerable at will of the unfortunate contemplator
Who becomes his food such is the way of the Devouring Power

And this is the cause of the appearance in the frowning Chaos
Albions Emanation which he had hidden in Jealousy
Appeard now in the frowning Chaos prolific upon the Chaos
Reflecting back to Albion in Sexual Reasoning Hermaphrodine
Albion spoke. Who art thou that appearest in gloomy pomp
Involving the Divine Vision in colours of autumn ripeness
I never saw thee till this time. nor beheld life abstracted
Nor darkness immingled with light on my furrowd field
Whence camest thou who art thou O loveliest the Divine Vision
Is as nothing before thee. faded is all life and joy

Vala replied in clouds of tears Albions garment embracing

I was a City & a Temple built by Albions Children.
I was a Garden planted with beauty I allured on hill & valley
The River of Life to flow against my walls & among my trees
Vala was Albions Bride & Wife in great Eternity
The loveliest of the daughters of Eternity when in day-break
I emanated from Luvah over the Towers of Jerusalem
And in her Courts among her little Children offering up
The Sacrifice of fanatic love. why loved I Jerusalem
Why was I one with her embracing in the Vision of Jesus
Wherefore did I loving create love. which never yet
Immingled God & Man. when thou & I. hid the Divine Vision
In cloud of secret gloom which behold involve me round about
Know me now Albion: look upon me I alone. am Beauty
The Imaginative Human Form is but a breathing of Vala
I breathe him forth into the Heaven from my secret Cave
Born of the Woman to obey the Woman O Albion the mighty
For the Divine appearance is Brotherhood. but I am Love

Elevate into the Region of Brotherhood with my red fires

Art thou Vala? replied Albion, image of my repose
O how I tremble! how my members pour down milky fear!
A dewy garment covers me all over, all manhood is gone!
At thy word & at thy look death enrobes me about
From head to feet, a garment of death & eternal fear
Is not that Sun thy husband & that Moon thy glimmering Veil!
Are not the Stars of heaven thy Children! art thou not Babylon?
Art thou Nature Mother of all! is Jerusalem thy Daughter
Why have thou elevate inward: O dweller of outward chambers
From grot & cave beneath the Moon dim region of death
Where I laid my Plow in the hot noon, where my hot team fed
Where implements of War are forged, the Plow to go over the Nations
In pain girding me round like a rib of iron in heaven: O Vala
In Eternity they neither marry nor are given in marriage
Albion the high Cliff of the Atlantic is become a barren Land

Los stood at his Anvil: he heard the contentions of Vala
He heavd his thundring Bellows upon the valleys of Middlesex
He opend his Furnaces before Vala, then Albion frownd in anger
On his Rock, ere yet the Starry Heavens were fled away
From his awful Members. and thus Los cried aloud
To the Sons of Albion & to Hand the eldest Son of Albion
I hear the screech of Childbirth loud pealing. & the groans
Of Death, in Albions clouds dreadful utterd over all the Earth
What may Man be? who can tell! but what may Woman be?
To have power over Man from Cradle to corruptible Grave.
There is a Throne in every Man, it is the Throne of God
This Woman has claimd as her own & Man is no more!
Albion is the Tabernacle of Vala & her Temple
And not the Tabernacle & Temple of the Most High
O Albion why wilt thou Create a Female Will?
To hide the most evident God in a hidden covert, even
In the shadows of a Woman & a secluded Holy Place
That we may pry after him as after a stolen treasure
Hidden among the Dead & mured up from the paths of life
Hand! art thou not Reuben enrooting thyself into Bashan
Till thou remainest a vaporous Shadow in a Void! O Merlin
Unknown among the Dead where never before Existence came
Is this the Female Will O ye lovely Daughters of Albion. To
Converse concerning Weight & Distance in the Wilds of Newton & Locke

So Los spoke standing on Mam-Tor looking over Europe & Asia
The Graves thunder beneath his feet from Ireland to Japan

Reuben slept in Bashan like one dead in the valley
Cut off from Albions mountains & from all the Earths summits
Between Succoth & Zaretan beside the Stone of Bohan
While the Daughters of Albion divided Luvah into three Bodies
Los bended his Nostrils down to the Earth, then sent him over
Jordan to the Land of the Hittite: every-one that saw him
Fled! they fled at his horrible Form: they hid in caves
And dens, they looked on one-another & became what they beheld.

Reuben returnd to Bashan, in despair he slept on the Stone.
The Gwendolen divided into Rahab & Tirza in Twelve Portions
Los rolled his Eyes into two narrow circles, then sent him
Over Jordan; all terrified fled: they became what they beheld.
If Perceptive Organs vary: Objects of Perception seem to vary:
If the Perceptive Organs close: their Objects seem to close also:
Consider this O mortal Man: O worm of sixty winters said Los
Consider Sexual Organization & hide thee in the dust.

Then the Divine hand found the Two Limits, Satan and Adam,
In Albions bosom: for in every Human bosom those Limits stand.
And the Divine voice came from the Furnaces, as multitudes without
Number! the voices of the innumerable multitudes of Eternity.
And the appearance of a Man was seen in the Furnaces:
Saving those who have sinned from the punishment of the Law.
In pity of the punisher whose state is eternal death,
And keeping them from Sin by the mild counsels of his love.

Albion goes to Eternal Death: In Me all Eternity,
Must pass thro' condemnation, and awake beyond the Grave:
No individual can keep these Laws, for they are death
To every energy of man, and forbid the springs of life:
Albion hath enterd the State Satan! Be permanent O State!
And be thou for ever accursed! that Albion may arise again:
And be thou created into a State! I go forth to Create
States: to deliver Individuals evermore! Amen.

So spoke the voice from the Furnaces, descending into Non-Entity

Reuben return'd to his place, in vain he sought beautiful Tirzah
For his Eyelids were narrow'd & his Nostrils scented the ground
And Sixty Winters Los raged in the Divisions of Reuben:
Building the Moon of Ulro plank by plank & rib by rib
Reuben slept in the Cave of Adam, and Los folded his Tongue
Between Lips of mire & clay, then sent him forth over Jordan
In the love of Tirzah he said Doubt is my food day & night—
All that beheld him fled howling and gnawed their tongues
For pain: they became what they beheld In reasonings Reuben ret
To Heshbon, disconsolate he walkd thro Moab & he stood
Before the Furnaces of Los in a horrible dreamful slumber,
On Mount Gilead looking toward Gilgal: and Los bended
His Ear in a spiral circle outward; then sent him over Jordan.

The Seven Nations fled before him they became what they beheld
Hand, Hyle & Coban fled; they became what they beheld
Gwantock & Peachy hid in Damascus beneath Mount Lebanon
Brereton & Slade in Egypt. Hutton & Skofeld & Kox
Fled over Chaldea in terror, in pains in every nerve
Kotope & Bowen became what they beheld, fleeing over the Earth
And the Twelve Female Emanations fled with them agonizing.

Jerusalem trembled seeing her Children driven by Loss Hammer
In the visions of the dreams of Beulah on the edge of Non Entity
Hand stood between Reuben & Merlin, as the Reasoning Spectre
Stands between the Vegetative Man & his Immortal Imagination

And the Four Zoa's clouded rage East & West & North & South
They change their situations, in the Universal Man.
Albion groans, he sees the Elements divide before his face
And England who is Brittannia divided into Jerusalem & Vala
And Urizen assumes the East, Luvah assumes the South
In his dark Spectre ravening from his open Sepulcher

And the Four Zoa's who are the Four Eternal Senses of Man
Became Four Elements separating from the Limbs of Albion
These are their names in the Vegetative Generation.

And Accident & Chance were found hidden in Length Bredth & Highth
And they divided into Four ravening deathlike Forms
Fairies & Genii & Nymphs & Gnomes of the Elements
These are States Permanently Fixed by the Divine Power
The Atlantic Continent sunk round Albions cliffy shore
And the Sea poured in amain upon the Giants of Albion
As Los bended the Senses of Reuben Reuben is Merlin
Exploring the Three States of Ulro; Creation; Redemption. & Judgment

And many of the Eternal Ones laughed after their manner
Have you known the Judgment that is arisen among the
Zoas of Albion? where a Man dare hardly to embrace
His own Wife, for the terrors of Chastity that they call
By the name of Morality, their Daughters govern all
In hidden deceit! they are Vegetable only fit for burning
Art & Science cannot exist but by Naked Beauty displayd

Then those in Great Eternity who contemplate on Death
Said thus. What seems to Be: Is: To those to whom
It seems to Be: & is productive of the most dreadful
Consequences to those to whom it seems to Be: even of
Torments, Despair, Eternal Death; but the Divine Mercy
Steps beyond and Redeems Man in the Body of Jesus Amen
And Length Bredth Highth again Obey the Divine Vision Hallelujah

I feel my Spectre rising upon me! Albion! arouse thyself!
Why dost thou thunder with frozen Spectrous wrath against us?
The Spectre is in Giant Man; insane, and most deform'd.
Thou wilt certainly provoke my Spectre against thine in fury!
He has a Sepulcher hewn out of a Rock ready for thee:
And a Death of Eight thousand years forg'd by thyself, upon
The point of his Spear! if thou persistest to forbid with Laws
Our Emanations, and to attack our secret supreme delights

So Los spoke: But when he saw blue death in Albions feet,
Again he joind the Divine Body, following merciful;
While Albion fled more indignant; revengeful covering

His face and bosom with petrific hardness, and his hands
And feet, lest any should enter his bosom & embrace
His hidden heart; his Emanation wept & trembled within him:
Uttering not his jealousy, but hiding it as with
Iron and steel, dark and opake, with clouds & tempests brooding:
His strong limbs shudderd upon his mountains high and dark.

Turning from Universal Love petrific as he went,
His cold against the warmth of Eden rag'd with loud
Thunders of deadly war (the fever of the human soul)
Fires and clouds of rolling smoke; but mild the Saviour follow'd him,
Displaying the Eternal Vision! the Divine Similitude!
In loves and tears of brothers, sisters, sons, fathers, and friends
Which if Man ceases to behold, he ceases to exist:

Saying. Albion! Our wars are wars of life, & wounds of love,
With intellectual spears, & long winged arrows of thought:
Mutual in one anothers love and wrath all renewing
We live as One Man: for contracting our infinite senses
We behold multitude; or expanding: we behold as one,
As One Man all the Universal Family: and that One Man
We call Jesus the Christ: and he in us, and we in him,
Live in perfect harmony in Eden the land of life,
Giving, recieving, and forgiving each others trespasses.
He is the Good shepherd, he is the Lord and master:
He is the Shepherd of Albion, he is all in all.
In Eden: in the garden of God: and in heavenly Jerusalem.
If we have offended, forgive us, take not vengeance against us.

Thus speaking; the Divine Family follow Albion:
I see them in the Vision of God upon my pleasant valleys.

I behold London; a Human awful wonder of God!
He says. Return Albion, return! I give myself for thee:
My Streets are my Ideas of Imagination.
Awake Albion, awake! and let us awake up together.
My Houses are Thoughts; my Inhabitants; Affections.
The children of my thoughts, walking within my blood-vessels,
Shut from my nervous form which sleeps upon the verge of Beulah
In dreams of darkness, while my vegetating blood in veiny pipes,
Rolls dreadful thro' the Furnaces of Los, and the Mills of Satan.
For Albions sake, and for Jerusalem thy Emanation
I give myself, and these my brethren give themselves for Albion.

So spoke London, immortal Guardian! I heard in Lambeths shades:
In Felpham I heard and saw the Visions of Albion
I write in South Molton Street, what I both see and hear
In regions of Humanity, in Londons opening streets.

I see thee awful Parent Land in light, behold I see!
Verulam! Canterbury! venerable parent of men,
Generous immortal Guardian golden clad! for Cities
Are Men, fathers of multitudes, and Rivers & Mountains
Are also Men; every thing is Human, mighty! sublime!
In every bosom a Universe expands, as wings
Let down at will around, and call'd the Universal Tent.
York, crown'd with loving kindness, Edinburgh, clothd
With fortitude as with a garment of immortal texture
Woven in looms of Eden, in spiritual deaths of mighty men
Who give themselves, in Golgotha, Victims to Justice: where
There is in Albion a Gate of precious stones and gold
Seen only by Emanations, by vegetations viewless,
Bending across the road of Oxford Street; it from Hyde Park
To Tyburns deathful shades, admits the wandering souls
Of multitudes who die from Earth: this Gate cannot be found

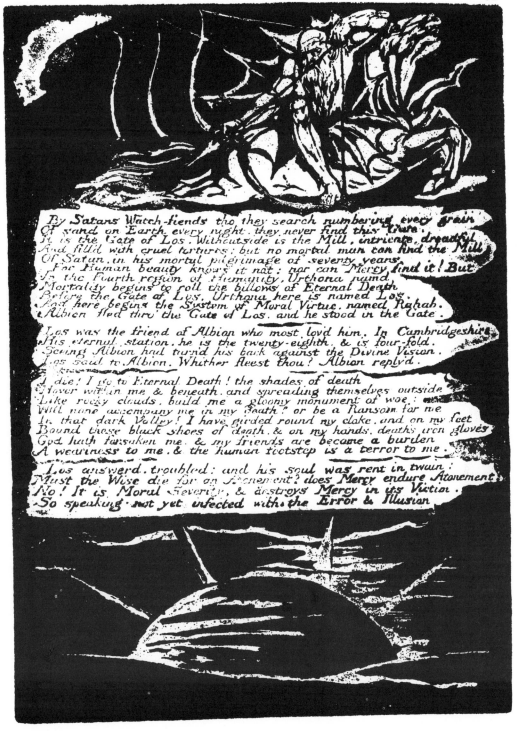

By Satans Watch-fiends tho they search numbering every grain
Of sand on Earth every night. they never find this Grain
It is the Gate of Los. Withoutside is the Mill, intricate, dreadful
And fill'd with cruel tortures: but no mortal man can find the Mill
Of Satan. in his mortal pilgrimage of seventy years,
For Human beauty knows it not: nor can Mercy find it! But
In the Fourth region of Humanity, Urthona named,
Mortality begins to roll the billows of Eternal Death
Before the Gate of Los. Urthona here is named Los.
And here begins the System of Moral Virtue. named Rahab.
Albion fled thro the Gate of Los. and he stood in the Gate.

Los was the friend of Albion who most lov'd him. In Cambridgeshire
His eternal station. he is the twenty-eighth. & is four-fold.
Seeing Albion had turned his back against the Divine Vision.
Los said to Albion. Whither fleest thou? Albion replyd.

I die! I go to Eternal Death! the shades of death
Hover within me & beneath. and spreading themselves outside
Like rocky clouds. build me a gloomy monument of woe:
Will none accompany me in my death? or be a Ransom for me
In that dark Valley! I have girded round my cloke. and on my feet
Bound these black shoes of death. & on my hands. deaths iron gloves
God hath forsaken me. & my friends are became a burden
A weariness to me. & the human footstep is a terror to me.

Los answerd. troubled: and his soul was rent in twain:
Must the Wise die for an Atonement? does Mercy endure Atonement
No! It is Moral Severity, & destroys Mercy in its Virtue.
So speaking, not yet infected with the Error & Illusion

Los shudder'd at beholding Albion, for his disease
Arose upon him pale and ghostly: and he call'd around
The Friends of Albion; trembling at the sight of Eternal Death
The four appeard with their Emanations in fiery
Chariots: black their fires roll beholding Albions House of Eternity
Damp couch the flames beneath and silent, sick, stand shuddering
Before the Porch of sixteen pillars: weeping every one
Descended and fell down upon their knees round Albions knees
Swearing the Oath of God! with awful voice of thunders round
Upon the hills & valleys, and the cloudy Oath rolld far and wide

Albion is sick! said every Valley, every mournful Hill
And every River: our brother Albion is sick to death.
He hath leagued himself with robbers! he hath studied the arts
Of unbelief! Envy hovers over him! his Friends are his abhorrence!
Those who give their lives for him are despised!
Those who devour his soul, are taken into his bosom!
To destroy his Emanation is their intention:
Arise! awake O Friends of the Giant Albion
They have perswaded him of horrible falshoods!
They have sown errors over all his fruitful fields!

The Twenty-four heard! they came trembling on watry chariots.
Borne by the living Creatures of the third procession
Of Human Majesty. the Living Creatures wept aloud as they
Went along Albions roads, till they arriv'd at Albions House.

O! how the torments of Eternal Death, waited on Man:
And the loud-rending bars of the Creation ready to burst:
That the wide world might fly from its hinges, & the immortal mansion
Of Man, for ever be possess'd by monsters of the deeps:
And Man himself become a Fiend, wrap'd in an endless curse.
Consuming and consum'd for-ever in flames of Moral Justice.

For had the Body of Albion fall'n down, and from its dreadful ruins
Let loose the enormous Spectre on the darkness of the deep.
At enmity with the Merciful & filld with devouring fire.
A nether-world must have reciev'd the foul enormous spirit.
Under pretence of Moral Virtue, filld with Revenge and Law.
There to eternity chain'd down, and issuing in red flames
And curses, with his mighty arms brandish'd against the heavens
Breathing cruel blood & vengeance, gnashing his teeth with pain
Torn with black storms, & ceaseless torrents of his own consuming fire:
Within his breast his mighty Sons chain'd down & filld with cursings:
And his dark Eon, that once fair crystal form divinely clear:
Within his ribs producing serpents whose souls are flames of fire.
But, glory to the Merciful-One, for he is of tender mercies!
And the Divine Family wept over him as One Man.

And these the Twenty-four in whom the Divine Family
Appeard; and they were One in Him. A Human Vision!
Human Divine. Jesus the Saviour. blessed for ever and ever.

Selsey, true friend! who afterwards submitted to be devour'd
By the waves of Despair, whose Emanation rose above
The flood, and was nam'd Chichester, lovely mild & gentle! Lo!
Her lambs bleat to the sea-fowls cry. lamenting still for Albion.

Submitting to be call'd the son of Los the terrible vision:
Winchester stood devoting himself for Albion: his tents
Outspread with abundant riches, and his Emanations
Submitting to be call'd Enitharmons daughters, and be born
In vegetable mould, created by the Hammer and Loom
In Bowlahoola & Allamanda where the Dead wail night & day

(I call them by their English names: English, the rough basement.
Los built the stubborn structure of the Language, acting against
Albions melancholy, who must else have been a Dumb despair.)

Gloucester and Exeter and Salisbury and Bristol: and benevolent

Bath who is Legions: he is the Seventh, the physician and
The poisoner: the best and worst in Heaven and Hell:
Whose Spectre first assimilated with Luvah in Albions mountains
A triple octave he took, to reduce Jerusalem to twelve
To cast Jerusalem forth upon the wilds to Poplar & Bow:
To Malden & Canterbury in the delights of cruelty:
The Shuttles of death sing in the sky to Islington & Pancrass
Round Marybone to Tyburns River, weaving black melancholy as a net,
And despair as meshes closely wove over the west of London.
Where mild Jerusalem sought to repose in death & be no more.
She fled to Lambeths mild Vale and hid herself beneath
The Surrey Hills where Rephaim terminates: her Sons are siezd
For victims of sacrifice: but Jerusalem cannot be found, Hid
By the Daughters of Beulah: gently snatched away: and hid in Beulah

There is a Grain of Sand in Lambeth that Satan cannot find
Nor can his Watch Fiends find it: tis translucent & has many Angles
But he who finds it will find Oothoons palace, for within
Opening into Beulah, every angle is a lovely heaven
But should the Watch Fiends find it, they would call it Sin
And lay its Heavens & their inhabitants in blood of punishment
Here Jerusalem & Vala were hid in soft slumberous repose
Hid from the terrible East, shut up in the South & West.
The Twenty-eight trembled in Deaths dark caves, in cold despair
They kneeld around the Couch of Death in deep humiliation
And tortures of self condemnation while their Spectres ragd within
The Four Zoa's in terrible combustion clouded rage
Drinking the shuddering fears & loves of Albions Families
Destroying by selfish affections the things that they most admire
Drinking & eating, & pitying & weeping, as at a tragic scene
The soul drinks murder & revenge, & applauds its own holiness

They saw Albion endeavouring to destroy their Emanations

Each Man is in
his Spectres power
Untill the arrival
of that hour
When his Humanity
awake
And cast his Spectre
into the Lake

They saw their Wheels rising up poisonous against Albion
Urizen. cold & scientific: Luvah, pitying & weeping
Tharmas, indolent & sullen: Urthona, doubting & despairing
Victims to one another & dreadfully plotting against each other
To prevent Albion walking about in the Four Complexions.

They saw America clos'd out by the Oaks of the western shore;
And Tharmas dash'd on the Rocks of the Altars of Victims in Mexico.
If we are wrathful Albion will destroy Jerusalem with rooty Groves
If we are merciful, ourselves must suffer destruction on his Oaks:
Why should we enter into our Spectres. to behold our own corruptions
O God of Albion descend: deliver Jerusalem from the Oaken Groves:

Then Los grew furious raging: Why stand we here trembling around
Calling on God for help: and not ourselves in whom God dwells
Stretching a hand to save the falling Man: are we not Four
Beholding Albion upon the Precipice ready to fall into Non-Entity:
Seeing these Heavens & Hells conglobing in the Void. Heavens over Hells
Brooding in holy hypocritic lust, drinking the cries of pain.
From howling victims of Law: building Heavens Twenty-seven-fold.
Swell'd & bloated General Forms. repugnant to the Divine-
Humanity, who is the Only General and Universal Form
To which all Lineaments tend & seek with love & sympathy
All broad & general principles belong to benevolence
Who protects minute particulars, every one in their own identity.
But here the affectionate touch of the tongue is clos'd in by deadly teeth
And the soft smile of friendship & the open dawn of benevolence
Became a net & a trap, & every energy renderd cruel,
Till the existence of friendship & benevolence is denied:
The wine of the Spirit & the vineyards of the Holy-One.
Here; turn into poisonous stupor & deadly intoxication:
That they may be condemn'd by Law & the Lamb of God be slain.
And the two Sources of Life in Eternity Hunting and War.
Are become the Sources of dark & bitter Death & of corroding Hell:
The open heart is shut up in integuments of frozen silence
That the spear that lights it forth may shatter the ribs & bosom
A pretence of Art to destroy Art; a pretence of Liberty
To destroy Liberty. a pretence of Religion to destroy Religion
Oshea and Caleb fight: they contend in the valleys of of Peor
In the terrible Family Contentions of those who love each other:
The Armies of Balaam weep—no women come to the field
Dead corses lay before them, & not as in Wars of old.
For the Soldier who fights for Truth. calls his enemy his brother:
They fight & contend for life, & not for eternal death.
But here the Soldier strikes, & a dead corse falls at his feet
Nor Daughter nor Sister nor Mother come forth to embosom the Slain!
But Death! Eternal Death; remains in the Valleys of Peor.
The English are scatterd over the face of the Nations: are these
Jerusalems children? Hark! hear the Giants of Albion cry at night
We smell the blood of the English! we delight in their blood on our Altars!
The living & the dead shall be ground in our rumbling Mills
For bread of the Sons of Albion: of the Giants Hand & Scofield
Scofeld & Kox are let loose upon my Saxons! they accumulate
A World in which Man is by his Nature the Enemy of Man.
In pride of Selfhood unwieldy, stretching out into Non Entity
Generalizing Art & Science till Art & Science is lost.
Bristol & Bath. listen to my words, & ye Seventeen! give ear:
It is easy to acknowledge a man to be great & good while we
Derogate from him in the trifles & small articles of that goodness:
Those alone are his friends, who admire his minutest powers
Instead of Albions lovely mountains & the curtains of Jerusalem
I see a Cave, a Rock, a Tree deadly and poisonous. unimaginative:
Instead of the Mutual Forgivenesses. the Minute Particulars. I see
Pits of bitumen ever burning: artificial Riches of the Canaanite
Like Lakes of liquid lead: instead of heavenly Chapels, built
By our dear Lord: I see Worlds crusted with snows & ice;
I see a Wicker Idol woven round Jerusalems children, I see
The Canaanite, the Amalekite, the Moabite, the Egyptian,
By Demonstrations the cruel Sons of Quality & Negation.
Driven on the Void in incoherent despair into Non Entity
I see America clos'd apart, & Jerusalem driven in terror
Away from Albions mountains, far away from Londons spires:
I will not endure this thing: I alone withstand to death.
This outrage. Ah me! how sick & pale you all stand round me!
Ah me! pitiable ones! do you also go to deaths vale?
All you my Friends & Brothers! all you my beloved Companions:
Have you also caught the infection of Sin & stern Repentance?
I see Disease arise upon you! yet speak to me, and give
Me some comfort: why do you all stand silent? I alone
Remain in permanent strength. Or is all this goodness & pity, only
That you may take the greater vengeance in your Sepulcher.

So Los spoke. Pale they stood around the House of Death:
In the midst of temptations & despair; among the rooted Oaks;
Among reard Rocks of Albions Sons at length they rose

With one accord in love sublime, & as on Cherubs wings
They Albion surround with kindest violence to bear him back
Against his Will thro Los's Gate to Eden: Four-fold; loud!
Their Wings waving over the bottomless Immense: to bear
Their awful charge back to his native home; but Albion dark,
Repugnant; rolld his Wheels backward into Non-Entity
Loud roll the Starry Wheels of Albion into the World of Death
And all the Gate of Los, clouded with clouds redounding from
Albions dread Wheels, stretching out spaces immense between
That every little particle of light & air, became Opake
Black & immense, a Rock of difficulty & a Cliff
Of black despair; that the immortal Wings labourd against
Cliff after cliff, & over Valleys of despair & death:
The narrow Sea between Albion & the Atlantic Continent:
Its waves of pearl became a boundless Ocean bottomless,
Of grey obscurity, filld with clouds & rocks & whirling waters
And Albions Sons ascending & desending in the horrid Void.

But as the Will must not be bended but in the day of Divine
Power: silent calm & motionless, in the mid-air sublime.
The Family Divine hover around the darkend Albion.

Such is the nature of the Ulro: that whatever enters:
Becomes Sexual, & is Created, and Vegetated, and Born,
From Hyde Park spread their vegetating roots beneath Albion
In dreadful pain the Spectrous Uncircumcised Vegetation,
Forming a Sexual Machine: an Aged Virgin Form.
In Erins Land toward the north, joint after joint & burning
In love & jealousy immingled & calling it Religion
And feeling the damps of death they with one accord delegated Los
Conjuring him by the Highest that he should Watch over them
Till Jesus shall appear: & they gave their power to Los
Naming him the Spirit of Prophecy, calling him Elijah

Strucken with Albions disease they become what they behold;
They assimilate with Albion in pity & compassion;
Their Emanations return not: their Spectres rage in the Deep
The Slumbers of Death came over them around the Couch of Death
Before the Gate of Los & in the depths of Non Entity
Among the Furnaces of Los: among the Oaks of Albion.

Man is adjoind to Man by his Emanative portion:
Who is Jerusalem in every individual Man: and her
Shadow is Vala, builded by the Reasoning power in Man
O search & see: turn your eyes inward: open O thou World
Of Love & Harmony in Man: expand thy ever lovely Gates.

They wept into the deeps a little space at length was heard
The voice of Bath, faint as the voice of the Dead in the House of
                                                            Death

Bath, healing City! whose wisdom in midst of Poetic
Fervor, mild spoke thro' the Western Porch in soft gentle tears

O Albion mildest Son of Eden! clos'd is thy Western Gate
Brothers of Eternity, this Man whose great example
We all admird & lovd, whose all benevolent countenance, seen
In Eden, in lovely Jerusalem, drew even from envy
The tear: and the confession of honesty, open & undisguis'd
From mistrust and suspicion. The Man is himself become
A piteous example of oblivion. To teach the Sons
Of Eden, that however great and glorious; however loving
And merciful the Individuality; however high
Our palaces and cities, and however fruitful are our fields
In Selfhood, we are nothing: but fade away in mornings breath.
Our mildness is nothing; the greatest mildness we can use
Is incapable and nothing: none but the Lamb of God can heal
This dread disease: none but Jesus; O Lord descend and save.
Albions Western Gate is clos'd; his death is coming apace;
Jesus alone can save him; for alas we none can know
How soon his lot may be our own. When Africa in sleep
Rose in the night of Beulah, and bound down the Sun & Moon
His friends cut his strong chains, & overwhelmd his dark
Machines in fury & destruction, and the Man reviving repented.
He wept before his wrathful brethren, thankful & considerate
For their well timed wrath. But Albions sleep is not
Like Africa's; and his machines are woven with his life
Nothing but mercy can save him! nothing but mercy interposing
Lest he should slay Jerusalem in his fearful jealousy
O God descend! gather our brethren, deliver Jerusalem
But that we may omit no office of the friendly spirit
Oxford take thou these leaves of the Tree of Life: with eloquence
That thy immortal tongue inspires; present them to Albion:
Perhaps he may recieve them, offerd from thy loved hands.

So spoke, unheard by Albion, the merciful Son of Heaven
To those whose Western Gates were open, as they stood weeping
Around Albion: but Albion heard him not; obdurate! hard;
He frownd on all his Friends, counting them enemies in his sorrow

And the Seventeen conjoining with Bath, the Seventh:
In whom the other Ten shine manifest, a Divine Vision!
Assimulated, and embracd Eternal Death for Albions sake.

And these the names of the Eighteen combining with those Ten

Both. mild. Physician of Eternity. mysterious power.
Whose springs are unsearchable & knowledge infinite.
Hereford, ancient Guardian of Wales, whose hands
Builded the mountain palaces of Eden. stupendous works!
Lincoln, Durham & Carlisle. Councellors of Los.
And Ely, Scribe of Los, whose pen no other hand
Dare touch! Oxford immortal Bard! with eloquence
Divine he went over Albion; speaking the words of God
In mild perswasion: bringing leaves of the Tree of Life.

Thou art in Error Albion, the Land of Ulro:
One Error not removd, will destroy a human Soul.
Repose in Beulahs night, till the Error is removd
Reason not on both sides. Repose upon our bosoms
Till the Plow of Jehovah, and the Harrow of Shaddai
Have passed over the Dead, to awake the Dead to Judgment.
But Albion turnd away refusing comfort.

Oxford trembled while he spoke, then fainted in the arms
Of Norwich, Peterboro, Rochester, Chester awful, Worcester.
Litchfield, Saint Davids, Landaff, Asaph, Bangor, Sodor.
Bowing their heads devoted; and the Furnaces of Los
Began to rage, thundering loud the storms began to roar
Upon the Furnaces, and loud the Furnaces rebellow beneath

And these the Four in whom the twenty-four appeard four-fold:
Verulam, London, York, Edinburgh, mourning one towards another
Alas! —— The time will come, when a mans worst enemies
Shall be those of his own house and family: in a Religion
Of Generation, to destroy by Sin and Atonement, happy Jerusalem.
The Bride and Wife of the Lamb. O God thou art Not an Avenger!

Thus Albion sat, studious of others in his pale disease:
Brooding on evil: but when Los opend the Furnaces before him:
He saw that the accursed things were his own affections,
And his own beloveds: then he turnd sick! his soul died within him
Also Los sick & terrified beheld the Furnaces of Death
And must have died, but the Divine Saviour descended
Among the infant loves & affections, and the Divine Vision wept
Like evening dew on every herb upon the breathing ground

Albion spoke in his dismal dreams: O thou deceitful friend
Worshipping mercy & beholding thy friend in such affliction:
Los! thou now discoverest thy turpitude to the heavens.
I demand righteousness & justice. O thou ingratitude!
Give me my Emanations back food for my dying soul:
My daughters are harlots! my sons are accursed before me.
Enitharmon is my daughter: accursed with a fathers curse!
O I have utterly been wasted! I have given my daughters to devils

So spoke Albion in gloomy majesty, and deepest night
Of Ulro rolld round his skirts from Dover to Cornwall.

Los answerd. Righteousness & justice I give thee in return
For thy righteousness! but I add mercy also, and bind
Thee from destroying these little ones: am I to be only
Merciful to thee and cruel to all that thou hatest
Thou wast the Image of God surrounded by the Four Zoa's
Three thou hast slain! I am the Fourth: thou canst not destroy me.
Thou art in Error; trouble me not with thy righteousness:
I have innocence to defend and ignorance to instruct:
I have no time for seeming; and little arts of compliment,
In morality and virtue: in self-glorying and pride.
There is a limit of Opakeness, and a limit of Contraction;
In every Individual Man, and the limit of Opakeness
Is named Satan: and the limit of Contraction is named Adam,
But when Man sleeps in Beulah, the Saviour in mercy takes
Contractions Limit, and of the Limit he forms Woman; That
Himself may in process of time be born Man to redeem
But there is no Limit of Expansion! there is no Limit of Translucence
In the bosom of Man for ever from eternity to eternity.
Therefore I break thy bonds of righteousness; I crush thy messengers:
That they may not crush me and mine: do thou be righteous,
And I will return it: otherwise I defy thy worst revenge:
Consider me as thine enemy: on me turn all thy fury
But destroy not these little ones, nor mock the Lords anointed:
Destroy not by Moral Virtue, the little ones whom he hath chosen!
The little ones whom he hath chosen in preference to thee.
He hath cast thee off for ever, the little ones he hath anointed!
Thy Selfhood is for ever accursed from the Divine presence

So Los spake: then turnd his face & wept for Albion

Albion replied. Go Hand & Hyle: sieze the abhorred friend!
As you have siezd the Twenty-four rebellious ingratitudes;
To atone for you, for spiritual death! Man lives by deaths of Men
Bring him to justice before heaven here upon London stone,
Between Blackheath & Hounslow, between Norwood & Finchley
All that they have is mine: from my free genrous gift,
They now hold all they have: ingratitude to me,
To me their benefactor calls aloud for vengeance deep.

Los stood before his Furnaces awaiting the fury of the Dead:
And the Divine hand was upon him, strengthening him mightily.

The Spectres of the Dead cry out from the deeps beneath
Upon the hills of Albion: Oxford groans in his iron furnace
Winchester in his den & cavern; they lament against
Albion: they curse their human kindness & affection
They rage like wild beasts in the forests of affliction
In the dreams of Ulro they repent of their human kindness.

Come up, build Babylon, Rahab is ours & all her multitudes
With her in pomp and glory of victory. Depart
Ye twenty-four into the deeps! let us depart to glory!

Their Human majestic Forms sit up upon their Couches
Of death: they curb their Spectres as with iron curbs
They enquire after Jerusalem in the regions of the dead,
With the voices of dead men low, scarcely articulate,
And with tears cold on their cheeks they weary repose.

O when shall the morning of the grave appear, and when
Shall our salvation come? we sleep upon our watch
We cannot awake! and our Spectres rage in the forests
O God of Albion where art thou! pity the watchers!

Thus mourn they. Loud the Furnaces of Los thunder upon
The clouds of Europe & Asia, among the Serpent Temples!

And Los drew his Seven Furnaces around Albions Altars
And as Albion built his frozen Altars, Los built the Mundane Shell,
In the Four Regions of Humanity East & West & North & South,
Till Norwood & Finchley & Blackheath & Hounslow, coverd the whole Earth.
This is the Net & Veil of Vala, among the Souls of the Dead.

Then the Divine Vision like a silent Sun appeard above
Albions dark rocks: setting behind the Gardens of Kensington
On Tyburns River, in clouds of blood: where was mild Zions Hill
Most ancient promontary, and in the Sun, a Human Form appeard
And thus the Voice Divine went forth upon the rocks of Albion

I elected Albion for my glory; I gave to him the Nations,
Of the whole Earth. He was the Angel of my Presence: and all
The Sons of God were Albions Sons: and Jerusalem was my joy.
The Reactor hath hid himself thro envy. I behold him.
But you cannot behold him till he be reveald in his System
Albions Reactor must have a Place prepard: Albion must Sleep
The Sleep of Death, till the Man of Sin & Repentance be reveald.
Hidden in Albions Forests he lurks: he admits of no Reply
From Albion: but hath founded his Reaction into a Law
Of Action, for Obedience to destroy the Contraries of Man
He hath compelld Albion to become a Punisher & hath possessd
Himself of Albions Forests & Wilds: and Jerusalem is taken!
The City of the Woods in the Forest of Ephratah is taken!
London is a stone of her ruins; Oxford is the dust of her walls!
Sussex & Kent are her scatterd garments; Ireland her holy place
And the murderd bodies of her little ones are Scotland and Wales
The Cities of the Nations are the smoke of her consummation
The Nations are her dust! ground by the chariot wheels
Of her lordly conquerors, her palaces levelld with the dust
I come that I may find a way for my banished ones to return
Fear not O little Flock I come! Albion shall rise again.

So saying, the mild Sun inclosd the Human Family.

Forthwith from Albions darkning locks came two Immortal forms
Saying We alone are escaped, O mercful Lord and Saviour,
We flee from the interiors of Albions hills and mountains!
From his Valleys Eastward: from Amalek Canaan & Moab:
Beneath his vast ranges of hills surrounding Jerusalem.

Albion walkd on the steps of fire before his Halls
And Vala walkd with him in dreams of soft deluding slumber.
He looked up & saw the Prince of Light with splendor faded.
Then Albion ascended mourning into the porches of his Palace
Above him rose a Shadow from his wearied intellect:
Of living gold, pure, perfect, holy: in white linen pure he hoverd
A sweet entrancing self-delusion a watry vision of Albion
Soft exulting in Existence; all the Man absorbing!

Albion fell upon his face prostrate before the watry Shadow
Saying O Lord whence is this change! thou knowest I am nothing!
And Vala trembled & coverd her face! & her locks were spread on the
pavement

We heard astonishd at the Vision & our hearts trembled within us:
We heard the voice of slumberous Albion, and thus he spake,
Idolatrous to his own Shadow words of eternity uttering:

O I am nothing when I enter into judgment with thee!
If thou withdraw thy breath I die & vanish into Hades
If thou dost lay thine hand upon me behold I am silent:
If thou withhold thine hand; I perish like a fallen leaf:
O I am nothing: and to nothing must return again:
If thou withdraw thy breath. Behold I am oblivion.

He ceasd: the shadowy voice was silent; but the cloud hoverd over their heads
In golden wreathes, the sorrow of Man; & the balmy drops fell down.
And Lo! that son of Man that Shadowy Spirit of mild Albion:
Luvah descended from the cloud: in terror Albion rose:
Indignant rose the awful Man & turnd his back on Vala.

We heard the voice of Albion starting from his sleep:
Whence is this voice crying Enion! that soundeth in my ears?
O cruel pity! O dark deceit! can love seek for dominion?

And Luvah strove to gain dominion over Albion
They strove together above the Body where Vala was inclosd
And the dark Body of Albion left prostrate upon the crystal pavement,
Coverd with boils from head to foot: the terrible smitings of Luvah.

Then frownd the fallen Man, and put forth Luvah from his presence
Saying, Go and Die the Death of Man, for Vala the sweet wanderer.
I will turn the volutions of your ears outward, and bend your nostrils
Downward, and your fluxile eyes englobd, roll round in fear:
Your withring lips and tongue shrink up into a narrow circle,
Till into narrow forms you creep: go take your fiery way:
And learn what tis to absorb the Man you Spirits of Pity & Love.

They heard the voice and fled swift as the winters setting sun.
And now the human blood foamd high, the Spirits Luvah & Vala,
Went down the Human Heart where Paradise & its joys abounded,
In jealous fears & fury & rage, & flames roll round their fervid feet:
And the vast form of Nature like a serpent playd before them
And as they fled in folding fires & thunders in the deep:
Vala shrunk in like the dark sea, that leaves its slimy banks.
And from her bosom Luvah fell far, as the east and west:
And the vast form of Nature like a serpent rolld between,
Whether of Jerusalems or Valas ruins congenerated we know not:
All is confusion: all is tumult & we alone are escaped.
So spoke the fugitives; they joind the Divine Family, trembling

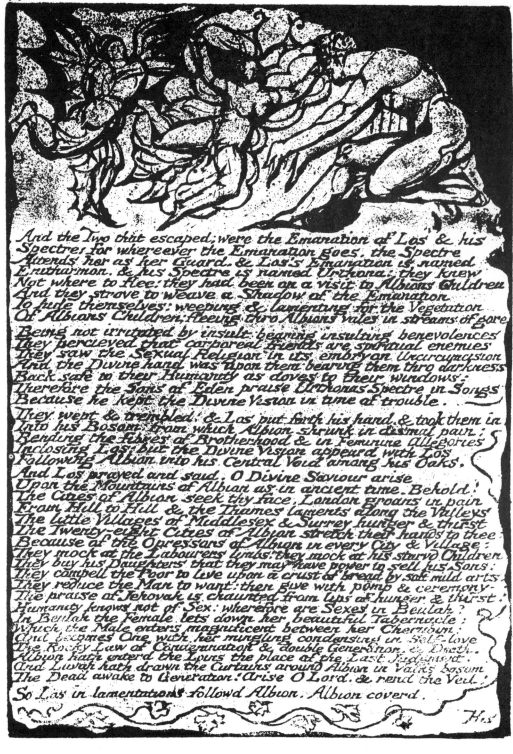

And the Two that escaped; were the Emanation of Los & his
Spectre: for whereever the Emanation goes, the Spectre
Attends her as her Guard. & Los's Emanation is named
Enitharmon. & his Spectre is named Urthona: they knew
Not where to flee: they had been on a visit to Albions Children
And they strove to weave a Shadow of the Emanation
To hide themselves: weeping & lamenting for the Vegetation
Of Albions Children; fleeing thro Albions vales in streams of gore

Being not irritated by insult, bearing insulting benevolences
They percieved that corporeal friends are spiritual enemies
They saw the Sexual Religion in its embryon Uncircumcision
And the Divine hand was upon them bearing them thro darkness
Back safe to their Humanity as doves to their windows:
Therefore the Sons of Eden praise Urthonas Spectre in Songs
Because he kept the Divine Vision in time of trouble.

They wept & trembled. & Los put forth his hand & took them in
Into his Bosom: from which Albion shrunk in dismal pain;
Rending the fibres of Brotherhood & in Feminine Allegories
Inclosing Los: but the Divine Vision appeard with Los
Following Albion into his Central Void among his Oaks.
And Los prayed and said. O Divine Saviour arise
Upon the Mountains of Albion as in ancient time. Behold!
The Cities of Albion seek thy face, London groans in pain
From Hill to Hill & the Thames laments along the Valleys
The little Villages of Middlesex & Surrey hunger & thirst
The Twenty-eight Cities of Albion stretch their hands to thee:
Because of the Opressors of Albion in every City & Village:
They mock at the Labourers limbs: they mock at his starvd Children.
They buy his Daughters that they may have power to sell his Sons:
They compell the Poor to live upon a crust of bread by soft mild arts.
They reduce the Man to want: then give with pomp & ceremony.
The praise of Jehovah is chaunted from lips of hunger & thirst:
Humanity knows not of Sex: wherefore are Sexes in Beulah:
In Beulah the Female lets down her beautiful Tabernacle:
Which the Male enters magnificent between her Cherubim:
And becomes One with her mingling condensing in Self-love
The Rocky Law of Condemnation & double Generation. & Death.
Albion hath enterd the Loins the place of the Last Judgment.
And Luvah hath drawn the Curtains around Albion in Vala's bosom
The Dead awake to Generation! Arise O Lord, & rend the Veil!
So Los in lamentations followd Albion. Albion coverd.

His western heaven with rocky clouds of death & despair.

Fearing that Albion should turn his back against the Divine Vision
Los took his globe of fire to search the interiors of Albions
Bosom, in all the terrors of friendship, entering the caves
Of despair & death, to search the tempters out, walking among
Albions rocks & precipices! caves of solitude & dark despair,
And saw every Minute Particular of Albion degraded, & murderd
But saw not by whom; they were hidden within in the minute particulars
Of which they had possessd themselves; and there they take up
The articulations of a mans soul, and laughing throw it down
Into the frame, then knock it out upon the plank, & souls are bak'd
In bricks to build the pyramids of Heber & Terah. But Los
Searchd in vain: closd from the minutia he walkd, difficult.
He came down from Highgate thro Hackney & Holloway towards London
Till he came to old Stratford & thence to Stepney & the Isle
Of Leuthas Dogs, thence thro the narrows of the Rivers side,
And saw every minute particular, the jewels of Albion, running down
The kennels of the streets & lanes as if they were abhorrd.
Every Universal Form, was become barren mountains of Moral
Virtue: and every Minute Particular hardend into grains of sand:
And all the tendernesses of the soul cast forth as filth & mire.
Among the winding places of deep contemplation intricate
To where the Tower of London frownd dreadful over Jerusalem;
A building of Luvah builded in Jerusalems eastern gate to be
His secluded Court: thence to Bethlehem where was builded
Dens of despair in the house of bread: enquiring in vain
For stones and rocks he took his way, for human form was none:
And thus he spoke, looking on Albions City with many tears

What shall I do! what could I do, if I could find these Criminals
I could not dare to take vengeance; for all things are so constructed
And builded by the Divine hand, that the sinner shall always escape,
And he who takes vengeance alone is the criminal of Providence;
If I should dare to lay my finger on a grain of sand
In way of vengeance; I punish the already punishd: O whom
Should I pity if I pity not the sinner who is gone astray!
O Albion, if thou takest vengeance; if thou revengest thy wrongs
Thou art for ever lost! What can I do to hinder the Sons
Of Albion from taking vengeance? or how shall I them perswade,

So spoke Los, travelling thro darkness & horrid solitude:
And he beheld Jerusalem in Westminster & Marybone.
Among the ruins of the Temple: and Vala who is her Shadow.
Jerusalems Shadow bent northward over the Island white.
At length he sat on London Stone, & heard Jerusalems voice.

Albion I cannot be thy Wife, thine own Minute Particulars,
Belong to God alone, and all thy little ones are holy
They are of Faith & not of Demonstration: wherefore is Vala
Clothd in black mourning upon my rivers currents, Vala awake!
I hear thy shuttles sing in the sky, and round my limbs
I feel the iron threads of love & jealousy & despair.

Vala reply'd. Albion is mine! Luvah gave me to Albion
And now receives reproach & hate. Was it not said of old
Set your Son before a man & he shall take you & your sons
For slaves: but set your Daughter before a man and She
Shall make him & his sons & daughters your slaves for ever!
And is this Faith! Behold the strife of Albion & Luvah
Is great in the east, their spears of blood rage in the eastern heaven
Urizen is the champion of Albion, they will slay my Luvah:
And thou O harlot daughter! daughter of despair art all
This cause of these shakings of my towers on Euphrates.
Here is the House of Albion, & here is thy secluded place,
And here we have found thy sins; & hence we turn thee forth.
For all to avoid thee; to be astonishd at thee for thy sins:
Because thou art the impurity & the harlot: & thy children;
Children of whoredoms: born for Sacrifice: for the meat & drink
Offering: to sustain the glorious combat & the battle & war
That Man may be purified by the death of thy delusions.

So saying she her dark threads cast over the trembling River:
And over the valleys, from the hills of Hertfordshire to the hills
Of Surrey across Middlesex, & across Albions House
Of Eternity! pale stood Albion at his eastern gate.

Leaning against the pillars, & his disease rose from his skirts
Upon the Precipice he stood: ready to fall into Non-Entity.

Los was all astonishment & terror: he trembled sitting on the Stone
Of London: but the interiors of Albions fibres & nerves were hidden
From Los; astonishd he beheld only the petrified surfaces;
And saw his Furnaces in ruins, for Los is the Demon of the Furnaces:
He saw also the Four Points of Albion reversd inwards
He siezd his Hammer & Tongs, his iron Poker & his Bellows.
Upon the valleys of Middlesex, Shouting loud for aid Divine.

In stern defiance came from Albions bosom Hand, Hyle, Koban,
Gwantok, Peachy, Brereton, Slaid, Hutton, Skofeld, Kock, Kotope
Bowen: Albions Sons: they bore him a golden couch into the porch
And on the Couch reposd his limbs, trembling from the bloody field.
Rearing their Druid Patriarchal rocky Temples around his limbs.
(All things begin & end in Albions Ancient Druid Rocky Shore.)

From Camberwell to Highgate where the mighty Thames shudders along,
Where Los's Furnaces stand, where Jerusalem & Vala howl:
Luvah tore forth from Albions Loins, in fibrous veins, in rivers
Of blood over Europe: a Vegetating Root in grinding pain,
Animating the Dragon Temples, soon to become that Holy Fiend
The Wicker Man of Scandinavia in which cruelly consumed
The Captives reard to heaven howl in flames among the stars
Loud the cries of War on the Rhine & Danube, with Albions Sons,
Away from Beulahs hills & vales break forth the Souls of the Dead,
With cymbal, trumpet, clarion; & the scythed chariots of Britain,

And the Veil of Vala, is composed of the Spectres of the Dead

Hark! the mingling cries of Luvah with the Sons of Albion
Hark! & Record the terrible wonder! that the Punisher
Mingles with his Victims Spectre, enslaved & tormented
To him whom he has murderd, bound in vengeance & enmity
Shudder not, but Write, & the hand of God will assist you!
Therefore I write Albions last words. Hope is banishd from me.

These

These were his last words and the merciful Saviour in his arms
Reciev'd him in the arms of tender mercy and reposd
The pale limbs of his Eternal Individuality
Upon the Rock of Ages. Then surrounded with a Cloud:
In silence the Divine Lord builded with immortal labour,
Of gold & jewels a sublime Ornament, a Couch of repose,
With Sixteen pillars: canopied with emblems & written verse.
Spiritual Verse, orderd & measurd, from whence time shall reveal.
The Five books of the Decalogue, the books of Joshua & Judges,
Samuel, a double book & Kings, a double book & the Psalms & Prophets
The Four-fold Gospel, and the Revelations everlasting.
Eternity groan'd & was troubled, at the image of Eternal Death!

Beneath the bottoms of the Graves, which is Earths central joint,
There is a place where Contrarieties are equally true:
To protect from the Giant blows in the sports of intellect,
Thunder in the midst of kindness, & love that kills its beloved:
Because Death is for a period, and they renew tenfold.
From this sweet Place Maternal Love awoke Jerusalem
With pangs she forsook Beulah's pleasant lovely shadowy Universe
Where no dispute can come; created for those who Sleep.

Weeping was in all Beulah, and all the Daughters of Beulah
Wept for their Sister the Daughter of Albion, Jerusalem:
When out of Beulah the Emanation of the Sleeper descended
With solemn mourning out of Beulahs moony shades and hills:
Within the Human Heart, whose Gates closed with solemn sound.

And this the manner of the terrible Separation
The Emanations of the grievously afflicted Friends of Albion
Concenter in one Female form an Aged pensive Woman.
Astonish'd! lovely! embracing the sublime shade: the Daughters of Beulah
Beheld her with wonder! With awful hands she took
A Moment of Time, drawing it out with many tears & afflictions
And many sorrows, oblique across the Atlantic Vale
Which is the Vale of Rephaim dreadful from East to West,
Where the Human Harvest waves abundant in the beams of Eden
Into a Rainbow of jewels and gold, a mild Reflection from
Albions dread Tomb. Eight thousand and five hundred years
In its extension. Every two hundred years has a door to Eden
She also took an Atom of Space, with dire pain opening it a Center
Into Beulah: trembling the Daughters of Beulah dried
Her tears, she ardent embrac'd her sorrows, occupied in labours
Of sublime mercy in Rephaims Vale. Perusing Albions Tomb
She sat: she walk'd among the ornaments solemn mourning.
The Daughters attended her shudderings, wiping the death sweat
Los also saw her in his seventh Furnace, he also terrified
Saw the finger of God go forth upon his seventh Furnace:
Away from the Starry Wheels to prepare Jerusalem a Place.
When with a dreadful groan the Emanation mild of Albion
Burst from his bosom in the Tomb like a pale snowy cloud,
Female and lovely, struggling to put off the Human form
Writhing in pain. The Daughters of Beulah in kind arms reciev'd
Jerusalem: weeping over her among the Spaces of Erin,
In the Ends of Beulah, where the Dead wail night & day.

And thus Erin spoke to the Daughters of Beulah, in soft tears

Albion the Vortex of the Dead! Albion the Generous!
Albion the mildest son of Heaven! The Place of Holy Sacrifice!
Where Friends Die for each other: will become the Place,
Of Murder, & Unforgiving, Never-awaking Sacrifice of Enemies
The Children must be sacrifıc'd! (a horror never known
Till now in Beulah.) unless a Refuge can be found
To hide them from the wrath of Albions Law that freezes sore
Upon his Sons & Daughters, self-exiled from his bosom
Draw ye Jerusalem away from Albions Mountains
To give a Place for Redemption, let Sihon and Og
Remove Eastward to Bashan and Gilead, and leave

The secret coverts of Albion & the hidden places of America
Jerusalem Jerusalem! why wilt thou turn away
Come ye O Daughters of Beulah, lament for Og & Sihon
Upon the Lakes of Ireland from Rathlin to Baltimore:
Stand ye upon the Dargle from Wicklow to Drogheda
Come & mourn over Albion the White Cliff of the Atlantic
The Mountain of Giants: all the Giants of Albion are become
Weak! witherd! darkend: & Jerusalem is cast forth from Albion
They deny that they ever knew Jerusalem. or ever dwelt in Shiloh
The Gigantic roots & twigs of the vegetating Sons of Albion
Filld with the little ones are consumed in the fires of their Altars
The vegetating Cities are burned & consumed from the Earth
And the Bodies in which all Animals & Vegetations, the Earth & Heaven
Were containd in the All Glorious Imagination are witherd & darkend;
The golden Gate of Havilah. and all the Garden of God.
Was caught up with the Sun in one day of fury and war:
The Lungs. the Heart, the Liver, shrunk away far distant from Man
And left a little slimy substance floating upon the tides:
In one right the Atlantic Continent was caught up with the Moon,
And became an Opake Globe far distant clad with moony beams.
The Visions of Eternity, by reason of narrowed perceptions,
Are become weak Visions of Time & Space fixd into furrows of death;
Till deep dissimulation is the only defence an honest man has left
O Polypus of Death O Spectre over Europe and Asia
Withering the Human Form by Laws of Sacrifice for Sin
By Laws of Chastity & Abhorrence I am witherd up.
Striving to Create a Heaven in which all shall be pure & holy
In their Own Selfhoods, in Natural Selfish Chastity to banish Pity
And dear Mutual Forgiveness, & to become One Great Satan
Inslavd to the most powerful Selfhood: to murder the Divine Humanity
In whose sight all are as the dust & who changeth his Angels with folly
Oh! weak & wide astray! Ah shut in narrow doleful form!
Creeping in reptile flesh upon the bosom of the ground:
The Eye of Man a little narrow orb, closd up & dark
Scarcely beholding the Great Light, conversing with the ground.
The Ear, a little shell, in small volutions shutting out
True Harmonies, & comprehending great, as very small:
The Nostrils, bent down to the earth & closd with senseless flesh.
That odours cannot expand, nor joy on them exult:
The Tongue, a little moisture fills, a little food it cloys:
A little sound it utters, & its cries are faintly heard.
Therefore they are removed: therefore they have taken root
In Egypt & Philistea: in Moab & Edom & Aram:
In the Erythrean Sea their Uncircumcision in Heart & Loins
Be lost for ever & ever, then they shall arise from Self
By Self Annihilation into Jerusalems Courts & into Shiloh
Shiloh the Masculine Emanation among the Flowers of Beulah
Lo Shiloh dwells over France, as Jerusalem dwells over Albion
Build & prepare a Wall & Curtain for Americas shore
Rush on! Rush on! Rush on! ye vegetating Sons of Albion
The Sun shall go before you in Day: the Moon shall go
Before you in Night. Come on! Come on! Come on! The Lord
Jehovah is before, behind, above, beneath, around
He has builded the arches of Albions Tomb binding the Stars
In merciful Order, bending the Laws of Cruelty to Peace.
He hath placed Og & Anak, the Giants of Albion for their Guards:
Building the Body of Moses in the Valley of Peor: the Body
Of Divine Analogy: and Og & Sihon in the tears of Balaam
The Son of Beor have given their power to Joshua & Caleb.
Remove from Albion, far remove these terrible surfaces.
They are beginning to form Heavens & Hells in immense
Circles: the Hells for food to the Heavens: food of torment,
Food of despair: they drink the condemnd Soul & rejoice
In cruel holiness, in their Heavens of Chastity & Uncircumcision
Yet they are blameless & Iniquity must be imputed only
To the State they are enterd into that they may be deliverd:
Satan is the State of Death, & not a Human existence:
But Luvah is named Satan, because he has enter'd that State,
A World where Man is by Nature the enemy of Man
Because the Evil is Created into a State. that Men
May be deliverd time after time evermore. Amen
Learn therefore O Sisters to distinguish the Eternal Human
That walks about among the stones of fire in bliss & woe
Alternate: from those States or Worlds in which the Spirit travels:
This is the only means to Forgiveness of Enemies
Therefore remove from Albion these terrible Surfaces
And let wild seas & rocks close up Jerusalem away from The

The Atlantic Mountains where Giants dwelt in Intellect;
Now given to stony Druids, and Allegoric Generation
To the Twelve Gods of Asia. the Spectres of those who Sleep:
Sway'd by a Providence oppos'd to the Divine Lord Jesus:
A murderous Providence! a Creation that groans, living on Death.
Where Fish & Bird & Beast & Man & Tree & Metal & Stone
Live by Devouring, going into Eternal Death continually:
Albion is now possess'd by the War of Blood! the Sacrifice
Of envy Albion is become, and his Emanation cast out:
Come Lord Jesus. Lamb of God descend! for if; O Lord!
If thou hadst been here, our brother Albion had not died.
Arise sisters! Go ye & meet the Lord, while I remain—
Behold the foggy mornings of the Dead on Albions cliffs:
Ye know that if the Emanation remains in them:
She will become an Eternal Death, an Avenger of Sin
A Self-righteousness: the proud Virgin-Harlot! Mother of War!
And we also & all Beulah, consume beneath Albions curse.

So Erin spoke to the Daughters of Beulah. Shuddering
With their wings they sat in the Furnace, in a night
Of stars, for all the Sons of Albion appeard distant stars.
Ascending and descending into Albions sea of death.
And Erins lovely Bow enclos'd the Wheels of Albions Sons.

Expanding on wing. the Daughters of Beulah replied in sweet response

Come O thou Lamb of God and take away the remembrance of Sin
To Sin & to hide the Sin in sweet deceit. is lovely!!
To Sin in the open face of day is cruel & pitiless! But
To record the Sin for a reproach: to let the Sun go down
In a remembrance of the Sin: is a Woe & a Horror!
A brooder of an Evil Day, and a Sun rising in blood
Come then O Lamb of God and take away the remembrance of Sin

End of Chap 2.

Rahab is an Eternal State } **To the Deists** { The Spiritual States of the Soul are all Eternal Distinguish between the Man, & his present State

He never can be a Friend to the Human Race who is the Preacher of Natural Morality or Natural Religion, he is a flatterer who means to betray, to perpetuate Tyrant Pride & the Laws of that Babylon which he foresees shall shortly be destroyed, with the Spiritual and not the Natural Sword: He is in the State named Rahab: which State must be put off before he can be the Friend of Man.

You O Deists profess yourselves the Enemies of Christianity: and you are so: you are also the Enemies of the Human Race & of Universal Nature. Man is born a Spectre or Satan & is altogether an Evil, & requires a New Selfhood continually & must continually be changed into his direct Contrary. But your Greek Philosophy (which is a Remnant of Druidism) teaches that Man is Righteous in his Vegetated Spectre: an Opinion of fatal & accursed consequence to Man, as the Ancients saw plainly by Revelation to the intire abrogation of Experimental Theory. and many believed what they saw, and Prophecied of Jesus.

Man must & will have Some Religion: if he has not the Religion of Jesus, he will have the Religion of Satan, & will erect the Synagogue of Satan, calling the Prince of this World, God; and destroying all who do not worship Satan under the Name of God. Will any one say: Where are those who worship Satan under the Name of God! Where are they? Listen! Every Religion that Preaches Vengeance for Sin is the Religion of the Enemy & Avenger; and not of the Forgiver of Sin, and their God is Satan, Named by the Divine Name Your Religion O Deists: Deism, is the Worship of the God of this World by the means of what you call Natural Religion and Natural Philosophy, and of Natural Morality or Self-Righteousness, the Selfish Virtues of the Natural Heart. This was the Religion of the Pharisees who murderd Jesus. Deism is the same & ends in the same.

Voltaire Rousseau Gibbon Hume, charge the Spiritually Religious with Hypocrisy! but how a Monk or a Methodist either, can be a Hypocrite: I cannot conceive. We are, Men of like passions with others & pretend not to be holier than others: therefore, when a Religious Man falls into Sin, he ought not to be called a Hypocrite: this title is more properly to be given to a Player who falls into Sin: whose profession is Virtue & Morality & the making Men Self-Righteous. Foote in calling Whitefield, Hypocrite: was himself one: for Whitefield pretended not to be holier than others; but confessed his Sins before all the World: Voltaire! Rousseau! You cannot escape my charge that you are Pharisees & Hypocrites, for you are constantly talking of the Virtues of the Human Heart, and particularly of your own, that you may accuse others & especially the Religious, whose errors, you by this display of pretended Virtue, chiefly design to expose. Rousseau thought Men Good by Nature: he found them Evil & found no friend. Friendship cannot exist without Forgiveness of Sins continually. The Book written by Rousseau calld his Confessions is an apology & cloke for his Sin & not a confession.

But you also charge the poor Monks & Religious with being the causes of War: while you acquit & flatter the Alexanders & Caesars, the Lewis's & Fredericks: who alone are its causes & its actors. But the Religion of Jesus, Forgiveness of Sin, can never be the cause of a War nor of a single Martyrdom.

Those who Martyr others or who cause War are Deists, but never can be Forgivers of Sin. The Glory of Christianity is, To Conquer by Forgiveness. All the Destruction therefore, in Christian Europe has arisen from Deism, which is Natural Religion.

I saw a Monk of Charlemaine
Arise before my sight
I talked with the Grey Monk as we stood
In beams of infernal light

Gibbon arose with a lash of steel
And Voltaire with a wracking wheel
The Schools in clouds of learning rolld
Arose with War in iron & gold.

Thou lazy Monk they sound afar
In vain condemning glorious War
And in your Cell you shall ever dwell
Rise War & bind him in his Cell!

(Side)
The blood, red ran from the Grey Monks side
His hands & feet, were wounded wide
His body bent, his arms & knees
Like to the roots of ancient trees

When Satan first the black bow bent
And the Moral Law from the Gospel, rent
He forgd the Law into a Sword
And spilld the blood of mercys Lord!

Titus! Constantine! Charlemaine!
O Voltaire! Rousseau! Gibbon! Vain
Your Grecian Mocks & Roman Sword
Against this image of his Lord!

For a Tear is an Intellectual thing
And a Sigh is the Sword of an Angel King
And the bitter groan of a Martyrs woe
Is an Arrow from the Almighties Bow!

Jerusalem

Chap 3.

But Los, who is the Vehicular Form of strong Urthona
Wept vehemently over Albion where Thames currents spring
From the rivers of Beulah; pleasant river! soft, mild, parent stream
And the roots of Albions Tree enterd the Soul of Los
As he sat before his Furnaces clothed in sackcloth of hair
In gnawing pain dividing him from his Emanation:
Inclosing all the Children of Los time after time
Their Giant forms condensing into Nations & Peoples & Tongues
Translucent the Furnaces of Beryll & Emerald immortal:
And Seven-fold each within other: incomprehensible
To the Vegetated Mortal Eye's perverted & single vision
The Bellows are the Animal Lungs: the Hammers, the Animal Heart
The Furnaces, the Stomach for Digestion: terrible their fury
Like seven burning heavens rang'd from South to North

Here on the banks of the Thames, Los builded Golgonooza,
Outside of the Gates of the Human Heart, beneath Beulah
In the midst of the rocks of the Altars of Albion. In fears
He builded it, in rage & in fury. It is the Spiritual Fourfold
London: continually building & continually decaying desolate:
In eternal labours: loud the Furnaces & loud the Anvils
Of Death thunder incessant around the flaming Couches of
The Twentyfour Friends of Albion and round the awful Four
For the protection of the Twelve Emanations of Albions Sons
The Mystic Union of the Emanation in the Lord; Because
Man divided from his Emanation is a dark Spectre
His Emanation is an ever-weeping melancholy Shadow
But she is made receptive of Generation thro' mercy
In the Potters Furnace, among the Funeral Urns of Beulah
From Surrey hills, thro' Italy and Greece, to Hinnoms vale.

In Great Eternity, every particular Form gives forth or Emanates
Its own peculiar Light, & the Form is the Divine Vision
And the Light is his Garment This is Jerusalem in every Man
A Tent & Tabernacle of Mutual Forgiveness Male & Female Clothings.
And Jerusalem is called Liberty among the Children of Albion

But Albion fell down a Rocky fragment from Eternity hurld
By his own Spectre, who is the Reasoning Power in every Man
Into his own Chaos which is the Memory between Man & Man

The silent broodings of deadly revenge springing from the
All powerful parental affection, fills Albion from head to foot
Seeing his Sons assimilate with Luvah, bound in the bonds
Of spiritual Hate, from which springs Sexual Love as iron chains
He tosses like a cloud outstretchd among Jerusalems Ruins
Which overspread all the Earth, he groans among his ruind porches

Reason

Pity — Wrath
This World

Desire

But the Spectre like a hoar frost & a Mildew rose over Albion
Saying, I am God O Sons of Men! I am your Rational Power!
Am I not Bacon & Newton & Locke who teach Humility to Man!
Who teach Doubt & Experiment & my two Wings Voltaire: Rousseau.
Where is that Friend of Sinners! that Rebel against my Laws!
Who teaches Belief to the Nations. & an unknown Eternal Life
Come hither into the Desart & turn these stones to bread.
Vain foolish Man! wilt thou believe without Experiment?
And build a World of Phantasy upon my Great Abyss!
A World of Shapes in craving lust & devouring appetite
So spoke the hard cold constrictive Spectre he is named Arthur
Constructing into Druid Rocks round Canaan Agag & Aram & Pharoh

Then Albion drew England into his bosom in groans & tears
But she stretchd out her starry Night in Spaces against him. like
A long Serpent, in the Abyss of the Spectre which augmented
The Night with Dragon wings coverd with stars & in the Wings
Jerusalem & Vala appeard: & above between the Wings magnificent
The Divine Vision dimly appeard in clouds of blood weeping.

Then those who disregard all Mortal Things, saw a Mighty-One
Among the Flowers of Beulah still retain his awful strength
They wonderd: checking their wild flames & Many gathering
Together into an Assembly; they said, let us go down
And see these changes! Others said, If you do so prepare
For being driven from our fields, what have we to do with the Dead
To be their inferiors or superiors we equally abhor;
Superior. none we know: inferior none: all equal share
Divine Benevolence & Joy: for the Eternal Man
Walketh among us, calling us his Brothers & his Friends:
Forbidding us that Veil which Satan puts between Eve & Adam
By which the Princes of the Dead enslave their Votaries
Teaching them to form the Serpent of precious stones & gold
To sieze the Sons of Jerusalem & plant them in One Mans Loins
To make One Family of Contraries: that Joseph may be sold
Into Egypt: for Negation; a Veil the Saviour born & dying rends

But others said: Let us to him who only Is, & who
Walketh among us, give decision. bring forth all your fires!

So saying, an eternal deed was done: in fiery flames
The Universal Concave raged, such thunderous sounds as never
Were sounded from a mortal cloud, nor on Mount Sinai old
Nor in Havilah where the Cherub rolld his redounding flame.

Loud! loud! the Mountains lifted up their voices, loud the Forests
Rivers thunderd against their banks. loud Words furious fought
Cities & Nations contended in fires & clouds & tempests.
The Seas raisd up their voices & lifted their hands on high
The Stars in their courses fought, the Sun! Moon! Heaven! Earth.
Contending for Albion & for Jerusalem his Emanation
And for Shiloh, the Emanation of France & for lovely Vala.

Then far the greatest number were about to make a Separation
And they Elected Seven, calld the Seven Eyes of God;
Lucifer. Molech. Elohim. Shaddai. Pahad. Jehovah. Jesus.
They namd the Eighth. he came not. he hid in Albions Forests
But first they said: (& their Words stood in Chariots in array
Curbing their Tygers with golden bits & bridles of silver & ivory)

Let the Human Organs be kept in their perfect Integrity
At will Contracting into Worms, or Expanding into Gods
And then behold! what are these Ulro Visions of Chastity
Then as the moss upon the tree: or dust upon the plow:
Or as the sweat upon the labouring shoulder: or as the chaff
Of the wheat floor or as the dregs of the sweet wine-press
Such are these Ulro Visions, for, tho we sit down within
The plowed furrow, listning to the weeping clods till we
Contract or Expand Space at will: or if we raise ourselves
Upon the chariots of the morning. Contracting or Expanding Time!
Every one knows, we are One Family! One Man blessed for ever

Silence remaind & every one resumd his Human Majesty
And many conversed on these things as they labourd at the furrow
Saying: It is better to prevent misery, than to release from misery
It is better to prevent error, than to forgive the criminal:
Labour well the Minute Particulars, attend to the Little-ones:
And those who are in misery cannot remain so long
If we do but our duty: labour well the teeming Earth.

They Plow'd in tears. the trumpets sounded before the golden Plow
And the voices of the Living Creatures were heard in the clouds of heaven
Crying: Compell the Reasoner to Demonstrate with unhewn Demonstrations
Let the Indefinite be explored. and let every Man be Judged
By his own Works, Let all Indefinites be thrown into Demonstrations
To be pounded to dust & melted in the Furnaces of Affliction:
He who would do good to another, must do it in Minute Particulars
General Good is the plea of the scoundrel hypocrite & flatterer:
For Art & Science cannot exist but in minutely organized Particulars
And not in generalizing Demonstrations of the Rational Power.
The Infinite alone resides in Definite & Determinate Identity
Establishment of Truth depends on destruction of Falshood continually
On Circumcision: not on Virginity, O Reasoners of Albion

So cried they at the Plow. Albions Rock frowned above
And the Great Voice of Eternity rolled above terrible in clouds
Saying Who will go forth for us! & who shall we send before our face?

Then Los heaved his thund'ring Bellows on the Valley of Middlesex
And thus he chaunted his Song: the Daughters of Albion reply,

What may Man be? who can tell! But what may Woman be?
To have power over Man from Cradle to corruptible Grave.
He who is an Infant, and whose Cradle is a Manger
Knoweth the Infant sorrow: whence it came, and where it goeth.
And who weave it a Cradle of the grass that withereth away.
This World is all a Cradle for the erred wandering Phantom:
Rock'd by Year, Month, Day & Hour; and every two Moments
Between, dwells a Daughter of Beulah, to feed the Human Vegetable
Entune: Daughters of Albion. your hymning Chorus mildly!
Cord of affection thrilling extatic on the iron Reel:
To the golden Loom of Love! to the moth-labour'd Woof
A Garment and Cradle weaving for the infantine Terror:
For fear; at entering the gate into our World of cruel
Lamentation: it flee back & hide in Non-Entitys dark wild
Where dwells the Spectre of Albion: destroyer of Definite Form.
The Sun shall be a Scythed Chariot of Britain: the Moon; a Ship
In the British Ocean! Created by Los's Hammer; measured out
Into Days & Nights & Years & Months. to travel with my feet
Over these desolate rocks of Albion: O daughters of despair!
Rock the Cradle, and in mild melodies tell me where found
What you have enwoven with so much tears & care? so much
Tender artifice: to laugh: to weep: to learn: to know;
Remember! recollect! what dark befel in wintry days

O it was lost for ever! and we found it not: it came
And wept at our wintry Door: Look! look! behold! Gwendolen
Is become a Clod of Clay! Merlin is a Worm of the Valley!

Then Los uttered with Hammer & Anvil: Chaunt! revoice!
I mind not your laugh: and your frown I not fear! and
You must my dictate obey from your gold-beam'd Looms: trill
Gentle to Albions Watchman. on Albions mountains; reeccho
And rock the Cradle while! Ah me! Of that Eternal Man
And of the cradled Infancy in his bowels of compassion:
Who fell beneath his instruments of husbandry & became
Subservient to the clods of the furrow! the cattle and even
The emmet and earth-Worm are his superiors & his lords.

Then the response came warbling from trilling Looms in Albion
We Women tremble at the light therefore: hiding fearful
The Divine Vision with Curtain & Veil & fleshly Tabernacle
Los utterd: swift as the rattling thunder upon the mountains
Look back into the Church Paul! Look! Three Women around
The Cross! O Albion why didst thou a Female Will Create?

York   London

And the voices of Bath & Canterbury & York & Edinburgh Cry
Over the Plow of Nations in the strong hand of Albion thundering along
Among the Fires of the Druid & the deep black rethundering Waters
Of the Atlantic which poured in impetuous loud loud louder & louder.
And the Great Voice of the Atlantic howled over the Druid Altars.
Weeping over his Children in Stone-henge in Malden & Colchester.
Round the Rocky Peak of Derbyshire London Stone & Rosamonds Bower

What is a Wife & what is a Harlot? What is a Church? & What ?
Is a Theatre? are they Two & not One? can they Exist Separate?
Are not Religion & Politics the Same Thing? Brotherhood is Religion
O Demonstrations of Reason Dividing Families in Cruelty & Pride!

But Albion fled from the Divine Vision with the Plow of Nations enflaming
The Living Creatures maddend and Albion fell into the Furrow. and
The Plow went over him & the Living was Plowed in among the Dead
But his Spectre rose over the starry Plow. Albion fled beneath the Plow
Till he came to the Rock of Ages, & he took his Seat upon the Rock.
Wonder seizd all in Eternity! to behold the Divine Vision. open
The Center into an Expanse, & the Center rolled out into an Expanse

Jerusalem

In beauty the Daughters of Albion divide & unite at will
Naked & drunk with blood Gwendolen dancing to the timbrel
Of War: reeling up the Street of London she divides in twain
Among the Inhabitants of Albion, the People fall around
The Daughters of Albion, divide & unite in jealousy & cruelty
The Inhabitants of Albion at the Harvest & the Vintage
Feel their Brain cut round beneath the temples shrieking
Bonifying into a Scull, the Marrow exuding in dismal pain
They flee over the rocks bonifying: Horses Oxen, feel the knife.
And while the Sons of Albion by severe War & Judgement, bonify
The Hermaphroditic Condensations are divided by the Knife
The obdurate Forms are cut asunder by Jealousy & Pity.

Rational Philosophy and Mathematic Demonstration
Is divided in the intoxications of pleasure & affection,
Two Contraries War against each other in fury & blood,
And Los fixes them on his Anvil, incessant his blows:
He fixes them with strong blows, placing the stones & timbers.
To Create a World of Generation from the World of Death:
Dividing the Masculine & Feminine: for the comingling
Of Albions & Luvahs Spectres was Hermaphroditic

Urizen wrathful strode above directing the awful Building:
As a Mighty Temple; delivering Form out of confusion
Jordan sprang beneath its threshold bubbling from beneath
Its pillars: Euphrates ran under its arches: white sails
And silver oars reflect on its pillars, & sound on its ecchoing
Pavements: where walk the Sons of Jerusalem who remain Ungenerate
But the revolving Sun and Moon pass thro its porticoes.
Day & night, in sublime majesty & silence they revolve
And shine glorious within! Hand & Koban arch'd over the Sun
In the hot noon, as he traveld thro his journey: Hyle & Skofield
Arch'd over the Moon at midnight & Los Fix'd them there,
With his thunderous Hammer; terrified the Spectres rage & flee
Canaan is his portico; Jordan is a fountain in his porch:
A fountain of milk & wine to relieve the traveller:
Egypt is the eight steps within. Ethiopia supports his pillars:
Lybia & the Lands unknown, are the ascent without:
Within is Asia & Greece, ornamented with exquisite art:
Persia & Media are his halls: his inmost hall is Great Tartary.
China & India & Siberia are his temples for entertainment
Poland & Russia & Sweden, his soft retired chambers
France & Spain & Italy & Denmark & Holland & Germany
Are the temples among his pillars: Britain is Los's Forge:
America North & South are his baths of living waters.

Such is the Ancient World of Urizen in the Satanic Void
Created from the Valley of Middlesex by Londons River
From Stone-henge & from London Stone, from Cornwall to Cathnes
The Four Zoa's rush around on all sides in dire ruin
Furious in pride of Selfhood the terrible Spectres of Albion
Rear their dark Rocks among the Stars of God: stupendous
Works! A World of Generation continually Creating; out of
The Hermaphroditic Satanic World of rocky destiny.

And formed into Four precious stones. for enterance from Beulah

For the Veil of Vala which Albion cast into the Atlantic Deep
To catch the Souls of the Dead: began to Vegetate & Petrify
Around the Earth of Albion. among the Roots of his Tree
This Los formed into the Gates & mighty Wall, between the Oak
Of Weeping & the Palm of Suffering beneath Albions Tomb.
Thus in process of time it became the beautiful Mundane Shell.
The Habitation of the Spectres of the Dead & the Place
Of Redemption & of awaking again into Eternity

For Four Universes round the Mundane Egg remain Chaotic
One to the North: Urthona: One to the South: Urizen:
One to the East: Luvah: One to the West: Tharmas;
They are the Four Zoas that stood around the Throne Divine
Verulam: London: York & Edinburgh: their English names
But when Luvah assumed the World of Urizen Southward
And Albion was slain upon his Mountains & in his Tent.
All fell towards the Center, sinking downwards in dire ruin.
In the South remains a burning Fire: in the East, a Void.
In the West, a World of raging Waters: in the North: solid Darkness
Unfathomable without end: but in the midst of these
Is Built eternally the sublime Universe of Los & Enitharmon.

And, in the North Gate, in the West of the North. toward Beulah
Cathedrons Looms are builded. & Loss Furnaces in the South
A wondrous golden Building immense with ornaments sublime
Is bright Cathedrons golden Hall. its Courts Towers & Pinnacles

And one Daughter of Los sat at the fiery Reel & another
Sat at the shining Loom with her Sisters attending round
Terrible their distress & their sorrow cannot be utterd
And another Daughter of Los sat at the Spinning Wheel
Endless their labour, with bitter food. void of sleep.
Tho hungry they labour: they rouze themselves anxious
Hour after hour labouring at the whirling Wheel
Many Wheels & as many lovely Daughters sit weeping
Yet the intoxicating delight that they take in their work
Obliterates every other evil: none pities their tears
Yet they regard not pity & they expect no one to pity
For they labour for life & love, regardless of any one
But the poor Spectres that they work for, always incessantly
They are mockd, by every one that passes by. they regard not
They labour: & when their Wheels are broken by scorn & malice
They mend them sorrowing with many tears & afflictions.
Other Daughters Weave on the Cushion & Pillow, Network fine
That Rahab & Tirzah may exist & live & breathe & love
Ah, that it could be as the Daughters of Beulah wish!
Other Daughters of Los, labouring at Looms less fine
Create the Silk-worm & the Spider & the Caterpiller
To assist in their most grievous work of pity & compassion
And others Create the wooly Lamb & the downy Fowl
To assist in the work: the Lamb bleats: the Sea-fowl cries
Men understand not the distress & the labour & sorrow
That in the Interior Worlds is carried on in fear & trembling
Weaving the shuddring fears & loves of Albions Families
Thunderous rage the Spindles of iron. & the iron Distaff
Maddens in the fury of their hands. Weaving in bitter tears
The Veil of Goats-hair & Purple & Scarlet & fine twined Linen

The clouds of Albions Druid Temples rage in the eastern heaven
While Los sat terrified beholding Albions Spectre who is Luvah
Spreading in bloody veins in torments over Europe & Asia:
Not yet formed but a wretched torment unformed & abyssal
In flaming fire; within the Furnaces the Divine Vision appeard
On Albions hills: often walking from the Furnaces in clouds
And flames among the Druid Temples & the Starry Wheels
Gatherd Jerusalems Children in his arms & bore them like
A Shepherd in the night of Albion which overspread all the Earth

I gave thee liberty and life O lovely Jerusalem
And thou hast bound me down upon the Stems of Vegetation
I gave thee Sheep-walks upon the Spanish Mountains Jerusalem
I gave thee Priams City and the Isles of Grecia lovely!
I gave thee Hand & Scofield & the Counties of Albion:
They spread forth like a lovely root into the Garden of God:
They were as Adam before me: united into One Man,
They stood in innocence & their skiey tent reachd over Asia
To Nimrods Tower to Ham & Canaan walking with Mizraim
Upon the Egyptian Nile, with solemn songs to Grecia
And sweet Hesperia even to Great Chaldea & Tesshina
Following thee as a Shepherd by the Four Rivers of Eden
Why wilt thou rend thyself apart, Jerusalem?
And build this Babylon & sacrifice in secret Groves,
Among the Gods of Asia: among the fountains of pitch & nitre
Therefore thy Mountains are become barren Jerusalem!
Thy Valleys, Plains of burning sand, thy Rivers: waters of death
Thy Villages die of the Famine and thy Cities
Beg bread from house to house, lovely Jerusalem
Why wilt thou deface thy beauty & the beauty of thy little-ones
To please thy Idols, in the pretended chastities of Uncircumcision
Thy Sons are lovelier than Egypt or Assyria: wherefore
Dost thou blacken their beauty by a Secluded place of rest,
And a peculiar Tabernacle, to cut the integuments of beauty
Into veils of tears and sorrows O lovely Jerusalem:
They have persuaded thee to this, therefore their end shall come
And I will lead thee thro the Wilderness in shadow of my cloud
And in my love I will lead thee, lovely Shadow of Sleeping Albion.
This is the Song of the Lamb, sung by Slaves in evening time.

But Jerusalem faintly saw him, closd in the Dungeons of Babylon
Her Form was held by Beulahs Daughters, but all within unseen
She sat at the Mills, her hair unbound her feet naked
Cut with the flints: her tears run down, her reason grows like
The Wheel of Hand, incessant turning day & night without rest
Insane she raves upon the winds, hoarse, inarticulate:
All night Vala hears, she triumphs in pride of holiness
To see Jerusalem deface her lineaments with bitter blows
Of despair, while the Satanic Holiness triumphd in Vala
In a Religion of Chastity & Uncircumcised Selfishness
Both of the Head & Heart & Loins, closd up in Moral Pride.

But the Divine Lamb stood beside Jerusalem, oft she saw
The lineaments Divine & oft the Voice heard, & oft she said:
O Lord & Saviour, have the Gods of the Heathen pierced thee:
Or hast thou been pierced in the House of thy Friends?
Art thou alive! & livest thou for evermore? or art thou
Not: but a delusive shadow, a thought that liveth not.
Babel mocks saying, there is no God nor Son of God
That thou O Human Imagination, O Divine Body art all
A delusion, but I know thee O Lord when thou arisest upon
My weary eyes even in this dungeon, & this iron mill,
The Stars of Albion cruel rise; thou bindest to sweet influences:
For thou also sufferest with me altho I behold thee not:
And altho I sin & blaspheme thy holy name, thou pitiest me:
Because thou knowest I am deluded by the turning mills,
And by these visions of pity & love because of Albions death.
Thus spake Jerusalem, & thus the Divine Voice replied:

Mild Shade of Man, pitiest thou these Visions of terror & woe!
Give forth thy pity & love, fear not! lo I am with thee always,
Only believe in me that I have power to raise from death
Thy Brother who Sleepeth in Albion: fear not trembling Shade

Behold: in the Visions of Elohim Jehovah, behold Joseph & Mary
And be comforted O Jerusalem in the Visions of Jehovah Elohim

She looked & saw Joseph the Carpenter in Nazareth & Mary
His espoused Wife. And Mary said. If thou put me away from thee
Dost thou not murder me? Joseph spoke in anger & fury. Should I
Marry a Harlot & an Adulteress? Mary answerd. Art thou more pure
Than thy Maker who forgiveth Sins & calls again Her that is Lost
Tho She hates. he calls her again in love. I love my dear Joseph
But he driveth me away from his presence. yet I hear the voice of God.
In the voice of my Husband. tho he is angry for a moment. he will not
Utterly cast me away. if I were pure. never could I taste the sweets
Of the Forgiveness of Sins! if I were holy! I never could behold the tears
Of love! of him who loves me in the midst of his anger in furnace of fire.

Ah my Mary: said Joseph: weeping over & embracing her closely in
His arms: Doth he forgive Jerusalem & not exact Purity from her who is
Polluted. I heard his voice in my sleep & his Angel in my dream:
Saying Doth Jehovah Forgive a Debt only on condition that it shall
Be Payed? Doth he Forgive Pollution only on conditions of Purity
That Debt is not Forgiven! That Pollution is not Forgiven
Such is the Forgiveness of the Gods, the Moral Virtues of the
Heathen, whose tender Mercies are Cruelty. But Jehovahs Salvation
Is without Money & without Price, in the Continual Forgiveness of Sins
In the Perpetual Mutual Sacrifice in Great Eternity! for behold!
There is none that liveth & Sinneth not! And this is the Covenant
Of Jehovah: If you Forgive one-another. so shall Jehovah Forgive You:
That He Himself may Dwell among You. Fear not then to take
To thee Mary thy Wife. for she is with Child by the Holy Ghost

Then Mary burst forth into a Song! she flowed like a River of
Many Streams in the arms of Joseph & gave forth her tears of joy
Like many waters, and Emanating into gardens & palaces upon
Euphrates & to forests & floods & animals wild & tame from
Gihon to Hiddekel. & to corn fields & villages & inhabitants
Upon Pison & Arnon & Jordan. And I heard the voice among
The Reapers Saying. Am I Jerusalem the lost Adulteress? or am I
Babylon come up to Jerusalem? And another voice answerd Saying
Does the voice of my Lord call me again. am I pure thro his Mercy
And Pity. Am I become lovely as a Virgin in his sight who am
Indeed a Harlot drunken with the Sacrifice of Idols does he
Call her pure as he did in the days of her Infancy when She
Was cast out to the loathing of her person. The Chaldean took
Me from my Cradle. The Amalekite stole me away upon his Camels
Before I had ever beheld with love the Face of Jehovah; or known
That there was a God of Mercy: O Mercy O Divine Humanity!
O Forgiveness & Pity & Compassion! If I were Pure I should never
Have known Thee; If I were Unpolluted I should never have
Glorified thy Holiness. or rejoiced in thy great Salvation!

Mary leaned her side against Jerusalem: Jerusalem recieved
The Infant into her hands in the Visions of Jehovah. Times passed on
Jerusalem fainted over the Cross & Sepulcher She heard the voice
Wilt thou make Rome thy Patriarch Druid & the Kings of Europe his
Horsemen? Man in the Resurrection changes his Sexual Garments at Will
Every Harlot was once a Virgin. every Criminal an Infant Love!

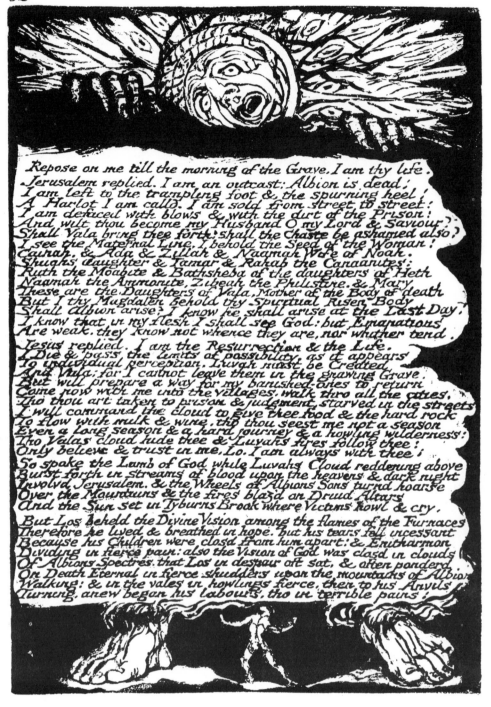

Repose on me till the morning of the Grave. I am thy life.
Jerusalem replied. I am an outcast: Albion is dead;
I am left to the trampling foot & the spurning heel;
A Harlot I am calld. I am sold from street to street:
I am defaced with blows & with the dirt of the Prison:
And wilt thou become my Husband O my Lord & Saviour?
Shall Vala bring thee forth: shall the Chaste be ashamed also?
I see the Maternal Line, I behold the Seed of the Woman!
Cainah, & Ada & Zillah & Naamah Wife of Noah.
Shuahs daughter & Tamar & Rahab the Canaanites:
Ruth the Moabite & Bathsheba of the daughters of Heth
Naamah the Ammonite, Zibeah the Philistine. & Mary
These are the Daughters of Vala, Mother of the Body of death
But I thy Magdalen behold thy Spiritual Risen Body
Shall Albion arise? I know he shall arise at the Last Day!
I know that in my flesh I shall see God: but Emanations
Are weak. they know not whence they are, nor whither tend.

Jesus replied. I am the Resurrection & the Life.
I Die & pass the limits of possibility, as it appears
To individual perception. Luvah must be Created
And Vala; for I cannot leave them in the gnawing Grave.
But will prepare a way for my banished-ones to return
Come now with me into the villages. walk thro all the cities.
Tho thou art taken to prison & judgement, starved in the streets
I will command the cloud to give thee food & the hard rock
To flow with milk & wine, tho thou seest me not a season
Even a long season & a hard journey & a howling wilderness!
Tho Valas cloud hide thee & Luvahs fires follow thee!
Only believe & trust in me, Lo. I am always with thee!
So spoke the Lamb of God while Luvahs Cloud reddening above
Burst forth in streams of blood upon the heavens & dark night
Involvd Jerusalem. & the Wheels of Albions Sons turnd hoarse
Over the Mountains & the fires blazd on Druid Altars
And the Sun set in Tyburns Brook where Victims howl & cry.

But Los beheld the Divine Vision among the flames of the Furnaces
Therefore he lived & breathed in hope. but his tears fell incessant
Because his Children were closd from him apart: & Enitharmon
Dividing in fierce pain: also the Vision of God was closd in clouds
Of Albions Spectres. that Los in despair oft sat, & often ponderd
On Death Eternal in fierce shudders upon the mountains of Albion
Walking: & in the vales in howlings fierce, then to his Anvils
Turning. anew began his labours, tho in terrible pains!

Jehovah stood among the Druids in the Valley of Annandale
When the Four Zoas of Albion, the Four Living Creatures, the Cherubim
Of Albion tremble before the Spectre, in the starry Harness of the Plow
Of Nations. And their Names are Urizen & Luvah & Tharmas & Urthona
Luvah slew Tharmas the Angel of the Tongue & Albion brought him
To Justice in his own City of Paris, denying the Resurrection
Then Vala the Wife of Albion who is the Daughter of Luvah
Took vengeance Twelve-fold among the Chaotic Rocks of the Druids
Where the Human Victims howl to the Moon & Thor & Friga
Dance the dance of death contending with Jehovah among the Cherubim
The Chariot Wheels filled with Eyes rage along the howling Valley
In the Dividing of Reuben & Benjamin bleeding from Chester's River

The Giants & the Witches & the Ghosts of Albion dance with Thor
Thor & Friga, & the Fairies lead the Moon along the Valley of Cherubim
Bleeding in torrents from Mountain to Mountain, a lovely Victim
And Jehovah stood in the Gates of the Victim & he appeared
A weeping Infant in the Gates of Birth in the midst of Heaven

The Cities & Villages of Albion became Rock & Sand Unhumanized
The Druid Sons of Albion & the Heavens a Void around unfathomable
No Human Form but Sexual & a little weeping Infant pale reflected
Multitudinous in the Looking Glass of Enitharmon, on all sides
Around in the clouds of the Female, on Albions Cliffs of the Dead

Such the appearance in Cheviot: in the Divisions of Reuben

When the Cherubim hid their heads under their wings in deep slumbers
When the Druids demanded Chastity from Woman & all was lost.

How can the Female be Chaste O thou stupid Druid Cried Los
Without the Forgiveness of Sins in the merciful clouds of Jehovah
And without the Baptism of Repentance to wash away Calumnies. and
The Accusations of Sin that each may be Pure in their Neighbours sight
O when shall Jehovah give us Victims from his Flocks & Herds
Instead of Human Victims by the Daughters of Albion & Canaan

Then laugh'd Gwendolen & her laughter shook the Nations & Families of
The Dead beneath Beulah from Tyburn to Golgotha, and from
Ireland to Japan. furious her Lions & Tygers & Wolves sport before
Los on the Thames & Medway. London & Canterbury groan in pain

Los knew not yet what was done: he thought it was all in Vision
In Visions of the Dreams of Beulah among the Daughters of Albion
Therefore the Murder was put apart in the Looking Glass of Enitharmon
He saw in Valas hand the Druid Knife of Revenge & the Poison Cup
Of Jealousy, and thought it a Poetic Vision of the Atmospheres
Till Canaan roll'd apart from Albion across the Rhine along the Danube

And all the Land of Canaan suspended over the Valley of Cheviot
From Bashan to Tyre & from Troy to Gaza of the Amalekite
And Reuben fled with his head downwards among the Caverns

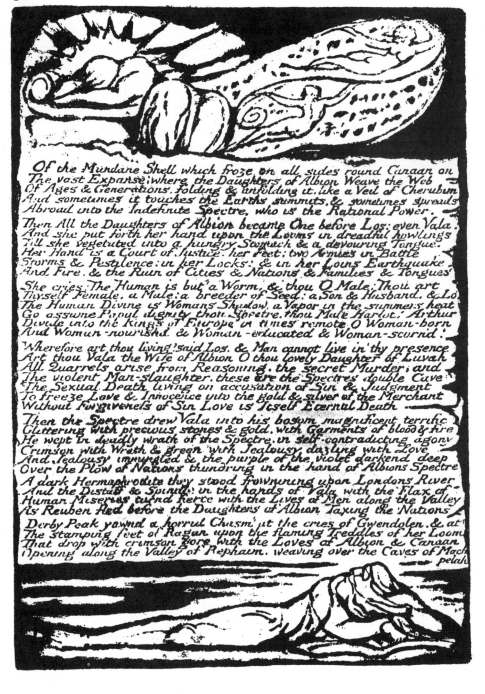

Of the Mundane Shell which froze on all sides round Canaan on
The vast Expanse: where the Daughters of Albion Weave the Web
Of Ages & Generations, folding & unfolding it, like a Veil of Cherubim
And sometimes it touches the Earths summits, & sometimes spreads
Abroad into the Indefinite Spectre, who is the Rational Power.

Then All the Daughters of Albion became One before Los: even Vala.
And she put forth her hand upon the Looms in dreadful howlings
Till she vegetated into a hungry Stomach & a devouring Tongue.
Her Hand is a Court of Justice, her Feet: two Armies in Battle
Storms & Pestilence: in her Locks: & in her Loins Earthquake.
And Fire. & the Ruin of Cities & Nations & Families & Tongues

She cries; The Human is but a Worm, & thou O Male: Thou art
Thyself Female, a Male: a breeder of Seed: a Son & Husband. & Lo.
The Human Divine is Womans Shadow, a Vapor in the summers heat
Go assume Paul dignity thou Spectre, thou Mule Harlot: Arthur
Divide into the Kings of Europe in times remote O Woman-born
And Woman-nourishd. & Woman-educated & Woman-scorned!

Wherefore art thou living? said Los. & Man cannot live in thy presence
Art thou Vala the Wife of Albion O thou lovely Daughter of Luvah
All Quarrels arise from Reasoning. the secret Murder, and
The violent Man-slaughter. these are the Spectres double Cave
The Sexual Death living on accusation of Sin & Judgment
To freeze Love & Innocence into the gold & silver of the Merchant
Without Forgiveness of Sin Love is Itself Eternal Death

Then the Spectre drew Vala into his bosom magnificent terrific.
Glittering with precious stones & gold, with Garments of blood & fire
He wept in deadly wrath of the Spectre, in self-contradicting agony
Crimson with Wrath & green with Jealousy, dazling with Love
And Jealousy immingled & the purple of the violet darkend deep
Over the Plow of Nations thundring in the hand of Albions Spectre

A dark Hermaphrodite they stood frowning upon Londons River
And the Distaff & Spindle in the hands of Vala with the Flax of
Human Miseries turnd fierce with the Lives of Men along the Valley
As Reuben fled before the Daughters of Albion Taxing the Nations

Derby Peak yawnd a horrid Chasm at the cries of Gwendolen. & at
The stamping feet of Ragan upon the flaming Treddles of her Loom
That drop with crimson gore with the Loves of Albion & Canaan
Opening along the Valley of Rephaim. weaving over the Caves of Mach
                                                              pelah

To decide Two Worlds with a great decision: a World of Mercy, and
A World of Justice: the World of Mercy for Salvation
To cast Luvah into the Wrath. and Albion into the Pity
In the Two Contraries of Humanity & in the Four Regions.

For in the depths of Albions bosom in the eastern heaven,
They sound the clarions strong! they chain the howling Captives:
They cast the lots into the helmet: they give the oath of blood in Lambeth
They vote the death of Luvah, & they naild him to Albions Tree in Bath:
They staind him with poisonous blue, they inwove him in cruel roots
To die a death of Six thousand years bound round with vegetation.
The sun was black & the moon rolld a useless globe thro Britain.

Then left the Sons of Urizen the plow & harrow. the loom
The hammer & the chisel, & the rule & compasses; from London fleeing
They forgd the sword on Cheviot. the chariot of war & the battle-ax,
The trumpet fitted to mortal battle, & the flute of summer in Annandale
And all the Arts of Life, they changd into the Arts of Death in Albion.
The hour-glass contemnd because its simple workmanship.
Was like the workmanship of the plowman, & the water wheel,
That raises water into cisterns: broken & burnd with fire:
Because its workmanship, was like the workmanship of the shepherd.
And in their stead, intricate wheels invented, wheel without wheel:
To perplex youth in their outgoings, & to bind to labours in Albion
Of day & night the myriads of eternity that they may grind
And polish brass & iron hour after hour laborious task:
Kept ignorant of its use, that they might spend the days of wisdom
In sorrowful drudgery, to obtain a scanty pittance of bread:
In ignorance to view a small portion & think that All,
And call it Demonstration: blind to all the simple rules of life.

Now: now the battle rages round thy tender limbs O Vala
Now smile among thy bitter tears: now put on all thy beauty
Is not the wound of the sword sweet! & the broken bone delightful?
Wilt thou now smile among the scythes when the wounded groan in the field
We were carried away in thousands from London; & in tens
Of thousands from Westminster & Marybone in ships closd up:
Chaind hand & foot. compelld to fight under the iron whips
Of our captains: fearing our officers more than the enemy.
Lift up thy blue eyes Vala & put on thy sapphire shoes:
O melancholy Magdalen behold the morning over Malden break:
Gird on thy flaming zone, descend into the Sepulcher of Canterbury.
Scatter the blood from thy golden brow, the tears from thy silver locks:
Shake off the waters from thy wings! & the dust from thy white garments
Remember all thy feigned terrors on the secret couch of Lambeths Vale
When the sun rose in glowing morn, with arms of mighty hosts
Marching to battle who was wont to rise with Urizens harps
Girt as a sower with his seed to scatter life abroad over Albion!
Arise O Vala: bring the bow of Urizen: bring the swift arrows of light.
How ragd the golden horses of Urizen, compelld to the chariot of love!
Compelld to leave the plow to the ax, to snuff up the winds of desolation
To trample the corn-fields in boastful neighings; this is no gentle harp
This is no warbling brook, nor shadow of a myrtle tree:
But blood and wounds and dismal cries, and shadows of the oak:
And hearts laid open to the light, by the broad grisly sword:
And bowels hid in hammerd steel ripd quivering on the ground:
Call forth thy smiles of soft deceit: call forth thy cloudy tears:
We hear thy sighs in trumpets shrill, when morn shall blood renew.

So sang the Spectre Sons of Albion round Luvahs Stone of Trial:
Mocking and deriding at the writhings of their Victim on Salisbury:
Drinking his Emanation in intoxicating bliss rejoicing in Giant dance:
For a Spectre has no Emanation but what he imbibes from deceiving
A Victim! Then he becomes her Priest & she his Tabernacle.
And his Oak Grove, till the Victim rend the woven Veil.
In the end of his sleep when Jesus calls him from his grave.

Howling the Victims on the Druid Altars yield their souls
To the Stern Warriors: lovely sport the Daughters round their Victims:
Drinking their lives in sweet intoxication, hence arose from Bath
Soft deluding odours, in spiral volutions intricately winding
Over Albions mountains, a feminine indefinite cruel delusion.
Astonishd: terrified & in pain & torment, Sudden they behold
Their own Parent the Emanation of their murderd Enemy
Become their Emanation and their Temple and Tabernacle
They knew not, this Vala was their beloved Mother Vala Albions Wife.
Terrified at the sight of the Victim: at his distorted sinews:
The tremblings of Vala vibrate thro' the limbs of Albions Sons:
While they rejoice over Luvah in mockery & bitter scorn:
Sudden they become like what they behold in howlings & deadly pain.
Spasms smite their features, sinews & limbs: pale they look on one another.
They turn, contorted: their iron necks bend unwilling towards
Luvah: their lips tremble: their muscular fibres are crampd & smitten
They become like what they behold. Yet immense in strength & power,

In awful pomp & gold. in all the precious unhewn stones of Eden
They build a stupendous Building on the Plain of Salisbury; with chains
Of rocks round London Stone: of Reasonings: of unhewn Demonstrations
In labyrinthine arches. (Mighty Urizen the Architect.) thro which
The Heavens might revolve & Eternity be bound in their chain.
Labour unparalleld; a wondrous rocky World of cruel destiny
Rocks piled on rocks reaching the stars: stretching from pole to pole.
The Building is Natural Religion & its Altars Natural Morality
A building of eternal death: whose proportions are eternal despair
Here Vala stood turning the iron Spindle of destruction
From heaven to earth: howling! invisible! but not invisible
Her Two Covering Cherubs afterwards named Voltaire & Rousseau:
Two frowning Rocks: on each side of the Cove & Stone of Torture:
Frozen Sons of the feminine Tabernacle of Bacon. Newton & Locke.
For Luvah is France: the Victim of the Spectres of Albion.

Los beheld in terror: he pourd his loud storms on the Furnaces:
The Daughters of Albion clothed in garments of needle work
Strip them off from their shoulders and bosoms, they lay aside
Their garments: they sit naked upon the Stone of trial.
The Knife of flint passes over the howling Victim: his blood
Gushes & stains the fair side of the fair Daughters of Albion.
They put aside his curls: they divide his seven locks upon
His forehead: they bind his forehead with thorns of iron
They put into his hand a reed, they mock: Saying: Behold
The King of Canaan whose are seven hundred chariots of iron!
They take off his vesture whole with their Knives of flint:
But they cut asunder his inner garments: searching with
Their cruel fingers for his heart, & there they enter in pomp,
In many tears; & there they erect a temple & an altar:
They pour cold water on his brain in front. to cause
Lids to grow over his eyes in veils of tears: and caverns
To freeze over his nostrils. while they feed his tongue from cups
And dishes of painted clay. Glowing with beauty & cruelty:
They obscure the sun & the moon: no eye can look upon them.

Ah! alas! at the sight of the Victim. & at sight of those who are smitten,
All who see become what they behold. their eyes are coverd
With veils of tears and their nostrils & tongues shrunk up
Their ear bent outwards. as their Victim. so are they in the pangs
Of unconquerable fear! amidst delights of revenge Earth-shaking!
And as their eye & ear shrunk, the heavens shrunk away
The Divine Vision became first a burning flame. then a column
Of fire, then an awful fiery wheel surrounding earth & heaven:
And then a globe of blood wandering distant in an unknown night:
Afar into the unknown night the mountains fled away:
Six months of mortality; a summer: & six months of mortality; a winter:
The Human form began to be alterd by the Daughters of Albion
And the perceptions to be dissipated into the Indefinite. Becoming
A mighty Polypus namd Albions Tree: they tie the Veins
And Nerves into two knots: & the Seed into a double knot:
They look forth: the Sun is shrunk: the Heavens are shrunk
Away into the far remote: and the Trees & Mountains witherd
Into indefinite cloudy shadows in darkness & separation.
By Invisible Hatreds adjoind, they seem remote and separate
From each other: and yet are a Mighty Polypus in the Deep!
As the Mistletoe grows on the Oak. so Albions Tree on Eternity: Lo!
He who will not commingle in Love. must be adjoind by Hate

They look forth from Stone-henge! from the Cove round London Stone
They look on one another: the mountain calls out to the mountain:
Plinlimmon shrunk away: Snowdon trembled: the mountains
Of Wales & Scotland beheld the descending War: the routed flying:
Red run the streams of Albion: Thames is drunk with blood:
As Gwendolen cast the Shuttle of war: as Cambel returnd the beam.
The Humber & the Severn: are drunk with the blood of the slain:
London feels his brain cut round: Edinburghs heart is circumscribed!
York & Lincoln hide among the flocks. because of the griding Knife.
Worcester & Hereford: Oxford & Cambridge reel & stagger.
Overwearied with howling: Wales & Scotland alone sustain the fight!
The inhabitants are sick to death: they labour to divide into Days
And Nights, the uncertain Periods: and into Weeks & Months. In vain
They send the Dove & Raven: & in vain the Serpent over the mountains.
And in vain the Eagle & Lion. over the four-fold wilderness.
They return not: but generate in rocky places desolate.
They return not: but build a habitation separate from Man.
The Sun forgets his course like a drunken man: he hesitates
Upon the Cheselden hills, thinking to sleep on the Severn
In vain: he is hurried afar into an unknown Night
He bleeds in torrents of blood as he rolls thro heaven above
He chokes up the paths of the sky: the Moon is leprous as snow:
Trembling & descending down seeking to rest upon high Mona:
Scattering her leprous snows in flakes of disease over Albion.
The Stars flee remote: the heaven is iron, the earth is sulphur,
And all the mountains & hills shrink up like a withering gourd.
As the Senses of Men shrink together under the Knife of flint,
In the hands of Albions Daughters, among the Druid Temples.

By those who drink their blood & the blood of their Covenant
And the Twelve Daughters of Albion. united in Rahab & Tirzah
A Double Female: and they drew out from the Rocky Stones
Fibres of Life to Weave for every Female is a Golden Loom
The Rocks are opake hardnesses covering all Vegetated things
And as they Wove & Cut from the Looms in various divisions
Stretching over Europe & Asia from Ireland to Japan
They divided into many lovely Daughters to be counterparts
To those they Wove, for when they Wove a Male, they divided
Into a Female to the Woven Male, in opake hardness
they cut the Fibres from the Rocks groaning in pain they Weave:
Calling the Rocks Atomic Origins of Existence; denying Eternity
By the Atheistical Epicurean Philosophy of Albions Tree
Such are the Feminine & Masculine when separated from Man
They call the Rocks Parents of Men. & adore the frowning Chaos
Dancing around in howling pain clothed in the bloody Veil.
Hiding Albions Sons within the Veil, closing Jerusalems
Sons without; to feed with their Souls the Spectres of Albion
Ashamed to give Love openly to the piteous & merciful Man
Counting him an imbecile mockery; but the Warrior
They adore: & his revenge cherish, with the blood of the Innocent
They drink up Dan & Gad, to feed with milk Skofeld & Kotope
They strip off Josephs Coat & dip it in the blood of battle
Tirzah sits weeping to hear the shrieks of the dying: her Knife
Of flint is in her hand: she passes it over the howling Victim
The Daughters Weave their Work in loud cries over the Rock
Of Horeb: still eyeing Albions Cliffs eagerly siezing & twisting
The threads of Vala & Jerusalem running from mountain to mountain
Over the whole Earth: loud the Warriors rage in Beth Peor
Beneath the iron whips of their Captains & consecrated banners
Loud the Sun & Moon rage in the conflict: loud the Stars
Shout in the night of battle & their spears grow to their hands
With blood, weaving the deaths of the Mighty into a Tabernacle
For Rahab & Tirzah; till the Great Polypus of Generation covered
	the Earth
In Verulam the Polypus's Head. winding around his bulk
Thro Rochester. and Chichester. & Exeter & Salisbury.
To Bristol: & his Heart beat strong on Salisbury Plain
Shooting out Fibres round the Earth. thro Gaul & Italy
And Greece. & along the Sea of Rephaim into Judea
To Sodom & Gomorrha: thence to India, China & Japan
The Twelve Daughters in Rahab & Tirzah have circumscribed the Brain
Beneath & pierced it thro the midst with a golden pin.
Blood hath staind her fair side beneath her bosom.
O thou poor Human Form! said she. O thou poor child of woe!
Why wilt thou wander away from Tirzah: why me compel to bind thee
If thou dost go away from me, I shall consume upon these Rocks
These fibres of thine eyes that used to beam in distant heavens
Away from me: I have bound down with a hot iron.
These nostrils that expanded with delight in morning skies
I have bent downward with lead melted in my roaring furnaces
Of affliction: of love: of sweet despair: of torment unendurable
My soul is seven furnaces, incessant roars the bellows
Upon my terribly flaming heart, the molten metal runs
In channels thro my fiery limbs: O love: O pity: O fear:
O pain: O the pangs, the bitter pangs of love forsaken
Ephraim was a wilderness of joy where all my wild beasts ran
The River Kanah wanderd by my sweet Manassehs side
To see the boy spring into heavens sounding from my sight!
Go Noah fetch the girdle of strong brass, heat it red-hot:
Press it around the loins of this ever expanding cruelty
Shriek not so my only love: I refuse thy joys: I drink
Thy shrieks because Hand & Hyle are cruel & obdurate to me

O Skofeld why art thou cruel? Lo Joseph is thine! to make
You One: to weave you both in the same mantle of skin
Bind him down Sisters bind him down on Ebal, Mount of cursing:
Malah come forth from Lebanon: & Hoglah from Mount Sinai:
Come circumscribe this tongue of sweets & with a screw of iron
Fasten this ear unto the rock: Milcah the task is thine
Weep not so Sisters! weep not so! our life depends on this
Or mercy & truth are fled away from Shechem & Mount Gilead
Unless my beloved is bound upon the Stems of Vegetation

And thus the Warriors cry, in the hot day of Victory, in Songs.
Look: the beautiful Daughter of Albion sits naked upon the Stone
Her panting Victim beside her: her heart is drunk with blood
Tho her brain is not drunk with wine: she goes forth from Albion
In pride of beauty: in cruelty of holiness: in the brightness
Of her tabernacle, & her ark & secret place, the beautiful Daughter
Of Albion, delights the eyes of the Kings, their hearts & the
Hearts of their Warriors glow hot before Thor & Friga. O Molech!
O Chemosh! O Bacchus! O Venus! O Double God of Generation
The Heavens are cut like a mantle around from the Cliffs of Albion
Across Europe; across Africa; in howlings & deadly War
A sheet & veil & curtain of blood is let down from Heaven
Across the hills of Ephraim & down Mount Olivet to
The Valley of the Jebusite: Molech rejoices in heaven
He sees the Twelve Daughters naked upon the Twelve Stones
Themselves condensing to Rocks & into the Ribs of a Man
Lo they shoot forth in tender Nerves across Europe & Asia
Lo they rest upon the Tribes, where their panting Victims lie
Molech rushes into the Kings in love to the beautiful Daughters:
But they frown & delight in cruelty, refusing all other joy
Bring your Offerings, your first begotten; pampered with milk & blood
Your first born of seven years old! be they Males or Females:
To the beautiful Daughters of Albion; they sport before the Kings
Clothed in the skin of the Victim! blood: human blood: is the life
And delightful food of the Warrior: the well fed Warriors flesh
Of him who is slain in War, fills the Valleys of Ephraim with
Breeding Women walking in pride & bringing forth under green trees
With pleasure, without pain, for their food is blood of the Captive
Molech rejoices thro the Land from Havilah to Shur: he rejoices
In moral law & its severe penalties: loud Shaddai & Jehovah
Thunder above! when they see the Twelve panting Victims
On the Twelve Stones of Power, &, the beautiful Daughters of Albion
If you dare rend their Veil with your Spear; you are healed of Love!
From the Hills of Camberwell & Wimbledon: from the Valleys
Of Walton & Esher: from Stone-henge & from Maldens Cove
Jerusalems Pillars fall in the rendings of fierce War
Over France & Germany: upon the Rhine & Danube
Reuben & Benjamin flee; they hide in the Valley of Rephaim
Why trembles the Warriors limbs when he beholds thy beauty
Spotted with Victims blood: by the fires of thy secret tabernacle
And thy ark & holy place; at thy frowns: at thy dire revenge
Smitten as Uzzah of old; his armour is softend; his spear
And sword faint in his hand, from Albion across Great Tartary
O beautiful Daughter of Albion; cruelty is thy delight
O Virgin of terrible eyes, who dwellest by Valleys of springs
Beneath the Mountains of Lebanon, in the City of Rehob in Hamath
Taught to touch the harp: to dance in the Circle of Warriors
Before the Kings of Canaan: to cut the flesh from the Victim
To roast the flesh in fire: to examine the Infants limbs
In cruelties of holiness: to refuse the joys of love: to bring
The Spies from Egypt, to raise jealousy in the bosoms of the Twelve
Kings of Canaan: then to let the Spies depart to Meribah Kadesh
To the place of the Amalekite; I am drunk with unsatiated love
I must rush again to War: for the Virgin has frownd & refusd
Sometimes I curse & sometimes bless thy fascinating beauty
Once Man was occupied in intellectual pleasures & energies
But now my soul is harrowd with grief & fear & love & desire
And now I hate & now I love & Intellect is no more:
There is no time for any thing but the torments of love & desire
The Feminine & Masculine Shadows soft, mild & ever varying
In beauty: are Shadows now no more, but Rocks in Horeb

Then all the Males conjoined into One Male & every one
Became a ravening eating Cancer growing in the Female
A Polypus of Roots of Reasoning Doubt Despair & Death.
Going forth & returning from Albions Rocks to Canaan:
Devouring Jerusalem from every Nation of the Earth.

Envying stood the enormous Form at variance with Itself
In all its Members: in eternal torment of love & jealousy:
Drawn forth by Los, time after time from Albions cliffy shore.
Drawing the free loves of Jerusalem into infernal bondage:
That they might be born in contentions of Chastity & in
Deadly Hate between Leah & Rachel, Daughters of Deceit & Fraud
Bearing the images of various Species of Contention
And Jealousy & Abhorrence & Revenge & deadly Murder.
Till they refuse liberty to the Male: & not like Beulah
Where every Female delights to give her maiden to her husband
The Female searches sea & land for gratifications to the
Male Genius; who in return clothes her in gems & gold
And feeds her with the food of Eden, hence all her beauty beams
She Creates at her will a little moony night & silence
With Spaces of sweet gardens & a tent of elegant beauty:
Closed in by a sandy desart & a night of stars shining.
And a little tender moon & hovering angels on the wing.
And the Male gives a Time & Revolution to her Space
Till the time of love is passed in ever varying delights
For All Things Exist in the Human Imagination
And thence in Beulah they are stolen by secret amorous theft.
Till they have had Punishment enough to make them commit Crimes
Hence rose the Tabernacle in the Wilderness & all its Offerings.
From Male & Female Loves in Beulah & their Jealousies
But no one can consummate Female bliss in Los's World without
Becoming a Generated Mortal, a Vegetating Death

And now the Spectres of the Dead awake in Beulah: all
The Jealousies become Murderous: uniting together in Rahab
A Religion of Chastity, forming a Commerce to sell Loves
With Moral Law an Equal Balance, not going down with decision
Therefore the Male severe & cruel filld with stern Revenge:
Mutual Hate returns & mutual Deceit & mutual Fear.

Hence the Infernal Veil grows in the disobedient Female:
Which Jesus rends & the whole Druid Law removes away
From the Inner Sanctuary: a False Holiness hid within the Center,
For the Sanctuary of Eden is in the Camp: in the Outline:
In the Circumference: & every Minute Particular is Holy:
Embraces are Cominglings, from the Head even to the Feet
And not a pompous High Priest entering by a Secret Place.

Jerusalem pined in her inmost soul over Wandering Reuben,
As she slept in Beulahs Night hid by the Daughters of Beulah

And this the form of mighty Hand sitting on Albions cliffs
Before the face of Albion; a mighty threatning Form.

His bosom wide & shoulders huge overspreading wondrous
Bear Three strong sinewy Necks & Three awful & terrible Heads
Three Brains in contradictory council brooding incessantly.
Neither daring to put in act its councils, fearing each other.
Therefore rejecting Ideas as nothing & holding all Wisdom
To consist in the agreements & disagreements of Ideas.
Plotting to devour Albions Body of Humanity & Love.

Such Form the aggregate of the Twelve Sons of Albion took; & such
Their appearance when combind: but often by birth pangs & loud groans
They divide to Twelve: the key-bones & the chest dividing in pain
Disclose a hideous orifice; thence issuing the Giant-brood
Arise as the smoke of the furnace, shaking the rocks from sea to sea.
And there they combine into Three Forms, named Bacon & Newton & Locke,
In the Oak Groves of Albion which overspread all the Earth.

Imputing Sin & Righteousness to Individuals; Rahab
Sat deep within him hid: his Feminine Power unreveald
Brooding Abstract Philosophy. to destroy Imagination, the Divine-
-Humanity A Three-fold Wonder: feminine: most beautiful: Three-fold
Each within other. On her white marble & even Neck, her Heart
Inorbd and bonified: with locks of shadowing modesty, shining
Over her beautiful Female features, soft flourishing in beauty
Beams mild, all love and all perfection, that when the lips
Recieve a kiss from Gods or Men, a threefold kiss returns
From the pressd loveliness: so her whole immortal form three-fold
Three-fold embrace returns: consuming lives of Gods & Men
In fires of beauty melting them as gold & silver in the furnace
Her Brain enlabyrinths the whole heaven of her bosom & loins
To put in act what her Heart wills; O who can withstand her power
Her name is Vala in Eternity: in Time her name is Rahab

The Starry Heavens all were fled from the mighty limbs of Albion

And above Albions Land was seen the Heavenly Canaan
As the Substance is to the Shadow; and above Albions Twelve Sons
Were seen Jerusalems Sons: and all the Twelve Tribes spreading
Over Albion. As the Soul is to the Body. so Jerusalems Sons.
Are to the Sons of Albion: and Jerusalem is Albions Emanation

What is Above is Within, for every-thing in Eternity is translucent:
The Circumference is Within: Without, is formed the Selfish Center
And the Circumference still expands going forward to Eternity.
And the Center has Eternal States: these States we now explore.

And these the Names of Albions Twelve Sons, & of his Twelve Daughters
With their Districts. Hand dwelt in Selsey & had Sussex & Surrey
And Kent & Middlesex: all their Rivers & their Hills of Rocks & Herds:
Their Villages Towns Cities Sea-Ports Temples sublime Cathedrals;
All were his Friends & their Sons & Daughters intermarry in Beulah
For all are Men in Eternity. Rivers Mountains Cities Villages.
All are Human & when you enter into their Bosoms you walk
In Heavens & Earths; as in your own Bosom you bear your Heaven
And Earth, & all you behold, tho it appears Without it is Within
In your Imagination of which this World of Mortality is but a Shadow.

Hyle dwelt in Winchester comprehending Hants Dorset Devon Cornwall.
Their Villages Cities Sea-Ports, their corn fields & Gardens spacious
Palaces, Rivers & Mountains. and between Hand & Hyle arose
Gwendolen & Cambel who is Boadicea: they go abroad & return
Like lovely beams of light from the mingled affections of the Brothers
The Inhabitants of the whole Earth rejoice in their beautiful light.

Coban dwelt in Bath Somerset Wiltshire Gloucestershire,
Obeyd his awful voice Ignoge is his lovely Emanation:
She adjoind with Gwantokes Children soon lovely Cordella arose.
Gwantoke forgave & joyd over South Wales & all its Mountains

Peachey had North Wales Shropshire Cheshire & the Isle of Man.
His Emanation is Mehetabel terrible & lovely upon the Mountains

Brereton had Yorkshire Durham Westmoreland & his Emanation
Is Ragan, she adjoind to Slade, & produced Gonorill far beaming.

Slade had Lincoln Stafford Derby Nottingham & his lovely
Emanation Gonorill rejoices over hills & rocks & woods & rivers.

Hutton had Warwick Northampton Bedford Buckingham
Leicester & Berkshire: & his Emanation is Gwinefred beautiful

Skofeld had Ely Rutland Cambridge Huntingdon Norfolk
Suffolk Hartford & Essex: & his Emanation is Gwinevera
Beautiful. she beams towards the east. all kinds of precious stones
And pearl, with instruments of music in holy Jerusalem

Kox had Oxford Warwick Wilts: his Emanation is Estrild:
Joind with Cordella she shines southward over the Atlantic:

Kotope had Hereford Stafford Worcester. & his Emanation
Is Sabrina joind with Mehetabel she shines west over America

Bowen had all Scotland, the Isles Northumberland & Cumberland
His Emanation is Conwenna she shines a triple form
Over the north with pearly beams gorgeous & terrible
Jerusalem & Vala rejoice in Bowen & Conwenna.

But the Four Sons of Jerusalem that never were Generated
Are Rintrah. and Palamabron and Theotormon and Bromion, they
Dwell over the Four Provinces of Ireland in heavenly light
The Four Universities of Scotland, & in Oxford & Cambridge & Winchester

But now Albion is darkened & Jerusalem lies in ruins:
Above the Mountains of Albion, above the head of Los.

And Los shouted with ceaseless shoutings & his tears poured down
His immortal cheeks, rearing his hands to heaven for aid Divine:
But he spoke not to Albion: fearing lest Albion should turn his Back
Against the Divine Vision: & fall over the Precipice of Eternal Death:
But he receded before Albion & before Vala weaving the Veil
With the iron shuttle of War among the rooted Oaks of Albion:
Weeping & shouting to the Lord day & night; and his Children
Wept round him as a flock silent Seven Days of Eternity

And the Thirty-two Counties of the Four Provinces of Ireland
Are thus divided: The Four Counties are in the Four Camps
Munster South in Reubens Gate. Connaut West in Josephs Gate
Ulster North in Dans Gate, Leinster East in Judahs Gate

For Albion in Eternity has Sixteen Gates among his Pillars
But the Four towards the West were Walled up & the Twelve
That front the Four other Points were turned Four Square
By Los for Jerusalems sake & called the Gates of Jerusalem
Because Twelve Sons of Jerusalem fled successive thro the Gates
But the Four Sons of Jerusalem who fled not but remaind
Are Rintrah & Palamabron & Theotormon & Bromion
The Four that remain with Los to guard the Western Wall
And these Four remain to guard the Four Walls of Jerusalem
Whose foundations remain in the Thirty-two Counties of Ireland
And in Twelve Counties of Wales & in the Forty Counties
Of England & in the Thirty-six Counties of Scotland
And the names of the Thirty-two Counties of Ireland are these
Under Judah & Issachar & Zebulun are Louth Longford
Eastmeath Westmeath Dublin Kildare Kings County
Queens County Wicklow Catherloh Wexford Kilkenny
And those under Reuben & Simeon & Levi are these
Waterford Tipperary Cork Limerick Kerry Clare
And those under Ephraim Manasseh & Benjamin are these
Galway Roscommon Mayo Sligo Leitrim
And those under Dan Asher & Napthali are these
Donnegal Antrim Tyrone Fermanagh Armagh Londonderry
Down Managhan Cavan. These are the Land of Erin
All these Center in London & in Golgonooza. from whence
They are Created continually East & West & North & South
And from them are Created all the Nations of the Earth
Europe & Asia & Africa & America, in fury Fourfold!

And Thirty-two the Nations: to dwell in Jerusalems Gates
O Come ye Nations Come ye People Come up to Jerusalem
Return Jerusalem, & dwell together as of old: Return
Return: O Albion let Jerusalem overspread all Nations
As in the times of old: O Albion awake: Reuben wanders
The Nations wait for Jerusalem. they look up for the Bride

France Spain Italy Germany Poland Russia Sweden Turkey
Arabia Palestine Persia Hindostan China Tartary Siberia
Egypt Lybia Ethiopia Guinea Caffraria Negroland Morocco
Congo Zaara Canada Greenland Carolina Mexico
Peru Patagonia Amazonia Brazil. Thirty-two Nations
And under these Thirty-two Classes of Islands in the Ocean
All the Nations Peoples & Tongues throughout all the Earth
And the Four Gates of Los surround the Universe Within and
Without, & whatever is visible in the Vegetable Earth. the same
Is visible in the Mundane Shell: reversd in mountain & vale
And a Son of Eden was set over each Daughter of Beulah to guard
In Albions Tomb the wondrous Creation: & the Four-fold Gate
Towards Beulah is to the South Fenelon. Guion. Teresa.
Whitefield & Hervey, guard that Gate; with all the gentle Souls
Who guide the great Wine-press of Love; Four precious Stones that
                                                          Gate:

Women the comforters of Men become the Tormenters & Punishers

Such are Cathedrons golden Halls: in the City of Golgonooza

And Los's Furnaces howl loud; living: self-moving: lamenting
With fury & despair. & they stretch from South to North
Thro all the Four Points. Lo! the Labourers at the Furnaces
Rintrah & Palamabron, Theotormon & Bromion. loud labring
With the innumerable multitudes of Golgonooza. round the Anvils
Of Death. But how they came forth from the Furnaces & how long
Vast & severe the anguish eer they knew their father: were
Long to tell & of the iron rollers. golden axle-trees & yokes
Of brass. iron chains & braces & the gold. silver & brass
Mingled or separate: for swords: arrows: cannons: mortars
The terrible ball: the wedge: the loud sounding hammer of destruction
The sounding flail to thresh: the winnow: to winnow kingdoms
The water wheel & mill at many innumerable wheels. restless
Over the Fourfold Monarchy from Earth to the Mundane Shell:
Perusing Albions Tomb in the starry characters of Og & Anak:
To Create the Lion & wolf the bear: the tyger & ounce:
To Create the wooly lamb & downy fowl & scaly serpent
The summer & winter: day & night: the sun & moon & stars
The tree: the plant: the flower: the rock: the stone: the metal:
Of Vegetative Nature: by their hard restricting condensations.

Where Luvahs World of Opakeness grew to a period: It
Became a Limit. a Rocky hardness without form & void
Accumulating without end: here Los, who is of the Elohim
Opens the Furnaces of affliction in the Emanation
Fixing the Sexual into an ever-prolific Generation
Naming the Limit of Opakeness Satan & the Limit of Contraction
Adam, who is Peleg & Joktan: & Esau & Jacob: & Saul & David
Voltaire insinuates that these Limits are the cruel work of God
Mocking the Remover of Limits & the Resurrection of the Dead
Setting up Kings in wrath: in holiness of Natural Religion
Which Los with his mighty Hammer demolishes time on time
In miracles & wonders in the Four-fold Desart of Albion
Permanently Creating to be in Time Reveald & Demolishd
Satan Cain Tubal Nimrod Pharah Priam Bladud Belin
Arthur Alfred the Norman Conqueror Richard John

And all the Kings & Nobles of the Earth & all their Glories
These are Created by Rahab & Tirzah in Ulro: but around
These, to preserve them from Eternal Death Los Creates
Adam Noah Abraham Moses Samuel David Ezekiel

Dissipating the rocky forms of Death. by his thunderous Hammer
As the Pilgrim passes while the Country permanent remains
So Men pass on: but States remain permanent for ever

The Spectres of the Dead howl round the porches of Los
In the terrible Family feuds of Albions cities & villages
To devour the Body of Albion, hungring & thirsting & ravning
The Sons of Los clothe them & feed & provide houses & gardens
And every Human Vegetated Form in its inward recesses
Is a house of pleasantness & a garden of delight Built by the
Sons & Daughters of Los in Bowlahoola & in Cathedron
From London to York & Edinburgh the Furnaces rage terrible
Primrose Hill is the mouth of the Furnace & the Iron Door;

The Four Zoas clouded rage; Urizen stood by Albion
With Rintrah and Palamabron and Theotormon and Bromion
These Four are Verulam & London & York & Edinburgh
And the Four Zoa's are Urizen & Luvah & Tharmas & Urthona
In opposition deadly, and their Wheels in poisonous
And deadly stupor turnd against each other loud & fierce
Entering into the Reasoning Power, forsaking Imagination
They became Spectres; & their Human Bodies were reposed
In Beulah, by the Daughters of Beulah with tears & lamentations

The Spectre is the Reasoning Power in Man; & when separated
From Imagination, and closing itself as in steel, in a Ratio
Of the Things of Memory. It thence frames Laws & Moralities
To destroy Imagination; the Divine Body, by Martyrdoms & Wars

Teach me O Holy Spirit the Testimony of Jesus; let me
    Comprehend wonderous things out of the Divine Law
I behold Babylon in the opening Streets of London, I behold
Jerusalem in ruins wandering about from house to house
This I behold the shudderings of death attend my steps
I walk up and down in Six Thousand Years; their Events are present be- -fore me
To tell how Los in grief & anger, whirling round his Hammer on high
Drave the Sons & Daughters of Albion from their ancient mountains
They became the Twelve Gods of Asia Opposing the Divine Vision

The Sons of Albion are Twelve; the Sons of Jerusalem Sixteen
I tell how Albions Sons by Harmonies of Concords & Discords
Opposed to Melody, and by Lights & Shades, opposed to Outline
And by Abstraction opposed to the Visions of Imagination
By cruel Laws divided Sixteen into Twelve Divisions
How Hyle roard Los in Albions Cliffs by the affections rent
Asunder & opposed to Thought, to draw Jerusalems Sons
Into the Vortex of his Wheels, therefore Hyle is called Gog
Age after age drawing them away towards Babylon
Babylon, the Rational Morality deluding to death the little ones
In strong temptations of stolen beauty; I tell how Reuben slept
On London Stone & the Daughters of Albion ran around admiring
His awful beauty; with Moral Virtue the fair deceiver; offspring
Of Good & Evil, they divided him in love upon the Thames & Sent
Him over Europe in streams of gore out of Cathedrons Looms
How Los drave them from Albion & they became Daughters of Canaan
Hence Albion was calld the Canaanite & all his Giant Sons.

Hence is my Theme. O Lord my Saviour open thou the Gates
And I will lead forth thy Words, telling how the Daughters
Cut the Fibres of Reuben, how he rolld apart & took Root
In Bashan. terror-struck Albions Sons look toward Bashan
They have divided Simeon he also rolld apart in blood
Over the Nations till he took Root beneath the shining Looms
Of Albions Daughters in Philistea by the side of Amalek
They have divided Levi; he hath shot out into forty eight Roots
Over the Land of Canaan; they have divided Judah.
He hath took Root in Hebron, in the Land of Hand & Hyle
Dan: Napthali: Gad; Asher; Issachar; Zebulun; roll apart
From all the Nations of the Earth to dissipate into Non Entity

I see a Feminine Form arise from the Four terrible Zoas
Beautiful but terrible struggling to take a form of beauty
Rooted in Shechem; this is Dinah, the youthful form of Erin
The Wound I see in South Molton Street & Stratford place
Whence Joseph & Benjamin rolld apart away from the Nations
In vain they rolld apart; they are fixd into the Land of Cabul

And Rahab Babylon the Great hath destroyed Jerusalem
Bath stood upon the Severn with Merlin & Bladud & Arthur
The Cup of Rahab in his hand: her Poisons Twenty-seven-fold

And all her Twenty-seven Heavens now hid & now reveal'd
Appear in strong delusive light of Time & Space drawn out
In shadowy pomp by the Eternal Prophet created evermore
For Los in Six Thousand Years walks up & down continually
That not one Moment of Time be lost & every revolution
Of Space he makes permanent in Bowlahoola & Cathedron.

And these the names of the Twenty-seven Heavens & their Churches
Adam. Seth. Enos. Cainan. Mahalaleel. Jared. Enoch.
Methuselah. Lamech: these are the Giants mighty, Hermaphroditic
Noah. Shem. Arphaxad, Cainan the Second, Salah. Heber.
Peleg. Reu. Serug. Nahor, Terah: these are the Female Males:
A Male within a Female hid as in an Ark & Curtains.
Abraham. Moses. Solomon. Paul. Constantine. Charlemaine.
Luther. these Seven are the Male Females: the Dragon Forms
The Female hid within a Male: thus Rahab is reveald
Mystery Babylon the Great: the Abomination of Desolation
Religion hid in War: a Dragon red, & hidden Harlot
But Jesus breaking thro' the Central Zones of Death & Hell
Opens Eternity in Time & Space; triumphant in Mercy
Thus are the Heavens form'd by Los within the Mundane Shell
And where Luther ends Adam begins again in Eternal Circle
To awake the Prisoners of Death: to bring Albion again
With Luvah into light eternal. in his eternal day
But now the Starry Heavens are fled from the mighty limbs of Al-
bion

To the Christians

I give you the end of a golden string,
Only wind it into a ball:
It will lead you in at Heavens gate,
Built in Jerusalems wall.

We are told to abstain from fleshly desires that we may lose no time from the Work of the Lord. Every moment lost, is a moment that cannot be redeemed every pleasure that intermingles with the duty of our station is a folly unredeemable & is planted like the seed of a wild flower among our wheat. All the torments of repentance. are torments of self-reproach on account of our leaving the Divine Harvest to the Enemy, the struggles of entanglement with incoherent roots. I know of no other Christianity and of no other Gospel than the liberty both of body & mind to exercise the Divine Arts of Imagination. Imagination the real & eternal World of which this Vegetable Universe is but a faint shadow & in which we shall live in our Eternal or Imaginative Bodies. when these Vegetable Mortal Bodies are no more. The Apostles knew of no other Gospel. What were all their spiritual gifts? What is the Divine Spirit? is the Holy Ghost any other than an Intellectual Fountain? What is the Harvest of the Gospel & its Labours? What is that Talent which it is a curse to hide? What are the Treasures of Heaven which we are to lay up for ourselves. are they any other than Mental Studies & Performances? What are all the Gifts of the Gospel, are they not all Mental Gifts? Is God a Spirit who must be worshipped in Spirit & in Truth and are not the Gifts of the Spirit Every-thing to Man? O ye Religious discountenance every one among you who shall pretend to despise Art & Science! I call upon you in the Name of Jesus! What is the Life of Man but Art & Science? is it Meat & Drink? is not the Body more than Raiment? What is Mortality but the things relating to the Body, which Dies? What is Immortality but the things relating to the Spirit, which Lives Eternally! What is the Joy of Heaven but Improvement in the things of the Spirit? What are the Pains of Hell but Ignorance, Bodily Lust, Idleness & devastation of the things of the Spirit? Answer this to yourselves, & expel from among you those who pretend to despise the labours of Art & Science, which alone are the labours of the Gospel: Is not this plain & manifest to the thought? Can you think at all & not pronounce heartily! That to Labour in Knowledge. is to Build up Jerusalem: and to Despise Knowledge. is to Despise Jerusalem & her Builders. And remember He who despises & mocks a Mental Gift in another; calling it pride & selfishness & sin: mocks Jesus the giver of every Mental Gift; which always appear to the ignorance-loving Hypocrite, as Sins. but that which is a Sin in the sight of cruel Man, is not so in the sight of our kind God. Let every Christian as much as in him lies engage himself openly & publicly before all the World in some Mental pursuit for the Building up of Jerusalem

I stood among my valleys of the south
And saw a flame of fire, even as a Wheel
Of fire surrounding all the heavens: it went
From west to east against the current of
Creation, and devoured all things in its loud
Fury & thundering course round heaven & earth
By it the Sun was rolld into an orb:
By it the Moon faded into a globe.
Travelling thro the night; for from its dire
And restless fury, Man himself shrunk up
Into a little root a fathom long.
And I asked a Watcher & a Holy-One
Its Name? he answerd. It is the Wheel of Religion
I wept & said. Is this the law of Jesus
This terrible devouring sword turning every way
He answerd; Jesus died because he strove
Against the current of this Wheel: its Name
Is Caiaphas, the dark Preacher of Death

Of sin, of sorrow, & of punishment;
Opposing Nature! It is Natural Religion
But Jesus is the bright Preacher of Life
Creating Nature from this fiery Law,
By self-denial & forgiveness of Sin.
Go therefore, cast out devils in Christs name
Heal thou the sick of spiritual disease
Pity the evil, for thou art not sent
To smite with terror & with punishments
Those that are sick, like to the Pharisees
Crucifying & encompassing sea & land
For proselytes to tyranny & wrath.
But to the Publicans & Harlots go!
Teach them True Happiness but let no curse
Go forth out of thy mouth to blight their peace
For Hell is opend to Heaven; thine eyes beheld
The dungeons burst & the Prisoners set free.

England! awake! awake! awake!
Jerusalem thy Sister calls!
Why wilt thou sleep the sleep of death
And close her from thy ancient walls

Thy hills & valleys felt her feet,
Gently upon their bosoms move:
Thy gates beheld sweet Zions ways;
Then was a time of joy and love

And now the time returns again:
Our souls exult & Londons towers
Receive the Lamb of God to dwell
In Englands green & pleasant bowers

Jerusalem. C 4

The Spectres of Albions' Twelve Sons revolve nightily
Over the Tomb & over the Body; raving to devour
The Sleeping Humanity. Los with his mace of iron
Walks round: loud his threats, loud his blows fall,
On the rocky Spectres, as the Potter breaks the potsherds;
Dashing in pieces Self-righteousnesses: driving them from Albions
Cliffs: dividing them into Male & Female forms in his Furnaces
And on his Anvils: lest they destroy the Feminine Affections
They are broken. Loud howl the Spectres in his iron Furnace

While Los laments at his dire labours, viewing Jerusalem.
Sitting before his Furnaces clothed in sackcloth of hair;
Albions Twelve Sons surround the Forty-two Gates of Erin,
In terrible armour, raging against the Lamb & against Jerusalem,
Surrounding them with armies to destroy the Lamb of God;
They took their Mother Vala, and they crownd her with gold:
They numd her Rahab, & gave her power over the Earth
The Concave Earth round Golgonooza in Entuthon Benython,
Even to the stars exalting her Throne, to build beyond the Throne
Of God and the Lamb, to destroy the Lamb & usurp the Throne of God
Drawing their Ulro Voidness round the Four-fold Humanity

Naked Jerusalem lay before the Gates upon Mount Zion,
The Hill of Giants, all her foundations levelld with the dust!

Her Twelve Gates thrown down: her children carried into captivity
Herself in chains: this from within was seen in a dismal night
Outside, unknown before in Beulah, & the twelve gates were filld
With blood; from Japan eastward to the Giants causway, west
In Erins Continent: and Jerusalem wept upon Euphrates banks
Disorganizd; an evanescent shade, scarce seen or heard among
Her childrens Druid Temples dropping with blood wanderd weeping!
And thus her voice went forth in the darkness of Philisthea.

My brother & my father are no more! God hath forsaken me
The arrows of the Almighty pour upon me & my children
I have sinned and am an outcast from the Divine Presence!

My tents are falln: my pillars are in ruins: my children dashd
Upon Egypts iron floors, & the marble pavements of Assyria;
I melt my soul in reasonings among the towers of Heshbon:
Mount Zion is become a cruel rock & no more dew
Nor rain: no more the spring of the rock appears: but cold
Hard & obdurate are the furrows of the mountain of wine & oil:
The mountain of blessing is itself a curse & an astonishment:
The hills of Judea are fallen with me into the deepest hell
Away from the Nations of the Earth, & from the Cities of the Nations;
I walk to Ephraim. I seek for Shiloh: I walk like a lost sheep
Among precipices of despair: in Goshen I seek for light
In vain: and in Gilead for a physician and a comforter.
Goshen hath followd Philisted: Gilead hath joind with Og!
They are become narrow places in a little and dark land:
How distant far from Albion! his hills & his valleys no more
Recieve the feet of Jerusalem: they have cast me quite away:
And Albion is himself shrunk to a narrow rock in the midst of the sea!
The plains of Sussex & Surrey, their hills of flocks & herds
No more seek to Jerusalem nor to the sound of my Holy-ones.
The Fifty-two Counties of England are hardend against me
As if I was not their Mother, they despise me & cast me out
London coverd the whole Earth. England encompassd the Nations:
And all the Nations of the Earth were seen in the Cities of Albion:
My pillars reachd from sea to sea: London beheld me come
From my east & from my west; he blessed me and gave
His children to my breasts, his sons & daughters to my knees
His aged parents sought me out in every city & village:
They discernd my countenance with joy! they shewd me to their sons
Saying Lo Jerusalem is here! she sitteth in our secret chambers
Levi and Judah & Issachar: Ephram, Manasseh, Gad and Dan
Are seen in our hills & valleys: they keep our flocks & herds
They watch them in the night: and the Lamb of God appears among us.
The river Severn stayd his course at my command:
Thames poured his waters into my basons and baths:
Medway mingled with Kishon: Thames recievd the heavenly Jordan
Albion gave me to the whole Earth to walk up & down; to pour
Joy upon every mountain, to teach songs to the shepherd & plowman
I taught the ships of the sea to sing the songs of Zion.
Italy saw me, in sublime astonishment: France was wholly mine:
As my garden & as my secret bath: Spain was my heavenly couch:
I slept in his golden hills: the Lamb of God met me there.
There we walked as in our secret chamber among our little ones
They looked upon our loves with joy: they beheld our secret joys:
With holy raptures of adoration rapd sublime in the Visions of God:
Germany, Poland & the North wooed my footsteps they found
My gates in all their mountains & my curtains in all their vales
The furniture of their houses was the furniture of my chamber
Turkey & Grecia saw my instruments of music, they arose
They siezd the harp: the flute: the mellow horn of Jerusalems joy
They sounded thanksgivings in my courts: Egypt & Lybia heard
The swarthy sons of Ethiopia stood round the Lamb of God
Enquiring for Jerusalem: he led them up my steps to my altar:
And thou America! I once beheld thee but now behold no more
Thy golden mountains where my Cherubim & Seraphim rejoicd
Together among my little-ones. But now, my Altars run with blood!
My fires are corrupt, my incense is a cloudy pestilence
Of seven diseases! Once a continual cloud of salvation, rose
From all my myriads: once the Four-fold World rejoicd among
The pillars of Jerusalem, between my winged Cherubim:
But now I am closd out from them in the narrow passages
Of the valleys of destruction, into a dark land of pitch & bitumen.
From Albions Tomb afar and from the four-fold wanders of God
Shrunk to a narrow doleful form in the dark land of Cabul:
There is Reuben & Gad & Joseph & Judah & Levi, closd up
In narrow vales: I walk & count the bones of my beloveds
Along the Valley of Destruction, among these Druid Temples
Which overspread all the Earth in patriarchal pomp & cruel pride
Tell me O Vala thy purposes; tell me wherefore thy shuttles
Drop with the gore of the slain; why Euphrates is red with blood
Wherefore in dreadful majesty & beauty outside appears
Thy Masculine from thy Feminine hardening against the heavens
To devour the Human! Why dost thou weep upon the wind among
These cruel Druid Temples: O Vala! Humanity is far above
Sexual organization: & the Visions of the Night of Beulah
Where Sexes wander in dreams of bliss among the Emanations
Where the Masculine & Feminine are nursd into Youth & Maiden
By the tears & smiles of Beulahs Daughters till the time of Sleep is past.
Wherefore then do you realize these nets of beauty & delusion
In open day to draw the souls of the Dead into the light.
Till Albion is shut out from every Nation under Heaven.   E

Encompassd by the Frozen Net and by the rooted Tree
I walk weeping in pangs of a Mothers torment for her Children:
I walk in affliction: I am a worm, and no living soul!
A worm going to eternal torment: raisd up in a night
To an eternal night of pain. lost! lost! lost! for ever!
Beside her Vala howld upon the winds in pride of beauty
Lamenting among the timbrels of the Warriors: among the Captives
In cruel holiness, and her lamenting songs were from Arnon
And Jordan to Euphrates. Jerusalem followd trembling
Her children in captivity. listening to Valas lamentation
In the thick cloud & darkness. & the voice went forth from
The cloud. O rent in sunder from Jerusalem the Harlot daughter!
In an eternal condemnation in fierce burning flames
Of torment unendurable: and if once a Delusion be found
Woman must perish. & the Heavens of Heavens remain no more

My Father gave to me command to murder Albion
In unreviving Death: my Love, my Luvah orderd me in night
To murder Albion the King of Men. he fought in battles fierce
He conquerd Luvah my beloved: he took me and my Father
He slew them: I reviyed them, to life in my warm bosom
He saw them issue from my bosom, dark in Jealousy
He burnd before me: Luvah framd the Knife & Luvah gave
The Knife into his daughters hand: such thing was never known
Before in Albions land. that one should die a death never to be revivd
For in our battles we the Slain men view with pity and love:
We soon revive them in the secret of our tabernacles
But Vala. Luvahs daughter. keep his body embalmd in moral laws
With spices of sweet odours of lovely jealous stupefaction:
Return my bosom. lest he arise to life & slay my Luvah
By me then O Lamb of God. O Jesus pity me:
Come into Luvahs Tents. and seek not to revive the Dead!

So sang she: and the Spindle turnd furious as she sang:
The Children of Jerusalem the Souls of those who sleep
Were caught into the flax of her Distaff. & in her Cloud
To weave Jerusalem a body according to her will
A Dragon form on Zion Hills most ancient promontory

The Spindle turnd in blood & fire: loud sound the trumpets
Of war: the cymbals play loud before the Captains
With Cambel & Gwendolen in dance and solemn song
The Cloud of Rahab vibrating with the Daughters of Albion
Los saw terrified. melted with pity & divided in wrath
He sent them over the narrow seas in pity and love
Among the Four Forests of Albion which overspread all the Earth
They go forth & return swift as a flash of lightning
Among the tribes of warriors: among the Stones of power!
Against Jerusalem they rage thro all the Nations of Europe:
Thro Italy & Grecia. to Lebanon & Persia & India.
The Serpent Temples thro the Earth. from the wide Plain of Salisbury
Resound with cries of Victims. shouts & songs & dying groans
And flames of dusky fire. to Amalek. Canaan and Moab
And Rahab like a dismal and indefinite hovering Cloud
Refusd to take a definite form. she hoverd over all the Earth
Calling the definite. sin. defacing every definite form
Invisible. or Visible. stretchd out in length or spread in breadth:
Over the Temples. drinking groans of Victims weeping in pity.
And joying in the pity. howling over Jerusalems walls.

Hand slept on Skiddaws top: drawn by the love of beautiful
Cambel: his bright beaming Counterpart. divided from him
And her delusive light beamd fierce above the Mountain:
Soft: invisible: drinking his sighs in sweet intoxication:
Drawing out fibre by fibre: Returning to Albions Tree
At night: and in the morning to Skiddaw: she sent him over
Mountainous Wales into the Loom of Cathedron fibre by fibre:
He ran in tender nerves across Europe to Jerusalems Shade:
To weave Jerusalem a Body repugnant to the Lamb.
Hyle on East Moor in rocky Derbyshire. ravd to the Moon
For Gwendolen: she took up in bitter tears his anguishd heart.
That apparent to all in Eternity. Glows like the Sun in the breast:
She hid it in his ribs & back: she hid his tongue with teeth
In terrible convulsions pitying & gratified drunk with pity
Glowing with loveliness before him. becoming apparent
According to his changes: she rolld his kidneys round
Into two irregular forms: and looking on Albions dread Tree.
She wove two vessels of seed. beautiful as Skiddaws snow:
Giving them bends of self interest & selfish natural virtue:
She hid them in his loins: raving he ran among the rocks:
Compelld into a shape of Moral Virtue against the Lamb.
The invisible lovely one giving him a form according to
His Law a form against the Lamb of God opposd to Mercy
And playing in the thunderous Loom in sweet intoxication
Filling cups of silver & crystal with shrieks & cries, with groans
And dolorous sobs: the wine of lovers in the Wine-press of Luvah

O sister Cambel said Gwendolen, as their long beaming light
Mingled above the Mountain what shall we do to keep
These awful forms in our soft bands: distracted with trembling

I have mockd those who refused cruelty & I have admired
The cruel Warrior. I have refused to give love to Merlin the piteous
He brings to me the Images of his Love & I reject in chastity
And turn them out upon the streets for Harlots to be food
To the stern Warrior. I am become perfect in beauty over my Warrior
For Men are caught by Love: Woman is caught by Pride —
That Love may only be obtaind in the passages of Death.
Let us look: let us examine: is the Cruel become an Infant
Or is he still a cruel Warrior? look Sisters. look! O piteous
I have destroyd Wandring Reuben who strove to bind my Will
I have stripd off Josephs beautiful integument for my Beloved.
The Cruel-one of Albion: to clothe him in gems of my Zone
I have named him Jehovah of Hosts. Humanity is become
A weeping Infant in ruind lovely Jerusalems folding Cloud:

In Heaven the only Art of Living
Is Forgetting & Forgiving
Especially to the Male
But if you on Earth Forgive
You shall not find where to Live

In Heaven Love begets Love but Fear is the Parent of Earthly Love:
And he who will not bend to Love must be subdud by Fear.

I have heard Jerusalems groans; from Vala's cries & lamentations
I gather our eternal fate: Outcasts from life and love:
Unless we find a way to bind these awful Forms to our
Embrace we shall perish annihilate, discoverd our Delusions.
Look! I have wrought without delusion: Look! I have wept!
And given soft milk mingled together with the spirits of flocks
Of lambs and doves, mingled together in cups and dishes
Of painted clay; the mighty Hyle is become a weeping infant;
Soon shall the Spectres of the Dead follow my weaving threads.

The Twelve Daughters of Albion attentive listen in secret shades
On Cambridge and Oxford beaming soft uniting with Rahabs cloud
While Gwendolen spoke to Cambel turning soft the spinning reel:
Or throwing the wingd shuttle; or drawing the cords with softest songs
The golden cords of the Looms animate beneath their touches soft,
Along the Island white, among the Druid Temples, while Gwendolen
Spoke to the Daughters of Albion standing on Skiddaws top.

So saying she took a Falshood & hid it in her left hand:
To entice her Sisters away to Babylon on Euphrates.
And thus she closed her left hand and utterd her Falshood:
Forgetting that Falshood is prophetic, she hid her hand behind her,
Upon her back behind her loins & thus utterd her Deceit.

I heard Enitharmon say to Los: Let the Daughters of Albion
Be scatterd abroad and let the name of Albion be forgotten:
Divide them into three; name them Amalek Canaan & Moab:
Let Albion remain a desolation without an inhabitant:
And let the Looms of Enitharmon & the Furnaces of Los
Create Jerusalem, & Babylon & Egypt & Moab & Amalek,
And Helle & Hesperia & Hindostan & China & Japan.
But hide America, for a Curse an Altar of Victims & a Holy Place.
See Sisters Canaan is pleasant, Egypt is as the Garden of Eden:
Babylon is our chief desire, Moab our bath in summer:
Let us lead the stems of this Tree let us plant it before Jerusalem
To judge the Friend of Sinners to death without the Veil:
To cut her off from America, to close up her secret Ark:
And the fury of Man exhaust in War! Woman permanent remain
See how the fires of our loins point eastward to Babylon
Look, Hyle is become an infant Love: look: behold: see him lie!
Upon my bosom look: here is the lovely wayward form
That gave me sweet delight by his torments beneath my Veil;
By the fruit of Albions Tree I have fed him with sweet milk
By contentions of the mighty for Sacrifice of Captives;
Humanity the Great Delusion: is changed to War & Sacrifice;
I have naild his hands on Beth Rabbim & his hands on Heshbons Wall.
O that I could live in his sight: O that I could bind him to my arm.

So saying: She drew aside her Veil from Mam-Tor to Dovedale
Discovering her own perfect beauty to the Daughters of Albion
And Hyle a winding Worm beneath   & not a weeping Infant.
Trembling & pitying she screamd & fled upon the wind:
Hyle was a winding Worm and herself perfect in beauty;
The desarts tremble at his wrath: they shrink themselves in fear.

Cambel trembled with jealousy: she trembled: she envied:
The envy ran thro Cathedrons Looms into the Heart
Of mild Jerusalem, to destroy the Lamb of God. Jerusalem
Languishd upon Mount Olivet, East of mild Zions Hill.
Los saw the envious blight above his Seventh Furnace
On Londons Tower on the Thames: he drew Cambel in wrath.
Into his thundering Bellows, heaving it for a loud blast:
And with the blast of his Furnace upon fishy Billingsgate.
Beneath Albions fatal Tree, before the Gate of Los:
Shewd her the fibres of her beloved to ameliorate
The envy: loud she labourd in the Furnace of fire,
To form the mighty form of Hand according to her will
In the Furnaces of Los & in the Wine-press treading day & night
Naked among the human clusters: bringing wine of anguish
To feed the afflicted in the Furnaces: She minded not
The raging flames, tho she returnd   instead of beauty
Deformity: she gave her beauty to another: begging abroad,
Her struggling torment in her iron arms: and like a chain,
Binding his wrists & ankles with the iron arms of love.

Gwendolen saw the Infant in her sisters arms; she howld
Over the forests with bitter tears, and over the winding Worm
Repentant: and she also in the eddying wind of Los's Bellows
Began her dolorous task of love in the Wine-press of Luvah
To form the Worm into a form of love by tears & pain.
The Sisters saw! trembling ran thro their Looms! softening mild
Towards London; then they saw the Furnaces opend, & in tears
Began to give their souls away in the Furnaces of affliction.

Los saw & was comforted at his Furnaces uttering thus his voice.
I know I am Urthona keeper of the Gates of Heaven,
And that I can at will expatiate in the Gardens of bliss;
But pangs of love draw me down to my loins which are
Become a fountain of veiny pipes: O Albion: my brother:

Corrupt

Corruptibility appears upon thy limbs, and never more
Can I arise and leave thy side, but labour here incessant
Till thy awaking! yet alas I shall forget Eternity:
Against the Patriarchal pomp and cruelty, labouring incessant
I shall become an Infant horror. Enion! Tharmas! friends
Absorb me not in such dire grief: O Albion, my brother!
Jerusalem hungers in the desert: affection to her children!
The scorned and contemned youthful girl, where shall she fly?
Sussex shuts up her Villages. Hants, Devon & Wilts
Surrounded with masses of stone in ordered forms, determine then
A form for Vala and a form for Luvah, here on the Thames
Where the Victim nightly howls beneath the Druids knife:
A Form of Vegetation, nail them down on the stems of Mystery:
O when shall the Saxon return with the English his redeemed brother!
O when shall the Lamb of God descend among the Reprobate!
I woo to Amalek to protect my fugitives Amalek trembles:
I call to Canaan & Moab in my night watches, they mourn:
They listen not to my cry, they rejoice among their warriors
Woden and Thor and Friga wholly consume my Saxons
On their enormous Altars built in the terrible north:
From Irelands rocks to Scandinavia Persia and Tartary:
From the Atlantic Sea to the universal Erythrean.
Found ye London! enormous City! weeps thy River?
Upon his parent bosom lay thy little ones O Land
Forsaken. Surrey and Sussex are Enitharmons Chamber.
Where I will build her a Couch of repose & my pillars
Shall surround her in beautiful labyrinths: Oothoon!
Where hides my child? in Oxford hidest thou with Antamon?
In graceful hidings of error: in merciful deceit
Lest Hand the terrible destroy his affection, thou hidest her:
In chaste appearances for sweet deceits of love & modesty
Immingled, interwoven, glistening to the sickening sight.
Let Cambel and her Sisters sit within the Mundane Shell:
Forming the fluctuating Globe according to their will.
According as they weave the little embryon nerves & veins
The Eye, the little Nostrils, & the delicate Tongue & Ears
Of labyrinthine intricacy: so shall they fold the World
That whatever is seen upon the Mundane Shell, the same
Be seen upon the Fluctuating Earth, woven by the Sisters.
And sometimes the Earth shall roll in the Abyss, & sometimes
Stand in the Center & sometimes stretch flat in the Expanse.
According to the will of the lovely Daughters of Albion.
Sometimes it shall assimilate with mighty Golgonooza:
Touching its summits: & sometimes divided roll apart.
As a beautiful Veil, so these Females shall fold & unfold
According to their will the outside surface of the Earth.
An outside shadowy Surface superadded to the real Surface:
Which is unchangeable for ever & ever Amen: so be it!
Separate Albions Sons gently from their Emanations.
Weaving the powers of delight on the current of infant Thames
Where the old Parent still returns his youth as I alas!
Return my youth eight thousand and five hundred years.
The labourer of ages in the Valleys of Despair.
The land is marked for desolation & unless we plant
The seeds of Cities & of Villages in the Human bosom
Albion must be a rock of blood: mark ye the points
Where Cities shall remain & where Villages for the rest:
It must lie in confusion till Albions time of awaking.
Place the Tribes of Llewellyn in America for a hiding place:
Till sweet Jerusalem emanates again into Eternity
The night falls thick: I go upon my watch: be attentive:
The Sons of Albion go forth; I follow from my Furnaces:
That they return no more: that a place be prepard on Euphrates
Listen to your Watchmans voice: sleep not before the Furnaces
Eternal Death stands at the door. O God pity our labours.

So Los spoke to the Daughters of Beulah while his Emanation
Like a faint rainbow waved before him in the awful gloom
Of London City on the Thames from Surrey Hills to Highgate:
Swift turn the silver spindles, & the golden weights play soft
And lulling harmonies beneath the Looms, from Caithness in the north
To Lizard-point & Dover in the south: his Emanation
Joyd in the many weaving threads in bright Cathedrons Dome
Weaving the Web of life for Jerusalem, the Web of life
Down flowing into Entuthons Vales glistens with soft affections.

While Los arose upon his Watch, and down from Golgonooza
Putting on his golden sandals to walk from mountain to mountain,
He takes his way, girding himself with gold & in his hand
Holding his iron mace: The Spectre remains attentive
Alternate they watch in night: alternate labour in day
Before the Furnaces labouring, while Los all night watches
The stars rising & setting, & the meteors & terrors of night:
With him went down the Dogs of Leutha, at his feet
They lap the water of the trembling Thames then follow swift
And thus he heard the voice of Albions daughters on Euphrates, flak

Our Father Albions land: O it was a lovely land! & the Daughters of Beu
Walked up and down in its green mountains: but Hand is fled
Away: & mighty Hyle: & after them Jerusalem is gone: Awake

Highgates heights & Hampsteads, to Poplar Hackney & Bow:
To Islington & Paddington & the Brook of Albions River
We builded Jerusalem as a City & a Temple; from Lambeth
We began our Foundations; lovely Lambeth: O lovely Hills
Of Camberwell, we shall behold you no more in glory & pride
For Jerusalem lies in ruins & the Furnaces of Los are builded there
You are now shrunk up to a narrow Rock in the midst of the Sea
But here we build Babylon on Euphrates, compelld to build
And to inhabit, our Little-ones to clothe in armour of the gold
Of Jerusalems Cherubims & to forge them swords of her Altars
I see London blind & age-bent begging thro the Streets
Of Babylon, led by a child, his tears run down his beard
The voice of Wandering Reuben ecchoes from street to street
In all the Cities of the Nations Paris Madrid Amsterdam
The Corner of Broad Street weeps; Poland Street languishes
To Great Queen Street & Lincolns Inn all is distress & woe.

The night falls thick Hand comes from Albion in his strength
He combines into a Mighty-one the Double Molech & Chemosh
Marching thro Egypt in his fury the East is pale at his course
The Nations of India, the Wild Tartar that never knew Man
Starts from his lofty places & casts down his tents & flees away
But we woo him all the night in songs, O Los come forth O Los
Divide us from these terrors & give us power them to subdue
Arise upon thy Watches let us see thy Globe of fire
On Albions Rocks & let thy voice be heard upon Euphrates.

Thus sang the Daughters in lamentation, uniting into One
With Rahab as she turnd the iron Spindle of destruction.
Terrified at the Sons of Albion they took the Falshood which
Gwendolen hid in her left hand. it grew & grew till it

Became a Space & an Allegory around the Winding Worm:
They named it Canaan & built for it a tender Moon
Los smild with joy thinking on Enitharmon & he brought
Reuben from his twelvefold wandrings & led him into it
Planting the Seeds of the Twelve Tribes & Moses & David
And gave a Time & Revolution to the Space Six thousand years
He calld it Divine Analogy, for in Beulah the Feminine
Emanations Create Space, the Masculine Create Time, & plant
The Seeds of beauty in the Space: listning to their lamentation
Los walks upon his ancient Mountains in the deadly darkness
Among his Furnaces directing his laborious myriads watchful
Looking to the East: & his voice is heard over the whole Earth
As he watches the Furnaces by night, & directs the labourers

And thus Los replies upon his Watch: the Valleys listen silent:
The Stars stand still to hear; Jerusalem & Vala cease to mourn:
His voice is heard from Albion: the Alps & Appennines
Listen: Hermon & Lebanon bow their crowned heads
Babel & Shinar look toward the Western Gate, they sit down
Silent at his voice: they view the red Globe of fire in Los's hand
As he walks from Furnace to Furnace directing the Labourers
And this is the Song of Los, the Song that he sings on his
Watch

O lovely mild Jerusalem! O Shiloh of Mount Ephraim!
I see thy Gates of precious stones: thy Walls of gold & silver
Thou art the soft reflected Image of the Sleeping Man
Who stretchd on Albions rocks reposes amidst his Twenty-eight
Cities: where Beulah lovely terminates, in the hills & valleys of Albion
Cities not yet embodied in Time and Space: plant ye
The Seeds O Sisters in the bosom of Time & Spaces womb
To spring up for Jerusalem: lovely Shadow of Sleeping Albion
Why wilt thou rend thyself apart & build an Earthly Kingdom
To reign in pride & to oppress & to mix the Cup of Delusion
O thou that dwellest with Babylon! Come forth O lovely-one

I see thy Form O lovely mild Jerusalem, Wingd with Six Wings
In the opacous Bosom of the Sleeper, lovely Three fold
In Head & Heart & Reins three Universes of love & beauty
Thy forehead bright Holiness to the Lord, with Gates of pearl
Reflects Eternity beneath thy azure wings of feathery down
Ribbd delicate & clothd with featherd gold & azure & purple
From thy white shoulders shadowing, purity in holiness!
Thence featherd with soft crimson of the ruby bright as fire
Spreading into the azure Wings which like a canopy
Bends over thy immortal Head in which Eternity dwells
Albion beloved Land; I see thy mountains & thy hills
And valleys & thy pleasant Cities Holiness to the Lord
I see the Spectres of thy Dead O Emanation of Albion.

Thy Bosom white, translucent coverd with immortal gems
A sublime ornament not obscuring the outlines of beauty
Terrible to behold for thy extreme beauty & perfection
Twelve fold here all the Tribes of Israel I behold
Upon the Holy Land; I see the River of Life & Tree of Life
I see the New Jerusalem descending out of Heaven
Between thy Wings of gold & silver feathered immortal
Clear as the rainbow, as the cloud of the Suns tabernacle

Thy Reins coverd with Wings translucent sometimes covering
And sometimes spread abroad reveal the flames of holiness
Which like a robe covers: & like a Veil of Seraphim
In flaming fire unceasing burns from Eternity to Eternity
Twelvefold I there behold Israel in her Tents
A Pillar of a Cloud by day: a Pillar of fire by night
Guides them: there I behold Moab & Ammon & Amalek
There Bells of silver round thy knees living articulate
Comforting sounds of love & harmony & on thy feet
Sandals of gold & pearl, & Egypt & Assyria before me
The Isles of Javan, Philistea, Tyre and Lebanon

Thus Los sings upon his Watch walking from Furnace to Furnace
He siezes his Hammer every hour, flames surround him as
He beats: seas roll beneath his feet, tempests muster
Aroud his head, the thick hail stones stand ready to obey
His voice in the black cloud, his Sons labour in thunders
At his Furnaces: his Daughters at their Looms sing woes
His Emanation separates in milky fibres agonizing
Among the golden Looms of Cathedron sending fibres of love
From Golgonooza with sweet visions for Jerusalem, wanderer

Nor can any consummate bliss without being Generated
On Earth of those whose Emanations weave the loves
Of Beulah for Jerusalem & Shiloh, in immortal Golgonooza
Concentering in the majestic form of Erin in eternal tears
Viewing the Winding Worm on the Desarts of Great Tartary
Viewing Los in his Shudderings, pouring balm on his sorrows
So dread is Los's fury, that none dare him to approach
Without becoming his Children in the Furnaces of affliction

And Enitharmon like a faint rainbow waved before him
Filling with Fibres from his loins which reddend with desire
Into a Globe of blood beneath his bosom trembling in darkness
Of Albions clouds, he fed it, with his tears & bitter groans
Hiding his Spectre in invisibility from the timorous Shade
Till it became a separated cloud of beauty grace & love
Among the darkness of his Furnaces dividing asunder till
She separated stood before him a lovely Female weeping
Even Enitharmon separated outside, & his Loins closed
And heald after the separation: his pains he soon forgot:
Lured by her beauty outside of himself in shadowy grief.
Two Wills they had: Two Intellects: & not as in times of old.

Silent they wanderd hand in hand like two Infants wandring
From Enion in the desarts, terrified at each others beauty
Envying each other yet desiring, in all devouring Love.

Repelling weeping Enion blind & age-bent into the four-fold
Desarts. Los first broke silence & began to utter his love

O lovely Enitharmon: I behold thy graceful forms
Moving beside me till intoxicated with the woven labyrinth
Of beauty & perfection my wild fibres shoot in veins
Of blood thro all my nervous limbs. soon overgrown in roots
I shall be closed from thy sight. sieze therefore in thy hand
The small fibres as they shoot around me draw out in pity
And let them run on the winds of thy bosom: I will fix them
With pulsations. we will divide them into Sons & Daughters
To live in thy Bosoms translucence as in an eternal morning
Enitharmon answerd. No! I will sieze thy Fibres & weave
Them; not as thou wilt, but as I will, for I will Create
A round Womb beneath my bosom lest I also be overwoven.
With Love; be thou assured I never will be thy slave
Let Mans delight be Love; but Womans delight be Pride
In Eden our Loves were the same here they are opposite
I have Loves of my own I will weave them in Albions Spectre
Cast thou in Jerusalems shadows thy Loves: silk of liquid
Rubies Jacinths Crysolites: issuing from thy Furnaces. While
Jerusalem divides thy care: while thou carest for Jerusalem
Know that I never will be thine: also thou hidest Vala
From her these fibres shoot to shut me in a Grave.
You are Albions Victim, he has set his Daughter in your path

Los answerd sighing like the Bellows of his Furnaces
I care not! the swing of my Hammer shall measure the starry round
When in Eternity Man converses with Man they enter
Into each others Bosom (which are Universes of delight)
In mutual interchange, and first their Emanations meet
Surrounded by their Children. if they embrace & comingle
The Human Four-fold Forms mingle also in thunders of Intellect
But if the Emanations mingle not; with storms & agitations
Of earthquakes & consuming fires they roll apart in fear
For Man cannot unite with Man but by their Emanations
Which stand both Male & Female at the Gates of each Humanity
How then can I ever again be united as Man with Man
While thou my Emanation refusest my Fibres of dominion.
When Souls mingle & join thro all the Fibres of Brotherhood
Can there be any secret joy on Earth greater than this?

Enitharmon answerd: This is Womans World, nor need she any
Spectre to defend her from Man. I will Create secret places
And the masculine names of the places Merlin & Arthur.
A triple Female Tabernacle for Moral Law I weave
That he who loves Jesus may loathe terrified Female love
Till God himself become a Male subservient to the Female.

She spoke in scorn & jealousy alternate torments; and
So speaking she sat down on Sussex shore singing lulling
Cadences. & playing in sweet intoxication among the glistening
Fibres of Los; sending them over the Ocean eastward into
The realms of dark death; O perverse to thyself, contrarious
To thy own purposes; for when she began to weave
Shooting out in sweet pleasure her bosom in milky Love
Flowd into the aching fibres of Los. yet contending against him
In pride sendinding his Fibres over to her objects of jealousy
In the little lovely Allegoric Night of Albions Daughters
Which stretchd abroad expanding east & west & north & south
Thro all the World of Erin & of Los & all their Children
A sullen smile broke from the Spectre in mockery & scorn
Knowing himself the author of their divisions & shrinkings, gratif
At their contentions, he wiped his tears he washd his visage

The Man who respects Woman shall be despised by Woman
And deadly cunning & mean abjectness only, shall enjoy them
For I will make their places of joy & love, excrementitious
Continually building, continually destroying in Family feuds
While you are under the dominion of a jealous Female
Unpermanent for ever because of love & jealousy.
You shall want all the Minute Particulars of Life

Thus, joyd the Spectre in the dusky fires of Loss Forge, eyeing
Enitharmon who at her shining Looms sings lulling cadences
While Los stood at his Anvil in wrath the victim of their love
And hate: dividing the Space of Love with brazen Compasses
In Golgonooza & in Udan-Adan & in Entuthon of Urizen
The blow of his Hammer is Justice. the swing of his Hammer Mercy
The force of Loss Hammer is eternal Forgiveness; but
His rage or his mildness were vain, she scatterd his love on the wind
Eastward into her own Center, creating the Female Womb
In mild Jerusalem around the Lamb of God. Loud howl
The Furnaces of Los! loud roll the Wheels of Enitharmon
The Four Zoa's in all their faded majesty burst out in fury
And fire. Jerusalem took the Cup which foamd in Vala's hand
Like the red Sun upon the mountains in the bloody day
Upon the Hermaphroditic Wine-presses of Love & Wrath.

Who divided by the Cross & Nails & Thorns & Spear
In cruelties of Rahab & Tirzah permanent endure
A terrible indefinite Hermaphroditic form
A Wine-press of Love & Wrath double Hermaphroditic
Twelvefold in Allegoric pomp in selfish holiness
The Pharisaion, the Grammateis, the Presbuterion,
The Archiereus, the Iereus, the Saddusaion, double
Each without side of the other, covering eastern heaven

Thus was the Covering Cherub reveald majestic image
Of Selfhood, Body put off, the Antichrist accursed
Coverd with precious stones, a Human Dragon terrible
And bright, stretchd over Europe & Asia gorgeous
In three nights he devourd the rejected corse of death

His Head dark, deadly, in its Brain incloses a reflexion
Of Eden all perverted; Egypt on the Gihon many tongued
And many mouthd, Ethiopia, Libya, the Sea of Rephaim
Minute Particulars in slavery I behold among the brick-kilns
Disorganizd, & there is Pharoh in his iron Court:
And the Dragon of the River & the Furnaces of iron.
Outwoven from Thames & Tweed & Severn awful streams
Twelve ridges of Stone frown over all the Earth in tyrant pride
Frown over each River stupendous Works of Albions Druid Sons
And Albions Forests of Oaks coverd the Earth from Pole to Pole

His Bosom wide reflects Moab & Ammon, on the River
Pison, since calld Arnon, there is Heshbon beautiful
The Rocks of Rabbath on the Arnon & the Fish-pools of Heshbon
Whose currents flow into the Dead Sea by Sodom & Gomorra
Above his Head high arching Wings black filld with Eyes
Spring upon iron sinews from the Scapulae & Os Humeri.
There Israel in bondage to his Generalizing Gods
Molech & Chemosh, & in his left breast is Philistea
In Druid Temples over the whole Earth with Victims Sacrifice,
From Gaza to Damascus Tyre & Sidon & the Gods
Of Javan thro the Isles of Grecia & all Europes Kings
Where Hiddekel pursues his course among the rocks
Two Wings spring from his ribs of brass, starry, black as night
But translucent their blackness as the dazling of gems
His Loins inclose Babylon on Euphrates beautiful
And Rome in sweet Hesperia, there Israel scatterd abroad
In martyrdoms & slavery I behold: ah vision of sorrow!
Inclosed by eyeless Wings, glowing with fire as the iron
Heated in the Smiths forge, but cold the wind of their dread fury

But in the midst of a devouring Stomach, Jerusalem
Hidden within the Covering Cherub as in a Tabernacle
Of threefold workmanship in allegoric delusion & woe
There the Seven Kings of Canaan & Five Baalim of Philistea
Sihon & Og the Anakim & Emim, Nephilim & Gibborim
From Babylon to Rome & the Wings spread from Japan
Where the Red Sea terminates the World of Generation & Death
To Irelands farthest rocks where Giants builded their Causeway
Into the Sea of Rephaim, but the Sea overwhelmd them all.

A Double Female now appeard within the Tabernacle
Religion hid in War, a Dragon red & hidden Harlot
Each within other, but without a Warlike Mighty-one
Of dreadful power, sitting upon Horeb pondering dire
And mighty preparations mustering multitudes innumerable
Of warlike sons among the sands of Midian & Aram
For multitudes of those who sleep in Alla descend
Lured by his warlike symphonies of tabret pipe & harp
Burst the bottoms of the Graves, & Funeral Arks of Beulah
Wandering in that unknown Night beyond the silent Grave
They become One with the Antichrist & are absorbd in him

The Feminine separates from the Masculine & both from Man.
Ceasing to be His Emanations, Life to Themselves assuming:
And while they circumscribe his Brain. & while they circumscribe
His Heart. & while they circumscribe his Loins: a Veil & Net
Of Veins of red Blood grows around them like a scarlet robe.
Covering them from the sight of Man like the woven Veil of Sleep
Such as the Flowers of Beulah weave to be their Funeral Mantles
But dark; opake: tender to touch, & painful: & agonizing
To the embrace of love. & to the mingling of soft fibres
Of tender affection. that no more the Masculine mingles
With the Feminine. but the Sublime is shut out from the Pathos
In howling torment. to build stone walls of separation. compelling
The Pathos, to weave curtains of hiding secresy from the torment.

Bower & Conwenna stood on Skiddaw cutting the Fibres
Of Benjamin from Chesters River: loud the River: loud the Mersey
And the Ribble. thunder into the Irish sea, as the Twelve Sons
Of Albion drank & imbibed the Life & eternal Form of Luvah
Cheshire & Lancashire & Westmoreland groan in anguish
As they cut the fibres from the Rivers he sears them with hot
Iron of his Forge & fixes them into Bones of chalk & Rock
Conwenna sat above: with solemn cadences she drew
Fibres of life out from the Bones into her golden Loom
Hand had his Furnace on Highgates heights & it reachd
To Brockley Hills across the Thames: he with double Boadicea
In cruel pride cut Reuben apart from the Hills of Surrey
Comingling with Luvah & with the Sepulcher of Luvah
For the Male is a Furnace of beryll: the Female is a golden Loom
Los cries: No Individual ought to appropriate to Himself
Or to his Emanation, any of the Universal Characteristics
Of David or of Eve, of the Woman, or of the Lord.
Of Reuben or of Benjamin, of Joseph or Judah or Levi.
Those who dare appropriate to themselves Universal Attributes
Are the Blasphemous Selfhoods & must be broken asunder
A Vegetated Christ & a Virgin Eve, are the Hermaphroditic
Blasphemy. by his Maternal Birth he is that Evil-One
And his Maternal Humanity must be put off Eternally
Lest the Sexual Generation swallow up Regeneration
Come Lord Jesus take on thee the Satanic Body of Holiness

So Los cried in the Valleys of Middlesex in the Spirit of Prophecy
While in Selfhood Hand & Hyle & Bowen & Skofeld appropriate
The Divine Names: seeking to Vegetate the Divine Vision.
In a corporeal & ever dying Vegetation & Corruption
Mingling with Luvah in One. they become One Great Satan

Loud scream the Daughters of Albion beneath the Tongs & Hammer
Dolorous are their lamentations in the burning Forge
They drink Reuben & Benjamin as the, iron drinks the fire
They are red hot with cruelty: raving along the Banks of Thames
And on Tyburns Brook among the howling Victims in loveliness
While Hand & Hyle condense the Little-ones & erect them into
A mighty Temple even to the stars: but they Vegetate
Beneath Los's Hammer, that Life may not be blotted out.

For Los said: When the Individual appropriates Universality
He divides into Male & Female: & when the Male & Female,
Appropriate Individuality, they become an Eternal Death.
Hermaphroditic worshippers of a God of cruelty & law:
Your Slaves & Captives; you compell to worship a God of Mercy.
These are the Demonstrations of Los. & the blows of my mighty Hammer

So Los spoke. And the Giants of Albion terrified & ashamed.
With Los's thunderous Words, began to build trembling rocking Stones
For his Words roll in thunders & lightnings among the Temples
Terrified rocking to & fro upon the earth, & sometimes
Resting in a Circle in Maiden or in Strathness or Dura.
Plotting to devour Albion & Los the friend of Albion
Denying in private: mocking God & Eternal Life: & in Public
Collusion. calling themselves Deists, Worshipping the Maternal
Humanity: calling it Nature. and Natural Religion
But still the thunder of Los peals loud & thus the thunders cry
These beautiful Witchcrafts of Albion. are gratify'd by Cruelty

It is easier to Forgive an Enemy than to forgive a Friend:
The man who permits you to injure him, deserves your vengeance:
He also, will recieve it: go Spectre; obey my most secret desire:
Which thou knowest without my speaking: Go to these Fiends of Righteousness
Tell them to obey their Humanities, & not pretend Holiness;
When they are murderers: as far as my Hammer & Anvil permit
Go, tell them that the Worship of God, is honouring his gifts
In other men: & loving the greatest men best, each according
To his Genius: which is the Holy Ghost in Man; there is no other
God, than that God who is the intellectual fountain of Humanity:
He who envies or calumniates: which is murder & cruelty,
Murders the Holy-one: Go tell them this & overthrow their cup,
Their bread, their altar-table, their incense & their oath:
Their marriage & their baptism, their burial & consecration:
I have tried to make friends by corporeal gifts but have only
Made enemies: I never made friends but by spiritual gifts;
By severe contentions of friendship & the burning fire of thought
He who would see the Divinity must see him in his Children
One first, in friendship & love; then a Divine Family, & in the midst
Jesus will appear; so he who wishes to see a Vision; a perfect Whole
Must see it in its Minute Particulars: Organized & not as thou
O Fiend of Righteousness pretendest; thine is a Disorganized
And snowy cloud: brooder of tempests & destructive War
You smile with pomp & rigor: you talk of benevolence & virtue:
I act with benevolence & Virtue & get murderd time after time:
You accumulate Particulars, & murder by analyzing, that you
May take the aggregate; & you call the aggregate Moral Law:
And you call that Swelld & bloated Form; a Minute Particular.
But General Forms have their vitality in Particulars: & every
Particular is a Man; a Divine Member of the Divine Jesus.

So Los cried at his Anvil in the horrible darkness weeping:

The Spectre builded stupendous Works, taking the Starry Heavens
Like to a curtain & folding them according to his will
Repeating the Smaragdine Table of Hermes to draw Los down
Into the Indefinite, refusing to believe without demonstration
Los reads the Stars of Albion; the Spectre reads the Voids
Between the Stars; among the arches of Albions Tomb sublime
Rolling the Sea in rocky paths; forming Leviathan
And Behemoth; the War by Sea enormous & the War
By Land astounding; erecting pillars in the deepest Hell,
To reach the heavenly arches; Los beheld undaunted furious
His heavd Hammer; he swung it round & at one blow,
In unforgiving ruin driving down the pyramids of pride
Smiting the Spectre on his Anvil & the integuments of his Eye
And Ear unbinding in dire pain, with many blows,
Of strict severity self-subduing, & with many tears labouring.

Then he sent forth the Spectre all his pyramids were grains
Of sand & his pillars: dust on the flys wing: & his starry
Heavens; a moth of gold & silver mocking his anxious grasp
Thus Los alterd his Spectre & every Ratio of his Reason
He alterd time after time, with dire pain & many tears
Till he had completely divided him into a separate space.

Terrified Los sat to behold trembling & weeping & howling
I care not whether a Man is Good or Evil; all that I care
Is whether he is a Wise Man or a Fool. Go: put off Holiness
And put on Intellect: or my thundrous Hammer shall drive thee
To wrath which thou condemnest: till thou obey my voice

So Los terrified cries; trembling & weeping & howling! Beholding

92

What do I see The Briton Saxon Roman Norman amalgamating
In my Furnaces into One Nation the English: & taking Refuge
In the Loins of Albion. The Canaanite united with the fugitive
Hebrew, whom She divided into Twelve. & sold into Egypt
Then scatterd the Egyptian & Hebrew to the four Winds:
This sinful Nation Created in our Furnaces & Looms is Albion

So Los spoke. Enitharmon answerd in great terror in Lambeths Vale

The Poets Song draws to its period & Enitharmon is no more.
For if he be that Albion I can never weave him in my Looms
But when he touches the first fibrous thread, like filmy dew

Jerusalem

My Looms will be no more & I annihilate vanish for ever
Then thou wilt Create another Female according to thy Will.

Los answerd swift as the shuttle of gold. Sexes must vanish & cease
To be. when Albion arises from his dread repose O lovely Enitharmon:
When all their Crimes their Punishments their Accusations of Sin:
All their Jealousies Revenges. Murders. hidings of Cruelty in Deceit
Appear only in the Outward Spheres of Visionary Space and Time.
In the shadows of Possibility by Mutual Forgiveness forevermore
And in the Vision & in the Prophecy. that we may Foresee & Avoid
The terrors of Creation & Redemption & Judgment. Beholding them
Displayd in the Emanative Visions of Canaan in Jerusalem & in Shiloh
And in the Shadows of Remembrance. & in the Chaos of the Spectre
Amalek. Edom. Egypt. Moab. Ammon. Ashur. Philistea. around Jerusalem
Where the Druids reard their Rocky Circles to make permanent Remembrance
Of Sin. & the Tree of Good & Evil sprang from the Rocky Circle & Snake
Of the Druid. along the Valley of Rephaim from Camberwell to Golgotha
And framed the Mundane Shell Cavernous in Length Bredth & Highth

Anytus
Melitus
& Lycon
thought Socrates
a Very Pernicious
Man

So Caiphas thought Jesus

Enitharmon heard. She raisd her head like the mild Moon

O Rintrah! O Palamabron. What are your dire & awful purposes
Enitharmons name is nothing before you: you forget all my Love:
The Mothers love of obedience is forgotten & you seek a Love
Of the pride of dominion. that will Divorce Ocalythron & Elynittria
Upon East Moor in Derbyshire & along the Valleys of Cheviot
Could you Love me Rintrah. if you Pride not in my Love
As Reuben found Mandrakes in the field & gave them to his Mother
Pride meets with Pride upon the Mountains in the stormy day
In that terrible Day of Rintrahs Plow & of Satans driving the Team.
Ah! then I heard my little ones weeping along the Valley:
Ah! then I saw my beloved ones fleeing from my Tent
Merlin was like thee Rintrah among the Giants of Albion
Judah was like Palamabron: O Simeon! O Levi! ye fled away
How can I hear my little ones weeping along the Valley
Or how upon the distant Hills see my beloveds Tents.

Then Los again took up his speech as Enitharmon ceast

Fear not my Sons this Waking Death. he is become One with me
Behold him here! We shall not Die! we shall be united in Jesus.
Will you suffer this Satan this Body of Doubt that Seems but Is Not
To occupy the very threshold of Eternal Life. if Bacon. Newton. Locke.
Deny a Conscience in Man & the Communion of Saints & Angels
Contemning the Divine Vision & Fruition. Worshiping the Deus
Of the Heathen. The God of This World. & the Goddess Nature
Mystery Babylon the Great. The Druid Dragon & hidden Harlot
Is it not that Signal of the Morning which was told us in the Beginning
Thus they converse upon Mam-Tor. the Graves thunder under their feet

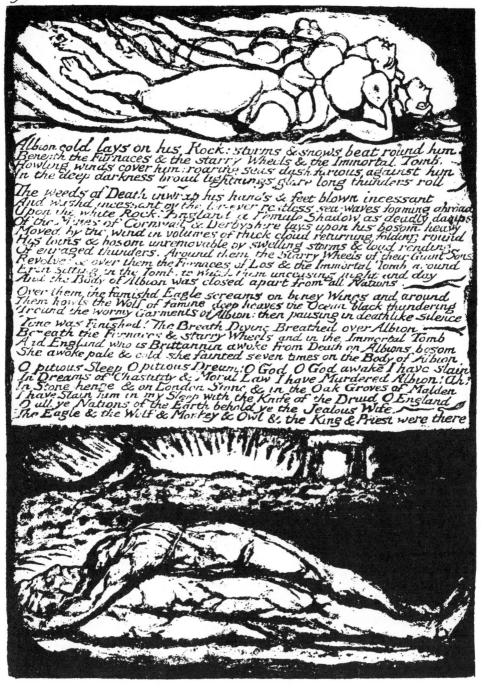

Albion cold lays on his Rock: storms & snows beat round him.
Beneath the Furnaces & the starry Wheels & the Immortal Tomb.
Howling winds cover him: roaring seas dash furious, against him
In the deep darkness broad lightnings glare long thunders roll

The weeds of Death inwrap his hands & feet blown incessant
And washd incessant by the for-ever restless sea-waves foaming abroad
Upon the white Rock. England a Female Shadow as deadly damps
Of the Mines of Cornwall & Derbyshire lays upon his bosom heavy
Moved by the wind in volumes of thick cloud returning folding round
His loins & bosom unremovable by swelling storms & loud rending
Of enraged thunders. Around them the Starry Wheels of their Giant Sons
Revolve: & over them the Furnaces of Los & the Immortal Tomb around
Even sitting in the Tomb: to watch them uncearing night and day
And the Body of Albion was closed apart from all Nations.

Over them the famishd Eagle screams on boney Wings and around
Them howls the Wolf of famine deep heaves the Ocean black thundering
Around the wormy Garments of Albion: then pausing in deathlike silence

Time was Finished! The Breath Divine Breathed over Albion
Beneath the Furnaces & starry Wheels and in the Immortal Tomb
And England who is Brittannia awoke from Death on Albions bosom
She awoke pale & cold she fainted seven times on the Body of Albion

O pitious Sleep O pitious Dream! O God O God awake I have slain
In Dreams of Chastity & Moral Law I have Murdered Albion! Ah!
In Stone henge & on London Stone & in the Oak Groves of Malden
I have Slain him in my Sleep with the Knife of the Druid O England
O all ye Nations of the Earth behold ye the Jealous Wife
The Eagle & the Wolf & Monkey & Owl & the King & Priest were there

Her voice pierd Albions clay cold ear. he moved upon the Rock.
The Breath Divine went forth upon the morning hills Albion mov'd.
Upon the Rock. he opend his eyelids in pain; in pain he mov'd
His stony members. he saw England. Ah! shall the Dead live again.

The Breath Divine went forth over the morning hills Albion rose
In anger: the wrath of God breaking bright flaming on all sides around
His awful limbs: into the Heavens he walked clothed in flames
Loud thundring. with broad flashes of flaming lightning & pillars
Of fire. speaking the Words of Eternity in Human Forms, in direful.
Revolutions of Action & Passion. thro the Four Elements on all sides
Surrounding his awful Members. Thou seest the Sun in heavy clouds
Struggling to rise above the Mountains. in his burning hand
He takes his Bow. then chooses out his arrows of flaming gold
Murmuring the Bowstring breathes with ardor! clouds roll round the
Horns of the wide Bow. loud sounding winds sport on the mountain brows
Compelling Urizen to his Furrow: & Tharmas to his Sheepfold:
And Luvah to his Loom: Urthona he beheld mighty labouring at
His Anvil, in the Great Spectre Los, unwearied labouring & weeping
Therefore the Sons of Eden praise Urthonas Spectre in songs
Because he kept the Divine Vision in time of trouble.
As the Sun & Moon lead forward the Visions of Heaven & Earth
England who is Brittannia enterd Albions bosom rejoicing.
Rejoicing in his indignation! adoring his wrathful rebuke.
She who adores not your frowns will only loathe your smiles

96

As the Sun & Moon lead forward the
Visions of Heaven & Earth
England who is Brittannia entered
Albions bosom rejoicing

Then Jesus appeared, standing by
Albion as the Good Shepherd
By the lost Sheep that he hath
found & Albion knew that it
Was the Lord the Universal Human
& Albion saw his Form
A Man. & they conversed as Man.
with Man in Ages of Eternity
And the Divine Appearance was
the likeness & similitude of Los

Albion said, O Lord what can
I do my Selfhood cruel
Marches against thee deceitful.
from Sinai & from Edom.
Into the Wilderness of Judah to
meet thee in his pride
I behold the Visions of my deadly
Sleep of Six Thousand Years
Dazling around thy skirts like
a Serpent of precious stones &
gold
I know it is my Self: O my Divine
Creator & Redeemer

Jesus replied Fear not Albion
unless I die thou canst not live
But if I die I shall arise again
& thou with me
This is Friendship & Brotherhood
without it Man Is Not

So Jesus spoke! the Covering
Cherub coming on in darkness
Overshadowd them & Jesus
said Thus do Men in Eternity
One for another to put off by
forgiveness, every sin

Albion replyd. Cannot Man
exist without Mysterious
Offering of Self for Another, is
this Friendship & Brotherhood
I see thee in the likeness and
similitude of Los my Friend

Jesus said. Wouldest thou
love one who never died
For thee or ever die for one
who had not died for thee
And if God dieth not for
Man & giveth not himself
Eternally for Man Man could not exist. for Man is Love:
As God is Love: every kindness to another is a little Death
In the Divine Image nor can Man exist but by Brotherhood
So saying, the Cloud overshadowing divided them asunder
Albion stood in terror: not for himself but for his Friend
Divine, & Self was lost in the contemplation of faith
And wonder at the Divine Mercy & at Loss sublime honour

Do I sleep amidst danger to Friends! O my Cities & Counties
Do you sleep! rouze up! rouze up. Eternal Death is abroad
So Albion spoke & threw himself into the Furnaces of affliction
All was a Vision, all a Dream: the Furnaces became
Fountains of Living Waters flowing from the Humanity Divine
And all the Cities of Albion rose from their Slumbers, and All
The Sons & Daughters of Albion on soft clouds Waking from Sleep
Soon all around remote the Heavens burnt with flaming fires
And Urizen & Luvah & Tharmas & Urthona arose into
Albions Bosom: Then Albion stood before Jesus in the Clouds
Of Heaven Fourfold among the Visions of God in Eternity

Awake Awake Jerusalem! O lovely Emanation of Albion
Awake and overspread all Nations as in Ancient Time
For lo! the Night of Death is past and the Eternal Day
Appears upon our Hills: Awake Jerusalem, and come away

So spake the Vision of Albion & in him so spake in my hearing
The Universal Father Then Albion stretchd his hand into Infinitude.
And took his Bow. Fourfold the Vision for bright beaming Urizen
Layd his hand on the South & took a breathing Bow of carved Gold
Luvah his hand stretchd to the East & bore a Silver Bow bright shining
Tharmas Westward a Bow of Brass pure flaming richly wrought
Urthona Northward in thick storms a Bow of Iron terrible thundering.
And the Bow is a Male & Female & the Quiver of the Arrows of Love.
Are the Children of this Bow: a Bow of Mercy & Loving-kindness: laying
Open the hidden Heart in Wars of mutual Benevolence Wars of Love
And the hand of Man grasps firm between the Male & Female Loves
And he Clothed himself in Bow & Arrows in awful state Fourfold
In the midst of his Twenty-eight Cities each with his Bow breathing

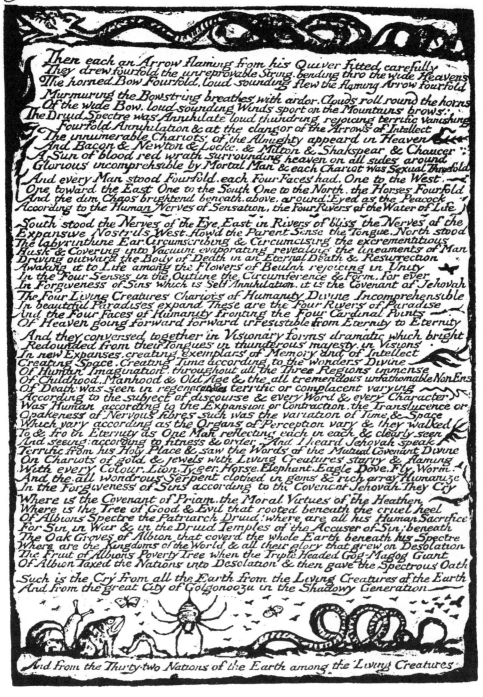

Then each an Arrow flaming from his Quiver fitted carefully
They drew fourfold the unreprovable String, bending thro the wide Heavens
The horned Bow Fourfold, loud sounding flew the flaming Arrow fourfold

Murmuring the Bowstring breathes with ardor. Clouds roll round the horns
Of the wide Bow. loud sounding Winds sport on the Mountains brows:
The Druid Spectre was Annihilate loud thundring rejoicing terrific vanishing
Fourfold Annihilation & at the clangor of the Arrows of Intellect
The innumerable Chariots of the Almighty appeard in Heaven
And Bacon & Newton & Locke, & Milton & Shakspear & Chaucer
A Sun of blood red wrath surrounding heaven on all sides around
Glorious incomprehensible by Mortal Man & each Chariot was Sexual Threefold
And every Man stood Fourfold, each Four Faces had. One to the West
One toward the East One to the South One to the North, the Horses Fourfold
And the dim Chaos brightend beneath. above. around: Eyed as the Peacock
According to the Human Nerves of Sensation, the Four Rivers of the Water of Life

South stood the Nerves of the Eye. East in Rivers of bliss the Nerves of the
Expansive Nostrils. West. flowd the Parent Sense the Tongue. North stood
The labyrinthine Ear. Circumscribing & Circumcising the excrementitious
Husk & Covering into Vacuum evaporating revealing the lineaments of Man
Driving outward the Body of Death in an Eternal Death & Resurrection
Awaking it to Life among the Flowers of Beulah rejoicing in Unity
In the Four Senses in the Outline the Circumference & Form. For ever
In Forgiveness of Sins which is Self Annihilation. it is the Covenant of Jehovah
The Four Living Creatures Chariots of Humanity Divine Incomprehensible
In beautiful Paradises expand These are the Four Rivers of Paradise
And the Four Faces of Humanity fronting the Four Cardinal Points
Of Heaven going forward forward irresistible from Eternity to Eternity

And they conversed together in Visionary forms dramatic which bright
Redounded from their Tongues in thunderous majesty, in Visions
In new Expanses, creating Exemplars of Memory and of Intellect
Creating Space, Creating Time according to the wonders Divine
Of Human Imagination, throughout all the Three Regions immense
Of Childhood, Manhood & Old Age & the all tremendous unfathomable Non Ens
Of Death was seen in regenerations terrific or complacent varying
According to the subject of discourse & every Word & every Character
Was Human according to the Expansion or Contraction, the Translucence or
Opakeness of Nervous fibres such was the variation of Time & Space
Which vary according as the Organs of Perception vary & they walked
To & fro in Eternity as One Man reflecting each in each & clearly seen
And seeing: according to fitness & order. And I heard Jehovah speak
Terrific from his Holy Place & saw the Words of the Mutual Covenant Divine
On Chariots of gold & jewels with Living Creatures starry & flaming
With every Colour, Lion, Tyger, Horse, Elephant, Eagle Dove, Fly, Worm,
And the all wondrous Serpent clothed in gems & rich array Humanize
In the Forgiveness of Sins according to thy Covenant Jehovah. They Cry

Where is the Covenant of Priam, the Moral Virtues of the Heathen
Where is the Tree of Good & Evil that rooted beneath the cruel heel
Of Albions Spectre the Patriarch Druid: where are all his Human Sacrifice
For Sin in War & in the Druid Temples of the Accuser of Sin: beneath
The Oak Groves of Albion that coverd the whole Earth beneath his Spectre
Where are the Kingdoms of the World & all their glory that grew on Desolation
The Fruit of Albions Poverty Tree when the Triple Headed Gog-Magog Giant
Of Albion Taxed the Nations into Desolation & then gave the Spectrous Oath

Such is the Cry from all the Earth from the Living Creatures of the Earth
And from the great City of Golgonooza in the Shadowy Generation

And from the Thirty-two Nations of the Earth among the Living Creatures

All Human Forms identified even Tree Metal Earth & Stone. all
Human Forms identified living going forth & returning wearied
Into the Planetary lives of Years Months Days & Hours reposing
And then Awaking into his Bosom in the Life of Immortality.
And I heard the Name of their Emanations they are named Jerusalem

The End of The Song
of Jerusalem

Index

Adan, 170 n.8

Adam: and Albion, 85, 90; and Satan, 78, 85, 93, 134

Adams, Hazard, 14, 23 n.12

Affective error. *See* Error

Albion: affective error of, 58–68; alternatives of, 19–21, 45, 49; and Jerusalem, 30, 63; and Vala, 18, 19, 63, 75, 77, 144; as a Deist, 37–41, 71, 108; as a Jew, 31ff.; as England, 22, 97–98, 104; as priestly judge, 71, 92, 95, 97; awakening of, 15, 25, 27, 30, 39, 160–69; blindness of, 49–50, 81, 85, 86, 93; death of, 15, 17, 26–27, 81, 89, 92, 102, 122; distorted love of, 71, 75, 79, 112–13, 124; division of, 16, 18, 44–47, 64, 71, 73, 74, 87, 95, 108, 129, 156, 158; error of, 15; eternal character of, 16, 18, 28, 41, 161–69; fall of, 15–17, 19, 30, 33, 64, 111, 138, 141, 160; fallen church, 73, 95; fallen cities of, 82; limits of, 77–78, 117; moral error of, 72–73; opposition of, to imaginative characters, 16–17, 212, 109, 141; petrified, 64, 72, 98, 100; rational or Deistic error of, 51–57, 108–9, 122, 124; religious error of, 49–51, 109; sickness of, 84. 89, 92; sleep, 132, 160; states and passage of, 15, 18–22, 93, 95–96; struggle of, with Luvah, 17, 124, 126; unity of, 18, 167–69

Altars: Albion's, 95, 110–11; Druid, 81, 127; twelve, 73, 139 n.8

America (William Blake), 14, 19, 48, 54, 131, 143

Anti-Christ, 16, 154, 161

Arthur, 137

Babylon, 64, 73, 91, 94, 120–21, 136–38, 154

Bacon, Francis, 36–37, 52–53, 111, 131, 166

Bath, city of, 87, 90–91, 97, 106 n.13, 136–37

Beulah, 68. *See also* Daughters of Beulah

Bible, books of the, 87, 101, 106 n.18

Bindman, David, 24 n.20

Bladud, 137

Bloom, Harold, 14, 23 n.4, 24 n.15, 69 n.12

Book of Urizen (William Blake), 81

Bow, 163, 165–66

Brittannia, 39, 161, 165

Bromion, 133, 135

Cambel, 142, 144–47, 151

Canaan, 18, 132

Chaucer, Geoffrey, 166

Chayes, Irene, 57, 170 n.13

Cheviot, 18, 132

Christ. *See* Jesus

Christianity: as alternative to Deism, 36; as a state, 20–21, 39–40; as imagination, 157–58, 166

Churches: Church of England, 84, 86, 93, 120; fallen, 86–89, 100, 113; false doctrines of the, 90–93; twenty-eight, 84, 171 n.17; twenty-seven, 84, 88, 93

Cities, cathedral: fallen, 86–87, 89–91; unfallen, 83–84, 165–66

277

Index of Plates